AF744908

Public Debt, Sustainability and Economic Growth

Alfred Greiner • Bettina Fincke

Public Debt, Sustainability and Economic Growth

Theory and Empirics

Springer

Alfred Greiner
Faculty of Economics
Bielefeld University
Bielefeld
Germany

Bettina Fincke
Faculty of Economics
Bielefeld University
Bielefeld
Germany

ISBN 978-3-319-09347-5 ISBN 978-3-319-09348-2 (eBook)
DOI 10.1007/978-3-319-09348-2
Springer Cham Heidelberg New York Dordrecht London

Library of Congress Control Number: 2014952604

© Springer International Publishing Switzerland 2015
This work is subject to copyright. All rights are reserved by the Publisher, whether the whole or part of the material is concerned, specifically the rights of translation, reprinting, reuse of illustrations, recitation, broadcasting, reproduction on microfilms or in any other physical way, and transmission or information storage and retrieval, electronic adaptation, computer software, or by similar or dissimilar methodology now known or hereafter developed. Exempted from this legal reservation are brief excerpts in connection with reviews or scholarly analysis or material supplied specifically for the purpose of being entered and executed on a computer system, for exclusive use by the purchaser of the work. Duplication of this publication or parts thereof is permitted only under the provisions of the Copyright Law of the Publisher's location, in its current version, and permission for use must always be obtained from Springer. Permissions for use may be obtained through RightsLink at the Copyright Clearance Center. Violations are liable to prosecution under the respective Copyright Law.
The use of general descriptive names, registered names, trademarks, service marks, etc. in this publication does not imply, even in the absence of a specific statement, that such names are exempt from the relevant protective laws and regulations and therefore free for general use.
While the advice and information in this book are believed to be true and accurate at the date of publication, neither the authors nor the editors nor the publisher can accept any legal responsibility for any errors or omissions that may be made. The publisher makes no warranty, express or implied, with respect to the material contained herein.

Printed on acid-free paper

Springer is part of Springer Science+Business Media (www.springer.com)

Preface

The financial crises that had begun as a sub-prime crisis in the USA in 2007 had plunged a great many economies throughout the world into deep economic recessions. It seemed that the slump had been overcome by 2010 when some countries reached their pre-crisis level of production. However, the sub-prime crisis turned into a public debt crisis because the bail-out of private financial institutions by governments led to a drastic increase of national debt to GDP ratios in some countries. Particularly in the euro area, economies still face severe problems and must be supported by other countries. This illustrates drastically that public debt does affect the evolution of market economies and the question arises which mechanisms one can identify that make public debt influence the real side of an economy. Whereas economic consequences of taxation can be readily derived, that does not hold for public debt since the latter does not have immediate consequences as concerns the allocation of resources. With this book, we intend to contribute to the research on how public debt affects the growth process of market economies in the medium- to long-run. In particular, we want to work out the mechanisms that make public debt affect the allocation of resources and that are not so easily understood as the economic effects of distortionary taxation.

Our book partly builds on papers by ourselves and extends our earlier book (Greiner and Fincke 2009). Thus, we develop new theoretical models of endogenous growth, we update empirical estimations and we present new empirical evidence as regards the relation between public debt and economic growth. The advantage of a monograph, compared to publications in the form of research papers, is that a book publication allows to get more into the details and also to be more precise about the effects that ensue when certain assumptions are changed and replaced by other ones, so that one can say more about the robustness of the results derived. Moreover, this book works out fundamental properties of public debt within basic models of endogenous economic growth. Therefore, it is also suited as a textbook for graduate students studying the relation between public debt, public deficits and the allocation of resources in an intertemporal context. We also owe our thanks to Peter Flaschel,

Göran Kauermann, Uwe Köller and Willi Semmler from whom we have benefited through earlier joint work and stimulating discussions. Further, we are indebted to Gaby Windhorst for typing some sections of the manuscript.

Parts of the material in this book have been presented at conferences, workshops and university seminars. Valuable comments that are gratefully acknowledged were provided by participants in the International Workshop on Advances in Macrodynamics at Bielefeld University, in the Conference on The Institutional and Social Dynamics of Growth and Distribution, Lucca, Italy, in the World Bank workshop on Modeling Fiscal Policy, Public Expenditure and Growth Linkages, Washington, D.C., in the Symposium on Nonlinear Dynamics and Econometrics, London, in the Workshop on Public Debt and Economic Growth of the European Commission, Economic and Financial Affairs, Brussels, in the DIW annual workshop on macroeconometric modelling, Berlin, at the UECE Conference on Economic and Financial Adjustments in Europe, Lisbon, at the SPERI Annual Conference Beyond Austerity vs Growth: The Future of the European Political Economy, Sheffield, as well as in seminars at the Université du Luxembourg, at the Vienna University of Technology and at the Université Paris 1 Panthéon-Sorbonne.

Bielefeld, Germany
June 2014

Alfred Greiner
Bettina Fincke

Contents

List of Figures

List of Tables

Chapter 1
Introduction

After World War II, in particular during the 1970s, the politico-economic principles had been largely dominated by the Keynesian approach according to which governments must play an active role in stabilizing market economies. The latter can be achieved by public expenditures in order to raise aggregate demand, with the spending being financed by public deficits. Particularly, in times of low aggregate demand and high unemployment the government must become active in order to restore the full employment equilibrium which, then, allows to reduce outstanding public debt. In addition, according to that view public debt does not pose a problem if the government runs into debt in the home country. This holds because no resources are lost and public deficits just imply a reallocation of resources from taxpayers to bondholders.

Another reason to resort to debt-financing is inter-generational redistribution. The aspect of inter-generational redistribution is also the justification for the so-called golden rule of public finance. According to that rule, governments should finance public investments that yield long-term benefits by public deficits in order to make future generations contribute to the financing. Since future generations will benefit from today's investment, their contribution to the financing is justified. Otherwise, the current generation would have to bear all the costs but benefit only to a certain degree which is considered as unfair.

As a consequence of the predominant Keynesian view, public debt rose considerably in the fourth quarter of the last century and, what is more, the increase in public debt was even larger than the growth rate of the gross domestic product (GDP), mainly in many European countries, so that the ratio of public debt to GDP grew, too. Even in the euro area, where countries participating in the European Economic and Monetary Union have signed the Maastricht treaty stating that the public deficit and the public debt relative to GDP must not exceed 3 and 60 %, respectively, quite a many economies have difficulties with their debt service and some even had to be bailed out by the European Stability Mechanism to prevent bankruptcy. This raises the question of whether and, more generally, under

© Springer International Publishing Switzerland 2015

A. Greiner, B. Fincke, *Public Debt, Sustainability and Economic Growth*,
DOI 10.1007/978-3-319-09348-2_1

which conditions a given path of public debt is sustainable. In economics, modern empirical research analyzing the sustainability of a time series of public debt has begun with the paper by Hamilton and Flavin (1986), who studied US government debt from the early 1960s to the mid 1980s.

When public debt rises in an economy, the government must increase future primary surpluses in order to fulfill its intertemporal budget constraint unless it accepts the possibility of a default, which is not a good option since a government default is usually accompanied by social riots that can endanger the whole political system. Higher primary surpluses can be achieved by raising taxes, by reducing public spending or by a rise in GDP that leads to more tax revenues where, of course, a combination of all three measures is feasible, too. Another possibility, that arises in monetary economics, is that the central bank raises the money supply and accepts a higher inflation rate such that the real value of public debt declines. In the extreme case when the inflation rate exceeds the interest rate on public debt, the real interest rate becomes negative leading to a decline in the public debt to GDP ratio.

When a monetary economy is considered, it is also possible to distinguish between Ricardian and non-Ricardian regimes, which goes back to Aiyagari and Gertler (1985), and that is based on the fiscal theory of the price level. According to that theory, the intertemporal budget constraint of the government must hold for some paths of the price level but not for all, in contrast to the budget constraint of private agents. If the intertemporal budget constraint of the government does not hold for any path of the price level, the government follows a non-Ricardian policy and the intertemporal budget constraint of the government only holds in equilibrium. If the intertemporal budget constraint holds for any price path, and not only for the equilibrium price path, the government pursues a Ricardian fiscal policy. Thus, in a non-Ricardian regime, the government would not commit itself in the future to completely match new public debt with future primary surpluses, because some part of the additional debt is to be financed through money creation. In a Ricardian regime, the opposite holds true and future fiscal revenues are expected to be equal to current public debt. For contributions as regards the fiscal theory of the price level see for example Leeper (1991), Sims (1994) and Woodford (1994). However, the fiscal theory of the price level is controversial and has been criticized, for example in the contribution by Buiter (2002) and in the paper by McCallum (2003). For a survey of the fiscal theory of the price level as well as for further studies criticizing that theory we refer to McCallum and Nelson (2006).

The research analyzing how public debt affects economies has had a long tradition. In the nineteenth century David Ricardo set up what is nowadays called the Ricardian equivalence theorem. According to that theorem budget deficits today require higher taxes in the future when a government cuts taxes without changing present or future public spending. Given that households are forward looking they will realize that they have to pay higher taxes in the future so that their total tax burden remains unchanged. As a consequence, households will reduce their consumption and increase savings in order to meet the future tax burden. The Ricardian equivalence theorem is based on the intertemporal budget constraint of the government and on the permanent income hypothesis. The first principle states that public debt must be sustainable in the sense that outstanding debt today must be equal to the present value of future government primary surpluses. The second principle states that households do not base their consumption on current income but on permanent income so that they will not raise consumption as long as their income increases only temporarily. The Ricardian equivalence theorem is intuitively plausible but rests on assumptions that may be difficult to find in real world economies, such as the absence of distortionary taxation or the non-consideration of economic growth, just to mention two.

With this book, our goal is to analyze the effects of public debt and to work out the mechanisms that make public affect the real side of an economy, using modern models of endogenous economic growth theory. Starting point of our analysis is the intertemporal budget constraint of the government to which the government must stick. When dealing with the question of under which conditions a given path of public debt is sustainable, we primarily focus on public spending and public revenues, ignoring the central bank of an economy in the majority of cases. We do so because governments should not rely on central banks to reduce public debt through money creation since central banks are independent and there is no obligation for them to assist governments in pursuing sustainable debt policies. Thus, we mostly neglect the possibility that a government can use seignorage or inflation to reduce the stock of outstanding real public debt.

In Chap. 2 we start with theoretical considerations dealing with the question of under which conditions a given path of public debt is sustainable. We put particular emphasis on the relation between the primary surplus and the public debt relative to GDP, respectively, and on the ratio of public debt to GDP. Among other things, we demonstrate that a permanently rising debt to GDP ratio is not compatible with a sustainable debt policy. The largest part of this chapter is dedicated to the empirical analysis of the sustainability of a given time series of public debt in real economies. We test Japan and the USA as well as member countries of the euro area, where we exemplarily show for Portugal and Spain how the 2007 financial crisis has affected their sustainability positions. In addition, we also take a brief look at some developing countries.

A basic endogenous growth model that allows for public debt is presented in Chap. 3. There, we study growth and welfare effects of different debt policies and we analyze how those debt policies affect the stability of market economies. We start with a basic model that, then, is generalized by assuming that it is the history of past debt that determines the primary surplus policy of a government. In that chapter, we also consider the central bank that can help the government to fulfill its intertemporal budget constraint by money creation. We analyze the interrelation between fiscal and monetary policies and how it affects growth and welfare as well as inflation and stability of an economy. Finally, the structure of this basic model is changed by assuming that the labor market is characterized by real wage rigidities that give rise to permanent unemployment. The effects of this assumption with respect to economic growth and stability of the economy are then analyzed and we highlight the difference to the model with a perfect labor market.

Chapter 4 extends the basic endogenous growth model from Chap. 3 by allowing for productive public spending. We assume that the government invests in a productive public capital stock that raises aggregate production possibilities. The government finances its expenditures by tax revenues and by public deficits and we again analyze the effects of different public debt policies with respect to growth and welfare as well as with respect to the stability of the economy. We, then, change the tax system and we study how the more realistic assumption of a progressive income tax scheme affects the outcome. In addition, we present and analyze a model where public spending directly affects production in an economy, where we pay particular attention to the emergence of underdevelopment traps and lock-in effects that may arise depending on the initial debt to GDP ratio. Further, we point out the effects that result when the labor market is not perfect but characterized by wage rigidities and unemployment. We present a detailed analysis of that model and we compare it to the one obtained with a perfect labor market.

The role of human capital accumulation for economic growth is analyzed in Chap. 5. There, it is supposed that the government hires teachers and finances additional teaching material to build up human capital in an economy. The government has access to the credit market and can finance its spending by running a deficit and with a distortionary income tax. We define appropriate equilibrium conditions and a balanced growth path and we study effects of different public debt policies. That model, then, is made more elaborate by allowing for a stock of knowledge capital that results as a by-product of production (learning-by-doing). However, knowledge accumulation is only possible if workers dispose of a certain amount of education so that human capital accumulation is an indispensable precondition for the generation of knowledge and, thus, for economic growth.

Finally, Chap. 6 presents empirical estimations analyzing the correlation between economic growth and public debt. In that chapter we perform panel data estimations including selected European economies and the USA for the time period from 1970 to 2012. We estimate both a pooled regression model and the random effects model with the GDP growth rate as the dependent variable that is explained by the public debt to GDP ratio at the beginning of the period under consideration and by other control variables, such as the initial GDP and inflation for example. The GDP growth rate is computed for a 1 year time period, for a 3-years time interval and for a 5-years interval. We also test for non-linearities by applying penalized spline estimation as in Chap. 2.

Chapter 7 summarizes the main findings of this book and points out in brief the effects of public debt and how it affects the allocation of resources in market economies.

Chapter 2
Sustainable Public Debt: Theory and Empirical Evidence

2.1 Theoretical Considerations

Modern research on sustainability of debt policies that applies statistical tests has started with the contribution by Hamilton and Flavin (1986) who analyzed whether the series of public debt in the USA contains a bubble term. Since then a great many papers have been written that try to answer the question of whether given debt policies can be considered as sustainable. The interest in that question is in part due to the fact that the latter question is not only of academic interest but that it has practical relevance, too. Hence, if tests reach the conclusion that given debt policies cannot be considered as sustainable governments should undertake corrective actions.

An important role in many of those studies on sustainability plays the interest rate, an aspect that was pointed out by Wilcox (1989) for example. Recalling that the intertemporal budget constraint of the government requires that the present value of public debt asymptotically converges to zero, the role of the interest rate that is resorted to in order to discount the stream of public debt becomes immediately clear. Therefore, tests have been conceived that reach results which are independent of the interest rate. One such test is to analyze whether public deficits inclusive of interest payments grow at most linearly, as suggested by Trehan and Walsh (1991). If that property is fulfilled a given series of public debt is sustainable because any time series that grows linearly converges to zero if it is exponentially discounted, provided the real interest rate is positive. Denoting by B public debt and by r the interest rate, another test proposed by Trehan and Walsh (1991) is to analyze whether a quasi-difference of public debt, $B_t - \vartheta B_{t-1}$ with $0 \leq \vartheta < 1 + r$, is stationary and whether public debt and primary surpluses are co-integrated. If government debt is quasi-difference stationary and public debt and primary surpluses are cointegrated, public debt is sustainable. Hence, these two tests present alternatives where the outcome is independent of the exact numerical value of the

© Springer International Publishing Switzerland 2015
A. Greiner, B. Fincke, *Public Debt, Sustainability and Economic Growth*,
DOI 10.1007/978-3-319-09348-2_2

interest rate. A survey of analyses that tested on sustainability of debt policies can be found in Afonso (2005), Neck and Sturm (2008) or Bohn (2008).

Another test that has received great attention in the economics literature is the one proposed by Bohn (1995). There, it is suggested to test whether the primary surplus relative to GDP is a positive function of the debt to GDP ratio. If that property holds, a given public debt policy can be shown to be sustainable. This test is very plausible because it has a nice economic intuition: if governments run into debt today they have to take corrective actions in the future by increasing the primary surplus. Otherwise, public debt will not be sustainable. Testing real world debt policies for that property one can indeed find evidence that countries behave like that (see for example Bohn 1998, for the USA and Ballabriga and Martinez-Mongay 2005, Greiner et al. 2007, or Fincke and Greiner 2008, Fincke and Greiner 2011b, for selected countries of the euro area).

From a statistical point of view, a rise in primary surpluses as a response to higher government debt implies that the series of public debt relative to GDP should become a mean-reverting process. This holds because higher debt ratios lead to an increase in the primary surplus relative to GDP, making the debt ratio decline and return to its mean. However, mean-reversion only holds if the reaction coefficient, determining how strongly the primary surplus reacts as public debt rises, is sufficiently large, as will be shown in detail in this section.

In this section, our goal is to elaborate on that test from a theoretical point of view. In particular, we are interested in the behavior of the debt to GDP ratio when governments pursue sustainable debt policies. For example, one question we address is whether a sustainable debt policy is compatible with a rising debt to GDP ratio. Another question we study is whether sustainability can be given if the government does not react to rising debt ratios and whether there probably exists a critical initial debt ratio that makes a sustainable debt policy impossible.

2.1.1 Public Debt and the Primary Surplus

We consider a real economy and we posit here that the government cannot use seignorage or inflation to reduce its outstanding debt. We do this because modern economies are characterized by independent central banks so that governments cannot control the money supply. Thus, governments should not rely on money creation to reduce the real value of outstanding public debt.

Starting point for the analysis of sustainability of public debt, then, is the accounting identity describing the accumulation of public debt in continuous time described by the following differential equation:

$$\dot{B}(t) = r(t)B(t) - S(t), \tag{2.1}$$

with $B(t)$ real public debt[1] at time t, $r(t)$ the real interest rate, $S(t)$ the real government surplus exclusive of interest payments on public debt and the dot over a variable stands for the derivative with respect to time d/dt. A government is said to follow a sustainable debt policy if the present value of public debt converges to zero asymptotically, that is if it does not play a Ponzi game. This implies that $\lim_{t\to\infty} e^{-C_1(t)} B(t) = 0$ holds, with $C_1(t) = \int_0^t r(\mu)d\mu$ the discount rate (see for example Blanchard and Fischer 1989, chapter 2).

Now, assume that the government in the economy chooses the primary surplus to GDP ratio, $s(t) = S(t)/Y(t)$, such that it is a positive linear function of the debt to GDP ratio, $b(t) = B(t)/Y(t)$, and of a term that is independent of public debt, $\phi(t)$ (see Bohn 1995, 1998; Canzoneri, Cumby, and Diba 2001, or Greiner 2008a). The primary surplus ratio, then, can be written as

$$s(t) = \psi(t)\, b(t) + \phi(t), \tag{2.2}$$

where $\psi(t)$ is the coefficient determining how strong the primary surplus reacts to changes in the public debt ratio and that is time-varying. It should be noted that any non-linear model can be approximated by a linear model with time-varying coefficients. Further, the approximation is good if the parameter changes smoothly (cf. Granger 2008). Thus, the modeling in (2.2) can be justified and there does not seem to be the need for a more general function describing the response of the primary surplus to public debt.

The term $\phi(t)$ is also time dependent and it is influenced by other economic variables, such as social spending or transitory government expenditures in general. As concerns $\phi(t)$ we suppose that it is bounded from above and below by a certain finite number that is constant over time. Since $\phi(t)$ gives the autonomous part of the primary surplus relative to GDP, that assumption is obvious and realistic. We should also like to point out that $\phi(t)$ cannot be completely controlled by the government. The government can influence that parameter to a certain degree but it has not complete control over it because $\phi(t)$ is also affected by the business cycle for example that can affect temporary government outlays.

In the next subsection, we analyze conditions that must be fulfilled such that the intertemporal budget constraint of the government holds and how the debt to GDP ratio evolves in that case.

2.1.2 Conditions for Sustainability of Public Debt

Before we start our analysis we make two additional assumptions. First, we posit that the interest rate on government bonds exceeds the growth rate of GDP on average so that $\int r(\mu)d\mu > \int g(\mu)d\mu$, with g denoting the growth rate of GDP.

[1] Strictly speaking, B should be real public net debt.

We make this assumption because otherwise the intertemporal budget constraint would not pose a problem for the government since it can grow out of debt in that case. In addition, this condition is fulfilled for countries of the euro area at least since the 1980s. Second, we neglect the case where public debt becomes negative meaning that the government would be a net lender. This is done for reasons of realism because a situation with negative public debt is of less relevance for real world economies.

In our analysis of sustainable debt policies we are particularly interested under which conditions sustainability of public debt is given and in the question of whether a sustainable debt policy is compatible with a rising debt to GDP ratio. To study those questions, we distinguish between two cases. First, we analyze the situation where the government sets the primary surplus according to Eq. (2.2), with $\psi(t) \neq 0$. Second, we study the case where the primary surplus does not react to variations in the debt ratio, implying that $\psi(t) = 0$ holds. In the latter case, we posit in addition that the government sets the primary surplus relative to GDP equal to its maximum value.

The Primary Surplus as a Function of Public Debt

In this subsection, we posit that the primary surplus is given by Eq. (2.2), with $\psi(t) \neq 0$. To study sustainability of public debt, we combine Eqs. (2.1) and (2.2) yielding

$$\dot{B}(t) = (r(t) - \psi(t))\, B(t) - \phi(t)\, Y(t). \tag{2.3}$$

With (2.3), the debt to GDP ratio evolves according to

$$\frac{\dot{b}}{b} = \frac{\dot{B}}{B} - \frac{\dot{Y}}{Y} \tag{2.4}$$

which is equivalent to

$$\dot{b}(t) = (r(t) - \psi(t))\, b(t) - \phi(t) - g(t)\, b(t). \tag{2.5}$$

With these two equations, we can derive our first result in Proposition 1.[2]

Proposition 1 *Assume that the upper bound of the primary surplus to GDP ratio is not binding. Then, a strictly positive reaction coefficient on average so that* $\int_0^t \psi(\mu) d\mu = \infty$ *holds for* $t \to \infty$ *guarantees sustainability of public debt.*

[2] In this book we consider deterministic economies. Sustainability of public debt with an additive stochastic term is briefly discussed in the appendix to this chapter.

For $\int_0^t \psi(\mu)d\mu > \int_0^t (r(\mu) - g(\mu))\, d\mu$, *the debt to GDP ratio converges to a constant and it diverges to plus or minus infinity for* $\int_0^t \psi(\mu)d\mu \leq \int_0^t (r(\mu) - g(\mu))\, d\mu$, *for* $t \to \infty$ *respectively.*

Proof See the appendix to this chapter.

This proposition demonstrates that a positive and sufficiently large reaction coefficient on average is sufficient for sustainability of public debt. If the reaction coefficient is strictly negative on average, the discounted value of public debt diverges to infinity. But Proposition 1 also shows that a positive value of the reaction coefficient does not necessarily imply that the debt to GDP ratio remains constant or that it asymptotically converges to zero. Only if the reaction coefficient exceeds the positive difference between the interest rate and the GDP growth rate on average, convergence can be guaranteed. Otherwise, the debt to GDP ratio diverges to infinity.

With the result of Proposition 1, one could reach the conclusion that a sustainable debt policy is compatible with a continuously rising debt to GDP ratio, in case the reaction coefficient ψ is positive on average but smaller than the difference between the average interest rate and the average growth rate, $r - g$. However, when the government sets the primary surplus according to rule (2.2), that possibility is not given as Proposition 2 demonstrates.

Proposition 2 *If the government pursues a sustainable debt policy and sets the primary surplus according to the rule given by* (2.2)*, the debt to GDP ratio remains bounded.*

Proof Assume that $b(t) \to \infty$. According to (2.2) this implies $s(t) \to \infty$ which, however, is excluded because the primary surplus cannot become larger than GDP implying that $s(t) < 1$ must always hold. □

The result in Proposition 2 is simply due to the fact that the primary surplus must be financed out of the GDP so that the ratio of the primary surplus to GDP must be smaller than a certain finite number that is lower one. Consequently, when the government pursues a sustainable debt policy and raises the primary surplus relative to GDP as the debt to GDP ratio increases, the debt ratio must remain bounded in the long-run.

Hence, a situation may be observed where the debt to GDP ratio rises over a certain time period although the primary surplus positively reacts to higher public debt. Such an evolution of public debt may be compatible with a sustainable debt policy but it cannot go on forever. Sooner or later, the public debt to GDP ratio must become constant or decline. Otherwise, sustainability is not given.

The Primary Surplus Independent of Public Debt

In our considerations up to now, it was assumed that the government sets the primary surplus according to the rule specified in Eq. (2.2). However, one could argue that governments can perform sustainable debt policies without reacting to higher public debt if they only chose the primary surplus sufficiently high, independent of public debt. Further, a situation is feasible where the government cannot react to higher debt since there is no scope for it because the primary surplus relative to GDP has already reached its upper bound. In both cases the reaction coefficient $\psi(t)$ would be zero.

In order to analyze that case we set $\psi(t) = 0$ and we denote by $m < 1$ the constant upper bound of the primary surplus to GDP ratio. In addition, we assume that the government sets the primary surplus to GDP ratio equal to that maximum value for all times, that is $s(t) = m$ for all t. Thus, the evolution of public debt is described by

$$\dot{B}(t) = r(t)\, B(t) - m\, Y(t) \tag{2.6}$$

and the debt to GDP ratio evolves according to

$$\dot{b}(t) = r(t)\, b(t) - m - g(t)\, b(t). \tag{2.7}$$

Given Eqs. (2.6) and (2.7), we can derive Proposition 3.

Proposition 3 *Assume that the initial debt to GDP ratio exceeds a certain threshold, given by* $b_{crit} = m \int_0^{\infty} e^{-(C_1(\mu)-C_2(\mu))} d\mu$, *with* $C_1(\mu) = \int_0^{\mu} r(\nu) d\nu$, $C_2(\mu) = \int_0^{\mu} g(\nu) d\nu$. *Then, a sustainable debt policy is excluded.*

If the initial debt to GDP ratio is smaller than or equal to the critical threshold, the government can pursue a sustainable debt policy. In this case, the debt to GDP ratio converges to a constant.

Proof See the appendix to this chapter.

Proposition 3 states that a sustainable debt policy cannot be pursued if the initial debt to GDP ratio is larger than a certain critical value. The critical value b_{crit} depends on how large the primary surplus relative to GDP can maximally become, m, and on the average difference between the interest rate and the growth rate, $r - g$. Hence, countries that do not stabilize their debt to GDP ratio but instead let it grow for a longer time period face the risk that they find themselves in a situation where they cannot react to higher debt to GDP ratios by raising their primary surplus relative to GDP. Then, it may become impossible to pursue a sustainable debt policy, independent of how large the primary surplus relative to GDP is set. In this case, the public debt to GDP ratio becomes unbounded asymptotically.

The proposition also demonstrates that the government can control public debt if it chooses the maximally possible value of the primary surplus, m, provided the initial debt to GDP ratio is not too large, that is if it is smaller than the critical value b_{crit}. In that case, sustainability of public debt is guaranteed and the debt to GDP ratio asymptotically converges to a constant. Of course, convergence to a constant is only given if the government always sets the primary surplus equal to its maximum value m and does not switch to a different debt policy.

It must also be pointed out that in the case when the primary surplus is set such that the debt to GDP ratio converges to a finite value, for example by following the primary surplus rule in Eq. (2.2), it cannot be guaranteed that $\lim_{t\to\infty} b(t) \leq b_{crit}$ holds, i.e. the critical debt to GDP ratio may be reached before the debt to GDP ratio has converged to its limiting value. If such a case occurs, the upper bound of the primary surplus to GDP ratio becomes binding so that the government violates its intertemporal budget constraint, unless it sets the primary surplus to GDP ratio equal to its maximum value as long as the debt to GDP ratio has not yet exceeded its critical value (see Greiner 2013a, for more details concerning that problem).

In the next section we perform empirical estimates based on the theoretical considerations of this section.

2.2 Empirics: Japan, Germany and the USA

With the financial crisis that had started in 2007 and the ensuing economic downturn countries have faced extensive pressure on their public budgets and are confronted with the difficult challenge to stabilize the economy while keeping the deficits moderate. Within this context the development of public debt is a central aspect that influences the budgets of governments because all measures and actions taken now have to be financed. Therefore, the currently accumulating deficits present a serious economic and political problem both now and in the future. This holds especially for European countries taking part in the Monetary Union, which are subject to the conditions of the Convergence Criteria of the Treaty on the European Union and the Stability and Growth Pact that imposes, among other things, an upper bound with respect to the public debt to GDP ratio. But it also affects other economies since problems of public debt, such as rising interest payments and redemptions, will appear at some point in the future, even in a long term perspective.

With this section we intend to perform a comparative study of the public debt situations in Japan, Germany and the United States. These countries have been selected because the United States represent the largest economy worldwide with a real GDP of 11,742.3 billion dollars and Japan is the second largest industrialized economy in the world with a real GDP of 3,597.6 billion dollars in 2008, respectively. Germany, finally, is clearly smaller than the other two countries, but it nevertheless is the third largest advanced country and it is the major economy in Europe with a real GDP of 2,351.8 billion dollars in 2008.[3]

In order to analyze the evolution of public debt in these economies we follow Fincke and Greiner (2011a) and first present a descriptive illustration of the debt situation for each country in a historical context, where we take into consideration particular circumstances the economy was exposed to in the past. We look at possible reasons for rising debt ratios and how governments have dealt with them

[3]For the Data see OECD (2009), base year 2000.

and how they managed the situation in the past. In a second step, we perform an econometric analysis in order to shed light on the question of whether the governments in the countries under consideration have performed sustainable debt policies.

2.2.1 *Descriptive Historical Approach*

We start with a historical perspective of the fiscal situation in the three countries under consideration to get a first impression of the dimension of public debt in those economies. As concerns the data we use annual fiscal year data, which is in part due to the availability of those data. For reasons of consistency we apply this concept to all countries considered.[4]

We start with the graphics of the historical debt ratios for at least the last 50 years, where we begin with Japan.

Japan

In order to get a first impression of the development of the National government debt in Japan, the time path of public debt relative to GDP is illustrated in Fig. 2.1.[5]

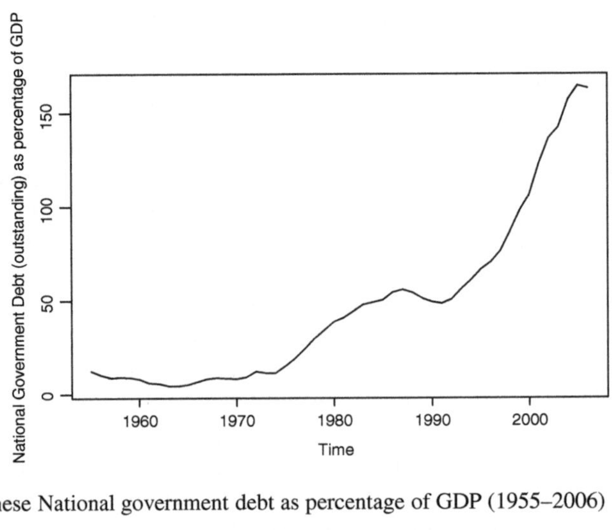

Fig. 2.1 Japanese National government debt as percentage of GDP (1955–2006)

[4]In Germany the fiscal year equals the calendar year. In Japan and in the United States a fiscal year lasts from April until March and from October until September, respectively. Whenever necessary, data have been adjusted.

[5] For the data see Japan Statistics Bureau (2009). We also have to thank Toichiro Asada for helping us understand particularities of the Japanese government account system.

With a drop in the tax revenue in 1965, the Japanese administration started to issue government bonds in the post-war period for the first time.[6] Further, slight rises in the debt ratio can be ascribed to the two oil crises in 1973 and 1979/1980, with the administration issuing an additional kind of bonds in 1975 to meet the economic slump, which ensued the first oil crisis.[7] Nevertheless, as regards Japan's debt situation, the distinctive feature is the enormous increase starting with the 1990s. This can, in part, be ascribed to the breakdown of the 'bubble economy' on the stock and land market in 1991. It was followed by an economic downturn and only in the recent past a slight recovery going along with a decline of the debt ratio can be observed.[8] In 2005, a maximum of 164.4 % of National government debt relative to GDP was attained. This is the worst situation of all OECD countries.[9]

Summarizing these historical aspects, the development since the 1990s seems to be really serious and asks for a closer study of the properties of the Japanese debt policy.

Germany

Next, we look at the fiscal situation in Germany. In Fig. 2.2 the evolution of Germany's public debt relative to GDP is depicted for the period from 1950 until 2007.[10]

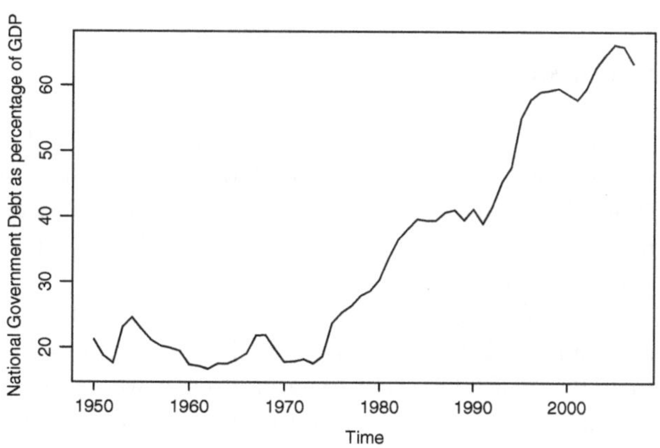

Fig. 2.2 German National government debt as percentage of GDP (1950–2007)

[6]See also for example Asako et al. (1991), pp. 452 and 453 and Ihori et al. (2001) especially sec. 1. For the tax revenue statistics of the selected economies see for example OECD (2009a).

[7]See Asako et al. (1991) also for additional characterizations of the Japanese deficits.

[8]See also Ihori et al. (2001) sec. 1.

[9]For a comparison of General government gross financial liabilities data see OECD (2009a).

[10]For the data see SVR (2008) and Statistisches Bundesamt (2008).

While debt ratios had remained at moderate levels during the 1950s, the time of the so called Wirtschaftswunder (economic miracle), as well as during the 1960s with values around 20 %, the debt ratio began to rise with the period of the oil crisis in the 1970s and even more rapidly during the 1980s to about 40 % of GDP. A unique feature that strongly affected the shape of the German debt to GDP ratio was the German Reunification in 1989/1990. Afterwards, with then 16 federal states, necessary adjustments and investments lead to a rapid increase of the debt ratio, soon approaching the 60 % benchmark during the 1990s. But this severe increase in public debt relative to GDP, starting in the middle of the 1970s until about 1990, cannot be explained by a heavy drop in tax revenues. Thus, other economic influences such as the aftermath of the oil crises 1973 and 1979/1980 on the expenditure side, for example, should be taken into consideration.

With the beginning of the new century, a stronger fiscal discipline and favorable economic conditions lead to a decline of the debt to GDP ratio. That evolution could, in part, be ascribed to the European Monetary Union with the criteria required to participate and conditions agreed upon. However, this trend did not last long and with 2002 the national government debt relative to GDP began to rise again.

Recapitulating the development of the German debt ratio, the almost monotonously rising time path of public debt relative to GDP presents a serious problem. In order to gain additional insight how German governments have coped with the rising debt ratio, we perform statistical tests in the next section. But before, we briefly consider the situation in the United States.

United States

For a meaningful representation of the history of the United States public debt, we use data for the years from 1940 until 2008. This time range allows to include World War II data but also allows to focus on the recent economic development of the public debt. In Fig. 2.3 the time path of United States Federal debt is shown as a percentage of GDP.[11]

Obviously, the graph is immensely shaped by the influences of World War II. The maximum of United States public debt was achieved in 1946 with debt amounting to 121.7 % of GDP. Thus, as a first result we can state that there have been more serious fiscal situations than the current one (although apparently influenced by war and its aftermath) and even those problems have been coped with and overcome.

This period of high debt ratios had been followed by a continuous decline until the 1970s. Then, some influence can be ascribed to the oil crisis and the resulting increases in the debt ratio. With the beginning of the 1980s, high budget deficits resulted in a sudden rise of the debt ratio to GDP. These high deficits during peace time are sometimes referred to as ‘Reagan deficits’ named after the president at that

[11]See United States Government (2008) for the data.

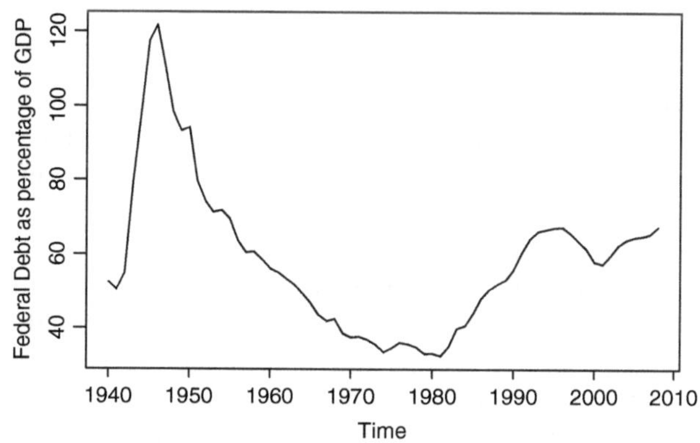

Fig. 2.3 US Federal debt at the end of year as percentage of GDP (1940–2008)

time. They were accompanied by a decline in tax revenues relative to GDP in the first years of that era.

During the early 1990s the debt ratio remained high although smaller primary deficits relative to GDP can be observed. These deficits might, among other things, be due to the gulf war in 1990/1991. But it was not until the middle of the 1990s, before the debt ratio began to decline. This was mostly the result of higher taxes and due to budgetary discipline, too. With the beginning of the new century, the debt ratio started to increase again. A possible reason for that can be seen in the aftermath of the terrorist attacks in September 2001 and the following 'war on terrorism'. Thus, concluding this descriptive part it can be summarized that there had been situations in the USA even worse than the current one and these had been coped with successfully. Therefore, although the current debt situation in the United States does not look too bright, it is not as severe as it seems viewn from a historical perspective.

2.2.2 Empirical Approach

Although the historical considerations from the previous subsection do indicate some important aspects with respect to the financial situation in Japan, Germany and the United States, they cannot replace statistical tests. Primarily, we are interested in the question of whether the past time series of public debt can be considered as sustainable. First, we test the reaction of the primary surplus relative to GDP to variations in the debt to GDP ratio.

Estimating the Response of the Primary Surplus to Public Debt

With the theoretical background from Sect. 2.1 we can now start testing for the correlation between the primary surplus to GDP ratio and the public debt ratio. To implement the test we estimate the following equation,

$$s(t) = \psi(t)\,b(t) + \phi^T Z(t) + \epsilon(t), \tag{2.8}$$

with $s(t)$ the primary surplus to GDP ratio at time t and $b(t)$ the public debt to GDP ratio. Other variables that influence the primary surplus ratio are included in the vector $Z(t)$. It contains 1 in its first element, yielding the intercept, and further variables in its other elements. The term $\epsilon(t)$ represents an error term, that is assumed to be i.i.d. $N(0, \sigma^2)$.

The variables included in $Z(t)$ are motivated by the tax smoothing hypothesis. According to that hypothesis public deficits should be used such that tax rates remain constant in order to minimize the excess burden of taxation. Thus, regular expenditures should be paid for by ordinary revenues. Unexpected spending should be financed by public deficits. We also include a business cycle variable, $YVar(t)$, to account for fluctuations in GDP. It is calculated by subtracting the long term trend of GDP from its realized values.[12] Positive values for *YVar* indicate booms and negative values indicate recessions. Moreover, deviations of real public expenditures from their long-run trend affect the primary surplus ratio, too. Like for the business cycle variable, we use the fluctuations of public expenditures around their trend, denoted by $GVar(t)$. The latter is computed as the realized values minus the trend values, that is $GVar_t = (G_t - G_t^*)$ with G_t for real public spending and G_t^* being its trend obtained by applying the Hodrick-Prescott filter to that time series. All data are annual.

For the estimation of Eq. (2.8), we substitute the debt to GDP ratio $b(t)$ by the lagged debt ratio $b(t-1)$ since budget plans are usually made one fiscal year ahead. Further, we thus also take account of the endogeneity problem of the public debt to GDP ratio. Hence, Eq. (2.8) can be rewritten as

$$s(t) = \phi_0 + \psi(t)b(t-1) + \phi_1 GVar(t) + \phi_2 YVar(t) + \epsilon(t). \tag{2.9}$$

Concerning the estimation technique, we resort to penalized spline estimation that is more flexible than OLS estimation (for a short introduction to penalized spline estimation see Appendix A or, for a more thorough introduction, Hastie and Tibshirani 1990 or Ruppert et al. 2003) and that allows us to obtain time-varying coefficients.[13] Thus, we can estimate the reaction coefficient $\psi(t)$ in Eq. (2.9) as a function of time. This makes it possible to show how that coefficient has evolved over the period under consideration.

Regarding the estimation results we will concentrate on the complete estimation with all three explanatory variables. Nevertheless, we also make estimations with different combinations of the variables in order to check the robustness of our results.

---

[12]This is computed by applying the Hodrick-Prescott-Filter (HP-Filter) to the real GDP series.

[13]All graphics and estimations have been performed with R (Version 2.5.0). The estimations were done with the package *mgcv* (Version 1.3–28) and for the unit root tests we used the package *urca*.

Japan

As seen in Fig. 2.1 the public debt situation in Japan has become more and more severe in the past 15–20 years, as already pointed out in the last subsection.

To get additional information on the public finance situation, we now perform the test with the Japanese data and consider the years from 1966 to 2006.[14] The Tables 2.1–2.4 summarize the estimation results for Japan for the period from 1966 until 2006. The year 1966 has been chosen as the starting point because in 1965 Japan issued national bonds for the first time after World War II.

Table 2.1 shows a positive average coefficient for the debt ratio, ψ, that, however, is not statistically significant. The only significant coefficients are the ones for the deviation of public spending from its trend, *GVar*, and for the business cycle variable, *YVar*. They have the expected sign, indicating that higher spending than usual leads to a lower primary surplus ratio and the primary surplus is higher in times of economic booms. The goodness of fit with $R^2(adj) = 0.937$ is quite high, indicating a good fit of the model, and the Durbin Watson test statistic $DW = 1.86$ does not indicate correlation of the residuals.

The deviation of the reaction coefficient from its average is reflected in the smooth term $sm(t)$. The estimated degrees of freedom (edf) are $edf = 6.789$,

Table 2.1 Equation (2.9) for Japan

	Coeff.	Stand. err. (t-stat)	Pr(>t)
Const.	−0.008	0.007(−1.163)	0.254
$b(t-1)$	0.015	0.031(0.464)	0.646
$GVar(t)$	−0.057	0.024(−2.375)	0.024
$YVar(t)$	0.168	0.030(5.558)	$4.71 \cdot 10^{-6}$
sm(t)	edf: 6.789	F:46.27	p-value: $3.17 \cdot 10^{-15}$
	GCV: $2.26 \cdot 10^{-5}$	R^2(adj):0.937	DW:1.86

Table 2.2 Equation (2.9) without *YVar*, Japan

	Coeff.	Stand. err. (t-stat)	Pr(>t)
Const.	−0.031	0.010(−3.029)	0.005
$b(t-1)$	0.112	0.044(2.550)	0.016
$GVar(t)$	−0.037	0.031(−1.203)	0.239
sm(t)	edf: 8.842	F:51.82	p-value: $1.59 \cdot 10^{-15}$
	GCV: $2.57 \cdot 10^{-5}$	R^2(adj):0.931	DW:1.88

[14]For the data see Japan Statistics Bureau (2009) and International Statistical Yearbook (2009). Please notice that for the primary surplus only the tax revenue is used and the social security payments have been subtracted from total expenditures in order to get reliable data.

Table 2.3 Equation (2.9) without *GVar*, Japan

	Coeff.	Stand. err. (t-stat)	Pr(>t)
Const.	−0.008	0.008(−1.026)	0.313
$b(t-1)$	0.016	0.036(0.441)	0.662
$YVar(t)$	0.147	0.031(4.807)	$3.82 \cdot 10^{-5}$
sm(t)	edf: 7.342	F:54.53	p-value: $<2 \cdot 10^{-16}$
	GCV: $2.32 \cdot 10^{-5}$	R^2(adj):0.934	DW:2.18

Table 2.4 Equation (2.9) with *b* only, Japan

	Coeff.	Stand. err. (t-stat)	Pr(>t)
Const.	−0.029	0.010(−2.891)	0.007
$b(t-1)$	0.107	0.044(2.427)	0.021
sm(t)	edf: 8.838	F:56.2	p-value: $<2 \cdot 10^{-16}$
	GCV: $2.54 \cdot 10^{-5}$	R^2(adj):0.929	DW:2.01

Fig. 2.4 Deviation $sm(t)$ from the average coefficient for $b(t-1)$ for Japan

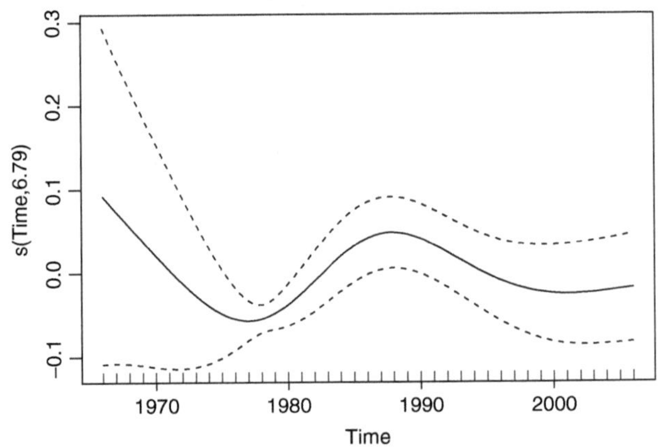

showing that the reaction coefficient $\psi(t)$ is not constant but time-varying. In addition, the smooth term is highly significant. The actual value of the reaction coefficient $\psi(t)$ at time t, then, is given by the average coefficient as reported in Table 2.1 plus the deviation from that value as shown in Fig. 2.4. The dashed lines show the 95 % confidence interval and the solid line represents the point estimation of the smooth term.[15]

The combination of the mean of the coefficient for $b(t-1)$ and the time-varying smooth term is negative for the period from 1971 until 1982 and then again from about 1996 onwards. The earlier period mentioned characterizes the first strong

[15]See also Wood (2001) especially p. 23.

increase of the debt ratio to GDP as shown in Fig. 2.1, that is followed by a phase of budgetary discipline with a stronger emphasis on responding to rising debt ratios. The other stage of negative response can be explained by the difficult fiscal situation after the burst of the bubble in the early 1990s.

Thus, although the mean of the reaction coefficient is positive in Table 2.1, it is not statistically significant so that the hypothesis of an unsustainable public debt cannot be rejected. But, the results in Table 2.4 and in Table 2.2 appear to be promising since the average of the coefficient is significantly positive and still a relatively high goodness of fit is achieved, leading to the conclusion that the hypothesis of sustainable debt policy should not be rejected too early. The most suitable model is the one shown in Table 2.1 since the GCV value is the smallest and that model best fits the data as can judged from R^2(adj).

Since the Japanese estimation results from above do not clearly indicate whether a sustainable debt policy has been implemented or rather not, we will now consider net debt, that is liabilities less assets, and see if this changes the implications and conclusion. Also we do that because financial assets in Japan are not negligible. They are more than twice as high as in the United States and in Germany, on average, over the period from 1970 to 2007. In 2007, the financial assets amounted to 84.7 % of GDP which is more than four times as high as in the United States and in Germany in that year.[16]

In order to obtain a first impression, the net debt is depicted as a percentage of GDP in Fig. 2.5 for the period from 1970 until 2006. Obviously, the general trend and the shape are similar to the public debt ratio shown in Fig. 2.1, with the two distinctive increases in the middle of the 1970s and after 1991, as already mentioned above.

Tables 2.5–2.8 present the estimation results with the net debt relative to GDP for the period from 1971 until 2006.

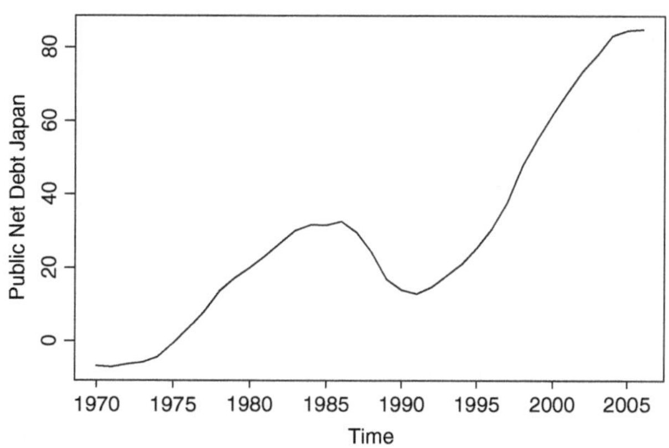

Fig. 2.5 General government net financial liabilities, Japan (1970–2006)

[16]For the net debt data see OECD (2009a) general government net financial liabilities, available from 1970 onwards. Apart from that, all other source are retained from the other estimations for Japan.

Table 2.5 Equation (2.9) for Japan (net debt)

	Coeff.	Stand. err. (t-stat)	Pr(>t)
Const.	−0.016	0.002(−8.650)	$7.20 \cdot 10^{-9}$
$b(t-1)$	0.036	0.007(5.181)	$2.57 \cdot 10^{-5}$
$GVar(t)$	−0.111	0.030(−3.690)	0.001
$YVar(t)$	0.365	0.056(6.586)	$7.89 \cdot 10^{-7}$
sm(t)	edf: 7.804	F:53.07	p-value: $9.54 \cdot 10^{-14}$
	GCV: $2.08 \cdot 10^{-5}$	R^2(adj):0.953	DW:2.31

Table 2.6 Without *YVar*, JAP (net debt)

	Coeff.	Stand. err. (t-stat)	Pr(>t)
Const.	−0.015	0.003(−5.751)	$4.77 \cdot 10^{-6}$
$b(t-1)$	0.015	0.009(1.668)	0.107
$GVar(t)$	−0.003	0.036(−0.069)	0.946
sm(t)	edf: 7.124	F:24.6	p-value: $1.69 \cdot 10^{-10}$
	GCV: $4.90 \cdot 10^{-5}$	R^2(adj):0.882	DW:1.67

Table 2.7 Without *GVar*, JAP (net debt)

	Coeff.	Stand. err. (t-stat)	Pr(>t)
Const.	−0.015	0.002(−7.205)	$1.33 \cdot 10^{-7}$
$b(t-1)$	0.025	0.007(3.469)	0.002
$YVar(t)$	0.263	0.053(4.937)	$4.17 \cdot 10^{-5}$
sm(t)	edf: 7.484	F:47.32	p-value: $1.12 \cdot 10^{-13}$
	GCV: $2.82 \cdot 10^{-5}$	R^2(adj):0.933	DW:2.38

Table 2.8 With *b* only, JAP (net debt)

	Coeff.	Stand. err. (t-stat)	Pr(>t)
Const.	−0.015	0.003(−5.776)	$4.02 \cdot 10^{-6}$
$b(t-1)$	0.015	0.009(1.717)	0.098
sm(t)	edf: 7.368	F:28.61	p-value: $1.88 \cdot 10^{-11}$
	GCV: $4.62 \cdot 10^{-5}$	R^2(adj):0.885	DW:1.68

As the tables show, the reaction coefficient now is positive on average and statistically significant for each estimation at least at the 10 % level (in Table 2.6 it has missed that mark only scarcely). When looking at the results in Table 2.5, one can realize that the mean of the coefficient for $b(t-1)$ is even significant at the 0.1 % level. The coefficients for public expenditures and for the business cycle again show the expected sign and are highly significant as well. The estimated

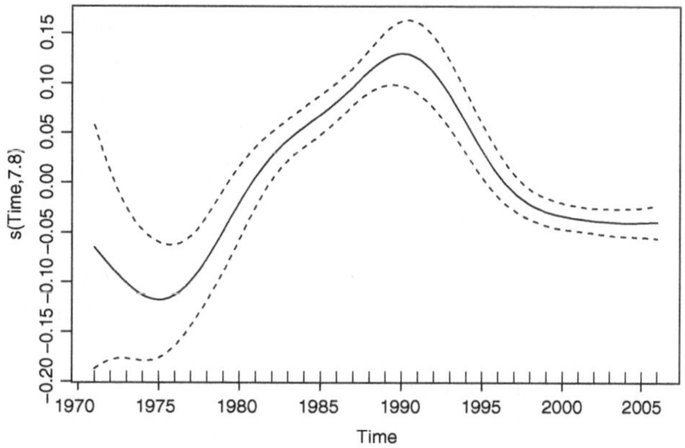

Fig. 2.6 Deviation $sm(t)$ from the average coefficient for $b(t-1)$ accounting for assets for Japan

degrees of freedom for the smooth term are $edf = 7.804$ and that term is statistically significant. Moreover, a really high goodness of fit has been achieved and the Durbin Watson test statistic does not indicate correlation of the residuals.

The actual value for the reaction coefficient $\psi(t)$ at time t is again given by the average value shown in Table 2.5 plus the deviation from that value as shown in Fig. 2.6. It can be realized that $\psi(t)$ has been negative only for the period before 1980 and after 2000. The shape of the smooth parameter in Fig. 2.6 is similar to that from Fig. 2.4. Both show an increase of the reaction since the late 1970s and a rapid fall since 1991 that only has slowed down towards the beginning of the new century.

The other estimation results in Tables 2.6–2.8 show that the average coefficient for $b(t-1)$ is significantly positive. As above, the most promising estimation model is the complete model with the results in Table 2.5, which are characterized by the smallest GCV value and by the highest R^2(adj). Therefore, the outcome of the estimations with net debt allows us to conclude that the primary surplus ratio increases as the debt to GDP ratio rises, thus indicating sustainability of public debt in Japan once government assets are taken into account.

Germany

Next we apply the test to German data. As shown in Fig. 2.2 the evolution of public debt has been affected by two distinctive increases, one starting in the middle of the 1970s and the other after German Reunification in 1990. For the empirical estimations, we use data from 1961 until 2006. The estimation results are presented in Tables 2.9–2.12.[17]

[17] See OECD (2003, 2009a) and International Statistical Yearbook (2009) for the data. From 1991 on, data for the united Germany are used. The estimations have been done without the data for 2000 since the primary surplus is biased in that year due to exceptional revenues from the UMTS auction.

Table 2.9 Equation (2.9) for Germany

	Coeff.	Stand. err. (t-stat)	Pr(>t)
Const.	−0.035	0.019(−1.793)	0.082
$b(t-1)$	0.121	0.068(1.794)	0.082
$GVar(t)$	−0.181	0.045(−4.021)	0.0003
$YVar(t)$	0.290	0.070(4.170)	0.0002
sm(t)	edf: 8.524	F:7.392	p-value: $8.81\cdot10^{-6}$
	GCV: $7.01\cdot10^{-5}$	R^2(adj):0.724	DW:2.27

Table 2.10 Equation (2.9) without *YVar*, GER

	Coeff.	Stand. err. (t-stat)	Pr(>t)
Const.	−0.038	0.023(−1.666)	0.105
$b(t-1)$	0.132	0.079(1.674)	0.103
$GVar(t)$	−0.150	0.053(−2.855)	0.007
sm(t)	edf: 8.115	F:4.155	p-value: 0.001
	GCV: $1.02\cdot10^{-4}$	R^2(adj):0.583	DW:1.88

Table 2.11 Equation (2.9) without *GVar*, GER

	Coeff.	Stand. err. (t-stat)	Pr(>t)
Const.	−0.066	0.021(−3.065)	0.004
$b(t-1)$	0.229	0.075(3.064)	0.004
$YVar(t)$	0.235	0.080(2.933)	0.006
sm(t)	edf: 8.669	F:9.189	p-value: $7.83\cdot10^{-7}$
	GCV: $9.41\cdot10^{-5}$	R^2(adj):0.62	DW:1.86

Table 2.12 Equation (2.9) with *b* only, GER

	Coeff.	Stand. err. (t-stat)	Pr(>t)
Const.	−0.064	0.023(−2.749)	0.009
$b(t-1)$	0.223	0.081(2.753)	0.009
sm(t)	edf: 8.432	F:6.599	p-value: $1.98\cdot10^{-5}$
	GCV: $1.13\cdot10^{-4}$	R^2(adj):0.528	DW:1.62

Looking at the estimation result presented in Table 2.9, one realizes that the average coefficient of the public debt to GDP ratio is positive and significant at the 10 % level. The intercept, the coefficient for public expenditure and the one for the business cycle are significant as well. Again, the negative sign of the spending coefficient indicates higher primary surpluses in periods with less spending and that

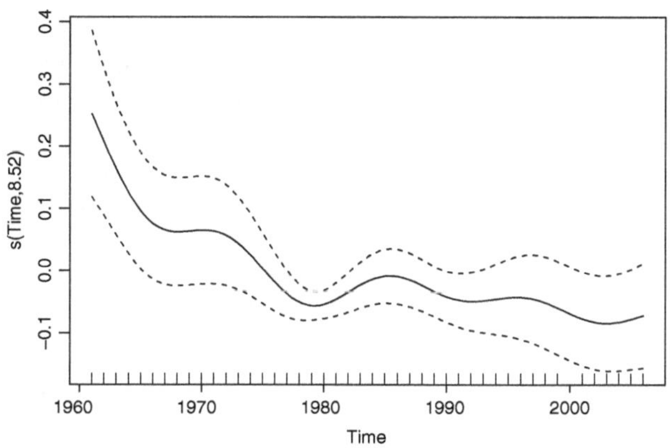

Fig. 2.7 Deviation $sm(t)$ from the average coefficient for $b(t-1)$ for Germany

of the business cycle variable implies higher primary surplus ratios in economic booms.

Once more, the parameter $sm(t)$ reflects the deviation from the mean of the coefficient over the period considered, which is statistically significant, and $edf = 8.524$ indicates fluctuations over time. The value of $R^2(adj)$ shows a fine goodness of fit and, concerning the correlation of the residuals, the Durbin Watson test statistic does not show evidence of autocorrelation.

In Fig. 2.7 the path of the smooth term is depicted.

Although the time path is alternating, the overall trend is decreasing. This shows that for the past 45 years the response of the primary surplus to public debt has become weaker but, nevertheless, it remained positive for the whole period under consideration. Adding the mean of the coefficient of the debt ratio and the smooth term leads to a positive reaction coefficient $\psi(t)$, indicating that Germany has followed a sustainable debt policy path for the years from 1961 until 2006. Once more, the model containing all variables, with the results shown in Table 2.9, replicates the true data generating process best, since it features the lowest GCV value and the highest R^2(adj).

United States

With an idea of the debt situation in the United States, which is depicted in Fig. 2.3, we now apply the test to United States data for the period from 1941 until 2007.[18] Tables 2.13–2.16 present the results from estimating Eq. (2.9) with different combinations of the variables. Only the debt to GDP ratio is contained in each estimation.

[18]The data have been obtained from United States Government (2008).

Table 2.13 Equation (2.9) for the USA

	Coeff.	Stand. err. (t-stat)	Pr(>t)
Const.	−0.128	0.018(−7.130)	$2.17 \cdot 10^{-9}$
$b(t-1)$	0.223	0.034(6.608)	$1.57 \cdot 10^{-8}$
$GVar(t)$	−0.204	0.017(−11.83)	$<2 \cdot 10^{-16}$
$YVar(t)$	0.347	0.091(3.806)	0.0004
sm(t)	edf: 7.317	F:53.28	p-value: $<2 \cdot 10^{-16}$
	GCV: $2.53 \cdot 10^{-4}$	R^2(adj):0.934	DW:1.58

Table 2.14 Equation (2.9) without *YVar*, USA

	Coeff.	Stand. err. (t-stat)	Pr(>t)
Const.	−0.189	0.026(−7.176)	$1.84 \cdot 10^{-9}$
$b(t-1)$	0.339	0.050(6.799)	$7.67 \cdot 10^{-9}$
$GVar(t)$	−0.146	0.009(−16.41)	$<2 \cdot 10^{-16}$
sm(t)	edf: 8.406	F:50.98	p-value: $<2 \cdot 10^{-16}$
	GCV: $2.83 \cdot 10^{-4}$	R^2(adj):0.926	DW:1.47

Table 2.15 Equation (2.9) without *GVar*, USA

	Coeff.	Stand. err. (t-stat)	Pr(>t)
Const.	−0.319	0.050(−6.418)	$3.33 \cdot 10^{-8}$
$b(t-1)$	0.586	0.094(6.213)	$7.19 \cdot 10^{-8}$
$YVar(t)$	−0.658	0.076(−8.706)	$6.08 \cdot 10^{-12}$
sm(t)	edf: 8.795	F:25.90	p-value: $<2 \cdot 10^{-16}$
	GCV: $6.98 \cdot 10^{-4}$	R^2(adj):0.819	DW:1.30

Table 2.16 Equation (2.9) with *b* only, USA

	Coeff.	Stand. err. (t-stat)	Pr(>t)
Const.	−0.150	0.032(−4.682)	$1.71 \cdot 10^{-5}$
$b(t-1)$	0.263	0.059(4.424)	$4.23 \cdot 10^{-5}$
sm(t)	edf: 5.913	F:11.09	p-value: $6.69 \cdot 10^{-10}$
	GCV: $1.53 \cdot 10^{-3}$	R^2(adj):0.58	DW:0.92

In Table 2.13 the results of the estimation of Eq. (2.9) including all variables are shown. All coefficients are highly significant and possess the expected sign. Especially, the coefficient of interest, that is $\psi(t)$, is positive on average and significant at the 0.1 % level. The value given for ψ in the table shows the average of that coefficient for the period considered. The deviation from the average over time is reflected by the smooth term $sm(t)$. The significantly positive coefficient

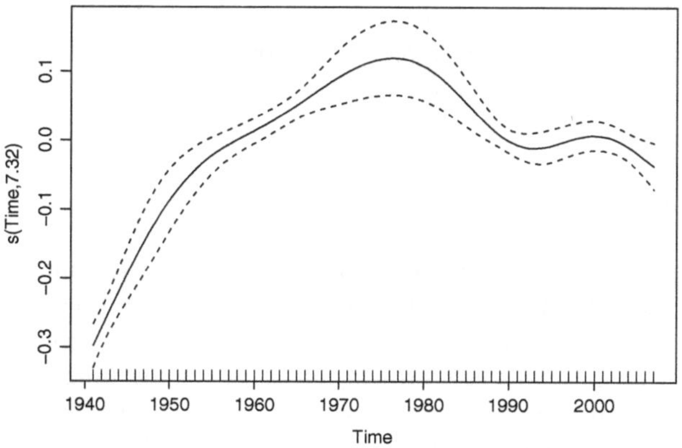

Fig. 2.8 Deviation $sm(t)$ from the average coefficient for $b(t-1)$ for the US

on average allows to conclude that sustainability of the United States public debt is given for the period under consideration. Concerning public expenditures the significantly negative coefficient for *GVar* indicates that the primary surplus ratio is smaller in periods with higher public expenditures, which is intuitively plausible. In addition, the positive and significant coefficient for *YVar* signifies that the primary surplus is higher in times of economic booms.

Potential time dependencies can be detected by the estimated degrees of freedom *edf* of the smooth term. The high value of $edf = 7.32$, which is significant at the 0.1 % level, shows that there have been variations of the reaction coefficient over time. The value of $R^2(adj) = 0.934$ indicates that a good fit of the model has been achieved. The Durbin Watson test statistic does not indicate that the residuals are correlated for a significance level of $\alpha = 0.01$.

As the information of Table 2.13 on the smooth term reveals the reaction coefficient has not been constant over time. The deviations from the average value, given in Table 2.13, are depicted in Fig. 2.8.

Figure 2.8 illustrates that the reaction of the primary surplus ratio to variations in the debt ratio had steadily increased from the World War II years until about 1975, which in turn explains the remarkable reduction in the debt to GDP ratio after World War II in Fig. 2.3. However, later on with the already mentioned less strict budget discipline during the Reagan Administration, the reaction coefficient declined. It was not until the early 1990s to tighten the reaction again, before it started to decay with the new century. Nevertheless, adding the time-varying smooth parameter and the mean of the coefficient gives a positive $\psi(t)$, except for the years of World War II. Hence, our estimations allow to conclude that the primary surplus ratio has been increased in response to rising debt ratios in the USA, which indicates sustainability of public debt.

The results presented in Tables 2.14–2.16 can be interpreted analogously. They have been included to show the robustness of the estimation result since the coefficient of interest, ψ, remains significant and positive for all combinations.

Concerning the choice of the most appropriate model to describe the United States debt situation, the results from Table 2.13 with the smallest GCV value and the highest goodness of fit indicator are the most suitable.

Comparing the Countries

When one compares the debt policies in the three countries one realizes that the United States have the highest average reaction coefficient giving the response of the primary surplus as public debt rises. In addition, the long-term real interest rate $r(t)$ falls short of the real GDP growth rate $g(t)$ for the time period considered in our study. That also holds if one considers the period from the 1960s to 2007 ($\text{mean}_{60,07}$: $r = 0.03266$, $g = 0.03272$). The reverse holds from the 1980s onwards ($\text{mean}_{80,07}$: $r = 0.0437$, $g = 0.0289$).[19] Thus, the United States had been able to grow out of their debt since the growth rate of GDP had exceeded the interest rate on government bonds for a long time period after World War II.

The latter does not hold for Germany. There, the long-term real interest rate exceeds the real GDP growth rate for both the period from 1961 until 2006, as well as from the 1980s onwards ($\text{mean}_{61,06}$: $r = 0.0356$, $g = 0.0254$; $\text{mean}_{80,06}$: $r = 0.0401$, $g = 0.0194$). Further, the reaction of the primary surplus to public debt has been smaller on average than in the United States. With these observations, it is not surprising that the ratio of public debt has been almost steadily rising in Germany since the 1970s.

For Japan the average increase of the primary surplus as a result of higher debt is smallest. This holds independent of whether gross debt or net debt is taken into consideration. But, as in the United States, the difference between the long-term real interest rate and the growth rate of real GDP was negative for the time period from the 1970s until the mid 2000s ($\text{mean}_{70,06}$: $r = 0.0249$, $g = 0.0298$). That fact also helped Japan to keep the increase in its public debt to GDP ratio relatively moderate until the mid 1990s. However, as for the United States, that changed with the beginning of the 1980s. If one takes the time period from 1980 to 2006 one realizes that the long-term real interest rate is larger than the growth rate of real GDP for that period ($\text{mean}_{80,06}$: $r = 0.0347$, $g = 0.0226$).

Finally, we briefly comment on the time path of the reaction coefficient $\psi(t)$. We do not go into the details because this has already been done for each country separately. We just want to point out that both for Japan and for the United States the coefficient is characterized by declines and increases over the period. In Germany, however, that coefficient has declined almost monotonously over the whole sample period.

---

[19]For the data see OECD (2003, 2009a), United States Government (2008), Japan Statistics Bureau (2009) and International Statistical Yearbook (2009). Please note that exceptionally we refer to calendar year data here and due to availability the periods do not always cover those of the estimations.

Additional Testing

As pointed out in the theoretical part, the empirical test resorted to in the last subsection does not take into account that the primary surplus relative GDP is bounded from above. Therefore, in order to gain additional insight in the question of whether the three countries have pursued sustainable debt policies, we now perform an additional test proposed by Trehan and Walsh (1991). Trehan and Walsh suggest to check if the total budget deficit, that is deficit inclusive of interest payments, is a stationary process. Stationarity of the deficit will be sufficient for the intertemporal budget constraint to be met if the real interest rate is positive. This holds because a time series that grows linearly, as public debt would in case of a stationary deficit, always converges to zero when multiplied by an exponential discount factor.

Testing whether a given time series is stationary can be accomplished by applying a unit root test, for example. Here, we use the augmented Dickey-Fuller test and test the hypothesis H_0, unit root in time series, against H_1, the series is stationary[20]:

$$H_0 : \pi = 0 \text{ versus } H_1 : \pi < 0.$$

Moreover, to account for possible correlation of the residuals, the augmented Dickey Fuller test contains lagged endogenous variables. We resort to the following three models in our analysis:

$$\Delta DEF_t = \pi DEF_{t-1} + \sum_{j=1}^{k} \gamma_j \Delta DEF_{t-j} + \epsilon_t, \tag{2.10}$$

$$\Delta DEF_t = \beta_0 + \pi DEF_{t-1} + \sum_{j=1}^{k} \gamma_j \Delta DEF_{t-j} + \epsilon_t, \tag{2.11}$$

$$\Delta DEF_t = \beta_0 + \pi DEF_{t-1} + \beta_2 t + \sum_{j=1}^{k} \gamma_j \Delta DEF_{t-j} + \epsilon_t. \tag{2.12}$$

The variable DEF_t denotes the total real budget deficit, i.e. inclusive of interest payments, and the types of model are specified plain, that is without drift and trend, in Eq. (2.10), with merely drift in Eq. (2.11) and with both drift and trend in (2.12).

The choice of the type of model depends on the data generating process which is usually unknown. To find the appropriate model we follow the guideline for the model selection as described for example in Enders (2004). According to that procedure one first estimates the most general model type (2.12) and proceeds

[20]See also Enders (2004) for example.

Table 2.17 ADF test for Japan (gross debt)

	Model:(2.10)	Lags:3	
Test statistic	$\hat{\tau}$		
	−1.25		
	Q(8):6.56	Q(10):7.87	Q(15):14.50

Table 2.18 ADF test for Japan (net debt)

	Model:(2.12)	Lags:6	
Test statistic	$\hat{\tau}$	ϕ_2	ϕ_3
	−3.32	3.73	5.58
	Q(15):15.40	Q(20):17.57	Q(25):18.26

Table 2.19 ADF test for the USA

	Model:(2.12)	Lags:1	
Test statistic	$\hat{\tau}$	ϕ_2	ϕ_3
	−4.62	7.18	10.77
	Q(8):7.32	Q(10):8.28	Q(15):9.79

Table 2.20 ADF test for Germany

	Model:(2.12)	Lags:3	
Test statistic	$\hat{\tau}$	ϕ_2	ϕ_3
	−4.07	5.59	8.37
	Q(8):4.30	Q(10):7.14	Q(15):12.02

to (2.11) and (2.10) in steps if necessary.[21] Here, the appropriate lag length has been chosen by the *General-to-specific* method, starting an estimation with a relative high number of lags, which is stepwise reduced until the t-statistic on the last lag is significant. This testing is now applied to Japanese, German and United States real public deficit data.[22]

Comparing the test statistics in Tables 2.17–2.20 with the critical values[23] shows that there is evidence for stationarity of the deficit series used in Tables 2.18–2.20, supporting our findings from the previous section. Information on possible correlation of the residuals is presented by the Box-Ljung test statistics Q. Here, they do not indicate correlation.

For Japanese data we again distinguish between public debt (1966–2006) and public debt minus assets (1971–2006). While stationarity does not seem to be given for the change of gross debt, the result changes once financial assets are taken into account. Then, a unit root in the series can be rejected at the 10 % level showing that for Japan the high level of assets make a significant difference when one evaluates

[21] See again for instance Enders (2004).

[22] Concerning the data, the same sources as above have been used and the estimation periods are maintained.

[23] For the critical values see for example Fuller (1976) table 8.5.2 on page 373 and Dickey and Fuller (1981) tables IV, V and VI on page 1063.

the situation of public finances, as already became clear in the last section. Testing the German data from 1961 until 2006 without the 2000 observation shows that there seems to be no evidence for a unit root in the real public deficit series at a significance level of 5 %. Concerning the United States the hypothesis of a unit root in the real public deficit series can be rejected at the 1 % level for the period from 1941 until 2007.

Therefore we can conclude that these test results are consistent with the findings from our first test such that the intertemporal budget constraint appears to be fulfilled for the countries under consideration.

In the next section we test how selected countries of the euro area have dealt with rising public debt to GDP ratios.

2.3 Empirical Results for Euro Area Countries

The growth of the public debt level is an important factor that affects the budget plan of a government. Without balanced budgets the ensuing deficits accumulate and lead to a rise of public debt in individual countries. Over the last decades, a lot of European countries have suffered from permanent and in part high public deficits. This trend has represented a serious problem from the economic and political point of view, especially for members of the European Monetary Union. Countries in the euro area have to stick to the Convergence Criteria of the Maastricht Treaty of the European Union and to the Stability and Growth Pact that imposes limitations with respect to fiscal policies.[24]

Europe has been hit hard by the financial and debt crisis and for more than 4 years the economic downswing with high unemployment, persistent budget deficits and rising public debt ratios has troubled the economies. This concerns central European countries, like Germany and France, but to a stronger degree economies at the periphery, like Portugal, Ireland, Italy or Spain. The situation is especially severe in Greece: faced with huge deficits and imminent fiscal problems, a first 'rescue program' was organized for the Greek economy in spring 2010. It was financed mainly bilaterally, including also IMF support, and covered 110 billion euros and was complemented by a second package of 130 billion euros. Being aware of the serious difficulties, the European governments and institutions, especially the European Central Bank (ECB) and the European Commission, agreed upon the organization of instruments such as the European Financial Stabilization Mechanism (EFSM), the European Financial Stability Facility (EFSF) and the European Stability Mechanism (ESM). In return for the financial assistance, the beneficiaries have to agree to implement rigid austerity programs.

[24]The data and the R-codes leading to the estimation results of this section can be downloaded from the website of the book on Springer.com in the box 'ADDITIONAL INFORMATION'.

When questions of public debt sustainability are studied, public debt is usually expressed in terms of ratios, mostly relative to GDP, in order to account for the size of the different countries. This measurement is also resorted to in the Convergence Criteria of the Maastricht Treaty of the European Union, which limits public deficits to 3 % of GDP and public debt to 60 % of GDP.[25] In the early 2000s, these criteria had been frequently violated by France, Germany and Portugal, for example.

As pointed out in the theoretical part of this chapter, an important aspect in this context is the question of whether governments are able to respond in a sustainable way to the above mentioned tendency of persistent budget deficits and growing levels of debt. Here, it is important to recall that the concept of sustainability is well compatible with indebtedness in the short run but it requires that the present value of debt converges to zero asymptotically. This raises the question of how governments react to higher public debt, which options they have to respond and if these actions are still effective.

Therefore, the starting point of our analysis is the test, where the response of the primary surplus (relative to GDP) with respect to variations in the public debt (relative to GDP) is analyzed. We take data until 2006 and we allow for a time varying coefficient giving the reaction of the primary surplus to GDP ratio to variations in the debt ratio, as in the previous section. Applying that estimation strategy, we are able to find whether the response of governments with respect to public debt have changed over time besides detecting whether the coefficient is positive at all. Thus, we intend to contribute to the literature that goes beyond OLS estimation in that area and that tries to find structural breaks, threshold or possible non-linearities (see for example Bajo-Rubio et al. 2004, Martin 2000, Payne et al. 2008, or Westerlund and Prohl 2010).

In this subsection we apply the test that is based on the theoretical considerations presented in Sect. 2.1 to data for six selected euro area countries. We analyze the correlation between the primary surplus and public debt all measured as ratios to GDP. For each selected country we estimate the reaction of the primary surplus to public debt, relative to GDP respectively, and present the results. To implement the test we estimate the following equation with annual data,[26]

$$s(t) = \psi(t)\, b(t) + \phi^T Z(t) + \epsilon(t), \tag{2.13}$$

with $s(t)$ the primary surplus to GDP ratio and $b(t)$ the public debt to GDP ratio at time t. $Z(t)$ is a vector of variables that includes 1 in its first element, for the intercept, and additional variables in its other elements, that influence the primary surplus ratio. $\epsilon(t)$ is an error term, which is assumed to be i.i.d. $N(0, \sigma^2)$.

As regards the variables included in $Z(t)$ we follow the same strategy as in the previous section. The choice of variables is again motivated by the tax smoothing

[25]See European Union (1992) Title VI Chap. 1, Art. 104c, Sect. 2. and Protocol 5 on the excessive deficit procedure.

[26]The data are taken from IMF (2010) and from OECD (2010).

hypothesis according to which public deficits should be used in order to keep tax rates constant which minimizes the excess burden of taxation. Hence, normal expenditures should be financed by regular revenues and deficits should be incurred to finance unexpected spending. Therefore, we include a business cycle variable, *YVar*, that accounts for fluctuations in revenues. It is calculated by subtracting the long term trend of GDP, which has been computed by applying the Hodrick-Prescott-Filter (HP-Filter) to the real GDP series, from its realized values. Moreover, deviations of real public expenditures from its long-run trend affect the primary surplus ratio, too. As for the business cycle variable we use the fluctuations of public expenditures around its trend, denoted by $GVar(t)$, that is computed as realized values minus trend values with the latter again estimated by the HP-Filter.

Further, for the estimation the lagged debt ratio $b(t-1)$ is used again in order to take account of problems of endogeneity. Thus, Eq. (2.13) can be written as

$$s(t) = \phi_0 + \psi(t)b(t-1) + \phi_1 GVar(t) + \phi_2 YVar(t) + \epsilon(t). \tag{2.14}$$

In order to estimate time-varying coefficients we resort to penalized spline estimation that is more robust than OLS estimation.[27] This allows to estimate the reaction coefficient $\psi(t)$ in Eq. (2.14) as a function of time showing how that coefficient evolves over time.

2.3.1 France

First, we estimate Eq. (2.14) for France.

For France we use data from 1975 until 2008. The result of the estimation is presented in Table 2.21.

The estimation outcome shown in Table 2.21 demonstrates that the average reaction coefficient of the primary surplus relative to GDP to variations in the debt

Table 2.21 Coefficients for Eq. (2.14) for France with data from 1975 to 2008

	Coefficient	Stand. error (t-stat)	Pr(>t)
Constant	−0.055	0.018(−3.088)	0.005
$b(t-1)$	0.073	0.03(2.471)	0.021
$GVar(t)$	−0.345	0.062(−5.543)	$1.07 \cdot 10^{-5}$
$YVar(t)$	0.396	0.073(5.449)	$1.35 \cdot 10^{-5}$
sm(t)	edf:6.567	F:10.26	p-value:$5.36 \cdot 10^{-6}$
	R^2(adj):0.86	DW:2.27	

[27] All equations have been estimated with R (Version 2.9.0) with the package *mgcv* (Version 1.6–1).

to GDP ratio takes a positive value of 7.3 % and is statistically significant at the 5 % level (second row in Table 2.21). Thus, France has pursued a sustainable debt policy if the time period considered can be taken as representative. It can also be realized that the time-varying component of the reaction coefficient, denoted by sm(t) in the fifth row, is statistically significant, too, and the estimated degrees of freedom (edf) of about 6.6 indicate that the reaction coefficient is not constant but a time-varying function.[28] In the appendix to this chapter we show the graph of the smooth term where the graph is drawn such that a value of 0 for the smooth term implies that the reaction coefficient just equals its average value. Thus, the actual value of the reaction coefficient at a certain point in time is equal to the average value plus the value of smooth term shown in the figure in the appendix. One can clearly recognize that the reaction coefficient has declined over the time period considered in our estimation which can explain the increase in the debt to GDP ratio in France.

Further one realizes that the primary surplus declines when public spending is above its trend, due to the negative coefficient of *GVar*, as well as when GDP is below its trend because of the positive sign of the coefficient of the variable *YVar*, as one would expect from economic theory. Finally, the adjusted R^2 of 86 % indicates a good overall fit of the model and the Durbin-Watson test statistics, DW, does not suggest that the residuals are autocorrelated.

2.3.2 *Ireland, Portugal and Spain*

In this subsection we report the outcome of our estimations for Ireland, Portugal and Spain which belong to the so-called group of PIIGS countries that have been characterized by very high deficits as a result of the financial crisis starting in 2007. However, looking at a longer time period those countries seem to be characterized by sustainable debt policies. The estimates of the average reaction coefficient describing the reaction of the primary surplus to higher public debt relative to GDP, respectively, is in all three countries positive and statistically significant. The estimations results are reported in Tables 2.22–2.24.

Tables 2.22–2.24 also demonstrate that the reaction coefficient is not constant but time-varying in all three countries. Nevertheless, there are also differences with respect to the debt policies in these three countries.

In Ireland the reaction coefficient has been steadily rising over time and the debt to GDP ratio that had increased to more than 100 % in the mid to late 1980s was reduced to less than 40 % in 2005.[29] The reduction in the debt to GDP ratio was also a result of the high GDP growth rates of more than 10 % in Ireland from the mid

[28]The edf give the estimated number of parameters for the smooth term. A value of 1 indicates that the coefficient does not depend on time.

[29]For the reaction coefficient as a function of time and for a plot of the data see again the appendix to this chapter.

Table 2.22 Coefficients for Eq. (2.14) for Ireland with data from 1975 to 2008

	Coefficient	Stand. error (t-stat)	Pr(>t)
Constant	−0.047	0.007(−7.069)	$8.92 \cdot 10^{-8}$
$b(t-1)$	0.041	0.005(8.48)	$2.41 \cdot 10^{-9}$
$GVar(t)$	−0.381	0.051(−7.487)	$2.98 \cdot 10^{-8}$
$YVar(t)$	0.323	0.069(4.651)	$6.69 \cdot 10^{-5}$
sm(t)	edf:1.5	F:54.84	p-value:$1.52 \cdot 10^{-9}$
	R^2(adj):0.916	DW:1.55	

Table 2.23 Coefficients for Eq. (2.14) for Portugal with data from 1977 to 2009

	Coefficient	Stand. error (t-stat)	Pr(>t)
Constant	−0.078	0.021(−3.724)	$9.54 \cdot 10^{-4}$
$b(t-1)$	0.073	0.02(3.578)	0.001
$GVar(t)$	−0.205	0.061(−3.359)	0.002
$YVar(t)$	0.294	0.099(2.965)	0.006
sm(t)	edf:3.478	F:9.264	p-value:$6.76 \cdot 10^{-5}$
	R^2(adj):0.71	DW:2.03	

Table 2.24 Coefficients for Eq. (2.14) for Spain with data from 1980 to 2009

	Coefficient	Stand. error (t-stat)	Pr(>t)
Constant	−0.053	0.035(−1.5)	0.15
$b(t-1)$	0.211	0.073(2.898)	0.009
$GVar(t)$	−0.196	0.113(−1.725)	0.101
$YVar(t)$	0.631	0.182(3.47)	0.003
sm(t)	edf:7.441	F:6.935	p-value:$2.3 \cdot 10^{-4}$
	R^2(adj):0.946	DW:2.29	

1990s to the early 2000s. In Spain, the debt ratio had been rising until the mid to late 1990s to more than 90 % before it was reduced again to about 40 % in the mid 2000s. The reaction coefficient slightly rises until the mid 2000s before it begins to decline again. Portugal, finally, has been characterized by an almost monotonic increase of the debt to GDP ratio in the time period under consideration from about 20 % to more than 80 %. The rise of the debt ratio was particularly pronounced from the late 1970s to the mid 1980s where it had increased from roughly 20 % to about 60 %. The reaction coefficient had remained virtually constant until the early 1990s when it began to slightly decline until the end of the time period we consider.

2.3.3 *Greece and Italy*

For Greece the result of our estimation is presented in the following table.

Table 2.25 Coefficients for Eq. (2.14) for Greece with data from 1976 to 2009

	Coefficient	Stand. error (t-stat)	Pr(>t)
Constant	−0.017	0.045(−0.377)	0.71
$b(t-1)$	−0.402	0.126(−3.202)	0.004
$GVar(t)$	−0.399	0.09(−4.415)	$2.37 \cdot 10^{-4}$
$YVar(t)$	0.504	0.127(3.957)	$7.12 \cdot 10^{-4}$
sm(t)	edf:9.343	F:19.88	p-value:$1.77 \cdot 10^{-8}$
	R^2(adj):0.886	DW:1.98	

Table 2.26 Coefficients for Eq. (2.14) for Italy with data from 1972 to 2009

	Coefficient	Stand. error (t-stat)	Pr(>t)
Constant	−0.078	0.044(−1.775)	0.087
$b(t-1)$	0.012	0.022(0.531)	0.599
$GVar(t)$	−0.026	0.115(−0.228)	0.821
$YVar(t)$	0.238	0.117(2.032)	0.052
sm(t)	edf:6.545	F:9.89	p-value:$2.39 \cdot 10^{-6}$
	R^2(adj):0.927	DW:1.82	

Table 2.25 shows that the average reaction coefficient of the primary surplus to public debt relative to GDP, respectively, is negative and statistically significant. This implies that the Greek government did not raise the primary surplus as government debt increased but rather reduced it, suggesting a Ponzi game. Consequently, the debt ratio in the period under consideration has increased from about 20 % to more than 110 %. Thus, it is not too surprising that Greece could not serve its debt obligations in early 2010 without support from other euro area countries and from the IMF.

The next table gives the estimation outcome for Italy.

From Table 2.26 one realizes that the estimation produces a positive average reaction coefficient that, however, is not statistically significant. Hence, one cannot conclude that Italian fiscal policy is sustainable. However, the estimation for Italy heavily depends on the time period under consideration. For example, taking the shorter period from 1981 to 2009 the estimation of Eq. (2.14) yields a positive and statistically significant reaction coefficient on average. Therefore, it is difficult to reach a definite answer as regards the Italian case.[30]

[30]That is also observed with data up to 2006. For 1975–2006, Greiner and Fincke (2009) obtain a significantly positive estimate which differs from the outcome in Greiner and Kauermann (2008) who took data from 1975 to 2003.

2.4 The Impact of the 2007 Financial Crisis: Portugal and Spain

In this section we want to study whether the financial crisis from 2007 changes the outcome with respect to the question of whether certain countries follow sustainable debt policies or not, where we closely follow Fincke (2013).

As already pointed out in the last section, many European countries have heavily suffered from the financial crisis starting in 2007. Midway through this unpleasant situation are also Portugal and Spain. Both applied for financial assistance by other euro countries, Portugal in spring 2011 and Spain for its banking sector in summer 2012. Despite the current crisis, even under 'normal' conditions sound fiscal performance is an important aspect. This especially holds true for monetary union members, such as economies in the euro zone for instance, as they commit to one single monetary policy. Concerning Europe, this relevance has been recognized by Article 121 of the Consolidated Version of the Treaty on European Union (cf. European Union 1997), which requires "the sustainability of the government financial position".

The Iberian Peninsula consists of the four states of Andorra, Gibraltar (British territory), Portugal and Spain – however, the focus of this analysis is set on the two main economies Portugal and Spain since they represent the major share of Iberia's economic power. For instance, in 2008 Spain contributed 86.1 % and Portugal 13.6 % to the GDP of the Iberian Peninsula, while Andorra's share was only 0.2 % and Gibraltar's of about 0.1 %.[31] Within the European context, the latter numbers diminish even further. Therefore, we concentrate on the Spanish and on the Portuguese economies.

A first impression of the economic situation after the beginning of the 2007 crisis can be gained by studying the interest rate spread of Portugal and of Spain. Here, the difference is based on calculations of the long-run government bond yield of the two Iberian economies relative to Germany. They are displayed in Fig. 2.9.[32]

Obviously, both economies had benefited from the proceeding European integration, both entering the EU in 1986, and from the preparatory steps for a common currency, with enforced sound fiscal performance, in terms of decreasing interest rates (compared to central European economies). This situation had lasted up to the mid 2000s, when the gaps started to widen again with the outbreak of the crisis. This development distinctly displays the dynamics of the economics of the European integration and accounts for the volatility in the Iberian economies.

An important aspect when dealing with questions of sustainability is the difference between the interest rate on public debt and the growth rate of GDP. When

---

[31]See World Bank (2013) and Government of Gibraltar (2013) for the data. Numbers have been converted to US $.

[32]Cf. IMF (2013) for the data, authors' calculations. All estimations and plots have been implemented in R 2.9.0.

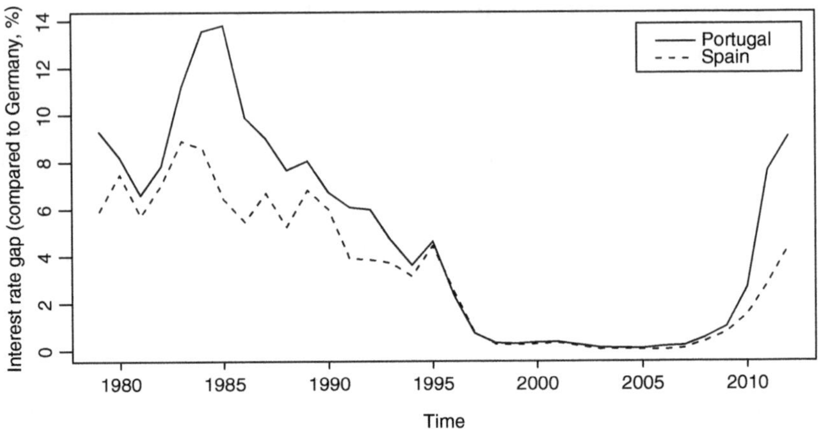

Fig. 2.9 Iberian interest rates compared to German bonds (1979–2012) in %

Table 2.27 Interest rate and growth rate gap for Portugal and Spain

$(\bar{r} - \bar{\gamma})$ in		
	1985–2012	1990–2012
Portugal	0.58	1.75
Spain	0.75	0.82

the growth rate exceeds the interest rate, public debt does not play a major problem since economies can grow out of debt in this case, as already pointed out in Sect. 2.1. Regarding the interest rate and the growth rate gap, the following Table 2.27 summarizes the past empirical observations for Portugal and Spain, respectively.[33] One can realize that this difference is strictly positive on average from the middle of the 1980s onwards.

As concerns the demarcation of the public sector, the general government classification is used here, meaning that all subordinate administrative levels and the social security system are included. Public debt is measured as gross financial liabilities, not taking into account assets. For the long run interest rate, i.e. for bond yields, we use IMF (2013) data, which have also been the basis for the spread and for the interest growth rate gap calculations. All data are measured in annual frequency.

To get a first impression, we look at the relationship between the primary surplus to GDP ratio, s, and the public debt to GDP ratio, b, for both Iberian economies. The following figures illustrate the situation for both countries: Portugal (1978–2012, solid lines), and Spain (1980–2012, dashed lines).

Regarding the primary balance in Fig. 2.10, Spain was able to reduce its deficits and to accomplish primary surpluses during the late 1990s and early 2000s, whereas for Portugal mainly deficits prevail. A corresponding pattern is shown in Fig. 2.11:

[33]See OECD (2013) and IMF (2013) for the data, authors' calculations.

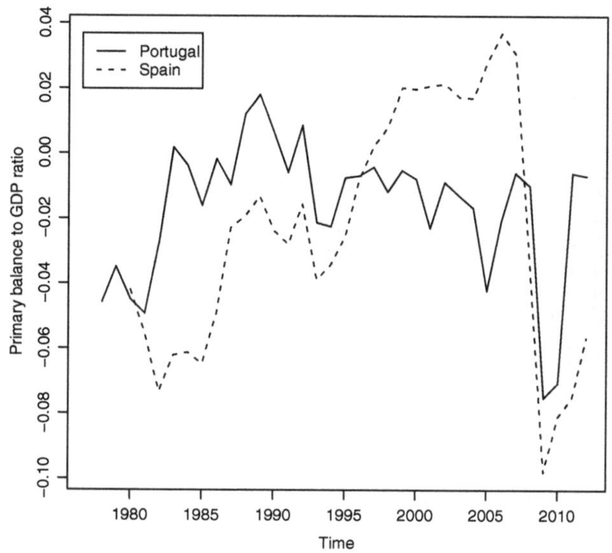

Fig. 2.10 Primary surplus to GDP ratio for Portugal and Spain

Fig. 2.11 Debt to GDP ratio for Portugal and Spain

while for Portugal the debt ratio shows an almost steadily increasing trend, the Spanish debt ratio rose until about 1995 then it dropped nearly by half. With the outbreak of the crisis, obviously, the debt ratios exploded in both economies.

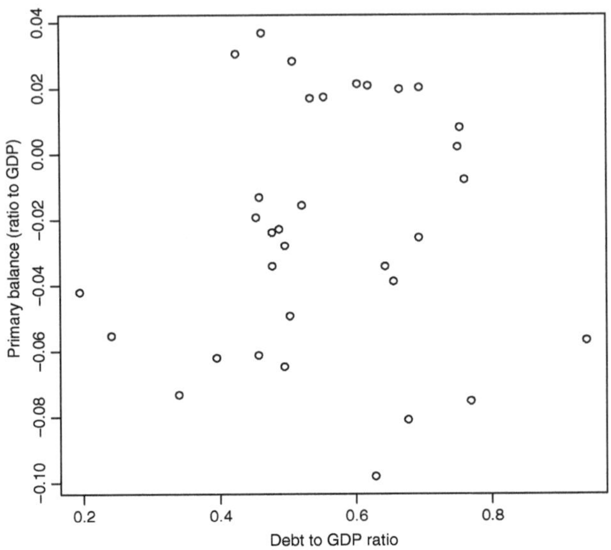

Fig. 2.12 Primary surplus and debt to GDP ratio for Spain (1980–2012)

Concentrating on the Spanish case for illustrative reasons, the subsequent plot in Fig. 2.12 presents the relationship between the primary surplus and public debt, both relative to GDP.

Apparently, no clear pattern can be observed. The observations are mainly clustered around the 60 % debt ratio with varying primary balances. Maybe, another explanatory variable modifies this original relationship. Since Spain is an EMU economy, which has been shaped by European integration and recently by the crisis, as already visualized by the spreads in Fig. 2.9 for instance, an evidently modifying variable is 'time'. Thus, Fig. 2.13 shows the primary surplus to GDP ratio relationship from above conditioned on time. Here, decades have been chosen with the last plot containing the crisis observations.

As Fig. 2.13 illustrates, the relationship between the Spanish primary surplus ratio and its debt ratio has changed over the years. While there is an increasing pattern in the 1980s and in the 1990s (enforcing a sound fiscal position), a stabilization can be observed in the 2000s with positive primary balances around 2.5 % and debt to GDP ratio values around 55 %, before the situation is plummeting due to the crisis that lead to strongly negative primary balances and high debt to GDP ratios.

In order to get an idea whether the financial 2007 crisis has changed and to answer the question of whether Portugal and Spain have pursued sustainable debt policies, we again estimate the relation between the primary surplus to GDP ratio and the debt to GDP ratio, but now with observations taken up to 2012. Including additional control variables, the full estimation model is described by:

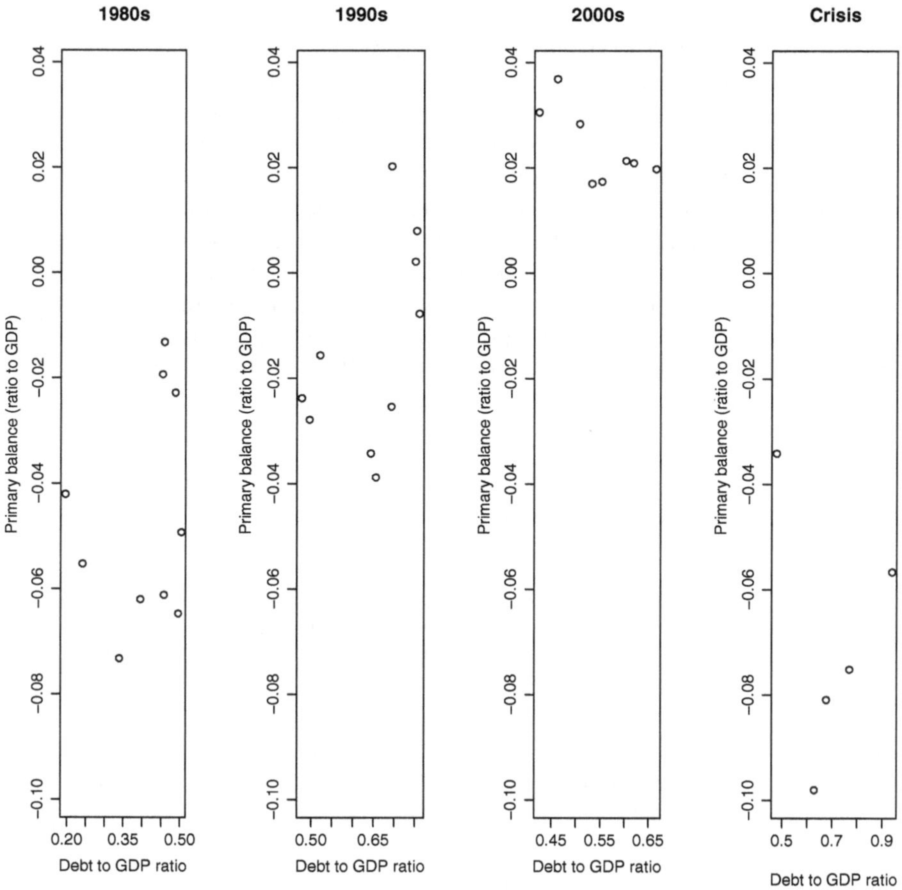

Fig. 2.13 Primary surplus and debt ratio for Spain (1980–2012) separated by decades

$$s(t) = \phi_0 + \psi(t)\, b(t-1) + \phi_1 YVar(t) + \phi_2 GVar(t) + \phi_3 Spread(t) + \epsilon(t), \qquad (2.15)$$

where we again include the public spending gap, *GVar*, and the output gap *YVar*, to account for business cycle variations, that have both been computed as in the last section. Furthermore, here the interest rate spread, *Spread*, illustrated in Fig. 2.9, has been included in order to take into account the volatility and to reflect the influence of the crisis.

With respect to the signs of the coefficients, a positive reaction coefficient is expected for the debt ratio, assuring sustainability, and for the business cycle variable, *YVar*, where a positive sign indicates counter-cyclical fiscal policy. As concerns the expenditure gap, *GVar*, a negative sign is to be expected, meaning that the primary surplus ratio declines in times of public spending above its trend value. The estimations of the regression equation (2.15) for Portugal (1978–2012) and for Spain (1980–2012) yield the following results[34]:

The result for Portugal yields a statistically significant and positive reaction coefficient, ψ, on average, indicating a sustainable debt policies. The estimated average reaction coefficient for Portugal is basically the same as in the last section with less past crisis observations (cf. Table 2.23). For Spain, however, the estimated average reaction coefficient is positive but not statistically significant. Moreover, it is considerably smaller in size than the one obtained in the last section with less past crisis observations (cf. Table 2.24). However, 2012 appears to be a special year for fiscal policy and sustainability in Spain. That holds because the reaction coefficient turns out to become positive and statistically significant, once this regression is run without the 2012 observations, i.e. until 2010 or 2011.[35] This change in 2012 is in line with the fact that Spain was forced to apply for financial assistance in summer 2012.

Table 2.28 Estimation results Spain (1980–2010)

	Coeff.	Std. error (t-stat)	Pr(>t)
Const.	−0.082	0.033(−2.51)	0.021
$b(t-1)$	0.172	0.064(2.70)	0.014
$YVar(t)$	0.663	0.198(3.35)	0.003
$GVar(t)$	−0.372	0.116(−3.22)	0.004
$Spread(t)$	$-1.9 \cdot 10^{-3}$	$2.6 \cdot 10^{-3}(-0.74)$	0.466
sm(t)	edf: 6.26	F: 6.3	p-value: 0.0005
	R^2(adj): 0.93	DW:2.04	

Table 2.29 Estimation results Spain (1980–2011)

	Coeff.	Std. error (t-stat)	Pr(>t)
Const.	−0.079	0.032(−2.47)	0.022
$b(t-1)$	0.136	0.064(2.14)	0.044
$YVar(t)$	0.701	0.191(3.67)	0.001
$GVar(t)$	−0.396	0.107(−3.71)	0.001
$Spread(t)$	$-2.3 \cdot 10^{-3}$	$2.6 \cdot 10^{-3}(-0.87)$	0.396
sm(t)	edf: 6.05	F: 8.7	p-value: $4.53 \cdot 10^{-5}$
	R^2(adj): 0.92	DW:1.80	

[34]See OECD (2013) and IMF (2013) for the data. Estimations were performed with package mgcv.

[35]See Tables 2.28 and 2.29 in the appendix for the results. A similar result is also obtained by Haskamp (2013), who analyses Spain's fiscal policy with the Bohn test from 1965 to 2010 finding sustainability.

Table 2.30 Estimation results Portugal

	Coeff.	Std. error (t-stat)	Pr(>t)
Const.	−0.090	0.021(−4.37)	0.0002
$b(t-1)$	0.081	0.022(3.62)	0.001
$YVar(t)$	0.362	0.094(3.87)	0.0006
$GVar(t)$	−0.226	0.061(−3.70)	0.001
$Spread(t)$	0.004	0.002(2.33)	0.028
sm(t)	edf: 3.47	F:10.8	p-val.: $1.51 \cdot 10^{-5}$
	R^2(adj): 0.68	DW:1.83	

Table 2.31 Estimation results Spain

	Coeff.	Std. error (t-stat)	Pr(>t)
Const.	−0.079	0.035(−2.26)	0.034
$b(t-1)$	0.083	0.084(0.99)	0.333
$YVar(t)$	0.728	0.207(3.52)	0.002
$GVar(t)$	−0.418	0.116(−3.61)	0.002
$Spread(t)$	−0.003	0.003(−1.05)	0.304
sm(t)	edf: 6.84	F:11.2	p-val.: $4.38 \cdot 10^{-6}$
	R^2(adj): 0.93	DW:1.92	

Moreover, the business cycle and spending parameters in Tables 2.30 and 2.31 all show the expected signs and are statistically significant, too. However, the interest rate gap is only significant for Portugal. The positive sign indicates that the spread has a similar effect as the debt ratio: it calls for fiscal counter-steering as the interest rate gap widens.

The diagnostics suggest a suitable fit of the model. The interesting part is the time-dependent smooth term, *sm*, which is also statistically significant and that indicates variations in the fiscal behavior over time. The plots of these smooth terms are depicted in Figs. 2.14 and 2.15 below. The plots are centered around the average value such that zero corresponds to the average value of the reaction coefficients in the Tables 2.30 and 2.31, respectively.

For Portugal, the graph shows an increasing pattern until the middle of the 1990s, afterwards a constantly decreasing shape. From an economic point of view, this implies a declining emphasis of the Portuguese government on debt stabilization from the late 1990s onwards. This means that the lack of the administration's willingness or ability to put more effort in correcting the trend resulted in an increasing debt to GDP ratio, which has been illustrated in Fig. 2.11, despite a positive reaction coefficient on average. Concerning the average, the strong positive effect in the first half of the sample may compensate the current deterioration of

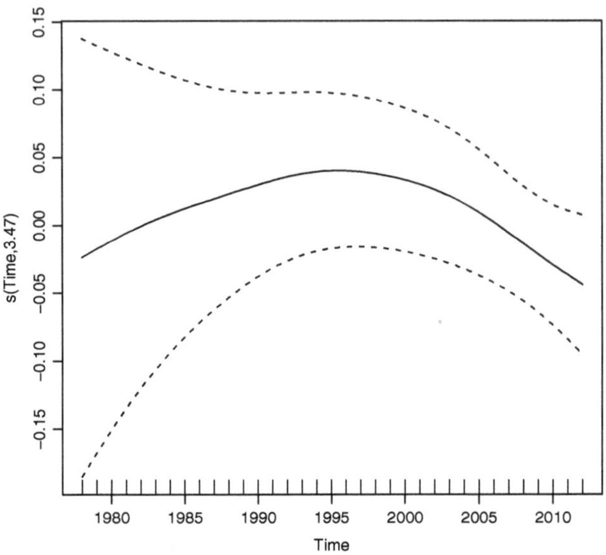

Fig. 2.14 Smooth term Portugal

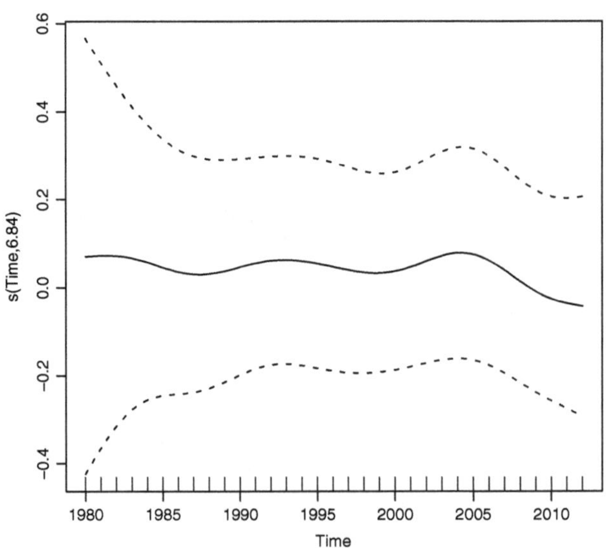

Fig. 2.15 Smooth term Spain

the fiscal reaction behavior in the crisis. However, the recent past and the latest development together with the financial crisis from 2007 can explain Portugal's application for financial assistance in 2011.

Corresponding to the decomposition by decades in Fig. 2.13, the evolution of the reaction coefficient for Spain over time is shown in Fig. 2.15: a more or less steady behavior until about the turn of the century was followed by an increasing value of that coefficient until the middle of the 2000s, when it started to decline with the beginning of the crisis. Obviously, the time-varying coefficient estimation yields a fair approximation of the underlying data generating process. However, compared to Portugal's pattern, for Spain there was not such a (past or historical) strong positive effect to rely on once the crisis affected the Spanish economy. Thus, the average reaction coefficient does no longer indicate sustainability.

These outcomes, however, do not state, that this situation is automatically given for the future. Moreover, the applications of fiscal consolidation programs underline this point: a stronger fiscal effort is indispensable for turning around the negative trend in the reaction coefficient that has lead to rising debt to GDP ratios. All in all, the tests suggest fiscal sustainability for Portugal despite the rising debt ratio during the 2007 crisis. For Spain, fiscal sustainability in terms of a statistically significant positive average reaction coefficient can only be indicated until 2011. Once the regression includes the 2012 observations, the result shows a positive but not significant effect of the public debt ratio on the primary balance ratio for Spain. This underlines the financial trouble and specific relevance of the year 2012, when Spain was forced to apply for financial assistance.

To finish our empirical tests regarding public debt sustainability, we analyze some developing economies in the next section.

2.5 Empirical Evidence for Developing Countries

Prevalent public deficits as well as growing debt levels and debt to GDP ratios have become a severe problem in many parts of the world, as already pointed out in the last section. Especially since the 1970s the unbalanced budgets have put a high burden on the governments of the affected countries. This fact is not only observed in the modern European and North American countries but in part also holds for newly industrializing and developing countries in Asia, Latin America and Africa (cf. Fincke and Greiner 2009). In particular, developing countries are rather vulnerable to debt crises as the 1980s and 1990s have shown. For some countries, this is due to the heavy dependence on raw materials as exporting goods but also to the fact that most of the debt is held by foreign countries in foreign currencies.

From the economic point of view the important question in this context is: are the governments of the developing countries able to react to the persistent budget deficits and growing debt in a sustainable manner? In this section we test whether governments of selected developing countries in Africa and Latin America have pursued sustainable debt policies.

The countries we consider are Botswana, Costa Rica, Mauritius, Panama, Rwanda and Tunisia. Rwanda is classified as low income country, Tunisia belongs to the lower middle income countries and Botswana, Costa Rica, Mauritius and

Panama belong to the upper middle income group.[36] Independent of the level of income, they all suffer from high and growing debt to GDP ratios, with the exception of Botswana. In contrast to a similar approach for mainly Asian and South American countries by Sawada (1994), who only considers external debt, we focus on analyzing the overall debt situation, with total debt being calculated by the sum of foreign and domestic debt, in order to reveal the particular economic conditions of the countries.

The economies have been chosen as a selection of different nations that represent diverse economies graded by the World Bank Atlas Method within the last three classifications, that is, low income group ($905 or less), Rwanda in this section, then lower middle income classification ($906–$3,595), Tunisia, and a bale of upper middle income countries ($3,596–$11,115) with different economic structures and country specific debt characteristics that, however, all face or had been confronted by high debt burdens. Each country of the two lowest classifications, Tunisia and Rwanda, offers interesting insight with observations over quite a long time period. With Botswana, Costa Rica, Mauritius and Panama four countries with completely different types of debt situations and debt paths can be combined as one cohort since they belong to the same group of income. However they show different debt patterns that need to be analyzed separately in order to catch the variety and diversity of the debt structure within that cohort. Botswana has remarkably reduced its debt and it still shows a declining trend, while for Panama the debt ratio shows an almost steadily increasing shape from the 1970s onwards. Concerning Mauritius, a peak had been reached in the early 1980s before the public debt to GDP ratio could again be considerably reduced, whereas for Costa Rica a relatively low value of the public debt to GDP ratio was achieved around 1990 that, however, has strongly increased since then. Therefore, these selected countries illustrate and cover a variety of different situations of developing countries and yield interesting insight and possibly useful examples.

Additionally, and maybe even more important, the relatively long, reliable and incessant time series allow a continuous observance and, thus, permit a more holistic approach.

2.5.1 The Estimation Strategy

Our estimation strategy is the same as the one applied in the last sections. We begin with a description of the fiscal situation for each country. Then, we analyze whether the governments were able to react to higher public debt by increasing their primary surpluses. Additionally, we test for stationarity of the overall deficits in the economies we consider. As concerns public debt, we take the sum of foreign and domestic debt.

[36] According to the 'World Bank Atlas Method' classification, see World Bank (2008b).

As regards the empirical estimation of the reaction of the primary surplus relative to GDP we recall that, as for developed countries, we assume that the tax smoothing hypothesis holds, according to which the primary deficit should be used to smooth variations in expenditures and revenues. Thus, we assume that the primary surplus relative to GDP depends on business cycles, *YVar*, and on deviations of public spending from its trend, *GVar*, besides depending on the public debt ratio. The variable *YVar* gives the deviation of real GDP from its trend and was computed using the Hodrick-Prescott filter. The variable *GVar* gives the deviation of real public spending from its normal value with positive values indicating expenditures above the normal level and vice versa.

Hence, we first estimate the following equation,

$$s(t) = \phi_0 + \psi(t)b(t-1) + \phi_1 GVar(t) + \phi_2 YVar(t) + \epsilon(t), \tag{2.16}$$

with $\epsilon(t)$ an error term, which is assumed to be i.i.d. $N(0, \sigma^2)$. Further, we assume again that the lagged debt to GDP ratio, $b(t-1)$, affects the primary surplus ratio, in order to take into account the problem of endogeneity.

For the second test, as supposed by Trehan and Walsh (1991), we estimate the following Augmented Dickey Fuller Test,[37]

$$H_0 : \pi = 0 \qquad H_1 : \pi < 0,$$

$$\Delta DEF_t = \beta_0 + \pi DEF_{t-1} + \beta_2 t + \sum_{j=1}^{k} \gamma_j \Delta DEF_{t-j} + \epsilon_t. \tag{2.17}$$

For the estimation, the suitable model type needs to be specified. The deficit *DEF* is the first difference of the level of real total debt, the sum of foreign and domestic debt, divided by the GDP deflator.

The estimations are done with R (Version 2.5.0). The first test is estimated with the package *mgcv* (Version 1.3–23) that uses penalized spline smoothing. Those results are more robust compared to OLS estimation results and it is possible for ψ to vary with time. The Durbin-Watson test statistic is calculated with the package *car*. The second test is estimated with the package *urca*. The Box-Ljung test is implemented in the package *stats*. All data are annual and have been taken from International Financial Statistics of the IMF Database, published in the International Statistical Yearbook 2007 unless otherwise stated.

2.5.2 Estimation Results

First, we analyze the South African country Botswana.

---

[37]For detailed information see again Enders (2004), for example.

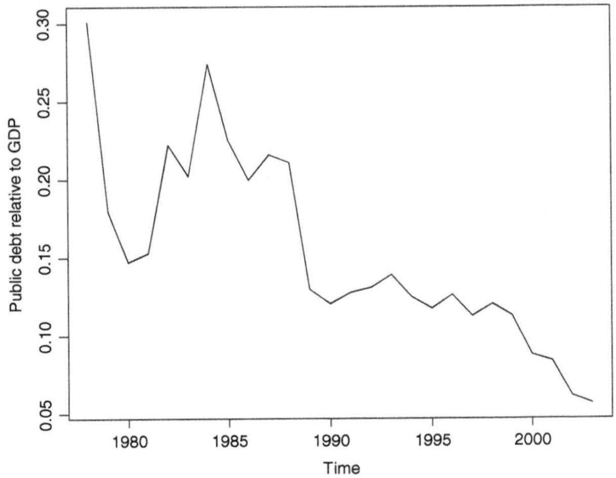

Fig. 2.16 Public debt to GDP ratio for Botswana (1978–2003)

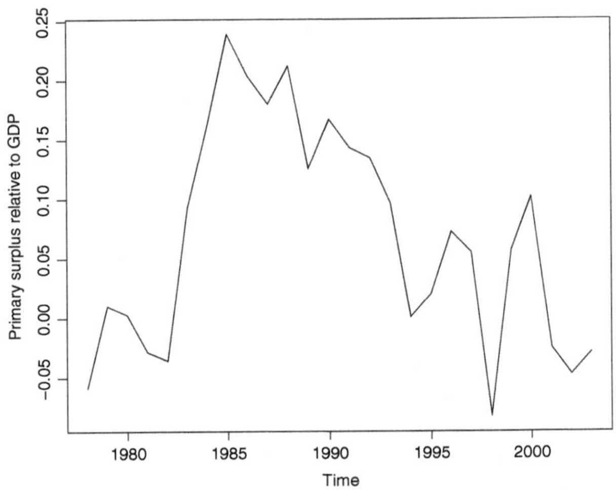

Fig. 2.17 Primary surplus to GDP ratio for Botswana (1978–2003)

Botswana

In Figs. 2.16 and 2.17 the public debt ratio and the primary surplus relative to GDP for the years from 1978 until 2003 are depicted.[38]

The overall trend of the debt ratio shown in Fig. 2.16 is declining. With an initial value of 30 % in 1978 and another rise in the early 1980s, which might be ascribed to bad weather and severe droughts around that time, the public debt relative to GDP continuously declined and in 2003 it amounted to less than 10 %.

[38]Due to data availability the data for Botswana have been taken from International Statistical Yearbook (2006).

Table 2.32 Coefficients for Eq. (2.16) for Botswana

	Coefficient	Stand. error (t-stat)	Pr(>t)
Constant	−0.122	0.055(−2.225)	0.038
$b(t-1)$	1.242	0.373(3.330)	0.003
$GVar(t)$	0.173	0.138(1.254)	0.225
$YVar(t)$	0.427	0.236(1.812)	0.086
sm(t)	edf:2.551	F:9.111	p-value:$8.18 \cdot 10^{-5}$
	R^2(adj):0.704	DW:2.05	

The primary balance in Fig. 2.17 shows almost only surpluses with remarkably high values starting at the middle of the 1980s. Hence, these surpluses can explain the steady decrease of the debt to GDP ratio. Thus, for the first test we expect a significantly positive reaction coefficient with this information. The fiscal success can be assigned to the mineral detections and the export strategy that caused large economic growth. The main exporting commodities are diamonds. For example only three mines sum up to more than two thirds of total export revenue and yield almost half of Botswana's GDP.[39]

Next, we apply the first test to examine how the primary surplus ratio responds to changes in the public debt ratio. The result is summarized in Table 2.32.

The estimated parameter for the debt ratio reflects the mean of that coefficient. Table 2.32 shows that the average of the debt ratio coefficient $\psi(t)$ is positive and significant at the 1 % level. Besides the reaction coefficient, only the intercept and the coefficient for the business cycle variable are statistically significant, the latter implying with its positive sign that the primary surplus rises in booms when GDP is above its trend value. Moreover, the coefficient for $GVar$ is not statistically significant. The goodness of fit is given by $R^2(adj) = 0.704$ and the Durbin-Watson test statistic does not indicate correlation of the residuals.

The deviation from the mean of the reaction coefficient is given by the smooth term $sm(t)$ shown in Fig. 2.18 which is highly significant. The dashed lines give the 95 % confidence interval and the solid line gives the point estimate of the smooth term.

The smooth term in Fig. 2.18 shows that the reaction coefficient $\psi(t)$ is steadily increasing until about 1990. From then on the curve decreases slowly. The rise until 1990 is in accordance with the Figs. 2.16 and 2.17 that the debt was significantly reduced and high primary surpluses were achieved. After that, the importance of debt reduction has diminished and a falling trend in primary balances supports that development. The smooth term apparently displays the reversed image of the debt ratio trend.

With both the smooth term and the positive value of the mean of the coefficient for $b(t-1)$ being significant, it is possible to state that $\psi(t)$ remained positive for

[39] See Government of Botswana (2008) for further information.

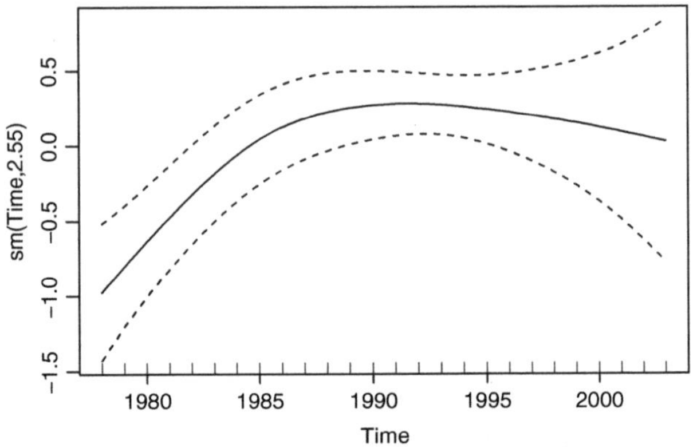

Fig. 2.18 Deviation sm(t) from the average coefficient for $b(t-1)$ for Botswana

Table 2.33 ADF test results for Botswana

	Model:drift, trend	Lags:0	
Test statistic	$\hat{\tau}$	ϕ_2	ϕ_3
	−5.54	10.23	15.34
	Q(8):1.90	Q(10):2.76	Q(15):3.61

the entire period. Therefore we conclude that there is evidence for sustainability of debt policy. If the estimation is implemented with only *GVar*, only *YVar* or just $b(t-1)$ the coefficient for the debt ratio remains positive and significant at least at the 5 % level.

Another informative indicator of the financial situation is the ratio of interest payments relative to GDP. For Botswana it amounts to 2.0 % (1986), 1.6 % (1996) and to 0.1 % (2005).[40] These low values are in accordance with the estimation result. Moreover, if only the external debt is considered, which indicates financial resources going abroad, the ratio of external debt to GDP for Botswana amounts to 15 % on average and clearly shows a decreasing trend. Starting at 27 % in 1978 it only amounts to 6 % in 2003. These ratios are additional important figures for developing countries since they supplement the information on the economic situation.

Next, as proposed by Trehan and Walsh (1991), we test for stationarity of the real deficit by applying the Augmented Dickey Fuller test to the budget deficit, which is calculated as the first difference of the real public debt. If the total government deficit is stationary public debt is sustainable unless the interest rate is negative. This holds because the present value of public debt asymptotically converges to zero when public debt rises linearly since it is discounted with an exponential factor. In Table 2.33 the result is given. The time period is the same as for the last test.

From the result in Table 2.33 one can realize that the value of the test statistic, when compared with the critical values, indicates stationarity of Botswana's deficit

[40]See World Bank (2008a) for the data.

Fig. 2.19 Budget deficit of Botswana (1978–2003)

at the 1 % significance level.[41] With the F-test related statistic ϕ it is possible to apply additional tests if necessary.[42] For possible autocorrelation of the residuals, the ACF and PACF have been checked and the Box-Ljung test statistic Q shows no evidence for correlation of the residuals.[43] Therefore, we can conclude that the intertemporal budget constraint holds and sustainability seems to be given for the period considered. In Fig. 2.19 the deficit is illustrated.

All in all, the results for Botswana support the hypothesis of debt sustainability as expected by the declining debt to GDP ratio over time. Thus, the findings show strong evidence for sustainability of public debt in that country.

Costa Rica

The next country we analyze is Costa Rica. Figures 2.20 and 2.21 show the public debt and primary balance relative to GDP, respectively, for Costa Rica from 1970 to 2002.

In Fig. 2.20 the sharp rise of the debt ratio towards 1980 might be due to the crisis in Latin America at the beginning of the 1980s. After that a fall of public debt until

[41]For the critical values see for example Fuller (1976) table 8.5.2 on page 373 and Dickey and Fuller (1981) tables IV, V and VI on page 1063. Here the critical values of a sample size of 25 are applied.

[42] Here it is not required since the null hypothesis can be rejected.

[43]For information on the Box-Ljung test see for example Enders (2004), especially chapter 2. Critical values can be taken from a χ^2 table.

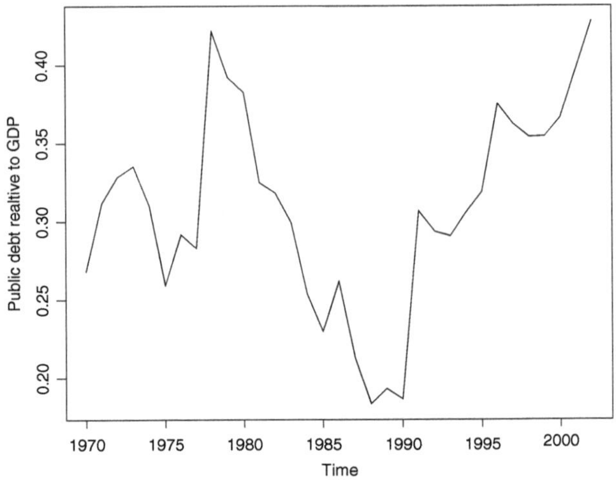

Fig. 2.20 Public debt to GDP ratio for Costa Rica (1970–2002)

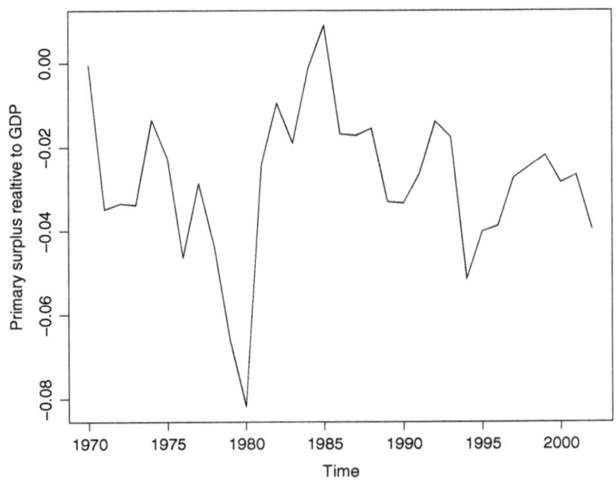

Fig. 2.21 Primary surplus to GDP ratio for Costa Rica (1970–2002)

about 1989 cut the debt by half to less then 20 % of GDP. This development goes along with a sudden drop of the primary surplus in 1980 as can be observed from Fig. 2.21. Later on, a rise in primary balances occurs and it shows even surpluses around 1985. Reasons for this decrease in the debt ratio starting in the late 1980s might in part be referred to the participation in debt rescheduling and refinancing of debt with the Brady-Plan.[44] However, this situation could not be preserved and beginning with the 1990s, the debt ratio has again steadily increased with a peak in 1996, which might in part be ascribed to the natural phenomenon *ElNiño* and a following drought.[45] In 2002, public debt to GDP amounted to 43 %. Parallel to

[44]See for instance Minkner-Buenjer (1999) especially pages 170 et seqq.

[45]See for example Minkner-Buenjer (1999) page 168.

Table 2.34 Coefficients for Eq. (2.16) for Costa Rica

	Coefficient	Stand. error (t-stat)	Pr(>t)
Constant	−0.030	0.011(−2.728)	0.012
$b(t-1)$	0.010	0.037(0.263)	0.795
$GVar(t)$	−0.125	0.013(−9.710)	$2.59 \cdot 10^{-9}$
$YVar(t)$	0.145	0.048(3.000)	0.007
sm(t)	edf:7.512	F:8.069	p-value:$3.82 \cdot 10^{-5}$
	R^2(adj):0.882	DW:2.28	

this rise in the debt ratio, the primary balance ratio tended to diminish from the beginning of the late 1980s until 2002, with persistent and growing primary deficits.

We estimate Eq. (2.16) for Costa Rica for the years from 1970 to 2002. The primary surplus and the public debt are measured relative to GDP. The results are presented in Table 2.34.

As Table 2.34 shows, the coefficient for public debt $b(t-1)$ is positive, but it is not statistically significant. The estimated parameter $\psi(t)$ gives the mean of that coefficient with $sm(t)$ again representing the deviation from that mean over time. Further, the estimated coefficient for public expenditures is negative and highly significant, implying that public spending above its normal value reduces the primary surplus ratio. The coefficient for the business cycle variable is positive and significant at the 1 % level which demonstrates that booms (recessions) cause a positive (negative) effect on the primary surplus ratio.

Information on time dependencies of the reaction coefficient is given by the degrees of freedom, *edf*, of the smooth term $sm(t)$. For Costa Rica $edf = 7.512$ and it is significant at the 1 % level, suggesting that the reaction coefficient is characterized by strong variations over time. The $R^2(adj)$ reflects the goodness of fit and with $R^2(adj) = 0.882$ a relative high goodness of fit is achieved. To check for correlation of the residuals the Durbin-Watson test statistic is calculated. There is no evidence for correlation of the residuals for Costa Rica.

If the estimation is performed without the business cycle variable or without expenditures or only with the debt ratio, the estimated average coefficient for $b(t-1)$ stays positive in all cases.

The results demonstrate that the reaction coefficient varies over time. The path of the deviation from the mean, $sm(t)$, is depicted in Fig. 2.22.

First a decline until 1979 can be observed, followed by a steep rise with a peak in the middle of the 1980s. Afterwards it dropped again. This can be interpreted as a loss of reaction over time, implying that the response of the primary surplus to GDP ratio with respect to variations in the debt ratio had declined. However, in the recent past $sm(t)$ has slightly increased.

As for Botswana, we calculate some economic key data for Costa Rica to get additional information on the financial situation. First, the interest payments to GDP

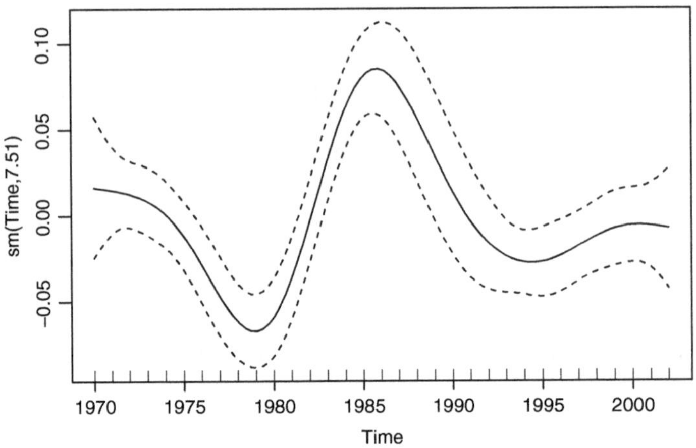

Fig. 2.22 Deviation sm(t) from the average coefficient for $b(t-1)$ for Costa Rica

Table 2.35 ADF test results for Costa Rica

	Model: drift, trend	Lags: 0	
Test statistic	$\hat{\tau}$	ϕ_2	ϕ_3
	−5.02	8.50	12.73
	Q(8):4.55	Q(10):9.12	Q(15):15.99

for Costa Rica are 4.0 % (1986), 1.6 % (1996) and 0.6 % (2005).[46] Although starting with a relatively high value, these three ratios show a decreasing trend. Furthermore, the average of the external debt to GDP ratio amounts to 9 % for the same period as the estimation was performed. However, this ratio is alternating and no explicit trend can be observed. These two indicators are in accordance with the positive but insignificant estimations. The ratios are relatively low but not as unambiguous as those for Botswana.

To get further insight we test the stationarity properties of the deficit inclusive of interest payments. Figure 2.23 shows the evolution of the situation for Costa Rica from 1970 to 2002.

For the test we calculate the first difference of the real public debt of Costa Rica for the years 1969–2002, so that the sample period from above is maintained. Table 2.35 summarizes the results.

As shown in Table 2.35, the deficit is stationary at the 1 % level. For possible autocorrelation of the residuals, the ACF and PACF are checked and the Box-Ljung test statistic Q shows no evidence for correlation of the residuals. Therefore, it is possible to conclude that the budget deficit of Costa Rica is stationary for the period considered. This indicates that the intertemporal budget constraint holds, hence the Costa Rican government has performed a sustainable debt policy.

[46]For the data see World Bank (2008a).

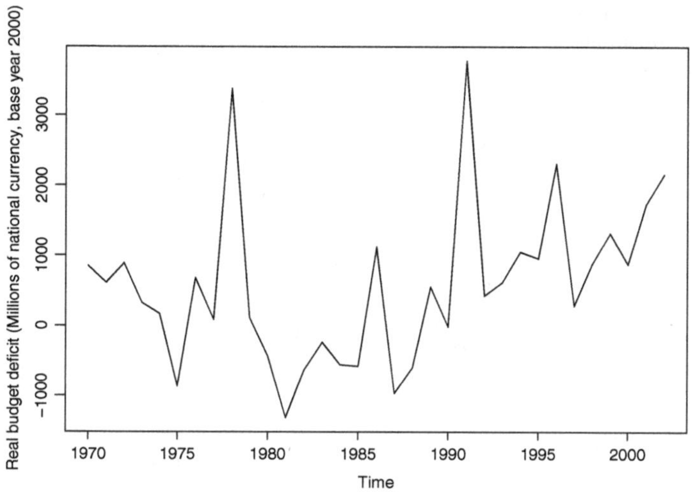

Fig. 2.23 Budget deficit of Costa Rica (1970–2002)

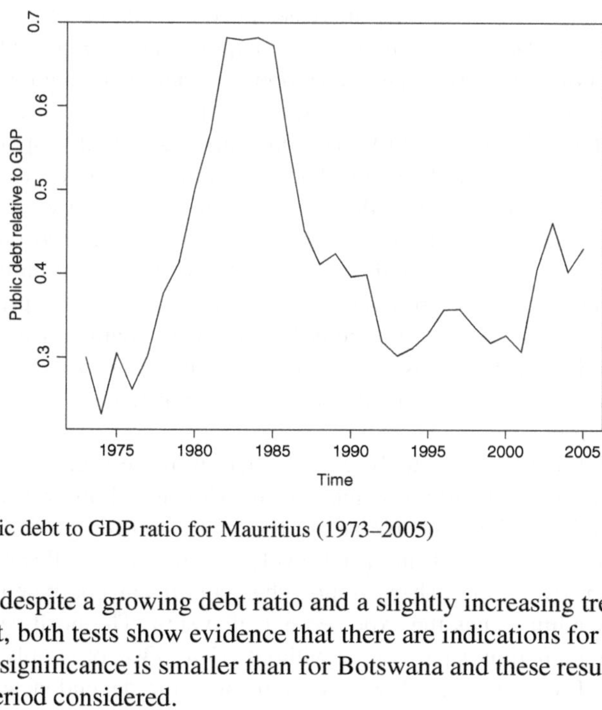

Fig. 2.24 Public debt to GDP ratio for Mauritius (1973–2005)

All in all, despite a growing debt ratio and a slightly increasing trend of the real budget deficit, both tests show evidence that there are indications for sustainability. However the significance is smaller than for Botswana and these results only allude to the time period considered.

Mauritius

The country we now consider is in South East Africa, namely Mauritius. Figures 2.24 and 2.25 illustrate the total public debt and the primary surplus to

Fig. 2.25 Primary surplus to GDP ratio for Mauritius (1973–2005)

GDP ratio from 1973 to 2005. The debt ratio in Fig. 2.24 shows a high value in the middle of the 1980s. The steep increase since the middle of the 1970s, might among other things, be due to a stagnation of exports and decreasing terms of trade which led to budget deficits.[47] This development, then, generated a growing debt ratio which might, at least partly, explain the peak around 1985. Later on, restrictive guidelines by the IMF and World Bank were imposed to limit imports in order to reduce deficits.[48] Then, the debt ratio had been gradually reduced and stabilized around a level of about 35 %. This decline might be explained by economic reform policies during that time. With a solid industrial base, the export commodity has changed from sugar to textile and apparel.[49] But with the beginning of the new century, another rise can be observed. Corresponding to that, the primary balance ratio in Fig. 2.25 shows primary deficits for the years characterized by high debt ratios in the middle of the 1980s. However, after that there is a remarkable increase in the primary surplus ratios until the late 1980s. Nonetheless, its trend has been decreasing recently.

Applying the first test that analyzes the reaction of the primary surplus ratio to variations in the debt to GDP ratio yields results shown in Table 2.36.

As shown in Table 2.36, the average of the coefficient for the debt ratio $\psi(t)$ is positive but not significant at the usual levels. Again, $sm(t)$ reflects the deviation from that mean over time. There is no other significant coefficient but the one for public expenditures has the expected negative sign. The positive sign of $\psi(t)$ remains if the estimation is performed without *GVar*, *YVar* or simply with the debt ratio included. The estimated $edf = 5.42$ indicates time-dependencies and $sm(t)$ is

[47] See for example Paul (1987), especially page 24.

[48] ibidem.

[49] See for example Embassy of the Republic of Mauritius (2008).

Table 2.36 Coefficients for Eq. (2.16) for Mauritius

	Coefficient	Stand. error (t-stat)	Pr(>t)
Constant	−0.034	0.020(−1.702)	0.102
$b(t-1)$	0.011	0.052(0.203)	0.841
$GVar(t)$	−0.059	0.052(−1.139)	0.266
$YVar(t)$	−0.038	0.094(−0.406)	0.688
sm(t)	edf:5.42	F:10.33	p-value:$2.82 \cdot 10^{-6}$
	R^2(adj):0.801	DW:1.94	

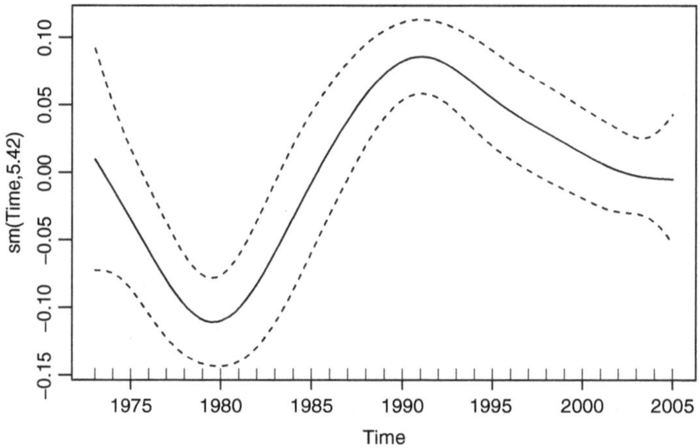

Fig. 2.26 Deviation sm(t) from the average coefficient for $b(t-1)$ for Mauritius

highly significant. The goodness of fit is relatively high and there seems to be no correlation of the residuals according to the Durbin-Watson test statistic. The time path of the smooth term is depicted in Fig. 2.26. It can be realized that the reaction coefficient had decreased until 1980. Then, it began to rise until the early 1990s before it started to decline again. The decreasing time path again indicates that the government put less importance on the stabilization of public debt. Nevertheless, adding the mean of the coefficient from Table 2.36 and the deviation from that mean gives a positive value, except for the period from the mid 1970s to the middle of the 1980s.

Again we look at the interest payments to GDP ratio and the external debt ratio. For Mauritius, the first relation accounts for 2.3 % (1986), 1.7 % (1996) and 0.5 % in 2005.[50] The average of the external debt relative to GDP from 1973 to 2005 is 13 %. However, for the period around the middle of the 1980s the ratio shows high values of more than 20 % and then decreases steadily to 5 % in 2005. This seems

[50]See World Bank (2008a).

Table 2.37 ADF test results for Mauritius

	Model: drift, trend	Lags: 0	
Test statistic	$\hat{\tau}$	ϕ_2	ϕ_3
	−5.11	8.73	13.07
	Q(8):4.35	Q(10):9.03	Q(15):11.21

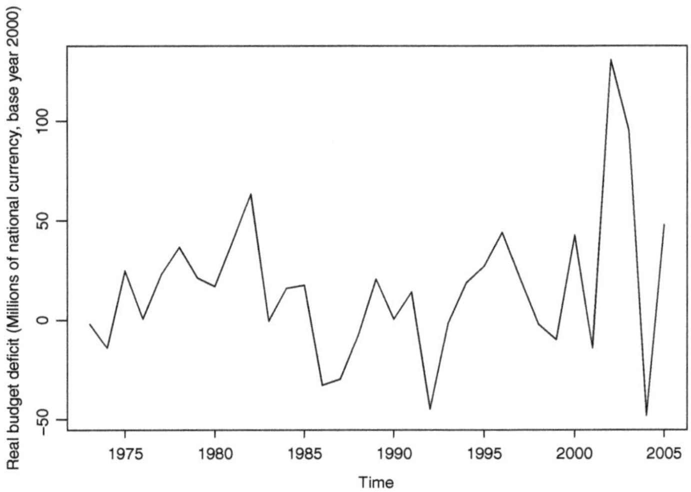

Fig. 2.27 Budget deficit of Mauritius (1973–2005)

to be in accordance with the development in Fig. 2.24, although it only refers to the external debt.

Next, we apply the stationarity test for Mauritius for the period considered. Again, the real deficit is calculated as the first difference of the real public debt. Table 2.37 shows the test result.

With the result from Table 2.37 we can conclude that the real budget deficit of Mauritius is stationary, which suggests that the intertemporal budget constraint of the government holds.

The real deficit of Mauritius is shown in Fig. 2.27. Apparently, the budget deficit is characterized by strong oscillations.

Summarizing the results for Mauritius, we conclude that both test results show evidence for sustainability of fiscal policy, although the statistical significance is smaller than for Botswana.

Panama

The second Latin American country we analyze is Panama. To get an idea of the situation, the Figs. 2.28 and 2.29 show the debt to GDP ratio and the primary surplus ratio for the years from 1970 until 2000.

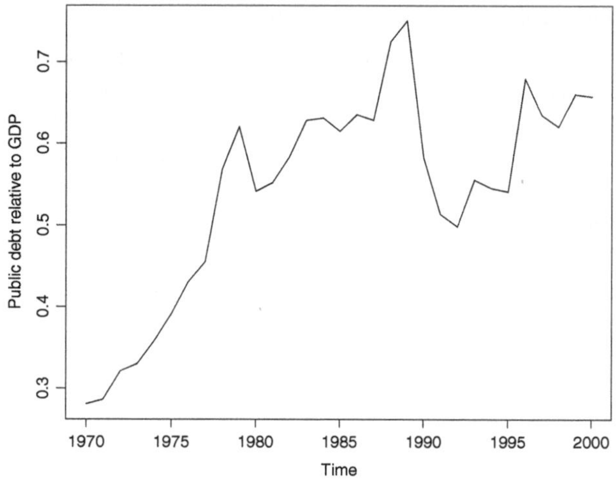

Fig. 2.28 Public debt to GDP ratio for Panama (1970–2000)

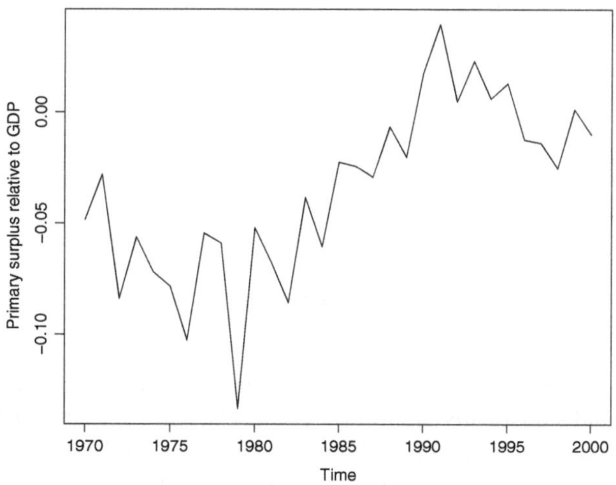

Fig. 2.29 Primary surplus to GDP ratio for Panama (1970–2000)

As Fig. 2.28 illustrates, the debt ratio rises over the whole sample period. Three abrupt increases can be observed. The first is a steady increase within the 1970s, another rise occurred at the end of the 1980s with a maximum peak of 75 % in 1989, when Panama endured an economic downturn. After a drop in the early and middle 1990s, that might be explained by economic reforms and later involvements of the IMF for example,[51] the debt ratio has begun to rise again since the late 1990s. This evolution of the debt ratio is accompanied by persistent primary deficits until the beginning of the 1990s, as shown in Fig. 2.29.

We now apply the first test on the Panamanian data for the years from 1970 to 2000. Table 2.38 presents the results.

[51]See also International Monetary Fund (1995).

Table 2.38 Coefficients for Eq. (2.16) for Panama

	Coefficient	Stand. error (t-stat)	Pr(>t)
Constant	0.023	0.020(1.184)	0.248
$b(t-1)$	−0.131	0.039(−3.351)	0.003
$GVar(t)$	−0.229	0.038(−6.101)	$2.53 \cdot 10^{-6}$
$YVar(t)$	0.243	0.073(3.314)	0.003
sm(t)	edf:2.706	F:17.43	p-value:$1.00 \cdot 10^{-7}$
	R^2(adj):0.876	DW:2.26	

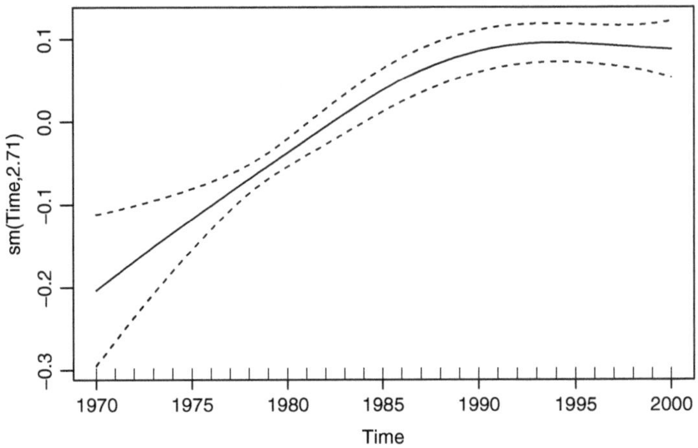

Fig. 2.30 Deviation sm(t) from the average coefficient for $b(t-1)$ for Panama

Table 2.38 illustrates that the mean of the parameter of interest $\psi(t)$ is negative and statistically significant at the 1 % level. Again, $sm(t)$ shows the deviation from that mean over time. This estimation result indicates that sustainability of the public debt policy might not be given for Panama for the sample period. The coefficient for public spending is negative as well, whereas the one for the business cycle variable shows a positive sign, both being statistically significant. The effect of a rise in the spending parameter indicates a decline in the primary surplus ratio and an economic boom raises the primary surplus to GDP ratio. Further, if the estimation is done without the business cycle variable, without the expenditure parameter or simply with $b(t-1)$, $\psi(t)$ remains significantly negative.

Again, time-dependencies are reflected by the degree of the *edf* of the smooth term, which is significant at the 1 % level. With $R^2(adj) = 0.876$ quite a high goodness of fit is achieved. The Durbin-Watson test does not indicate correlation of the residuals. With the information from Table 2.38 on the smooth term, a variation over time can be assumed. Figure 2.30 illustrates the time path of that function.

As shown in Fig. 2.30, the reaction of the primary surplus to public debt steadily increased until around 1990. From then on, the time path remained relatively stable.

Table 2.39 ADF test results for Panama

	Model: no drift, no trend	Lags: 7	
Test statistic	$\hat{\tau}$	ϕ_2	ϕ_3
	−0.93	–	–
	Q(12):9.40	Q(14):12.31	Q(20):17.52

In spite of this increasing slope, the response has not been increased enough to achieve a positive reaction coefficient on average.

Once more, we use the indicators interest payments to GDP and external debt relative to GDP to gain additional insight on the financial situation of Panama. The interest payments to GDP ratio amounts to 5.6 % (1986), 4.1 % (1996) and 4.2 % in 2005.[52] Moreover, the external debt ratio for the same period as above, shows an average value of 37 % and a clearly increasing trend, starting at 14 % in 1970 and reaching 48 % in 2000. These high figures support the estimation result from above.

For additional information we now apply the Augmented Dickey Fuller Test to the budget deficit of Panama. Therefore, the first difference of the real debt from 1969 to 2000 is calculated in order to keep the time period identical. In Table 2.39 the result is presented.

The results from Table 2.39 support the findings from the first test. The deficit is not stationary at any significance level. For possible correlation of the residuals, we looked at the ACF and PACF and calculated the Box-Ljung test statistic Q. There are no indications of autocorrelation. Thus, according to both test results, there is doubt whether the intertemporal budget constraint holds and whether the Panamanian government has pursued a sustainable fiscal policy.

In Fig. 2.31 the real budget deficit of Panama is depicted.

As shown in Fig. 2.31, there are three particular outliers, two surpluses in 1980 and 1990 and a high deficit in the middle of the 1990s. The time-path of the deficit had been relatively stable until the middle of the 1970s but began to show strong oscillations from the 1980s onwards.

To summarize the Panamanian situation, both tests suggest that sustainability of public debt does not seem to be given for the period considered.

Rwanda

The next state we consider is the East African country Rwanda. In Figs. 2.32 and 2.33, the public debt ratio and the primary balance ratio for the years from 1978 to 2004 are shown. Apparently, the debt ratio increases over the whole sample period as shown in Fig. 2.32. The two outliers in 1994 and 1995 can be ascribed to the Rwandan Genocide of 1994. The overall trend of the primary surplus ratio is

[52] See also World Bank (2008a).

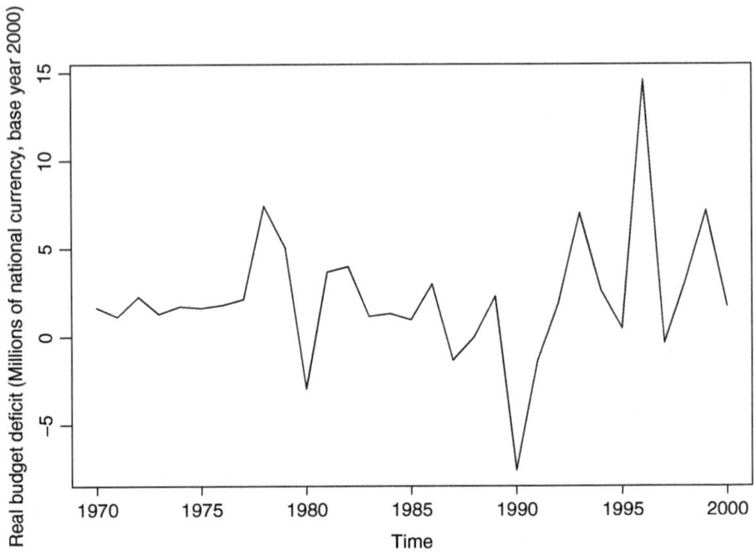

Fig. 2.31 Budget deficit of Panama (1970–2000)

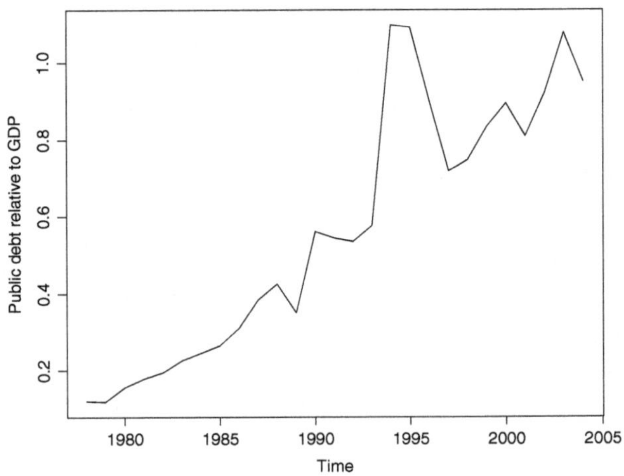

Fig. 2.32 Public debt to GDP ratio for Rwanda (1978–2004)

declining, again with the lowest values around the middle of the 1990s, as depicted in Fig. 2.33. Moreover, Rwanda is one of the countries taking part in the Heavily Indebted Poor Countries (HIPC) Debt Initiative, which is a device for debt relief and support of countries facing a high debt burden.[53]

[53]See also International Monetary Fund (2008), for example.

Fig. 2.33 Primary surplus to GDP ratio for Rwanda (1978–2004)

Table 2.40 Coefficients for Eq. (2.16) for Rwanda

	Coefficient	Stand. error (t-stat)	Pr(>t)
Constant	−0.110	0.016(−7.112)	$4.66 \cdot 10^{-6}$
$b(t-1)$	0.172	0.051(3.393)	0.004
$GVar(t)$	−0.199	0.028(−7.011)	$5.47 \cdot 10^{-6}$
$YVar(t)$	0.279	0.052(5.331)	$9.88 \cdot 10^{-5}$
sm(t)	edf:7.703	F:21.98	p-value:$7.35 \cdot 10^{-7}$
	R^2(adj):0.951	DW:2.88	

Next, we apply the first test to analyze the response of the primary surplus ratio to changes in the debt to GDP ratio for the sample period, where we neglect the year 1994, in which the Genocide occurred, in order to avoid leverage effects. Table 2.40 summarizes the results.

The average of the coefficient of interest, ψ, is positive and significant at the 1 % level, as shown in Table 2.40. The deviation from that mean is again given by the smooth term $sm(t)$. All other coefficients are significant as well. The ones for the expenditure variable and for the business cycle show the expected negative and positive signs, respectively. If the estimation is done without the business cycle variable, without the expenditures or with only the debt ratio, the mean of the coefficient for the debt ratio remains positive. Further, Table 2.40 shows that the estimated smooth term $sm(t)$ suggests a time-varying reaction coefficient because the estimated degrees of freedom are high and because it is significant at the 1 % level. The estimated $R^2(adj) = 0.951$ indicates a high goodness of fit for the model. Possible correlations of the residuals are studied with the Durbin-Watson test statistic. However, the test is inconclusive so that correlation of the residuals cannot be excluded.

As mentioned above, our findings suggest a time-varying smooth term. In Fig. 2.34 the time path is illustrated.

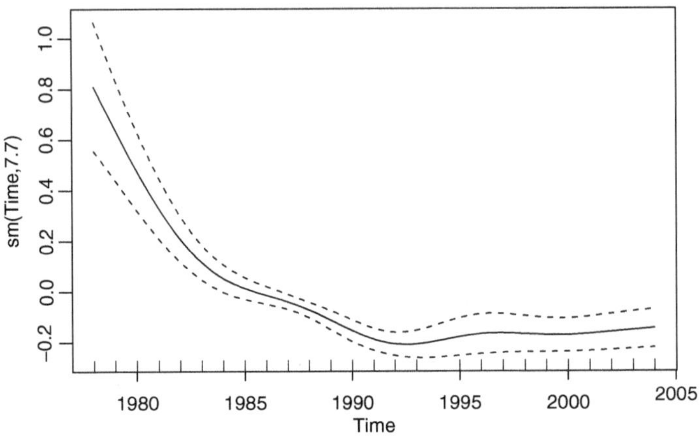

Fig. 2.34 Deviation sm(t) from the average coefficient for $b(t-1)$ for Rwanda

Table 2.41 ADF test results for Rwanda

	Model: drift, trend	Lags: 5	
Test statistic	$\hat{\tau}$	ϕ_2	ϕ_3
	−3.30	3.81	5.47
	Q(10):8.79	Q(15):12.63	Q(18):12.77

The function is decreasing over time but the estimated reaction coefficient $\psi(t)$ stays positive except for the critical years around the Genocide. The negative trend indicates a decreasing reaction of the primary surplus ratio to variations in the public debt to GDP ratio. However, it had remained relatively stable since the late 1990s.

The indicator interest payments to GDP shows low values, with 0.3 % (1986), 0.5 % (1996) and 0.4 % in 2005.[54] These figures are consistent with the estimation results. However, the external debt relative to GDP accounts for 44 % on average for the years from 1978 to 2004. Besides that high mean, the ratio shows a rising trend with 11 % in 1978 and 85 % in 2004.

To gain further insight, we use the Augmented Dickey Fuller test to analyze stationarity of the deficit inclusive of interest payments. In order to get the real budget deficit we compute the first difference of the real public debt. Table 2.41 summarizes the results for the period from 1978 to 2004 for Rwanda.[55]

From Table 2.41 we can conclude that the budget deficit is stationary for the sample period considered and, therefore, the test indicates that the intertemporal budget constraint holds. Hence, it confirms the findings from the first test. The

[54] See also World Bank (2008a).

[55] Without the 1994 observation, as above.

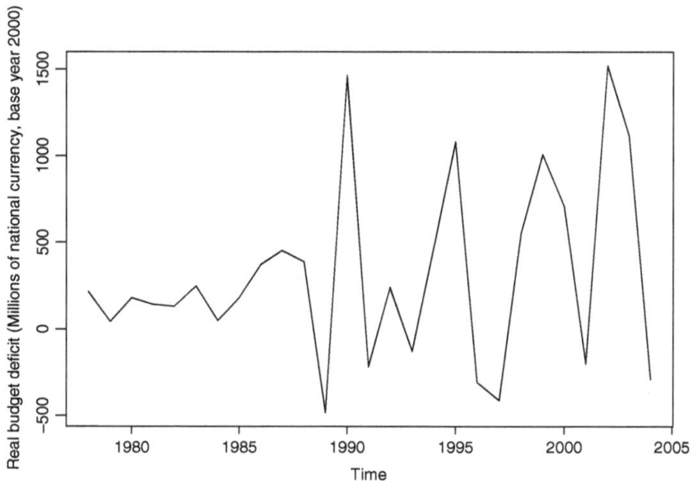

Fig. 2.35 Budget deficit of Rwanda (1978–2004)

Box-Ljung test statistic suggests that there are no hints for autocorrelation of the residuals.

Figure 2.35 shows the Rwandan real deficit situation, which has been used for the Unit Root test.

After a relatively constant time path until the middle of the 1980s, the deficits are characterized by a strongly oscillating development, henceforth. For Rwanda, the grants received seem to be quite important because they amount to 4.5 % of GDP on average, for the years considered, although we did not explicitly taken this into account in our model. The importance of those grants results from the fact that they are expected to determine the evolution of public debt, even if they are not directly used to reduce the budget deficit. Nevertheless, our analysis demonstrates that the government in Rwanda has performed a responsible debt policy. This is important for those who give grants to that country.

Figure 2.36 shows the grants received by Rwanda, relative to GDP, for the period from 1978 to 2004. Obviously, the overall trend is increasing. The two outliers in 1994 and in 1995 again refer to the Rwandan Genocide.

Summarizing the analysis of the Rwandan data, both test results indicate that there is evidence for sustainability of the public debt policy in that country.

Tunisia

Finally, we analyze the North African state Tunisia. Figures 2.37 and 2.38 show the public debt and the primary surplus to GDP ratio for the time period from 1972 to 1998. The debt to GDP ratio was increasing as can be seen in Fig. 2.37. There is a remarkable rise starting with the early 1980s until the end of that decade.

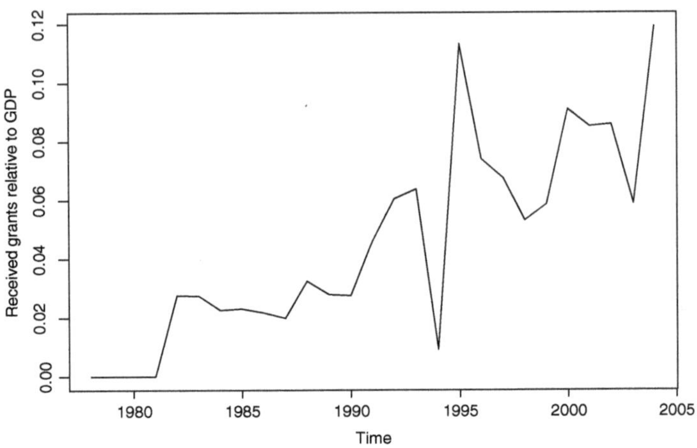

Fig. 2.36 Rwanda's received grants relative to GDP (1978–2004)

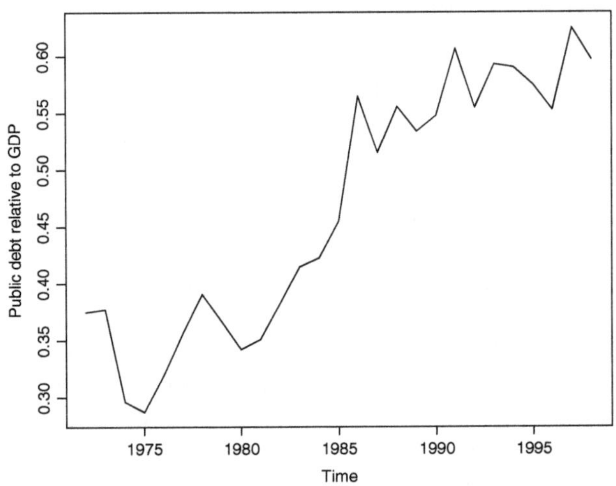

Fig. 2.37 Public debt to GDP ratio for Tunisia (1972–1998)

Reasons for this increase might have been bad weather and locusts that destroyed crops and harvest to a great degree in 1988.[56] Moreover, structural problems such as an increased role of government and emerging public enterprises intensified the situation. Adjustments by cutting public expenditures and investments were not effective immediately and could not stop the decline of public finances. However, reforms decelerated this situation afterwards.[57] From then on, the debt to GDP

[56]See for example Stork (1990) especially page 7.

[57]See also Nsouli et al. (1993), especially page 1 et seqq.

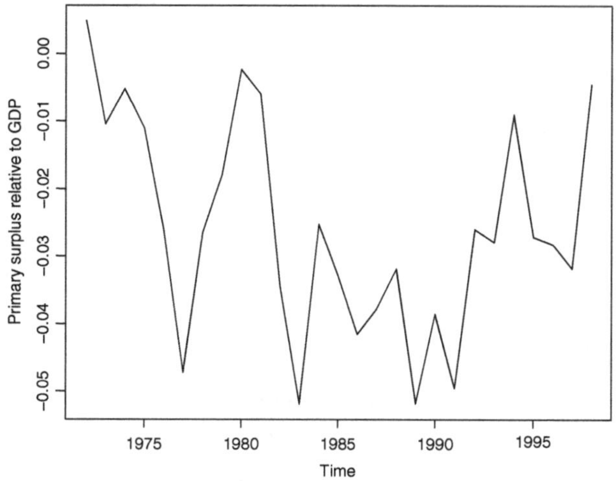

Fig. 2.38 Primary surplus to GDP ratio for Tunisia (1972–1998)

Table 2.42 Coefficients for Eq. (2.16) for Tunisia

	Coefficient	Stand. error (t-stat)	Pr(>t)
Constant	−0.025	0.022(−1.122)	0.275
$b(t-1)$	0.001	0.051(0.016)	0.988
$GVar(t)$	−0.193	0.059(−3.279)	0.004
$YVar(t)$	0.310	0.084(3.683)	0.001
sm(t)	edf:2.677	F:4.384	p-value:0.005
	R^2(adj):0.675	DW:2.28	

ratio grew rather slowly and has fluctuated around a high level of about 55 %. The primary balance ratio in Fig. 2.38 shows merely primary deficits, except for the first observation in 1972, with an overall decreasing trend.

Now, we apply the first test to study the reaction of the primary surplus ratio to variations in the debt to GDP ratio. In Table 2.42 the results are presented.

As Table 2.42 shows the average of the coefficient for the debt ratio is positive but not significant at the usual levels. As above, the deviation from that mean is given by $sm(t)$. The other coefficients, except for the intercept, are statistically significant and they show the expected signs. For the coefficient of interest, ψ, the positive sign remains if the estimation is run with only *GVar*, *YVar* or only with the debt ratio.[58] Further, Table 2.42 shows that $edf = 2.677$ and the smooth term is significant at the 1 % level. Moreover, $R^2(adj) = 0.675$ gives a fair goodness of fit and the Durbin-Watson test statistic does not indicate possible correlations of the residuals. In Fig. 2.39 the time path of the smooth term is pictured. The time

[58]For the estimation without *GVar*, ψ is significant at the 10 % level.

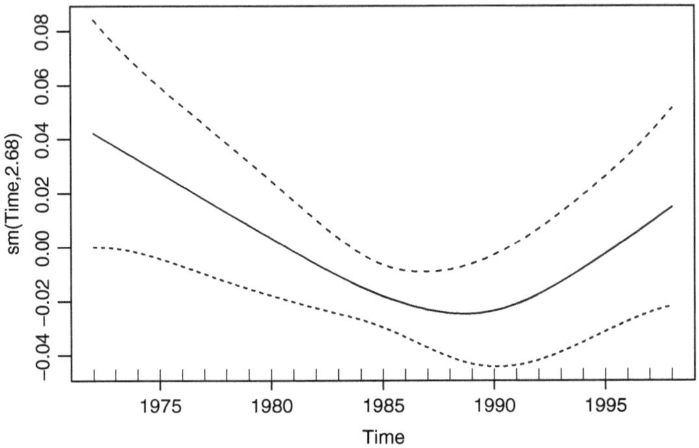

Fig. 2.39 Deviation sm(t) from the average coefficient for $b(t-1)$ for Tunisia

Table 2.43 ADF test results for Tunisia

	Model: drift, trend	Lags: 0	
Test statistic	$\hat{\tau}$	ϕ_2	ϕ_3
	−6.76	15.30	22.95
	Q(8):5.31	Q(10):8.21	Q(15):11.17

path of $sm(t)$ shows a decreasing trend until 1983. This decline indicates that the Tunisian government has put less importance on the stabilization of public debt over time. Nevertheless, the sum of the mean of the coefficient from Table 2.42 and the deviation from that mean remains positive except for the years from the early 1980s to the middle of the 1990s, but the estimated mean of the coefficient is not statistically significant. All in all, a positive but not statistically significant reaction coefficient $\psi(t)$ results from the test for Tunisia.

Again, the economic figures interest payments to GDP and external debt to GDP are consulted. For Tunisia, the interest payments relative to GDP amount to 3.4 % (1986), 2.6 % (1996) and 2.4 % in 2005.[59] Compared to those values, the average of the external debt to GDP ratio is 33 % for the years from 1972 to 1998. These figures yield some extra information on the economic situation of Tunisia.

Additionally, we apply the second test for stationarity to the budget deficit of Tunisia. As above, the deficit is calculated by the first difference of the real public debt. In Table 2.43 the test result is presented.

The result in Table 2.43 indicates that the real budget deficit is stationary. This finding suggests that the intertemporal budget constraint holds.

In Fig. 2.40 the deficit situation of Tunisia, which is used for the Dickey Fuller test, is depicted with the time period as above. Obviously, the real budget

[59]See also World Bank (2008a).

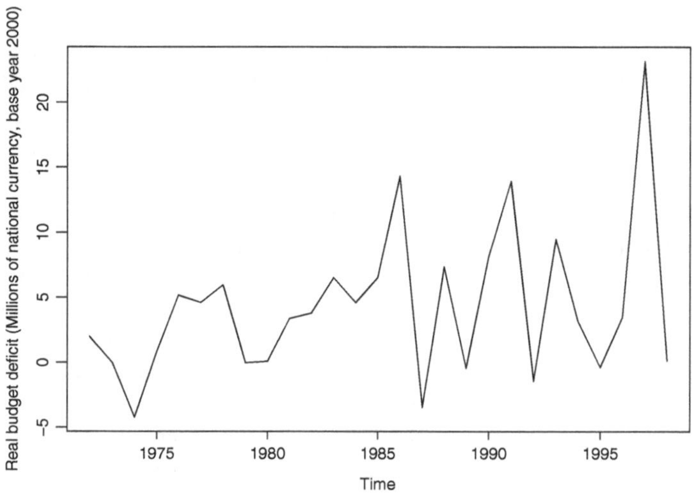

Fig. 2.40 Budget deficit of Tunisia (1972–1998)

deficit fluctuates over time with higher amplitudes in the recent past. To sum up the outcome for Tunisia, the results of the tests indicate that there seems to be sustainability of fiscal policy despite a growing debt ratio. Nevertheless, it must be pointed out that the estimated coefficient giving the reaction of the primary surplus to variations in public debt is not statistically significant. Therefore, there is some need for the government to put more weight on debt stabilization.

Conclusion

In this chapter, we have first studied conditions under which governments can pursue sustainable debt policies. When the interest rate exceeds the growth rate of GDP on average, a given debt policy is sustainable if the primary surplus relative to GDP is a positive function of the debt to GDP ratio and if the reaction coefficient is sufficiently large. The latter means that the average reaction coefficient must exceed the average difference between the interest rate on public debt and the GDP growth rate such that the debt to GDP ratio remains bounded and converges to a finite value.[60] If the reaction coefficient is positive but smaller than the difference between the interest rate and the GDP growth rate, the debt to GDP ratio becomes asymptotically unbounded that, however, implies an unsustainable debt policy. That holds because a rising debt to GDP ratio must be accompanied by a rising primary surplus

(continued)

[60]But even that does not guarantee that the critical debt to GDP ratio may be reached before the debt to GDP ratio has converged to its limiting value.

relative to GDP. But, the ratio of the primary surplus to GDP is bounded from above because the primary surplus must be financed out of GDP and it will be definitely much lower than the GDP of an economy. Consequently, a permanently rising debt to GDP ratio is not compatible with sustainability.

A sustainable debt policy is always excluded if the initial debt to GDP ratio exceeds a certain threshold, independent of how large the primary surplus is chosen, where it must be recalled that the primary surplus relative to GDP is bounded from above. If the initial debt to GDP ratio is smaller than the critical value it is possible that public debt remains sustainable, provided that the ratio of the primary surplus relative to GDP is sufficiently large. If the primary surplus is not a positive function of public debt, relative to GDP respectively, the debt ratio asymptotically converges to a constant if the government sets the primary surplus relative to GDP equal to its maximum value for ever.

We, then, applied the theoretical test methods to several countries where we started with Japan, Germany and the USA, in order to study whether the intertemporal budget constraint holds and solvency is given. The empirical part has demonstrated that a facile check on public debt might not be meaningful in the case of Japan because that country disposes of a large stock of financial assets. Looking at gross public debt did not give a statistically significant positive reaction coefficient of the primary surplus with respect to public debt. However, concentrating on public net debt, there is evidence of sustainability of Japanese public debt policy. We also found that the time path of the reaction coefficient declined until the mid 1970s, rose until the 1990s before it began to decline again and stabilized in the early 2000s.

For Germany the tests indicate sustainability of public debt, too, the statistical significance of the reaction coefficient, however, is relatively small. Further, the reaction of the primary surplus to rising public debt ratios has almost monotonously declined since 1960. Only from the early to the mid 1980s, the reaction coefficient shows a slight increase and the decline was stopped only in the early 2000s, when the parameter seems to have been stabilized.

Thus, both for Japan and Germany our analysis suggests that these two countries have performed sustainable debt policies since World War II, although the debt to GDP ratio has been rising. However, it must be pointed that a rising debt to GDP ratio is not compatible with sustainability in the long-run, as demonstrated in our theoretical part. Sooner or later public debt relative to GDP must become constant or decline. Economies that let their debt to GDP ratios grow over a longer time period face the danger that their debt ratios may exceed a certain critical value beyond which sustainability is excluded.

For the United States the high significance of the test results is encouraging despite the increasing debt ratio in the recent past. Our findings indicate that

(continued)

the intertemporal budget constraint seems to be fulfilled and that the United States government has followed a sustainable public debt policy. The reaction of the primary surplus to public debt continuously increased after World War II up to the mid 1970s, when it began to decline again, except for the early 1990s when it slightly increased.

An additional conclusion we can draw from that analysis is that the coefficient describing the reaction of the government to rising public debt ratios has not been constant. Instead, there is very strong empirical evidence that this coefficient is time-varying in all three countries under consideration.

With respect to euro area countries, our estimation results suggest that the second largest economies of the euro area, France, has pursued sustainable debt policies over the time period considered in our estimation. The average reaction coefficient giving the response of the primary surplus to public debt, relative to GDP respectively, has been positive and statistically significant. But, we also found that the reaction coefficient that was allowed to vary over time has not been constant but declined over time. This explains the rise in the debt to GDP ratio that can be compatible with a sustainable debt policy for a certain time period but not in the long-run.

As regards sustainability of public debt in the other euro area countries that have particularly suffered from the financial crises starting in 2007, we found that Ireland, Portugal and Spain seem to follow a sustainable debt policy if one takes the last three decades as representative for their public debt policies. Greece clearly has conducted an unsustainable debt policy that culminated in the Greek debt crisis in early 2010. For Italy, finally, the hypothesis of an unsustainable debt policy cannot be rejected if one takes the whole observation period. However, for a shorter time horizon a positive and statistically significant reaction coefficient could be obtained indicating a sustainable debt policy. Thus, we cannot draw a clear-cut conclusion in the case of Italy.

As concerns impacts of the 2007 financial crisis, we exemplarily studied the two Iberian countries Portugal and Spain. We found that for Portugal the crisis did not change the fundamental outcome of the previous estimations that this country seems to follow a sustainable debt policy. For Spain, however, this changes. There, debt sustainability seems to be given when observations are taken until 2010 and 2011, but not any longer when the year 2012 is included. This suggests that the financial crisis affected the sustainability position of Spain. It also underlines that several tests should be performed to get an idea about the sustainability of a given debt policy since one test alone may be rather fragile.[61] Nevertheless,

(continued)

[61] See also Tanner (2013) who argues that sustainability analyses should be more than mere mechanical estimation exercises.

our tests give an impression of how governments have dealt with rising debt to GDP ratios and how much importance they attach to performing sound fiscal policies and to control public debt.

For the developing economies, the results of our tests show that Botswana clearly has followed a sustainable debt policy and that country can be considered as an ideal as concerns its debt policy. As regards Rwanda, sustainability of fiscal policy seems to be given although the country is characterized by a growing debt ratio. This conclusion is based on a positive and statistically significant reaction of the primary surplus to variations in public debt and on stationary public deficits. Allowing for a time-varying reaction coefficient in the first test, it can also be realized that the reaction coefficient has declined over time.

The debt situation in Costa Rica, Mauritius and Tunisia also seems to be stable since the estimated reaction coefficient is positive on average and since the budget deficit is stationary. However, the estimated reaction coefficient is not statistically significant so that this coefficient should be considered with caution. In addition, it suggests that the governments in these countries should put more weight on stabilizing public debt. In contrast to that, for Panama both tests indicate that sustainability might not be given and a debt overhang problem might occur. The debt ratio is rising and although the smooth term of the first test shows an increasing time trend, the reaction coefficient is significantly negative on average. According to the second test stationarity of the deficit does not seem to be given for Panama. Thus, our results can be interpreted as a signal that corrective actions should be taken and the efforts on enforcing a stabilization policy should be intensified in Panama.

But these tests and the results have their limits. They only offer a partial view and for a detailed analysis of a developing country's situation more aspects should be taken into account. For example, characteristics of the real sector of an economy, such as aggregate indicators like trade, production and investments or monetary aspects, including the exchange rate play an important role, too. That, however, is beyond the scope of this analysis. Nevertheless, the tests performed provide meaningful results and offer some insight into the fiscal situations of the countries under consideration.

Appendix

Proof of Proposition 1

To prove that proposition we note that the evolution of public debt is given by Eq. (2.3). Integrating that equation and multiplying the resulting expression by $e^{-\int_0^t r(\mu)d\mu}$ to get present values gives,[62]

$$e^{-C_1(t)}B(t) = e^{-C_3(t)}B(0) - Y(0)e^{-C_3(t)} \int_0^t e^{-C_1(\mu)+C_2(\mu)+C_3(\mu)}\phi(\mu)d\mu, \tag{2.18}$$

with

$$\int_0^t r(\mu)d\mu =: C_1(t), \int_0^\mu r(\nu)d\nu =: C_1(\mu), \int_0^\mu g(\nu)d\nu =: C_2(\mu),$$
$$\int_0^\mu \psi(\nu)d\nu =: C_3(\mu).$$

For $\lim_{t\to\infty} C_3(t) = \lim_{t\to\infty} \int_0^t \psi(\nu)d\nu = \infty$, the first term on the right hand side in (2.18), that is $e^{-C_3(t)}\,B(0)$, converges to zero.

The second term on the right hand side in (2.18) can be written as

$$\frac{Y(0)\int_0^t e^{-C_1(\mu)+C_2(\mu)+C_3(\mu)}\phi(\mu)d\mu}{e^{C_3(t)}} =: K_1(t).$$

Since $|\phi| < \infty$ we can set $\phi Y(0) = 1$. If $\int_0^\infty e^{-C_1(\mu)+C_2(\mu)+C_3(\mu)}d\mu$ remains bounded $\lim_{t\to\infty} C_3(t) = \infty$ guarantees that K_1 converges to zero. If $\lim_{t\to\infty} \int_0^t e^{-C_1(\mu)+C_2(\mu)+C_3(\mu)}\,d\mu = \infty$, applying l'Hôpital gives the limit of K_1 as

$$\lim_{t\to\infty} K_1(t) = \lim_{t\to\infty} \frac{e^{-C_1(t)+C_2(t)}}{\psi(t)},$$

where we have set $\phi Y(0) = 1$ since $|\phi(t)|$ is bounded. Since $-C_1(t) + C_2(t) < 0$ we can find a constant $k > 0$ such that $K_1 \le e^{-kt}/\psi(t)$. The right hand side in the former inequality does not converge to zero if $\psi(t)$ converged to zero exponentially. However, in that case $\lim_{t\to\infty} \int_0^t \psi(\mu)d\mu < \infty$ would hold. Consequently, in case that $\lim_{t\to\infty} \int_0^t \psi(\mu)d\mu = \infty$ holds, $\psi(t)$ cannot decline exponentially, and $K_1(t)$ converges to zero.

[62]Equation (2.18) illustrates that a government can grow out of debt when $g > r$ holds with $\phi > 0$.

These considerations demonstrate that the intertemporal budget constraint holds for $\lim_{t\to\infty}\int_0^t \psi(\mu)d\mu = \infty$ which means that the reaction coefficient $\psi(t)$ is positive on average.

The debt ratio is obtained from (2.5) as

$$b(t) = e^{(C_1(t)-C_2(t)-C_3(t))}b(0) - e^{(C_1(t)-C_2(t)-C_3(t))}\int_0^t e^{-(C_1(\mu)-C_2(\mu)-C_3(\mu))}\phi(\mu)d\mu.$$

That expression shows that the debt to GDP ratio diverges to plus or minus infinity in the case of $\int_0^t \psi(\mu)d\mu \le \int_0^t (r(\mu)-g(\mu))\,d\mu$, while it remains constant or converges in all other cases. □

Proof of Proposition 3

To prove that proposition we note that the present value of public debt is now obtained from (2.6) as

$$e^{-C_1(t)}B(t) = B(0) - mY(0)\int_0^t e^{-(C_1(\mu)-C_2(\mu))}d\mu.$$

The intertemporal budget constraint is fulfilled for $\lim_{t\to\infty} e^{-C_1(t)}B(t) = 0$ which implies $b(0) = m\int_0^\infty e^{-(C_1(\mu)-C_2(\mu))}d\mu$. If the initial debt to GDP ratio, $b(0)$, is larger than $m\int_0^\infty e^{-(C_1(\mu)-C_2(\mu))}d\mu$ sustainability of public debt is excluded.

The debt to GDP ratio is obtained from (2.7) as

$$b(t) = e^{(C_1(t)-C_2(t))}\left(b(0) - m\int_0^t e^{-(C_1(\mu)-C_2(\mu))}d\mu\right).$$

If the intertemporal budget constraint holds we have $b(0) = m\int_0^\infty e^{-(C_1(\mu)-C_2(\mu))}d\mu$ giving $b(t) = -m\int_\infty^t e^{-(C_1(\mu)-C_2(\mu))}d\mu/e^{-(C_1(t)-C_2(t))}$. Using l'Hôpital gives $\lim_{t\to\infty} b(t) = m/(r-g)$ for asymptotically constant values of r and g. □

Public Debt Accumulation with a Stochastic Disturbance

Assume that the evolution of public debt is described by a stochastic differential equation with an additive noise. Equation (2.3), then, can be written as,

$$dB_t = (h(t)B_t - \phi(t)Y(t))\,dt + \sigma_d\,dW_t,$$

with $h(t) := r(t) - \psi(t)$ and W is a Wiener process with constant diffusion σ_d which is set equal to one, $\sigma_d = 1$. Solving that equation yields

$$B_t = e^{\int_0^t h(\tau)d\tau}\left(B_0 - \int_0^t e^{-\int_0^\tau h(\mu)d\mu}\phi(\tau)Y(\tau)d\tau + \int_0^t e^{-\int_0^\tau h(\mu)d\mu}dW_\tau\right)$$

with B_0 public debt at time $t = 0$. Multiplying both sides by the discount factor $e^{-\int_0^t r(\tau)d\tau}$ and rewriting gives

$$e^{-C_1(t)}B_t = e^{-C_3(t)}B_0 - Y_0 e^{-C_3(t)}\int_0^t e^{C_3(\tau)}e^{C_2(\tau)}e^{-C_1(\tau)}\phi(\tau)d\tau + e^{-C_3(t)}\int_0^t e^{C_3(\tau)}e^{-C_1(\tau)}dW_\tau \tag{2.19}$$

with

$$\int_0^t \psi(\tau)d\tau =: C_3(t), \int_0^\tau \psi(\mu)d\mu =: C_3(\tau), \int_0^\tau g(\mu)d\mu =: C_2(\tau), \int_0^\tau r(\mu)d\mu =: C_1(\tau),$$

where g gives the growth rate of Y. The first two terms are as in Eq. (2.18) above so that we do not have to consider them again.

The third term on the right hand side in (2.19) is stochastic with the expected value equal to zero. Defining the third term as $X_t(\omega) := e^{-C_3(t)}\int_0^t e^{C_3(\tau)}e^{-C_1(\tau)} dW_\tau(\omega)$, the second moment can be written as

$$E[X_t^2(\omega)] = E\left[\left(\frac{\int_0^t e^{C_3(\tau)}e^{-C_1(\tau)}dW_\tau(\omega)}{e^{C_3(t)}}\right)^2\right] = \left(\frac{\int_0^t E\left[e^{2C_3(\tau)}e^{-2C_1(\tau)}\right]d\tau}{e^{2C_3(t)}}\right),$$

because $E\left[\left(\int_0^t e^{C_3(\tau)}e^{-C_1(\tau)}dW_\tau(\omega)\right)^2\right] = \int_0^t E\left[\left(e^{C_3(\tau)}e^{-C_1(\tau)}\right)^2\right]d\tau$.

Since the mean of the realized real interest rate is strictly positive, we can find a constant $\bar{r} > 0$ so that $-C_1(\tau) = -\int_0^\tau r(\mu)d\mu \leq -\int_0^\tau \bar{r}\,d\mu$. Then, we can write

$$\frac{\int_0^t e^{2C_3(\tau)}E\left[e^{-2C_1(\tau)}\right]d\tau}{e^{2C_3(t)}} \leq \frac{\int_0^t e^{2C_3(\tau)}e^{-2\bar{r}\tau}d\tau}{e^{2C_3(t)}}.$$

If $\int_0^t e^{2C_3(\tau)}e^{-2\bar{r}\tau}d\tau$ remains bounded and if $\lim_{t\to\infty} C_3(t) = \infty$ holds, the expression converges to zero. If $\int_0^t e^{2C_3(\tau)}e^{-2\bar{r}\tau}d\tau$ diverges, applying l'Hôpital gives the right hand side as $e^{-2\bar{r}t}/2\psi(t)$ showing that $\psi(t)$ must not converge to zero faster than $e^{-2\bar{r}t}$ if that term is to converge to zero asymptotically. Now, assume that $\psi(t)$ declines exponentially. This would imply that $\lim_{t\to\infty} C_3(t) =$

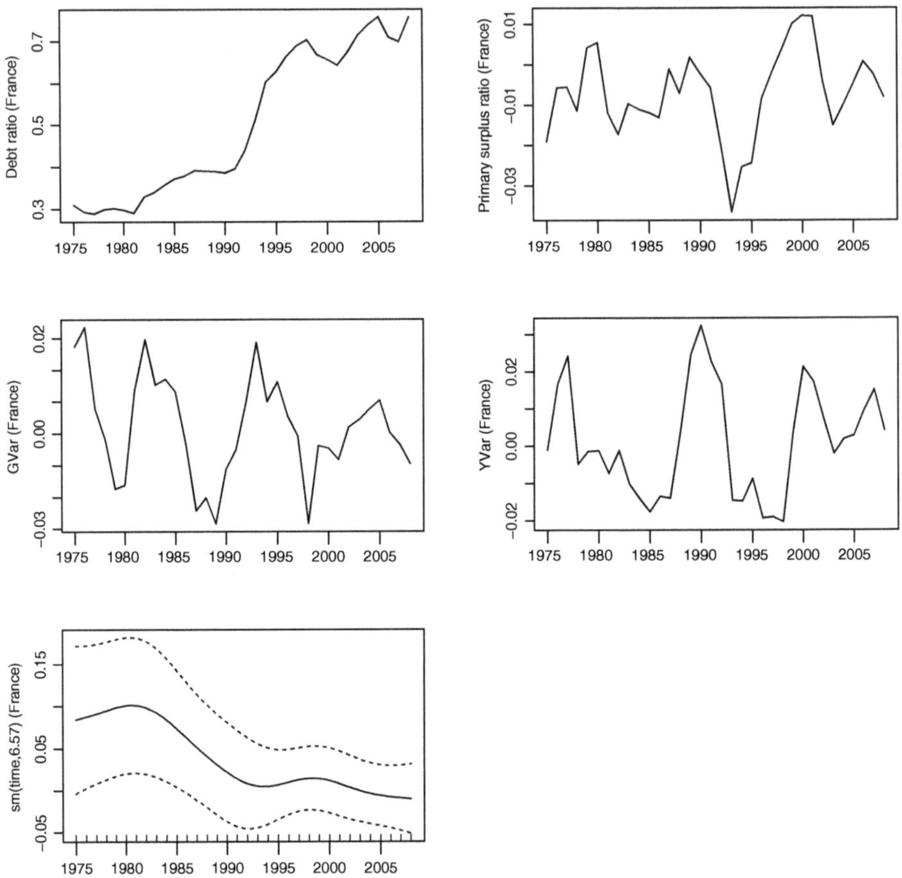

Fig. 2.41 Plot of variables and smooth term sm(t) for France

$\lim_{t\to\infty} \int_0^t \psi(\tau)d\tau < \infty$ holds. Consequently, if $\lim_{t\to\infty} C_3(t) = \infty$ holds, $\psi(t)$ cannot decline exponentially so that the expression $E[X_t^2(\omega)]$ converges to zero. □

Time-Varying Reaction Coefficients and Plots of the Data Used

The following figures show plots of the variables used in the estimations as well as the smooth term sm(t) giving the deviation of the reaction coefficient from its average value (Figs. 2.41–2.46).

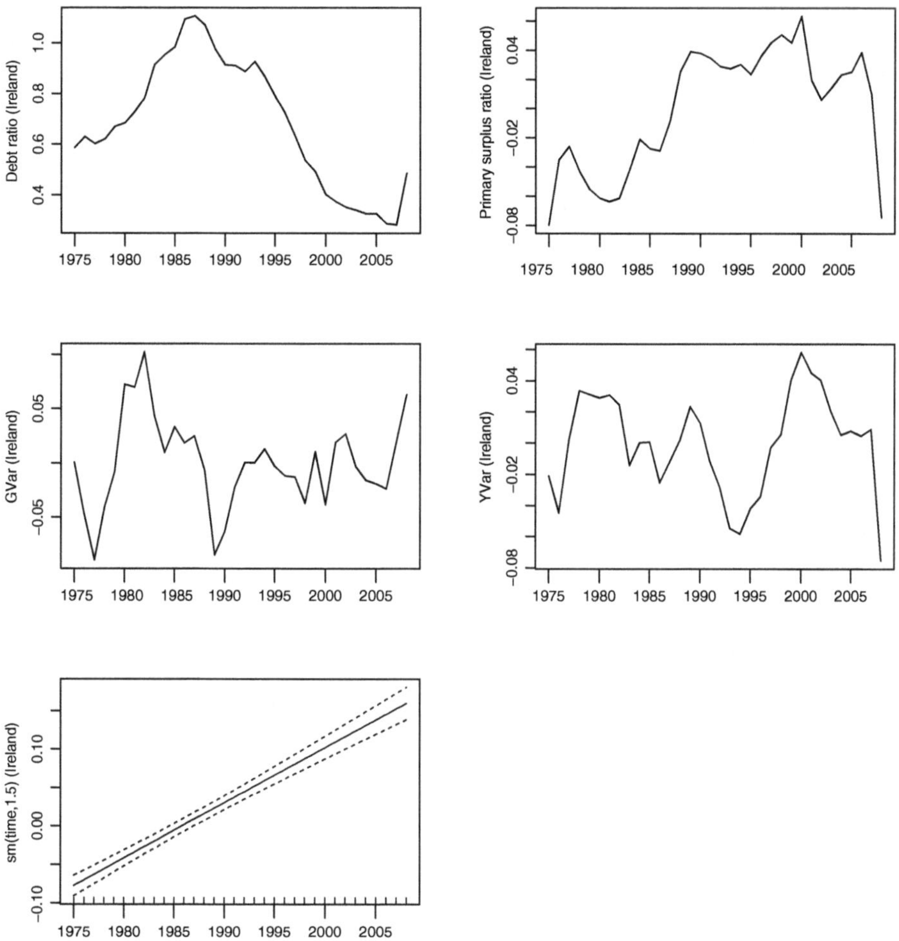

Fig. 2.42 Plot of variables and smooth term sm(t) for Ireland

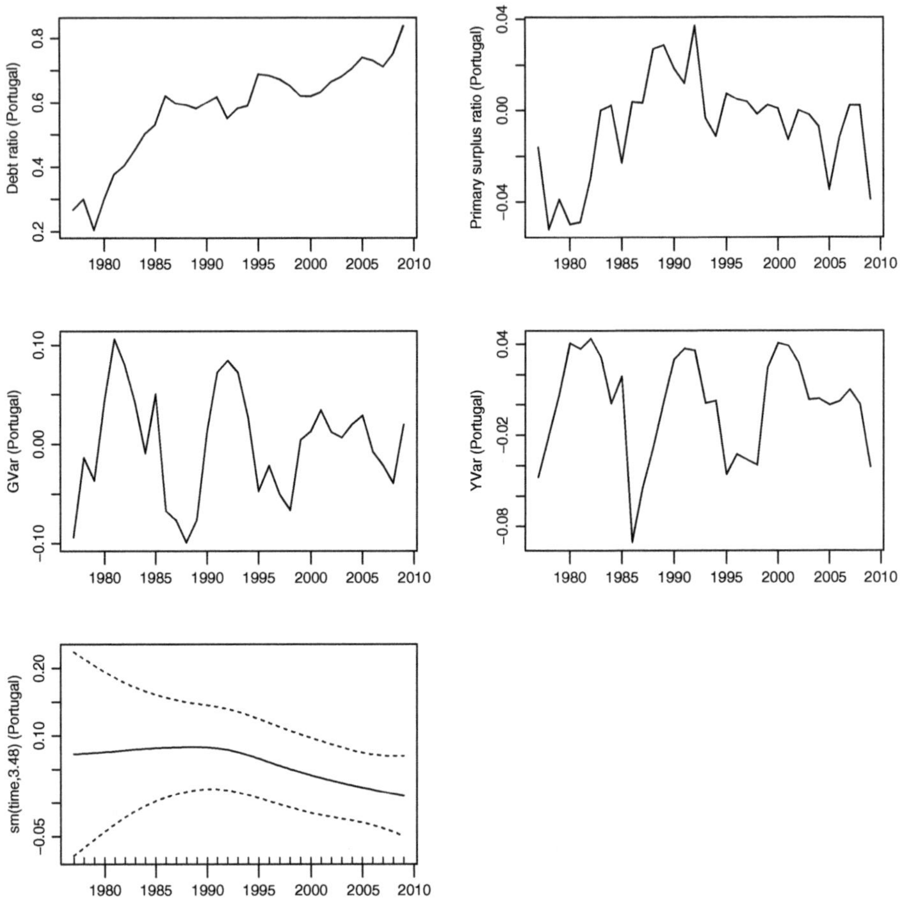

Fig. 2.43 Plot of variables and smooth term sm(t) for Portugal

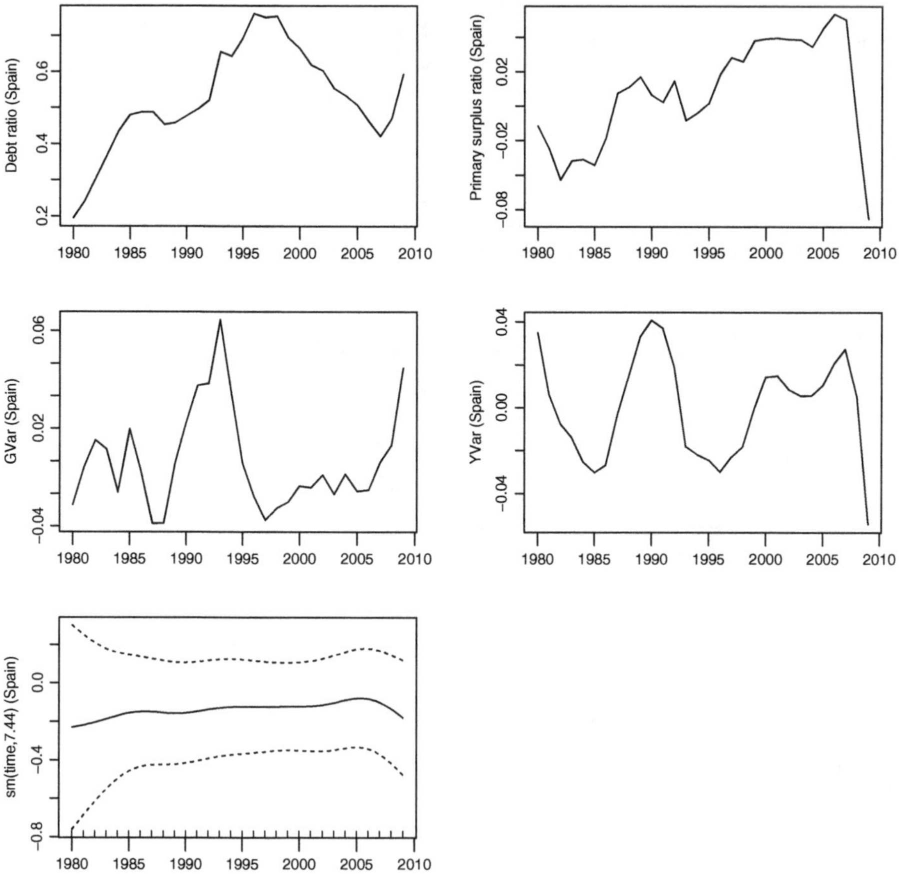

Fig. 2.44 Plot of variables and smooth term sm(t) for Spain

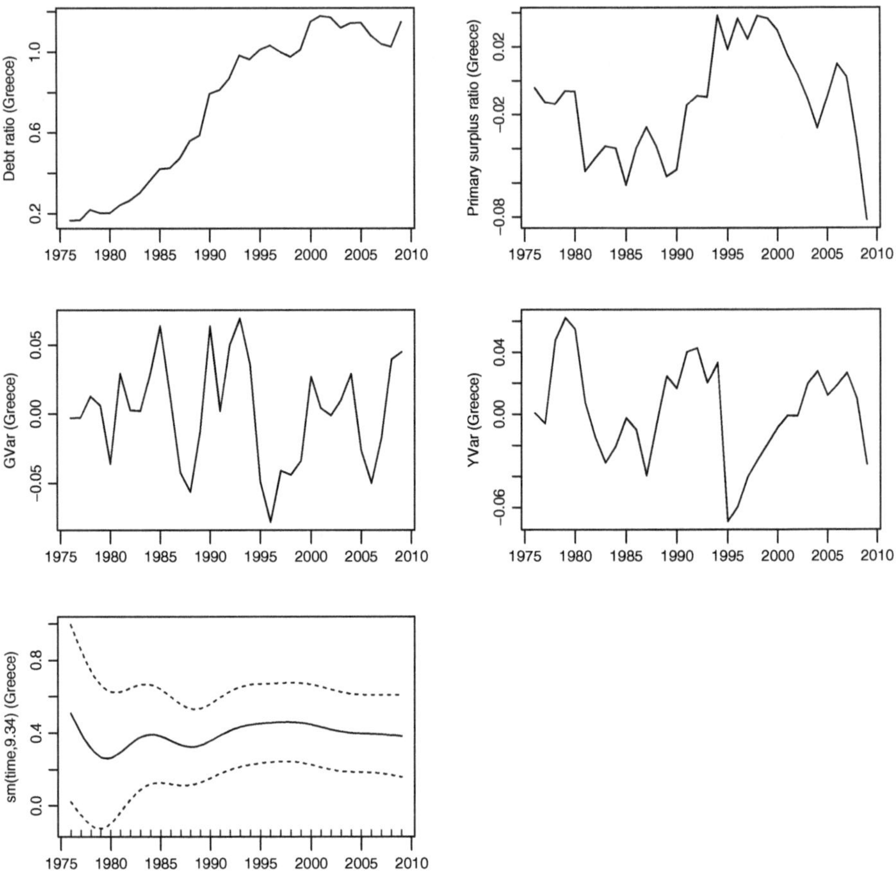

Fig. 2.45 Plot of variables and smooth term sm(t) for Greece

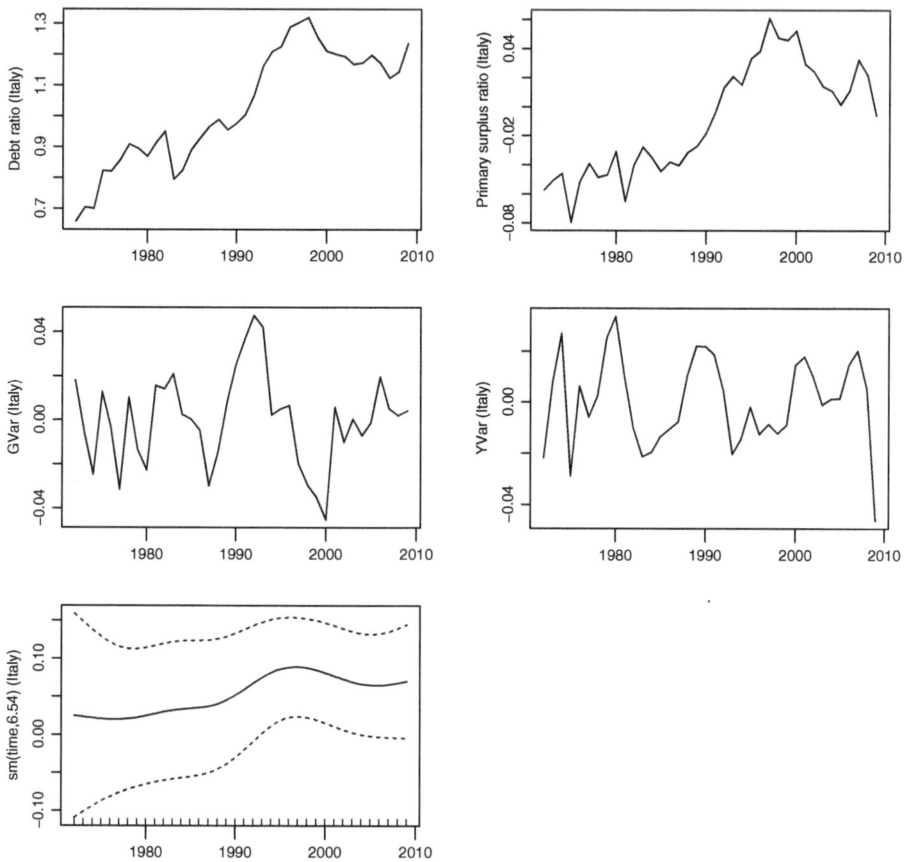

Fig. 2.46 Plot of variables and smooth term sm(t) for Italy

Additional Regressions for Spain

The subsequent tables summarize the regression outcomes for Eq. (2.15) for Spain once the sample only consists of observations until 2010 and 2011, respectively.

As these tables show, for a shorter time period the coefficient of interest, i.e. the reaction coefficient in the second line, shows a statistically significant and positive value indicating fiscal sustainability for Spain. The other significant variables possess the expected signs and the diagnostics suggest that the model is suited to replicate the data generating process. Concerning the plots of the smooth term, their shape remains similar as depicted in Fig. 2.15.

Chapter 3
Debt and Growth: A Basic Endogenous Growth Model

In the last chapter we tested for sustainability of public debt in developed as well as in developing economies. One test we resorted to was to analyze the reaction of the primary surplus, relative to GDP, to variations in the public debt to GDP ratio. We found that there is empirical evidence that the primary surplus is a positive function of public debt for most developed economies and also for some developing countries. In this chapter we will analyze the effect of this outcome for economic growth in a basic endogenous growth models.

Endogenous growth models have become popular in the economics literature with the publication of the papers by Romer (1986, 1990) and Aghion and Howitt (1992). With the emergence of that line of research the long-run growth rate of economies is no longer an exogenous variable but becomes itself an endogenous variable that depends on parameters. Hence, governments cannot only influence the levels of economic variables in the long-run but also their growth rates through fiscal policies.

Further, it is well known that the government can affect the dynamics of economies by its debt and deficit policy. For example, Schmitt-Grohé and Uribe (1997) demonstrate that a balanced government budget may lead to multiple equilibria if the distortionary income tax rate is used to balance the government budget for given public expenditures. The reason for that outcome is that there is a negative relation between aggregate activity and the income tax rate. If economic agents expect that the after-tax return rises they will increase their supply of production factors leading to a rise in the tax revenue. If public spending is fixed a balanced government budget leads to a lower tax rate such that the initial expectations are fulfilled. As a consequence, there exist multiple equilibria implying that the steady state is indeterminate. The paper by Schmitt-Grohé and Uribe is interesting because it nicely illustrates how self-fulfilling expectations can lead to multiple equilibria. However, neglecting a stock of outstanding public debt raises the question of how relevant their result is for real world economies. This holds because almost all countries are faced with the problem of public debt.

© Springer International Publishing Switzerland 2015

A. Greiner, B. Fincke, *Public Debt, Sustainability and Economic Growth*,
DOI 10.1007/978-3-319-09348-2_3

Guo and Harrison (2004) show that the result derived by Schmitt-Grohé and Uribe (1997) does not hold any longer when the tax rate is fixed and public spending is adjusted so that the budget of the government is balanced at each point in time. Then, the equilibrium is unique and saddle point stable. Thus, it is not the fact that the government budget is balanced but rather the adjustment through variations in the income tax rate that generates the outcome of Schmitt-Grohé and Uribe (1997). The contribution of Guo and Harrison (2004) is remarkable because if one accepts the tax smoothing rule derived by Barro (1979), the question arises why the government should balance its budget through adjustments in the tax rate when a non-constant tax rate leads to an excess burden that can be avoided.

In the present chapter, we want to extend this line of research in several respects as in Greiner (2007), where we follow Greiner (2011a). First, we allow for endogenous growth by assuming that there are positive externalities of investment which prevent the marginal product of capital from converging to zero as capital is accumulated. As a consequence, the economy is characterized by ongoing growth, a fact which does not hold for the models by Schmitt-Grohé and Uribe (1997) and Guo and Harrison (2004) where the economy converges to a steady state with zero growth. Taking into account that sustained per-capita growth is an important stylized fact in growth economics this extension is justified. Further, we consider that most industrialized countries are characterized by public debt so that we explicitly take into account a stock of government bonds in our model. The motivation for this lies in the observation that public debt plays an important role in real world economies so that analyzing budget rules without public debt seems to neglect an important aspect.

Within our model we, then, study three policy rules. The first rule we consider is the balanced budget rule implying that the level of public debt is constant over time, leading to a zero debt to GDP ratio in the long-run. The second rule is a rule where the government runs public deficits that are such that public debt grows but less than all other endogenous variables, such as GDP and the capital stock, for example. As for the balanced budget rule, this second rule also leads to a zero debt to GDP ratio in the long-run. The third rule is simply the intertemporal budget constraint stating that the present value of future surpluses must equal the current stock of public debt. To make that constraint operable we posit that the primary surplus of the government is a positive linear function of public debt and a function of GDP. It should be noted that, neglecting seignorage and inflation, this rule leaves three possibilities for a government to react to higher public debt: it can raise taxes, it can reduce public spending or/and public debt is repaid due to a high GDP growth rate leading to large tax revenues.

This basic model, then, is extended in several directions. Thus, we integrate a monetary sector and analyze how the interaction between fiscal and monetary policy affects the economy. Further, we also study how wage rigidities leading to persistent unemployment affect the allocative effects of public deficit and debt policies.

The goal of our contribution is to study how these budgetary rules affect stability and the growth rate of economies as well as welfare. Since public deficits and public debt play an important role in the euro area, as pointed out in the last chapter, our considerations are not only of theoretical interest but also have consequences for policy makers.

In the next section, we present the structure of our model.

3.1 The Growth Model

The structure of our model is basically the same as in Guo and Harrison (2004). Our economy consists of three sectors: A household sector which receives labor income and income from its saving, a productive sector and the government. First, we describe the household sector.

3.1.1 The Household Sector

The household sector is represented by one household which maximizes the discounted stream of utility arising from per-capita consumption, $C(t)$, and from leisure, $L^m - L(t)$, over an infinite time horizon subject to its budget constraint, taking factor prices as given. L^m denotes the maximum available amount of time and $L(t)$ is the actual labor input. The maximization problem of the household can be written as[1]

$$\max_{C,L} \int_0^\infty e^{-\rho t} \left(\ln(C C_p^{\kappa}) - L^{1+\gamma}/(1+\gamma) \right) dt, \tag{3.1}$$

subject to

$$(1-\tau)\left(wL + rK + r_B B + \pi_p\right) = \dot{W} + C + \delta K, \tag{3.2}$$

with C_p public spending that is welfare enhancing. The parameter $\rho \in (0,1)$ is the household's rate of time preference, $\gamma \geq 0$ is the inverse of the elasticity of labor supply and $\delta \in (0,1)$ is the depreciation rate of capital. The intertemporal elasticity of substitution of consumption is set equal to one so that the utility of the household is given by the natural logarithm of consumption.[2] The wage rate is denoted by w and r is the return to capital and r_B is the interest rate on government bonds. The wealth of the household is given by $W \equiv B + K$ which is equal to public debt, B, and capital, K, and π_p gives possible profits of the productive sector, the household

[1] From now on we omit the time argument t if no ambiguity arises.

[2] In the appendix to this chapter we briefly explain the elasticity of labor supply and the intertemporal elasticity of substitution of consumption.

takes as given in solving its optimization problem. Finally, $\tau \in (0,1)$ is the constant income tax rate. The dot gives the derivative with respect to time.

A no-arbitrage condition requires that the return to capital equals the return to government bonds yielding $r_B = r - \delta/(1-\tau)$. Thus, the budget constraint of the household can be written as

$$\dot{W} = (1-\tau)\left(wL + rW + \pi_p\right) - \delta W - C. \tag{3.3}$$

The current-value Hamiltonian[3] for this optimization problem is written as

$$\mathcal{H} = \ln(CC_p^{\kappa}) - L^{1+\gamma}/(1+\gamma) + \lambda((1-\tau)\left(wL + rW + \pi_p\right) - \delta W - C), \tag{3.4}$$

where λ is the co-state variable or the shadow price of wealth.

The necessary optimality conditions are given by

$$C = w(1-\tau)L^{-\gamma} \tag{3.5}$$

$$\dot{C} = C(1-\tau)r - C(\rho+\delta) \tag{3.6}$$

If the transversality condition $\lim_{t\to\infty} e^{-\rho t} W/C = 0$ holds, which is fulfilled for a time path on which assets grow at the same rate as consumption, the necessary conditions are also sufficient.

3.1.2 The Productive Sector

The productive sector is represented by one firm which behaves competitively and which maximizes static profits. The production function of the firm is given by,

$$Y = AK^{1-\alpha}\bar{K}^{\xi}L^{\beta}, \tag{3.7}$$

with $(1-\alpha) \in (0,1)$ the capital share, $\beta \in (0,1)$ the labor share and $(1-\alpha)+\beta \leq 1$ and A is a technology coefficient that is set equal to one, $A = 1$, unless mentioned otherwise. The variable Y is output and $\bar{K}$ represents the average economy-wide level of capital and we assume constant returns to capital in the economy, that is $(1-\alpha)+\xi = 1$.

Using $(1-\alpha)+\xi = 1$ and that $K = \bar{K}$ in equilibrium, profit maximization gives

$$r = (1-\alpha)L^{\beta} \tag{3.8}$$

$$w = \beta L^{\beta-1}K \tag{3.9}$$

[3] For a brief introduction into dynamic optimization see Appendix B of the book.

3.1.3 The Government

The government in our economy receives tax revenues from income taxation and has revenues from issuing government bonds. As concerns public spending we assume that it is used to finance public goods that raise the utility of the household. Further, the government sets the primary surplus such that it is a positive linear function of public debt which guarantees that public debt is sustainable, as shown in Sect. 2.1.

The accounting identity describing the accumulation of public debt in continuous time is given by:

$$\dot{B} = r_B B(1-\tau) - S, \tag{3.10}$$

where S is the government surplus exclusive of net interest payments.

The intertemporal budget constraint of the government is fulfilled if

$$\lim_{t\to\infty} e^{-\int_0^t (1-\tau) r_B(\mu) d\mu} B(t) = 0 \tag{3.11}$$

holds, which is the no-Ponzi game condition.

Now, assume that the ratio of the primary surplus to GDP is a positive linear function of the debt to GDP ratio and of a constant. The primary surplus ratio, then, can be written as

$$\frac{S}{Y} = \phi + \psi \frac{B}{Y}, \tag{3.12}$$

where $\phi \in \mathbb{R}$, $\psi \in \mathbb{R}_{++}$ are constants. The parameter ψ determines how strongly the primary surplus reacts to changes in public debt and ϕ determines whether the level of the primary surplus rises or falls with an increase in GDP. Using (3.12) the differential equation describing the evolution of public debt can be written as

$$\dot{B} = (r_B(1-\tau) - \psi)\, B - \phi\, Y. \tag{3.13}$$

From our considerations in Sect. 2.1 we know that, given the rule assumed in (3.12), a positive linear dependence of the primary surplus to GDP ratio on the debt ratio on average, that is $\psi > 0$, guarantees that the intertemporal budget constraint of the government is met. Further, Sect. 2.2 has shown that there is empirical evidence that developed countries raise their primary surplus as public debt rises. Therefore, we posit that the government sets the primary surplus according to (3.12) so that the evolution of public debt is given by (3.13). We should also like to point out that, in principle, public debt could be negative implying that the government is creditor. In this chapter, however, we assume throughout that public debt is positive.[4]

---

[4]If the government was a creditor there would be no need for the government to stick to the rule defined in (3.12) nor for the balanced budget rule.

Before we go on, we briefly discuss the rule given in Eq. (3.12). Intuitively, it is clear that economic agents have to run primary surpluses in the future, when they run deficits today, in order to avoid playing a Ponzi game. This also holds true for the government sector as shown above. But assuming that public debt is the only determinant of the primary surplus would be too short-sighted because the government has some discretionary scope and because other variables such as the surplus of social insurances, for example, affect the primary surplus in reality. Therefore, it is reasonable to posit that the primary surplus also depends on the level of GDP in a country that determines the total tax revenue and temporary government spending. But it should be pointed out that sustainability of public debt is independent of how GDP affects the primary surplus as long as the primary surplus is a positive linear function of public debt.

3.1.4 Analysis of the Model Structure

Before we analyze our model we give the definition of an equilibrium and of a balanced growth path. An equilibrium allocation for our economy is defined as follows.

Definition 1 An equilibrium is a sequence of variables $\{C(t), K(t), B(t)\}_{t=0}^{\infty}$ and a sequence of prices $\{w(t), r(t)\}_{t=0}^{\infty}$ such that, given prices and fiscal rules, the firm maximizes profits, the household solves (3.1) subject to (3.2) and the budget constraint of the government (3.10) is fulfilled with the primary surplus set according to (3.12).

In Definition 2 we define a balanced growth path.

Definition 2 A balanced growth path (BGP) is a path such that the economy is in equilibrium and such that consumption and capital grow at the same strictly positive constant growth rate, that is $\dot{C}/C = \dot{K}/K = g$, $g > 0$, $g = constant$, and either

(i) $\dot{B} = 0$ or
(ii) $\dot{B}/B = g_B$, with $0 < g_B < g$, $g_B = constant$, or
(iii) $\dot{B}/B = \dot{C}/C = \dot{K}/K = g$.

Definition 2 shows that we consider three different budgetary rules. Scenario (i) gives the balanced budget rule which implies that the debt to GDP ratio converges to zero in the long-run. Of course, such a situation is sustainable and we can even speak of strong sustainability in this case since the government balances its budget. It should be noted that the debt to GDP ratio asymptotically converges to zero in this scenario. In scenario (ii), the government runs permanent deficits and public debt grows over time. However, the deficits are such that public debt grows less than capital and GDP such that the debt to GDP ratio asymptotically converges to zero, too. This situation may be called quasi strong sustainability because it is less strict than the balanced budget rule but, nevertheless, the debt to GDP ratio also converges to zero in the long-run. We call this scenario the asymptotically zero debt ratio scenario. Finally, scenario (iii) describes a situation which is characterized by public deficits where the government debt grows at the same rate as all other endogenous variables in the long-run. Since the government sets the primary surplus according to Eq. (3.12) it does not play a Ponzi game in this case but fulfills the intertemporal budget constraint. This situation can be called weak sustainability since it only guarantees that the government does not play a Ponzi game but public debt grows at the same rate as GDP in the long-run.[5]

Thus, in equilibrium, our model economy is completely described by the following differential equations,

$$\frac{\dot{C}}{C} = (1-\tau)\,(1-\alpha)\,\omega\;(C/K)^{-\beta/(1-\beta+\gamma)} - (\rho+\delta),\; C(0) > 0, \tag{3.14}$$

$$\frac{\dot{K}}{K} = \omega\;(C/K)^{-\beta/(1-\beta+\gamma)}\;(1-\tau+\phi) - (C/K) - \delta + \psi\,(B/K)\,,\; K_0 > 0, \tag{3.15}$$

$$\frac{\dot{B}}{B} = (1-\tau)(1-\alpha)\omega\,(C/K)^{-\beta/(1-\beta+\gamma)} - \phi\,\omega\,(C/K)^{-\beta/(1-\beta+\gamma)}\,(K/B) - \delta - \psi,$$
$$B_0 > 0, \tag{3.16}$$

with $\omega = (\beta(1-\tau))^{\beta/(1-\beta+\gamma)}$ and where we used $r_B = r - \delta/(1-\tau)$. The initial conditions with respect to capital and public debt are assumed to be given while consumption can be chosen by the household at time $t = 0$.

To analyze our economy around a BGP we define the new variables $c := C/K$ and $b := B/K$. Differentiating these variables with respect to time leads to a two dimensional system of differential equations given by

$$\dot{c} = c\left(c - c^{-\beta/(1-\beta+\gamma)}\,\omega\,((1-\tau)\alpha+\phi) - \rho - \psi\,b\right), \tag{3.17}$$

$$\dot{b} = b\left(c - c^{-\beta/(1-\beta+\gamma)}\,\omega\,((1-\tau)\alpha+\phi) - \phi\,\omega\,c^{-\beta/(1-\beta+\gamma)}\,b^{-1}\right) -$$
$$b\,(\psi+\psi\,b)\,. \tag{3.18}$$

A solution of $\dot{c} = \dot{b} = 0$ with respect to c, b gives a BGP for our model and the corresponding ratios $b^\star, c^\star$ on the BGP.[6]

In the next subsection, we study our model where the government runs permanent deficits but sticks to the rule as defined in (3.12) so that the intertemporal budget constraint is fulfilled.

---

[5] A similar definition can be used in the analysis of a model with natural capital, see Greiner and Semmler (2008) or Greiner (2011b).

[6] The $\star$ denotes BGP values.

Permanent Deficits and the Intertemporal Budget Constraint

When permanent deficits are allowed one can distinguish between a purely discretionary policy where the primary surplus does not depend on the outstanding public debt, on the one hand, and, on the other hand, a rule based policy where the primary surplus is a positive function of the debt to GDP ratio. The first is modeled by setting $\psi = 0$ such that the primary surplus only depends on the parameter ϕ that is chosen arbitrarily. However, such a policy implies that the government violates its intertemporal budget constraint, as we have demonstrated in Sect. 2.1. In addition, in the appendix to this chapter we show within an endogenous growth framework that a discretionary policy in general violates the intertemporal budget constraint along a balanced growth path, because the present value of public debt converges to a positive or negative finite value or to plus or minus infinity, depending on the initial debt to GDP ratio and depending on the primary surplus policy of the government. Therefore, we limit our analysis to the case $\psi > 0$.

We should also like to recall that the rule based policy given by Eq. (3.12) with $\psi > 0$ nevertheless gives the government some discretionary scope. This holds because with (3.12) public spending relative to GDP, C_p/Y, is given by

$$C_p/Y = (\tau - \phi) - \psi\, B/Y. \tag{3.19}$$

Equation (3.19) shows that, given fiscal parameters τ, ϕ, ψ, public spending relative to GDP is an endogenous variable depending on the public debt ratio. However, the government can control C_p/Y to a certain degree by the choice of ϕ for example.

Proposition 4 below gives results as concerns existence, uniqueness and stability of a balanced growth path for our economy where the government runs deficits but sticks to the intertemporal budget constraint.

Proposition 4 *Assume that the household's time preference and the depreciation rate are sufficiently small. Then, there exists a unique BGP if the government runs permanent deficits but obeys the intertemporal budget constraint. For $\psi > \rho$ the BGP is saddle point stable, for $\psi < \rho$ the BGP is unstable.*

Proof See the appendix to this chapter.

The requirement that the rate of time preference and the depreciation rate must not be too large for a BGP to exist can be seen from (3.14). This is not a strict assumption. From an economic point of view it just states that the after-tax return to capital must be sufficiently large for ongoing growth.

Then, our economy is characterized by a unique BGP which is a saddle point if the reaction of the government to variations in public debt is sufficiently large, that is for $\psi > \rho$. This condition states that the primary surplus must rise sufficiently as public debt increases. In the opposite case, that is for $\psi < \rho$, the economy is unstable. In this case, the reaction of the primary surplus to increases in public debt is not large enough to stabilize the economy. Thus, the debt policy of the government is decisive as to whether the economy is stable or unstable.[7]

It should be noted that the condition for stability of the BGP in Proposition 4 makes sense from an economic point of view. Noting that $\rho = r(1 - \tau) - g$ holds on the BGP, we can state that the BGP is stable if and only if the reaction coefficient exceeds the difference between the net interest rate and the balanced growth rate. This is intuitively plausible because a rise of public debt relative to GDP, or relative to capital, by one unit implies that the public deficit ratio increases by $(1-\tau)r$, that is by the net return to public debt per unit. This tends to make the debt process unstable and to make the debt ratio explosive. On the other hand, in a growing economy the primary surplus rises at the balanced growth rate which stabilizes the process of debt accumulation. Since the net return to public debt equals the one to capital and exceeds the balanced growth rate, the debt ratio tends to become explosive unless the reaction coefficient is larger than that difference so that the debt ratio becomes a mean-reverting process.

Proposition 4 also implies that both global and local indeterminacy are excluded. Global indeterminacy refers to the balanced growth rate that is obtained in the long run and states that the initial value of consumption, which can be chosen freely by society, crucially determines to which BGP the economy converges and, thus, the long-run balanced growth rate. It should be noted that consumption is not a predetermined variable at time $t = 0$ in contrast to the initial stock of physical capital that is given. Local indeterminacy means that the transitional dynamics of two economies, which converge to the same BGP in the long run, crucially depend on the choice of initial consumption, $C(0)$. Thus, the transitional growth rates of those economies are determined by $C(0)$ but not the long-run growth rate, which is the same (see for example Benhabib and Perli 1994, for a more thorough treatment of those two concepts and Buiter 1982, for an exact definition of predetermined and non-predetermined variables).

Next, we analyze the balanced budget rule.

The Balanced Budget Rule and the Rule with an Asymptotically Zero Debt Ratio

To model the balanced budget rule, we set $\phi = 0$ and $\psi = (1 - \tau)r - \delta$. From Eq. (3.12) one immediately realizes that this implies $\dot{B} = 0$, that is a balanced budget and, thus, a constant level of public debt. Rule (ii) is obtained by setting $\phi = 0$ and ψ such that $\rho < \psi < (1 - \tau)r - \delta$ holds for all $t \in [0, \infty)$.[8] With those two rules the ratio of public spending to GDP, C_p/Y, is again a variable

---

[7]It should be noted that $\dot{C}/C = \dot{B}/B$ implies $\rho = \psi + \phi Y/B$. Hence, for the stable case with $\psi > \rho$, $\phi < 0$ must hold when B is positive (see the proof of Proposition 4 in the appendix to this chapter).

[8]The first inequality is necessary for $\dot{C}/C < \dot{B}/B$, the second for $\dot{B}/B > 0$.

that depends on the interest rate and on the debt ratio on the transition path. In the long-run rules, the debt ratio equals zero and the spending ratio equals the income tax rate, that is $C_p/Y = \tau$ holds, on the BGP.[9] Proposition 5 gives results for our economy assuming a balanced government budget or the asymptotically zero debt ratio rule.

Proposition 5 *Assume that the household's time preference and the depreciation rate are sufficiently small. Then, there exists a unique saddle point stable BGP if the government runs a balanced budget or if it runs public deficits such that the debt to GDP ratio asymptotically converges to zero.*

Proof See the appendix to this chapter.

Proposition 5 states that the balanced budget rule and the rule with an asymptotically zero debt ratio both yield a unique and saddle point stable BGP, in contrast to the case with permanent public deficits where the economy turned out to be unstable if the reaction of the primary surplus to higher public debt was not sufficiently large. As in the case where the government runs deficits but sticks to the intertemporal budget constraint, global and local indeterminacy are again excluded. But, in contrast to the former rule, the economy is always saddle point stable with a balanced government budget or an asymptotically zero debt ratio scenario.

Thus, the overall conclusion we can draw is that stability is the more likely, the more weight the government puts on debt stabilization. This holds because the balanced budget rule and the asymptotically zero debt ratio scenario always yield a saddle point stable BGP while the model with permanent public deficits is stable only if the reaction of the government to higher debt is sufficiently strong.

Next, we compare the long-run growth rate of the scenario with permanent deficits to that of the balanced budget rule and with that where the public debt grows but less than GDP. The following proposition gives the result.

Proposition 6 *The long-run growth rate in the economy under the balanced budget rule is equal to that under the asymptotically zero debt ratio scenario, where the public debt grows but less than GDP. The long-run growth rate in the economy with the balanced budget rule exceeds the long-run growth rate of the economy with permanent deficits.*

Proof See the appendix to this chapter.

The fact that the balanced budget rule and the asymptotically zero debt ratio scenario give the same balanced growth rate is simply due to the fact that the long-run debt to GDP ratio equals zero under both budgetary rules. Therefore, those two rules are equivalent as concerns the balanced growth rate.

The result stated in Proposition 6 is far-reaching. It says that an economy where the government runs a balanced budget gives a higher growth rate in the long-run

---

[9]Note that in case of permanent deficits a positive value for C_p/Y is not guaranteed on the BGP unless the tax rate is sufficiently large.

than an economy where the government runs deficits. The economic reason for that outcome is that a positive public debt ratio leads to a crowding out of investment which does not occur with the balanced budget rule where the debt to GDP ratio asymptotically equals zero.

But, the crowding-out mechanism is not so obvious. This holds because a higher public debt implies that public spending automatically declines because the government sticks to the primary surplus rule, Eq. (3.12). Since public spending is non-distortionary and has no productive effects anyway, the negative growth effect of a positive debt ratio is not so clear. Further, from a technical point of view that outcome is not obvious either because the growth rate of private capital in the economy-wide resource constraint, given in Eq. (3.15), does not depend negatively on the debt ratio so that there is no direct crowding out of aggregate private investment by a positive public debt ratio.

In order to understand what generates the crowding-out, we note that the economic mechanism behind it is as follows. A positive debt ratio implies that a certain part of aggregate savings is used for a non-productive purpose, i.e. for the debt service. This reduces the shadow price of private wealth and leads to a lower supply of labor and, consequently, the incentive to save and invest and, thus, the balanced growth rate decline. It is in this way that public debt affects the allocation of resources in the long-run.

Integrating Public Transfers

In the last subsection we assumed that public spending is used to finance public goods that raise the utility of the households in the economy. Now, we want to posit that public spending can be divided between spending for public goods that are welfare enhancing and spending for lump-sum public transfers to the household sector, as in Greiner (2012a). Neglecting depreciation of capital, i.e. setting $\delta = 0$, the budget constraint of the representative household, then, changes to

$$\dot{W} = (1 - \tau)\left(wL + rW + \pi_p\right) - C + T_p, \tag{3.20}$$

with T_p denoting lum-sum public transfers.

The period budget constraint of the government is now given by

$$\dot{B} = r_B B(1 - \tau) - S = r_B B(1 - \tau) - \left(\tau Y - c_p Y - t_p Y\right), \tag{3.21}$$

with $C_p = c_p Y$ and $T_p = t_p Y, c_p + t_p < \tau, 0 < c_p, t_p < 1$. The government again sets the primary surplus such that it is a positive function of public debt so that the intertemporal budget constraint is fulfilled. That is we have again

$$\frac{S}{Y} = \phi + \psi \frac{B}{Y}, \tag{3.22}$$

where $\phi \in \mathbb{R}$, $\psi \in \mathbb{R}_{++}$ are constants.

With a fixed income tax rate, the government can now adjust either public consumption or transfer payments as public debt rises. In the first case, public spending is given by $C_p = (\tau - t_p - \phi)Y - \psi B$ and the economy-wide resource constraint is obtained as

$$\frac{\dot{K}}{K} = \omega\ (C/K)^{-\beta/(1-\beta+\gamma)}\ (1 - \tau + \phi + t_p) - (C/K) + \psi\ (B/K)\,,\ K_0 > 0, \tag{3.23}$$

that is equivalent to (3.15) for $t_p = 0$.

In the second case, public transfers are $T_p = (\tau - c_p - \phi)Y - \psi B$ and the economy-wide resource constraint, then, becomes

$$\frac{\dot{K}}{K} = \omega\ (C/K)^{-\beta/(1-\beta+\gamma)}\ (1 - c_p) - (C/K)\,,\ K_0 > 0. \tag{3.24}$$

The equations describing the evolution of private consumption and of public debt are identical to those of the last subsections, that is they are given by (3.14) and by (3.16), respectively. Taking into account that the economy-wide resource constraint is given by (3.23) when public consumption is adjusted, one immediately realizes that the model structure is the same as above, implying that there exists a unique BGP that is saddle point stable for $\psi > \rho$.[10] However, when the government adjusts public transfers, the two differential equations describing the dynamics around a BGP are slightly different and obtained as

$$\dot{c} = c\left(c - c^{-\beta/(1-\beta+\gamma)}\,\omega\,(\tau - c_p + (1-\tau)\alpha) - \rho\right), \tag{3.25}$$

$$\dot{b} = b\left(c - c^{-\beta/(1-\beta+\gamma)}\,\omega\,(\tau - c_p + (1-\tau)\alpha) - \phi\,\omega\,c^{-\beta/(1-\beta+\gamma)}\,b^{-1} - \psi\right). \tag{3.26}$$

Noting that $\tau - c_p + (1-\tau)\alpha > 0$ we have

$$\lim_{c\to 0}(\dot{c}/c) = -\infty,\ \lim_{c\to\infty}(\dot{c}/c) = +\infty,\ \partial(\dot{c}/c)/\partial c > 0$$

showing that there exists a unique $c^\star$ that solves $\dot{c} = 0$ so that there is a unique BGP. As concerns stability we note that $\dot{c}$ is independent of b. Hence, there are no transition dynamics of c since c is set to its BGP value at $t = 0$ such that $\dot{c} = 0$ holds for all $t \in [0, \infty)$. For b to converge to a finite value, we must have $\partial(\dot{b}/b)/\partial b < 0$. The equation $\dot{b}/b$ is written as

$$\dot{b} = b(1-\tau)r - \psi b - \phi - b(\dot{K}/K), \tag{3.27}$$

[10] Here, we only consider the scenario where public debt grows at the same rate as all other endogenous variables on the BGP.

with $\dot{K}/K$ given by Eq. (3.24). Noting that $\dot{K}/K$ does not depend on b, differentiating $\dot{b}$ with respect to b leads to

$$\frac{\partial \dot{b}}{\partial b} = (1-\tau)r - \psi - g < 0 \leftrightarrow \psi > (1-\tau)r - g. \tag{3.28}$$

This shows that the model is again stable, in the case of permanent public deficits, if the government puts a sufficiently high weight on stabilizing public debt, that is if the reaction coefficient exceeds the difference between the net interest rate and the balanced growth rate.

Next, we analyze how the balanced growth rate depends on the debt policy when the government adjusts public consumption and when it adjusts public transfers, respectively. The result is given in Proposition 7.

Proposition 7 *If the government adjusts public spending to meet its intertemporal budget constraint the balanced growth rate is higher the smaller the public debt ratio. If the government adjusts transfers the balanced growth rate is independent of the debt ratio.*

Proof See the appendix to this chapter.

Proposition 7 demonstrates that the public debt ratio has a negative impact on the balanced growth rate if the government adjusts the public spending ratio, meaning that public debt crowds out government spending. But, again, since public spending is non-distortionary and has no productive effects anyway, the negative growth effect of a higher debt ratio is not so obvious. Further, it should be recalled that, from a technical point of view, this outcome is not obvious either because the growth rate of private capital in the economy-wide resource constraint, given in Eq. (3.23), does not depend negatively on the debt ratio so that there is no direct crowding out of aggregate private investment by public debt.

As above, the crowding out results from the fact that the shadow price of wealth is smaller if the government runs deficits because it implies that less of the household's savings can be used for the formation of productive private capital. That gives a return to capital, r, that is the lower the higher the debt to GDP ratio is. Consequently, the share of consumption relative to GDP is larger and the investment share is smaller leading to a lower balanced growth rate in the long-run, as a result of a higher debt to GDP ratio.

If the government adjusts transfer payments this effect does not occur. The reason is that in this case public debt does not appear in the economy-wide resource constraint, which is now given by Eq. (3.24), because the reduction of lump-sum transfers is used to meet the higher debt service. Then, the shadow price of capital and the labor supply remain unchanged so that a higher debt ratio does not lead to a reallocation of resources between saving and investment, on the one hand, and consumption, on the other hand. Thus, the long-run growth rate remains unaffected. It should be noted that the reduction in lump-sum transfers can be seen as a sort of lump-sum tax that is used to meet the higher debt service requiring higher primary surpluses.

That analysis has shown under which conditions a higher debt to capital ratio and, of course, also a higher debt to GDP ratio reduce the long-run balanced growth rate. It must be pointed out that the debt ratio is an endogenous variable which is larger the less strict the fiscal policy of a country is. In our framework, the fiscal policy of a country is determined by the income tax rate, by the transfer share and by the share of public consumption relative to GDP. When the government adjusts public consumption to fulfill its intertemporal budget constraint the government can set the transfer share and the income tax rate. It is easily seen that an increase in the income tax rate τ raises the debt ratio implying a lower long-run growth rate. It is true that a higher tax rate leads to a higher tax revenue but it also reduces capital accumulation such that the ratio of public debt to capital rises. On the other hand, a higher transfer share t_p reduces the debt ratio because a rise in the transfer share goes along with a decrease in public consumption relative to GDP since public consumption adjusts to meet the intertemporal budget constraint. Since lump-sum transfers do not affect the allocation of resources while a reduction in public consumption raises economic growth, this policy leads to higher growth and to a smaller debt ratio. When public transfers are adjusted a rise in the public consumption share c_p raises (reduces) the public debt ratio for $\phi < 0$ ($\phi > 0$). Recall that the parameter ϕ determines whether the level of the primary surplus declines (for $\phi < 0$) or rises (for $\phi > 0$) with a higher GDP. Consequently, an increase in the share of public consumption relative to GDP goes along with a decline (rise) in the primary surplus to GDP ratio in the case of $\phi < 0$ ($\phi > 0$) such that the debt ratio rises (declines).

In the next section we study welfare effects of different debt policies.

3.1.5 *Welfare Effects of Debt Policy*

It is well known that growth and welfare maximization may be different goals when transition dynamics occur (cf. Futagami et al. 1993). Therefore, we analyze in this section how the different budgetary rules affect welfare in our model economy, where we neglect public transfers, that is we set $t_p = 0$. Welfare is given by the expression

$$F = \max_{C,L} \int_0^\infty e^{-\rho t} (\ln(C C_p^\kappa) - L^{1+\gamma}/(1+\gamma)) dt. \tag{3.29}$$

In order to study welfare effects of the budgetary rules we resort to simulations since it is not possible to get results for the analytical model. To do so, we numerically compute the time paths of the variables $c(t)$ and $b(t)$ for the linearized version of the system (3.17)–(3.18) for a given initial debt to capital ratio taking into account transition dynamics. Given the time paths of $c(t)$ and $b(t)$ we numerically solve the differential equation system (3.14)–(3.16) yielding the values for $C(t)$, $K(t)$ and $B(t)$ as well as for labor supply $L(t)$. With these values we can compute the integral (3.29) where we set $K(0) = 1$ so that $C(0) = c(0)$ and $B(0) = b(0)$ hold.

As regards the parameter values we set the capital share to $1 - \alpha = 0.25$ and the labor share to $\beta = 0.75$. The labor share seems a bit high but it is nevertheless in the range of EU-15 countries. In the mid 2000s the average labor income share in the EU-15 countries, measured as a percentage of gross national income, was about 65 %, with the highest value of about 75 % in Sweden and in the UK and the lowest values of roughly 55 and 30 % in Ireland and Greece, respectively (see figures 1a and 1b in Breuss 2007). The depreciation rate of physical capital is 7.5 % i.e. $\delta = 0.075$. The income tax rate is $\tau = 0.25$ and the rate if time preference is set to $\rho = 0.05$. As regards the parameter γ we consider two different values, namely $\gamma = 0.15$ and $\gamma = 0.3$ that can be considered as plausible values. According to Benhabib and Farmer (1994), a value of $\gamma = 0.25$ can be considered as realistic and they take this value as benchmark. But they also consider other values for that parameter in the interval between 0 and 0.3, since higher and lower elasticities of labor supply cannot be excluded. The parameter κ, finally, is set to $\kappa = 0.25$, implying that the marginal rate of substitution between private and publicly provided goods is 0.25 (C/C_p).

Further, for the budgetary rule (iii) we have to specify the parameter values ϕ and ψ. These are set to $\phi = -0.00305$ and $\psi = 0.1$ that are compatible with empirical observations for euro area countries. Thus, empirical estimations for the reaction coefficient φ gave values between 0.077 and 0.199 for countries of the euro area (see e.g. Greiner et al. 2007). As to the parameter ϕ, estimations have been performed for Germany and Italy (cf. Greiner and Kauermann 2008, for example). We should also like to point out that different values for ψ lead to different values for the debt to GDP ratio with higher values of ψ going along with a lower debt ratio, ceteris paribus, thus affecting long-run growth and welfare. However, we do not go further into the details since our goal is to compare the outcome of the different rules we specified in Definition 2.

Given these parameter values the long-run growth rate for the balanced budget rule and for the rule with an asymptotically zero debt ratio is $g = 0.052$ for $\gamma = 0.15$ and $g = 0.053$ for $\gamma = 0.3$. The balanced growth rate in the case of permanent deficits is $g = 0.045$ for $\gamma = 0.15$ and $g = 0.047$ for $\gamma = 0.3$ with a debt to GDP ratio of about 70 % in both cases.

In Table 3.1 we report the values obtained for the welfare functional (3.29) where the initial condition with respect to $b(0)$ is set to $b(0) = 0.32$.[11]

Table 3.1 demonstrates that the rule where public debt grows in the long-run at the same rate as all other economic variables (rule (iii) denoted by ‘positive debt ratio’ in Table 3.1) clearly yields the lowest welfare. The reason for this outcome is that this rule yields a lower growth rate than the other two rules and a higher debt ratio that negatively affects public spending and, thus, welfare. Comparing the balanced budget rule (rule (i)) with the rule where public debt grows but less than all

[11] In the appendix to this chapter we report the results for a different initial condition with respect to $b(0)$ and also for $\kappa = 1$, showing that the qualitative outcome remains unchanged for those cases.

Table 3.1 Welfare F for the different budgetary rules with $\kappa = 0.25$ and $b(0) = 0.32$

	$\gamma = 0.15$		
	balanced budget	Asympt. zero debt ratio	Positive debt ratio
F	−9.283	−9.257	−9.951
	$\gamma = 0.3$		
	Balanced budget	Asympt. zero debt ratio	Positive debt ratio
F	−6.434	−6.392	−7.107

other economic variables (rule (ii) denoted by 'asympt. zero debt ratio' in Table 3.1), shows that the balanced budget rule gives lower welfare.

The economic reason behind this result is that public spending on the transition path under the balanced budget rule is smaller than under the rule where public debt grows but less than all other economic variables.[12] This can be seen by setting $\kappa = 0$ implying that public spending is not welfare enhancing. Then, the outcome changes and the balanced budget rule yields higher welfare than the rule where public debt grows but less than all other economic variables. Consequently, the fact that the balanced budget rule leads to lower welfare than the rule where public debt grows but less than all other economic variables, in case of welfare enhancing public spending, must be due to the lower level of public spending on the transition path under the balanced budget rule. The lower level of public spending with a balanced budget results form the fact that the parameter ψ, which determines how strong the debt to capital ratio reduces public spending on the transition path, is higher under the balanced budget rule compared to the rule where public debt grows but less than all other economic variables.

Since it is public spending that gives lower welfare under the balanced budget rule compared to the rule where debt grows but less than GDP, there is a critical value for κ which determines utility from public spending, below which that outcome changes. Hence, only if public spending is sufficiently welfare enhancing, a deficit policy with a slightly growing level of public debt can perform better than the balanced budget rule. That holds because under the rule where debt grows, but less than GDP, overall (i.e. private and public) consumption is higher and capital accumulation is lower along the transition path compared to the balanced budget rule. In our numerical example with $b(0) = 0.32$, the balanced budget rule performs still worse than the rule where public debt grows but less than GDP for $\kappa = 0.1$ with $\gamma = 0.3$. However, setting $\gamma = 0.15$ and leaving all other parameter values unchanged, the outcome changes and now the balanced budget rule yields higher welfare than the rule where debt grows but less than GDP, independent of the value of γ.

We should also like to point out that in our simulation, rule (iii), where public debt grows at the same rate as all other variables, always performs worse than

[12]Note that public spending is the same under these two rules on the BGP.

the other two rules, rule (i) and rule (ii), for the parameter values we considered. The reason is that rule (i) and rule (ii) yield the same growth rate in the long-run that exceeds the one obtained under rule (iii). Therefore, both private consumption and publicly provided goods grow at a smaller rate under rule (iii) in the long-run compared to rule (i) and (ii) giving higher welfare under the latter two rules.

3.2 Debt Cycles

In contrast to the approach presented above we now assume that the primary surplus does not only depend on the public debt of the current period but that the history of government debt is decisive as regards the determination of the primary surplus as in Greiner (2014a). Hence, the primary surplus is a function of cumulated past levels of public debt with exponentially declining weights put on debt further back in time. With this assumption we get a more complex outcome. We demonstrate that the stability of the economy with the balanced budget depends on the weight given to more recent levels of public debt. The economy with permanent public deficits may either give rise to no balanced growth path, to a unique balanced growth path or to two balanced growth paths. The paths are either stable or unstable and for a certain parameter constellation the dynamic system gives rise to a limit cycle. Finally, the economy with a balanced government budget always experiences a higher long-run growth rate than the economy with permanent public deficits, as in the previous sections.

For models where the household sector is characterized by an OLG structure, two interesting contributions have been presented by Bräuninger (2005) and by Yakita (2008). Bräuninger analyzes an OLG economy and demonstrates that for a fixed deficit ratio there exist two balanced growth paths as long as the deficit ratio is below a certain threshold. As the deficit ratio rises the growth rate declines and once the critical deficit ratio is exceeded sustained growth does not occur any longer. Yakita presents and studies an OLG model with productive public capital and demonstrates that there exists an upper bound for the level of public debt that is compatible with a sustainable debt policy. This critical level is determined by the stock of public capital and once the critical value of public debt relative to public capital is exceeded a sustainable debt policy of the government is excluded. Taking into account that the stock of public capital determines the level of GDP in his model, this result makes sense from an economic point of view.

3.2.1 Structure of the Model

The household sector and the productive sector are identical to those presented in Sect. 3.1. The government in our economy receives tax revenues from income taxation and has revenues from issuing government bonds and it only finances public spending, C_p, that now is a pure waste of resources, i.e. it neither enhances welfare nor raises production possibilities in the economy. The reason for that assumption is that in this section we are interested in effects of government debt per se, meaning that we neglect any distortions resulting from variations in government spending going along with changes in public debt. The period budget constraint of the government describing the accumulation of public debt in continuous time is given by:

$$\dot{B} = r_B B(1-\tau) - S, \tag{3.30}$$

where S is government surplus exclusive of net interest payments. The intertemporal budget constraint of the government is fulfilled if

$$B(0) = \int_0^\infty e^{-\int_0^\mu (1-\tau) r_B(\nu) d\nu} S(\mu) d\mu \Leftrightarrow \lim_{t\to\infty} e^{-\int_0^t (1-\tau) r_B(\mu) d\mu} B(t) = 0 \tag{3.31}$$

holds, which is the no-Ponzi game condition.

Now, assume that the history of government debt is decisive as regards the determination of the primary surplus. We do so because governments will make their budget plans dependent on how the public debt has evolved over time. Thus, a continuous rise in public debt relative to GDP may affect the budget plans of a government differently compared to a time path of the public debt ratio that has also shown a tendency to decline in the past. Thus, Legrenzi and Milas (2011) find empirical evidence that governments take corrective actions only when the debt exceeds a certain threshold that depends on the history of the government debt. Thus, it is the history of public debt that is decisive as regards the determination of the primary surplus. Therefore, we posit that the primary surplus relative to GDP depends on cumulated past debt with an exponentially declining weight put on investment flows further back in time. Further, in all empirical estimations performed in Chap. 2 it is the debt ratio of the previous period that has a statistically significant effect on the primary surplus to GDP ratio.

Therefore, the equation determining the primary surplus is now written as,

$$S = \phi Y + \int_{-\infty}^t e^{\theta(\mu - t)} \psi B(\mu) d\mu, \tag{3.32}$$

with $\phi \in \mathbb{R}$ the parameter determining whether a rise in GDP goes along with a higher or lower level of the primary surplus. The parameter $\psi \in \mathbb{R}_{++}$, which is the average of the reaction parameter that may vary over time, determines how strong the primary surplus reacts to cumulated past levels of public debt with an exponentially declining weight put on debt further back in time. The parameter θ determines how strong more recent levels of public debt affect the primary surplus where the influence of more recent public debt is the stronger the higher θ. It should be noted that for $\theta \to \infty$ we get the limit case where only public debt of the current period affects the primary surplus.

If the primary surplus depends on cumulated past debt with exponentially declining weights on debt further back in time, the reaction of the government to public debt is larger than in the case where public debt only depends on the current level of public debt, since $\psi B(t) < \psi B(t) + \int_{-\infty}^{t-\epsilon} e^{\theta(\mu-t)} \psi B(\mu) d\mu$. Thus, C_1 is larger and a positive average reaction coefficient guarantees sustainability if the reaction of the government to public debt is as in Eq. (3.32).

In the next subsection we derive the differential equations that describe our economy.

3.2.2 The Differential Equations

To study our model, we introduce the new variable $R = \int_{-\infty}^{t} e^{\theta(\mu-t)} \psi\, B(\mu) d\mu$ giving the reaction of the primary surplus to cumulated past public debt. Further, we note that (3.5) and (3.9) imply $L = (C/K)^{1/(\beta-\gamma-1)} \omega^{1/\beta}$, with $\omega = (\beta(1-\tau))^{\beta/(1-\beta+\gamma)}$. Thus, in equilibrium[13] our economy is completely described by the following differential equations,

$$\frac{\dot{C}}{C} = (1-\tau)(1-\alpha)\omega\, (C/K)^{-\beta/(1-\beta+\gamma)} - (\rho+\delta), \tag{3.33}$$

$$\frac{\dot{K}}{K} = \omega\, (C/K)^{-\beta/(1-\beta+\gamma)}\, (1-\tau+\phi) - (C/K) - \delta + R/K, \tag{3.34}$$

$$\frac{\dot{B}}{B} = \omega\, (C/K)^{-\beta/(1-\beta+\gamma)}\, ((1-\tau)(1-\alpha) - \phi(K/B)) - \delta - R/B, \tag{3.35}$$

$$\frac{\dot{R}}{R} = \psi\, (B/R) - \theta \tag{3.36}$$

where we used $r_B = r - \delta/(1-\tau)$ that results from the no-arbitrage condition. The initial conditions with respect to capital, K_0, public debt, B_0, and the reaction to cumulated past debt, R_0, are assumed to be given while consumption can be chosen by the household at time $t = 0$.

It should be mentioned that Eq. (3.33) is identical to (3.14) and obtained as above. The resource constraint of the economy, Eq. (3.34) is obtained by combining the budget constraint of the household with the government budget constraint that is now given by Eq. (3.30) and (3.32), where again (3.8) and (3.9) have been resorted to. Equation (3.35), finally, is obtained from (3.30), where Eqs. (3.5), (3.8) and (3.9)

[13]The equilibrium definition is the same as in the previous sections.

as well as the production function (3.7) have been used. The last equation, (3.36), finally is obtained by differentiating R with respect to time.

To analyze our economy around a BGP we define the new variables $c := C/K$, $b := B/K$ and $z := R/K$. Differentiating these variables with respect to time leads to a three dimensional system of differential equations given by,

$$\dot{c} = c\left(c - c^{-\beta/(1-\beta+\gamma)}\omega((1-\tau)\alpha + \phi) - \rho - z\right) \tag{3.37}$$

$$\dot{b} = b\left(c - c^{-\beta/(1-\beta+\gamma)}\omega((1-\tau)\alpha + \phi) - \phi\omega c^{-\beta/(1-\beta+\gamma)}b^{-1} - z(1+b^{-1})\right) \tag{3.38}$$

$$\dot{z} = z\left(\psi(b/z) - \theta + c + \delta - z - c^{-\beta/(1-\beta+\gamma)}\omega(1-\tau+\phi)\right) \tag{3.39}$$

In this section we consider only the balanced budget scenario and the scenario where public debt grows at the same rate as all other variables. Since the balanced budget scenario is equivalent to the scenario where public debt grows, but less than all other variables, concerning allocative aspects in the long-run and since we do not intend to study welfare effects, this can be justified. In the next section we first analyze the balanced budget scenario.

3.2.3 Balanced Government Budget

To model the balanced budget scenario we set $\phi = 0$ and ψ and θ are set such that $\dot{B} = 0$ holds. Setting $\dot{B} = 0$ implies that the ratio of public debt to private capital equals zero on the BGP, i.e. $b^\star = 0$ holds.[14] A constant value of public debt implies $R = B(r(1-\tau) - \delta) = const.$ so that $\dot{R} = 0$ and $z^\star = 0$ hold along the BGP. The condition $\dot{R} = 0$ gives $\psi B = \theta R$ which, together with $R = B(r(1-\tau) - \delta)$, leads to $\psi = \theta(r(1-\tau) - \delta)$. With $b^\star = z^\star = 0$ the economy is completely described by Eq. (3.37) and a rest point of that equation gives a balanced growth path for the economy. Proposition 8 shows that there exists a unique BGP for the balanced budget scenario under a slight additional assumption.

Proposition 8 *Assume that the rate of time preference and the depreciation rate are sufficiently small. Then, there exists a unique balanced growth path if the government runs a balanced budget.*

Proof A rest point of the equation $\dot{c}/c = c - c^{-\beta/(1-\beta+\gamma)}\omega(1-\tau)\alpha - \rho$ gives a BGP. It is easily seen that $\lim_{c\to 0} \dot{c}/c = -\infty$ and $\lim_{c\to\infty} \dot{c}/c = +\infty$ hold. Further, we have $\partial(\dot{c}/c)/\partial c > 0$ so that there exists a unique $c^\star$ that solves $\dot{c}/c = 0$. □

Proposition 8 shows that there exists a unique balanced growth path if the government runs a balanced budget. Hence, multiplicity of long-run growth rates

[14]The * again denotes BGP values.

can again be excluded. It should be noted that the assumption of a sufficiently small rate of time preference and of the depreciation rate of capital must be made, just as in the previous section, because we can only prove that there exists a unique rest point of the system (3.37)–(3.39) but we cannot show that this rest point implies a positive growth rate.

In order to analyze stability of the BGP we first state the following lemma.

Lemma 1 *The eigenvalues of the Jacobian evaluated at the balanced growth path are given by* $ev_1 = \partial\dot{c}/\partial c > 0$, $ev_2 = -g$, $ev_3 = \rho - \theta$.

Proof See appendix to this chapter. □

Given this lemma it is easy to derive a condition assuring that the BGP is saddle point stable. This is done in Proposition 9.

Proposition 9 *The balanced growth path is saddle point stable if and only if* $\theta > \rho$ *holds.*

Proof Follows immediately from Lemma 1. □

Proposition 9 states that the government must put a sufficiently high weight on more recent levels of public debt when setting the primary surplus so that saddle point stability is given. We should also like to point out that on the BGP we have $\rho = (r(1-\tau) - \delta) - g$, i.e. the rate of time preference is equal to the net return on wealth minus the balanced growth rate. Thus, we can state that the parameter θ must exceed the difference between the net return on wealth and the growth rate for the model economy to be stable. We also recall that the balanced budget scenario implies $\psi = \theta(r(1-\tau) - \delta)$ so that a high value for θ implies a high value for ψ, too. Hence, saddle point stability is only given if the government puts a sufficiently high weight on stabilization, i.e. if the primary surplus reacts strongly to past public debt, and if the primary surplus reacts soon to higher public debt, i.e. the weight given to more recent levels of public debt in setting the primary surplus must be large.

This shows that in this more complex model the balanced budget scenario is not saddle point stable unless the government puts a sufficiently high weight on stabilizing debt. In the next subsection, we analyze the economy with permanent public deficits.

3.2.4 Permanent Public Deficits

In the following we limit the analysis to the case $\omega((1-\tau)\alpha + \phi) > 0$. From an economic point of view this states that the government can reduce the primary surplus as GDP grows but that effect must not be too large, i.e. ϕ may become negative but its absolute value must be smaller than $(1-\tau)\alpha$. For the model with permanent public deficits we then see that the long-run dynamics is more complex than for the balanced budget case. Proposition 3 gives the different possible long-run outcomes.

Proposition 10 *Assume that the rate of time preference and the depreciation rate are sufficiently small. Then, the following holds true:*

(i) *For* $(\psi/\rho) + \rho + \delta < \theta$ *and* $\phi < 0$ *there exists no balanced growth.*
(ii) *For* $(\psi/\rho) + \rho + \delta < \theta$ *and* $\phi > 0$ *there exists a unique balanced growth path.*
(iii) *For* $(\psi/\rho) + \rho + \delta > \theta$ *and* $\phi < 0$ *there exists a unique balanced growth path.*
(iv) *For* $(\psi/\rho) + \rho + \delta > \theta$ *and* $\phi > 0$ *there exists either no balanced growth path or there exist two balanced growth paths.*

Proof See the appendix to this chapter. □

Proposition 10 demonstrates that the reaction of the government to higher public debt is crucial as regards existence of a BGP, given the structural parameters ρ and δ. If the parameter ψ is relatively small given a certain value for θ, such that $(\psi/\rho) + \rho + \delta < \theta$ (case (i) and (ii)), the primary surplus must increase as GDP rises so that a BGP exists, i.e. $\phi > 0$ must hold. Otherwise, i.e. for $\phi < 0$, no BGP exists since fiscal policy is too loose in the sense that the primary surplus declines with a rising GDP and the reaction of the primary surplus to cumulated past debt is small, too. Thus, with a governmental policy that does not pay sufficient attention to stabilizing public debt sustained growth is not possible.

If ψ is relatively large given a certain value for θ, so that $(\psi/\rho)+\rho+\delta > \theta$ holds (case (iii) in Proposition 3), there exists a unique BGP for $\phi < 0$. This holds because the reaction of the government to higher cumulated public debt, ψ, is relatively large so that a BGP can exist even if the primary surplus declines as GDP rises. If the reaction of the government to cumulated public debt is relatively large and the primary surplus rises with GDP, $\phi > 0$, case (iv), there exists either no BGP or two BGPs. If a BGP does not exist, the government puts too high a weight on stabilizing public debt in the sense that the primary surplus rises as GDP increases and it strongly reacts to cumulated past levels of public debt. Hence, a situation may exist where the government puts too high a weight on stabilizing debt implying that the growth rate of public debt falls short of the growth rates of capital and consumption. In this case, reducing the reaction to cumulated past debt, i.e. lowering ψ, or reducing ϕ, giving the increase of the primary surplus as GDP rises, can lead to endogenous growth. However, in this situation there then exist two BGPs, the stability of which remains to be determined, meaning that the economy is globally indeterminate.

Before we study stability of the BGP we first derive a lemma that gives the relation between the balanced growth rate and the debt ratio. That is the contents of Lemma 2.

Lemma 2 *Assume that there exists at least one BGP. Then, on the BGP the following relation holds:*

$$\frac{dg}{db} < 0$$

Proof See the appendix to this chapter. □

Lemma 2 shows that the balanced growth rate is the smaller the higher the debt ratio which confirms the outcome of the previous section. The economic mechanism behind that result is the same, namely that a higher debt ratio implies that more resources in the economy must be used for the debt service. As a consequence, the shadow price of wealth is smaller which gives a lower incentive to save and invest and a lower labor supply. Therefore, the balanced growth rate and the debt ratio are negatively correlated. Proposition 11 gives an immediate consequence of that result.

Proposition 11 *The long-run growth rate in the economy with permanent public deficits is smaller than in the economy with a balanced government budget.*

Proof Follows immediately from Lemma 2. □

That proposition which is an immediate consequence of Lemma 2 states that economies with a balanced government budget will always experience a higher growth rate than economies with permanent deficits that are such public debt grows at the same rate as capital and GDP. The reason is that the shadow price of wealth is smaller if the government runs deficits because it implies that less of the household's savings is used for the formation of private capital. That leads to a lower return to capital, r, and also to a lower labor supply, L, so that there will be less saving and less investment when the government requires a certain part of the savings in the economy for its debt service.

In order to study stability of the BGP for the situation with permanent public deficits we resort to numerical examples. We do so because the analytical model turns out to be too complex to gain insight into its stability properties. We should also like to point out that we do not intend to perform a calibration exercise that replicates real economies. The goal of our simulations is to get additional insight into the qualitative behavior of our model economy.

As regards the parameter values we set the capital share to 30 %, $1-\alpha = 0.3$, and the labor share is set to 70 %, $\beta = 0.7$. The depreciation rate of capital is 7.5 %, $\delta = 0.075$, and the income tax rate is 25 %, $\tau = 0.25$. The rate of time preference is 5 %, $\rho = 0.05$, and the inverse of the labor supply elasticity is set to $\gamma = 0.15$ which is in the range of the values considered by Benhabib and Farmer (1994) for example. For a further discussion of plausible values for the labor supply elasticity we refer to the previous section and to Benhabib and Farmer (1994), p. 32–33.

First, we consider the case (ii) in Proposition 10 where we set $\theta = 0.25$, $\phi = 0.001$ and $\psi = 0.003$. With these parameter values the system is unstable with two positive real eigenvalues and one negative. When we increase the parameter ψ implying that the reaction to cumulated public debt becomes larger, the qualitative outcome does not change. The largest value of ψ we considered was $\psi = 0.006$ because for values of ψ larger than 0.006 gives case (iv) of Proposition 10.

For case (iii) in Proposition 10 we set $\theta = 0.01$, $\phi = -0.001$ and $\psi = 0.0039$. With these parameter values the economy is stable with one pair of complex conjugate eigenvalues and one positive real eigenvalue. If we continuously decrease the parameter ψ implying that the government puts less weight on stabilizing public debt, we realize that for $\psi = \psi_{crit} = 3.712708 \cdot 10^{-3}$ two eigenvalues

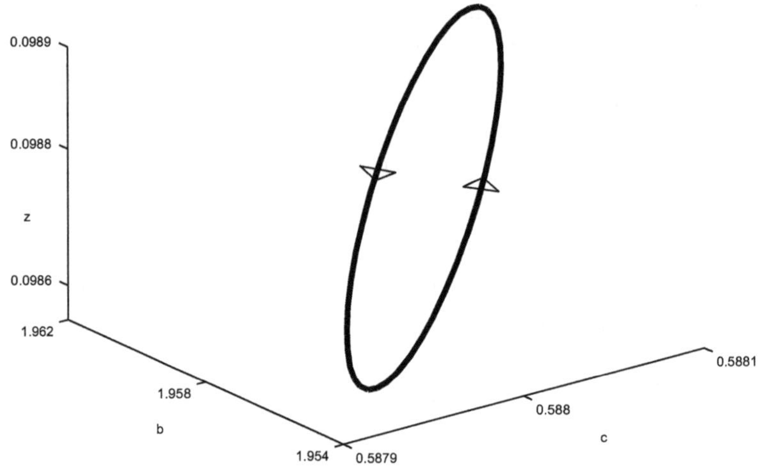

Fig. 3.1 Limit cycle in the $(b - z - c)$ phase space with $\psi = 3.7127 \cdot 10^{-3}$

are purely imaginary and a Hopf bifurcation occurs.[15] The Hopf bifurcation gives rise to stable limit cycles since the first Lyapunov coefficient L_1 is negative,[16] $L_1 = -5.36271 \cdot 10^{-2}$. The limit cycles exist for an interval of values of ψ which are smaller than ψ_{crit}. From an economic point of view the emergence of limit cycles means that the economy is not characterized by a constant growth rate at which all variables grow but the growth rates are cyclically fluctuating over time. If ψ is further decreased the economy becomes unstable. Figure 3.1 shows the limit cycle in the $(b - z - c)$ phase space where the orientation is as indicated by the arrows.[17]

In case (iv) there exist two BGPs where the one with the higher growth rate is unstable (two positive and one negative real eigenvalue) while the BGP yielding the lower balanced growth rate is stable (one positive real eigenvalue and one complex conjugate with negative real part) for $\theta = 0.01$, $\phi = 0.001$ and $\psi = 0.0039$. As in case (iii) two eigenvalues become purely imaginary as ψ is continuously reduced and for $\psi = \psi_{crit} = 3.638542 \cdot 10^{-3}$ a Hopf bifurcation occurs giving rise to limit cycles. Again, the limit cycles are stable because the first Lyapunov coefficient is negative, $L_1 = -5.85141 \cdot 10^{-2}$.

Thus, this section has demonstrated that the dynamics of this basic endogenous growth model with public debt become more complex once we posit that it is the

[15]A formal statement of the Hopf bifurcation theorem is given in Appendix C at the end of the book.

[16]For those computations we used the software LOCBIF, see Khibnik et al. (1993).

[17]To detect the limit cycle we used the software MATCONT, see Dhooge et al. (2003).

history of public debt that determines the debt policy of the government. Next, we analyze the interaction between fiscal and monetary policy.

3.3 The Interaction of Fiscal and Monetary Policy

With this section we intend to contribute to the research dealing with the question of how the interplay between public debt policy and monetary policy affects growth, inflation and welfare of economies, where we adopt the approach presented by Greiner (2014b). Among other things, we want to see whether central banks can compensate loose debt policies of governments by a higher growth rate of nominal money supply.

When a monetary sector is to be integrated in economic growth models the question of arises how that can be achieved. In economics, usually three approaches can be found (for a survey see Wang and Yip 1992). First, there is the so-called money-in-the-utility-function approach that assumes that real money holdings have a positive effect on the utility of agents. The second way of integrating real money is the cash-in-advance approach that posits that consumption goods and a part of the investment goods must be purchased out of existing real money balances. The third approach is the transactions-costs approach where money is introduced through a shopping-time technology that states that the time spent for shopping is the smaller the higher the real money holdings are. Resorting to those approaches, the interaction between monetary and fiscal policy can be studied then.[18]

There also exist studies dealing with money in endogenous growth models. For example, Jones and Manuelli (1995) analyze different types and show that in some models of endogenous growth inflation has direct effects on the growth rate of the economy by distorting the choice of households between consumption and leisure. That effect also characterizes the models presented by Wu and Zhang (1998) and by Gomme (1993). There, a rise in the inflation rate reduces the level of employment, thus, leading to lower growth. Gillman and Kejak (2005) set up a nesting model in order to analyze the theoretical literature on inflation and endogenous growth. They can show that a large array of models can all generate negative effects of inflation on economic growth. Further, they point out that the models can be distinguished whether there is a nonlinear relationship between inflation and growth so that the effect becomes smaller as inflation rises, or, whether this relation remains constant over the range of inflation rates.

In this section we adopt the money-in-the-utility approach and assume that real money holding yields utility for the representative household. Sustained growth in our model is the result of positive externalities leading to constant returns to capital in the economy. We can show for our model that a balanced government

---

[18]See for example Piergallini and Rodano (2012) who also present a good survey of such analyses for models characterized by exogenous growth.

budget always gives rise to a higher balanced growth rate compared to an economy with permanent public deficits, as in the model without a monetary sector analyzed above. That also holds with respect to welfare unless governments put a high weight on stabilizing public debt when running permanent deficits. In that case, welfare effects of the balanced budget scenario compared to the scenario with permanent deficits depend on the initial conditions with respect to public debt. When governments run permanent deficits, a stricter debt policy implies higher long-run growth as well as higher welfare. Further, the central bank can compensate a loose debt policy by increasing the nominal money growth rate. Such a policy raises the long-run growth rate but goes a along with higher inflation and less welfare. In addition, that is possible only up to a certain point, meaning that sustained growth is not feasible once the debt policy of the government falls short of a critical value.

The economy we analyze consists of a household sector, of a productive sector and of the public sector. The latter is composed of the government that collects taxes and runs into public debt to finance its spending and of the central bank that determines the nominal money growth rate. Basically, the model structure is the same as in the previous sections. However, we now have to distinguish between nominal and real variables. Therefore, we describe the structure of the model in detail. First, we describe the household sector.

3.3.1 The Household Sector

The household sector consists of many identical households of mass one where each household has measure zero. One household is representative for the whole household sector and maximizes the discounted stream of utility arising from real consumption, $c(t)$, from real money holdings, $m(t)$, and it has disutility from working with $l(t)$ denoting labor supply. In this section capital letters give nominal variables and lowercase letters stand for real variables. Further, we delete the time argument t as long as no unambiguity arises. The utility function is assumed to be logarithmic in c and m and the household maximizes its utility over an infinite time horizon subject to its budget constraint, taking factor prices as given. Thus, the maximization problem of the household can be written as

$$\max_{c,l} \int_0^\infty e^{-\rho t} \left(\ln c + \ln m - l^{1+\gamma}/(1+\gamma)\right) dt, \tag{3.40}$$

subject to

$$c + \dot{a} + \dot{m} = (1-\tau)\,(wl + ra) + t_p\, y - \pi\, m. \tag{3.41}$$

The parameter $\rho \in (0, 1)$ is the rate of time preference and $\gamma \geq 0$ gives the inverse of the elasticity of labor supply. The variable a denotes the assets of the household that are composed of real capital, k, where we neglect depreciation, and of real government bonds, b, and m stands for real money holdings. The income tax rate is denoted by $\tau \in (0, 1)$ and w and r give the real wage rate and the real interest rate, respectively. Finally, $t_p \in (0, \tau)$, gives lump-sum transfers as a share of real GDP, y, and π stands for the inflation rate. It should be mentioned that we do not consider negative transfers that would imply an additional tax for the household and that the transfer share is smaller than the tax rate.

We should like to point out that the budget constraint in real terms is derived from the nominal budget constraint, $Pc + P\dot{k} + \dot{M} + \dot{B} = (wl + rk)P(1 - \tau) + iB - \tau(i - \pi)B + t_{pY}$, with P the price level, $i = r + \pi$ the nominal interest rate and capital letters denoting nominal variables. This implies that the government only taxes the real return to government bonds which must hold for one unit of physical capital to yield the same return as one unit of government bonds in real terms. This is a no-arbitrage condition that makes the household indifferent between investing in physical capital and in government bonds.

To solve this problem we formulate the current-value Hamiltonian which is written as

$$\mathcal{H} = \left(\ln c + \ln m - l^{1+\gamma}/(1+\gamma)\right) + \lambda_1 \left((1-\tau)(wl + ra) + t_p\, y - \pi\, m - c\right) \\ + \lambda_2 (s_h - a - m), \tag{3.42}$$

with λ_1 the shadow price of private savings, s_h, and λ_2 a Lagrange multiplier. The necessary optimality conditions are obtained as,

$$c^{-1} = \lambda_1 \tag{3.43}$$

$$l^{\gamma} = \lambda_1 w (1 - \tau) \tag{3.44}$$

$$\dot{\lambda}_1 = \rho \lambda_1 - \lambda_2. \tag{3.45}$$

In addition, the return to assets must equal the value of money holdings at the margin, implying the following two conditions,

$$\lambda_2 = \lambda_1 r (1 - \tau) \tag{3.46}$$

$$\lambda_2 = m^{-1} - \lambda_1 \pi. \tag{3.47}$$

Combining Eqs. (3.43)–(3.47) leads to the following conditions that characterize an optimum,

$$c = m\left((1-\tau) r + \pi\right) \tag{3.48}$$

$$l^{\gamma} = w (1 - \tau) c^{-1} \tag{3.49}$$

$$\dot{c} = c\left((1-\tau) r - \rho\right) \tag{3.50}$$

If the transversality condition $\lim_{t\to\infty} e^{-\rho t} s_h / c = 0$ holds, which is the standard household's no-Ponzi game condition, that is fulfilled for a time path on which savings grow at the same rate as consumption, the necessary conditions are also sufficient.

3.3.2 The Productive Sector

The productive sector is represented by one firm which behaves competitively and which maximizes static profits. The production function of the firm is given by,

$$y = Ak^{1-\alpha}\bar{k}^{\xi}l^{\alpha}, \tag{3.51}$$

with $(1-\alpha) \in (0,1)$ the capital share and $\alpha \in (0,1)$ the labor share, y real output and $\bar{k}$ represents the average economy-wide level of capital. The parameter $A > 0$ reflects total productivity and we assume constant returns to capital in the economy, i.e. $(1-\alpha)+\xi = 1$.

Using $(1-\alpha)+\xi = 1$ and that $k = \bar{k}$ holds in equilibrium, profit maximization gives the real interest rate and the real wage rate as

$$r = (1-\alpha)Al^{\alpha} \tag{3.52}$$

$$w = \alpha Al^{\alpha-1}k \tag{3.53}$$

3.3.3 The Public Sector

The government in our economy receives tax revenues from income taxation and has revenues from issuing government bonds it uses to finance lump-sum transfers, $p = t_p y$, and public spending that is neither welfare enhancing nor productive. The period budget constraint of the government describing the accumulation of public debt in real terms is given by,

$$\dot{b} + \dot{m} = rb(1-\tau) - s - \pi\, m, \tag{3.54}$$

where s is the real primary surplus, i.e. government surplus exclusive of net interest payments.

The intertemporal budget constraint of the government is fulfilled if

$$\lim_{t\to\infty} P_0 e^{-\int_0^t (1-\tau)r(\mu)d\mu} b(t) = 0 \tag{3.55}$$

holds with P_0 the price level at $t = 0$ which is set equal to one.

Concerning the primary surplus, the government sets the primary surplus according to the rule assumed in the previous sections,

$$s = \phi\, y + \psi\, b. \tag{3.56}$$

The parameter $\psi \in \mathbb{R}_{++}$ determines how strong the primary surplus reacts to changes in public debt and will be denoted as the reaction coefficient and $\phi \in \mathbb{R}$ determines whether the level of the primary surplus rises or falls with an increase in GDP.

The monetary authority determines the growth rate of the money supply by setting the parameter $\theta > 0$ that gives the growth rate of nominal money supply, M. Thus, real money supply is determined as,

$$\frac{\dot{m}}{m} = \frac{\dot{M}}{M} - \pi = \theta - \pi. \tag{3.57}$$

In the next subsection we define equilibrium conditions and the balanced growth path.

3.3.4 The Balanced Growth Path

The economy-wide resource constraint for our economy is obtained by combining the budget constraint of the household, Eq. (3.41), with that of the government, Eq. (3.54), as,

$$\dot{k} = y(1 - \tau + \phi) - c + t_p\, y + \psi\, b, \tag{3.58}$$

where the primary surplus rule (3.56) has been used and y has been obtained from Eq. (3.51) as $y = kA^{(1+\gamma)/(1-\alpha+\gamma)}((k/c)\alpha(1-\tau))^{\alpha/(1-\alpha+\gamma)}$, where $k = \bar{k}$ has been used. Using the optimality conditions determining the factor prices, Eqs. (3.52) and (3.53), the evolution of private consumption is described by,

$$\dot{c} = c\left((1-\tau)\,(1-\alpha)\,(y/k) - \rho\right). \tag{3.59}$$

Given the primary surplus rule (3.56), the evolution of public debt is obtained from (3.54) as follows,

$$\dot{b} = (1-\tau)\,(1-\alpha)\,b\,(y/k) - \theta\, m - \phi\, y - \psi\, b \tag{3.60}$$

and the growth of real money supply is given by

$$\dot{m} = m\,\theta - c + m\,(1-\tau)\,(1-\alpha)\,(y/k), \tag{3.61}$$

with the inflation rate π determined by Eq. (3.48). Thus, in equilibrium the economy is completely described by the four differential equations (3.58)–(3.61).

We are interested in a situation with permanent growth. Therefore, we define a balanced growth path (BGP) as a path on which all economic variables grow at the same constant rate, possibly with the exception of public debt. As concerns public debt we consider two scenarios: Either, the government budget is balanced such that public debt is constant or the government runs permanent deficits such that public debt grows at the same rate as all other economic variables on the BGP.

To analyze our economy around a BGP we define the following variables, $x := c/k$, $z := m/k$ and $v := b/k$. The differential equation system that describes our economy around a BGP, then, is obtained as,

$$\dot{x} = x\left((1-\tau)(1-\alpha)(y/k) - \rho - (y/k)(1-\tau+\phi+t_p) + x - \psi v\right), \quad (3.62)$$

$$\dot{z} = z\left(\theta - x/z + (1-\tau)(1-\alpha)(y/k) - (y/k)(1-\tau+\phi+t_p) + x - \psi v\right), \quad (3.63)$$

$$\dot{v} = v\left(x - \theta(z/v) - \phi v^{-1}(y/k) - \psi - (y/k)(\alpha(1-\tau)+\phi+t_p) - \psi v\right), \quad (3.64)$$

with y/k given by $y/k = A^{(1+\gamma)/(1-\alpha+\gamma)} x^{-\alpha/(1-\alpha+\gamma)} (\alpha(1-\tau))^{\alpha/(1-\alpha+\gamma)}$. A rest point of (3.62)–(3.64) yields a BGP which implies $g := \dot{c}/c = \dot{m}/m = \dot{k}/k$, $\dot{b} = 0$, $v^\star = 0$, for a balanced government budget[19] and $g = \dot{c}/c = \dot{m}/m = \dot{k}/k = \dot{b}/b$ with permanent public deficits.

In the next section we analyze our model with respect to growth and welfare effects of different fiscal policy scenarios.

3.3.5 *Analysis of the Model*

First, we analyze our model with respect to existence and stability of a BGP and we study growth effects of fiscal and monetary policy.

Analyzing the Structure of the Model and Growth Effects of Policy Measures

To start with we consider the balanced budget scenario and compare it to the scenario with permanent public deficits.

The Balanced Budget Scenario

A balanced budget means $\dot{b} = 0$ which implies $\phi = -\theta z(k/y)$, where $v^\star = 0$ has been used. Further, $\dot{c}/c = \dot{m}/m$ implies $z = x/(\rho+\theta)$. Using those relations we get for $q_1(\cdot) := \dot{x}$,

[19]The * denotes BGP values.

$$q_1 = x\left(x - (x^{-1}A^{(1+\gamma)/\alpha}\alpha(1-\tau))^{\alpha/(1-\alpha+\gamma)}(t_p + \alpha(1-\tau)) + \theta x(\theta+\rho)^{-1} - \rho\right). \tag{3.65}$$

It is easily seen that $q_1(\cdot)$ is continuous and has the following properties, $q_1 \to -\infty(+\infty)$ for $x \to 0(\infty)$, and $\partial q_1/\partial x > 0$ for $\dot{x} = 0$. This shows that there exists a unique $x^\star$ that solves $\dot{x} = 0$ and, thus, a unique BGP for the balanced budget scenario.

The local stability of the dynamic system is determined by the eigenvalues of the Jacobian matrix corresponding to the system (3.62)–(3.64). In the appendix it is demonstrated that the Jacobian has one negative eigenvalue implying that there is a one-dimensional stable manifold of the dynamic system. Taking the initial capital stock and the initial public debt as given, this implies that there exists a unique value of initial consumption, $c(0)$, and of the initial stock of money, $m(0)$, such that the economy converges to the BGP in the long-run.

Another analytical result can be obtained for the long-run growth rate of the balanced budget scenario compared to that of the scenario with permanent public deficits. To do so, we note that for the balanced budget scenario we get from $\dot{c}/c = \dot{k}/k$ on the BGP,

$$-\rho+(1-\tau)(1-\alpha)(y/k) = -x+(1-\tau+t_p)x^{-\alpha/(1-\alpha+\gamma)}C_1-\theta x/(\theta+\rho), \tag{3.66}$$

where used $z = x/(\theta + \rho)$ and with $C_1 = A^{(1+\gamma)/(1-\alpha+\gamma)}(\alpha(1-\tau))^{\alpha/(1-\alpha+\gamma)}$. In addition, we used $\phi = -\theta z x^{\alpha/(1-\alpha+\gamma)}C_1$ that holds for a balanced government budget.

With permanent public deficits we obtain from $\dot{c}/c = \dot{k}/k$ on the BGP,

$$-\rho+(1-\tau)(1-\alpha)(y/k) = -x+(1-\tau+t_p)x^{-\alpha/(1-\alpha+\gamma)}C_1+\psi v+\phi x^{-\alpha/(1-\alpha+\gamma)}C_1. \tag{3.67}$$

From $\dot{c}/c = \dot{b}/b$ that must also hold on the BGP we get,

$$\psi v + \phi x^{-\alpha/(1-\alpha+\gamma)}C_1 = -\theta z + \rho v, \tag{3.68}$$

so that (3.67) can be rewritten as,

$$-\rho+(1-\tau)(1-\alpha)(y/k) = -x+(1-\tau+t_p)x^{-\alpha/(1-\alpha+\gamma)}C_1-\theta x/(\theta+\rho)+\rho v. \tag{3.69}$$

Comparing Eq. (3.66) with (3.69) shows that the left hand side is identical in both equations and monotonically rising with x. The right hand side in those two equations is monotonically declining with the graph of Eq. (3.69) always above that of (3.66), because of $v > 0$, which implies that the consumption share on the BGP, $x^\star$, with permanent deficits is larger than the consumption share with a balanced government budget. Consequently, the balanced growth rate in the scenario with permanent deficits is lower than that of the balanced budget scenario.

Next, we analyze our model with permanent public deficits.

Permanent Public Deficits

When we consider the model with permanent public deficits we see that it becomes rather complex such that we cannot gain analytical results. Therefore, we resort to simulations in order to gain insight into our model economy.

To do so we first specify the structural parameters of our model and the income tax rate as well as the share of lump-sum transfers. We set the labor share to 70 %, i.e. $\alpha = 0.7$, and A is set to $A = 0.3$. The rate of time preference is assumed to be 5 %, $\rho = 0.05$. As concerns the inverse of the elasticity of labor supply, values between 0.15 and 0.3 are considered as plausible (see our discussion in the previous sections) and we choose $\gamma = 0.3$. The income tax rate is 10 %, $\tau = 0.1$, and the share of lump-sum transfers is set to $t_p = 0.075$. Those parameters are left unchanged throughout our simulations.[20]

To start with we study how public debt policy affects economic growth for a given monetary policy. Table 3.2 shows how the balanced growth rate, the debt to capital ratio and the inflation rate react when the government reduces the reaction coefficient ψ, that is when it puts less weight on stabilizing public debt, where the growth rate of nominal money supply is set to $\theta = 0.07$ and $\phi = -0.33$.

Table 3.2 demonstrates that the balanced growth rate declines as the government puts less weight on stabilizing public debt, that is when it reduces the reaction coefficient ψ, which implies a higher debt to capital ratio. The economic mechanism behind that result is that a less strict public debt policy implies that less savings of the private sector are used for private capital formation but, instead, for unproductive public spending. This makes the household save and invest less and reduce its labor supply, thus, leading to a lower growth rate in the long-run. Table 3.2 also shows that a less strict debt policy leads to a higher inflation rate. That holds because the decline in the investment share implies a rise in the consumption share that goes along with higher inflation. With the parameter values underlying Table 3.2

Table 3.2 The balanced growth rate, g, the debt to capital ratio, v, and the inflation rate, π, for different values of the reaction coefficient, ψ, on the BGP

ψ	g (%)	v	π (%)
0.1	3.72	0.0625	3.28
0.075	3.69	0.0966	3.31
0.05	3.58	0.2126	3.42
0.035	3.09	0.7682	3.91

[20] Qualitatively, the outcome does not change for $\gamma = 0.15$. But to get plausible quantitative results we have to set A and the fiscal parameters τ and t_p to different values then.

the Jacobian matrix of the dynamic system (3.62)–(3.64) has one negative and two positive real eigenvalues. Thus, there exists a unique combination $\{c(0), m(0)\}$ such that the economy converges to the BGP in the long-run.

When we further reduce the reaction coefficient ψ, we see that for about $\psi \leq 0.03$ no BGP exists any longer or there exists a BGP that, however, goes along with a negative government debt and that is unstable, i.e. the Jacobian has three positive real eigenvalues. This implies that ongoing growth is not possible if the government puts too low a value on stabilizing public debt or only in case the government is a creditor that lends money to the private sector. But it must also be pointed out that the latter situation is unstable which means that the economy cannot reach that BGP unless it starts on the BGP at the beginning.

These considerations demonstrate that a less strict public debt policy leads to a lower balanced growth rate, to a higher debt ratio and to higher inflation, for a given monetary policy. In addition, if the public debt policy is too loose sustained growth may not be feasible at all with the government being a debtor. The question we address next is how monetary policy affects growth and whether it can compensate a loose debt policy. Table 3.3 gives the results of varying the nominal money growth rate θ with $\psi = 0.1$ and the other parameter values as for Table 3.2.

Table 3.3 illustrates the following. A higher growth rate of the money supply leads to a lower debt to capital ratio and to a higher balanced growth rate. However, that goes at the cost of higher inflation that monotonically rises when the money supply is increased. It must also be pointed out that this cannot go on forever. Hence, once a certain critical value of θ is exceeded, in our example for about $\theta \geq 0.85$, a balanced growth path with the government being a debtor does not exists any longer. Then, for ongoing growth to be feasible, the government must be a creditor.

Thus, we can conclude that monetary policy can compensate a loose debt policy of the government, but only up to a certain point. When the nominal money growth rate becomes too large, sustained growth is not possible unless the government disposes of a capital reserve it uses to lend money to the private sector. For the sake of completeness, we state that the stability properties of the system (3.62)–(3.64) with the parameter values underlying Table 3.3 are identical to those in Table 3.2, i.e. the Jacobian has one negative and two positive real eigenvalues.

In Table 3.3 we have seen allocative effects of monetary policy for the case that the government runs permanent deficits. In the following table we show how variations in the nominal money growth rate affects the balanced growth rate and the inflation rate assuming that the government runs a balanced budget that implies a zero debt to capital ratio in the long-run.

Table 3.3 The balanced growth rate, g, the debt to capital ratio, v, and the inflation rate, π, for different values of the nominal money growth rate, θ, on the BGP

θ	g (%)	v	π (%)
0.025	2.49	0.4821	0.01
0.05	3.33	0.1894	1.67
0.075	3.8	0.0384	3.7
0.08	3.87	0.0164	4.13

Table 3.4 The balanced growth rate, g, the debt to capital ratio, v, and the inflation rate, π, for different nominal money growth rates, θ, on the BGP with a balanced government budget

θ	g (%)	v	π (%)
0.035	3.2	0	0.03
0.07	3.22	0	3.78
0.1	4.05	0	5.95
0.15	4.58	0	20.42

Table 3.4 shows that a higher nominal money growth rate goes along with a higher balanced growth rate that, however, implies higher inflation as in Table 3.3. Further, the increase in the inflation rate is rather drastic and the rise is faster than that of the balanced growth rate. Setting $\theta = 0.5$ implies an inflation rate of 45 % while the growth rate only attains a value of 4.8 %. Due to the balanced government budget the debt to capital ratio does not change with variations in the monetary policy and always equals zero. Thus, with a balanced government budget the economy can attain a higher long-run growth rate through appropriate monetary policy. But, such a policy goes at the expense of price stability and the question of arises whether such a policy is also welfare enhancing.

Therefore, in the next subsection we study welfare effects of public debt policy and of monetary policy for our model economy.

Welfare Effects

In the last subsection we have seen how fiscal and monetary policy affect the allocation of resources and, thus, economic growth and inflation. In this subsection we want to analyze whether welfare reacts to policy measures in the same way as the balanced growth rate. To do so we solve the linearized differential equation system (3.62)–(3.64), taking into account transition dynamics, that gives the time paths for the variables $x(t)$, $z(t)$ and $v(t)$ for a given value of initial public debt relative to capital, v_0. With these variables we can solve the differential equations (3.59) and (3.61), where we set $K_0 = 1$ such that $x(0) = c(0)$ and $z(0) = m(0)$ and we get the time path for labor supply $l(t)$. Then, we can compute the value of the utility functional (3.40) that gives welfare in our economy for a given policy as,

$$F := \max \int_0^{\infty} e^{-\rho t} \left(\ln c + \ln m - l^{1+\gamma}/(1+\gamma) \right) dt. \tag{3.70}$$

The last result of the previous subsection was that a higher nominal money growth leads to a higher balanced growth rate but also to higher inflation in the

Table 3.5 Welfare, F, for different nominal money growth rates, θ, with a balanced government budget

θ	0.035	0.05	0.1
F	−6.875	−9.998	−17.854

Table 3.6 Welfare, F, for different values of the nominal money growth rate, θ

θ	0.035	0.05	0.07
F	−6.978	−9.269	−12.097

Table 3.7 Welfare, F, for different values of the reaction coefficient, ψ

ψ	0.035	0.05	0.1
F	−14.953	−14.122	−12.097

case of a balanced government budget.[21] Table 3.5 shows how welfare reacts to such a monetary policy.

From Table 3.5 we see that a higher growth rate of nominal money supply reduces welfare. There are the following opposite effects of such a monetary policy. On the one hand, raising the nominal money growth increases the balanced growth rate and leads to higher consumption that tends to raise welfare. However, on the other hand, a high inflation rate reduces the real money stock and a large growth rate implies a high labor supply. Those two latter effects dominate and make welfare decline as a result of a higher growth rate of nominal money supply.

Next, we analyze welfare effects of monetary policy assuming that the government does not run a balanced budget. From Table 3.3 we know that in this case a higher growth rate of nominal money supply leads to higher growth and to higher inflation. The results are shown in Table 3.6, with $\psi = 0.1$.

The outcome is equivalent to that in Table 3.5, that is the negative welfare effect of higher inflation and of a higher labor supply dominate the positive welfare effect of higher consumption growth as a result of increasing the nominal money supply. These outcomes demonstrate that a rise in the growth rate of nominal money supply raises the balanced growth rate but leads to lower welfare.

When we analyze how different debt policies affect welfare we see that a higher reaction coefficient ψ leads to higher welfare as Table 3.7 demonstrates, where we set the nominal money growth rate to $\theta = 0.07$. The reason for that outcome is that a stricter fiscal policy, in the sense that the government puts a higher weight on stabilizing public debt by setting the reaction coefficient ψ to a large value, generates a higher growth rate, a lower inflation rate and a higher labor supply. The first two effects raise welfare while the third leads to less welfare which, however, is dominated by the first two positive welfare effects.

[21] The initial condition of v is set to $v_0 = 0.5$ for the simulations in Tables 3.5–3.7. The qualitative outcome in those tables, however, is independent from v_0 anyway.

Table 3.8 Welfare, F, for a balanced government budget compared to permanent deficits

	$v_0 = 0.05$	$v_0 = 0.5$	$v_0 = 1$	
F	−14.513	−13.519	−12.491	(Balanced gov. budget)
F	−15.02	−14.122	−13.19	(Perm. deficits, $\psi = 0.05$)
F	−14.723	−12.097	−9.484	(Perm. deficits, $\psi = 0.1$)

The last exercise we perform is a comparison of welfare of the scenario with a balanced government debt and of the scenario with permanent deficits for different initial conditions with respect to public debt and for different reaction coefficients ψ. Table 3.8 shows the results with θ set to $\theta = 0.07$.

Table 3.8 demonstrates that the balanced budget scenario always yields higher welfare than the scenario with permanent deficits for small values of the reaction coefficient, independent of the initial conditions. That is, when the government puts a small weight on stabilizing public debt, a balanced government budget leads to higher welfare. That general result does not hold any longer when the government runs permanent deficits but puts a high weight on stabilizing debt, i.e. when it selects a high ψ. Then, the debt ratio is relatively small so that its negative effects (low growth, high inflation) are not too large. In that situation, the outcome depends on the initial conditions and for high values of the initial stock of public debt, the scenario with permanent deficits gives higher welfare than the balanced budget scenario. Only if the initial public debt is small, the balanced budget scenario performs better. The reason for that outcome is that with a high initial debt, the initial values of consumption and of the real money supply are clearly higher so that the time paths of consumption and of real money are above those obtained for smaller initial values of public debt. Therefore, a scenario where the government runs deficits but puts a high weight on stabilizing debt, so that the debt ratio and its negative effects are small, can perform better when the economy is relatively far away from its balanced growth path.

In the next section, we contribute to the research on the effects of public debt as regards economic growth and the stability of an economy, assuming that the latter is characterized by wage rigidities giving rise to permanent unemployment.

3.4 Effects of Wage Rigidities and Unemployment

Fiscal policy and, in particular, the debt policy of a government are generally expected to affect the evolution of market economies, as we have shown in the last sections. While that topic has been frequently analyzed for perfect labor markets, the question arises whether the effects are different when that assumption does not hold. Therefore, in contrast to most of what we see in the economics literature, we now posit that labor markets are incomplete, which generates persistent unemployment in an economy, where we closely follow Greiner (2013b).

Usually, endogenous growth models do not consider unemployment but instead presuppose that the economy is characterized by full employment. This is justified by assuming that growth models adopt a medium to long-run perspective and that all markets, including the labor market, are sufficiently flexible to equate supply and demand. But, if one looks at the real world, one realizes that unemployment in many economies, especially European ones, seems to present a long-run phenomenon which justifies incorporating unemployment into growth models. Arico (2003) presents a survey of how unemployment can be incorporated in endogenous growth models. Pissarides (1990), for example, identifies a link between economic growth and the labor market through a capitalization effect, which means that firms are more willing to create jobs when growth is high. A different model has been proposed by Aghion and Howitt (1994), whose model is based upon the Schumpeterian idea of creative destruction, wherein innovation make existing technologies obsolete, thus leading to reallocations of labor across firms. If each vacancy needs specific skills that job searchers do not possess, persistent unemployment can arise. Another mechanism has been worked out by Acemoglu (1997). In his model, strategic interactions between firms affect their decisions to invest in new technologies and to accumulate human capital. The analysis of the model shows that multiple equilibria can arise that generate an unemployment trap. Besides these contributions, one can also find models in the economics literature where unemployment is due to wage rigidities that prevent the wage rate from falling to the market-clearing level. These models give rise to a relationship between the wage rate and unemployment that describes the change of the wage rate as a function of labor demand or of the unemployment rate. In their book, Flaschel et al. (1997) analyze models of exogenous growth featuring unemployment and demonstrate how stability can be lost in this type of models.

Often, it is argued that the existence of lower bounds for wages, i.e. minimum wages, leads to low growth and unemployment. However, that is not necessarily the case as demonstrated by Cahuc and Michel (1996), for example, who show that a minimum wage legislation may have positive growth effects by raising human capital accumulation. In an open-economy endogenous growth model, Askenazy (2003) finds that a minimum wage raises long-run growth relative to exports which enhances economic growth. Flaschel and Greiner (2011) present a growth model that contains minimum wages as one important element of a flexicurity economy where heterogeneous labor and real wage rigidities are take into consideration. There, it is shown that the wage-setting process is crucial as regards stability of the economy and minimum wages can alleviate the negative consequences of economic downturns and help stabilize the economy.

Therefore, in this section we present a different endogenous growth model that allows to derive analytical results and we work out in detail the economic mechanisms. In particular, we want to explore whether the results obtained for the model with perfect labor markets also hold if the economy is characterized by rigid labor markets giving rise to persistent unemployment. To do so we resort to the endogenous growth model of the previous sections, where we allow for unemployment and where we integrate a government sector that may run into debt, but one which must obey its intertemporal budget constraint. Unemployment results from wage rigidities that give rise to a relationship between the change in the wage rate and unemployment such that labor demand becomes a function of the wage rate. Wage rigidities are the result of labor market imperfections due to trade unions maximizing the wage sum; thus our relationship between wage changes and unemployment can be termed "micro-founded".

3.4.1 The Structure of the Growth Model

We consider an economy that consists of a household sector which receives labor income and income from its saving, a productive sector, and the government. To begin with, we describe the household sector.

Consumers

The household sector consists of many identical households that are represented by one household, which maximizes the discounted stream of utility arising from per-capita consumption, $C(t)$, over an infinite time horizon subject to its budget constraint and that takes factor prices as given. We suppose a logarithmic utility function[22] such that $U(C) = \ln C$. labor supply L is constant and inelastic and L^d denotes labor demand by the productive sector so that $L - L^d > 0$ is unemployed. The household receives unemployment benefits of ϱw per unemployed labor with w denoting the wage rate and $\varrho \in (0, 1)$. The optimization problem of the household, then, is given by,

$$\max_{C} \int_0^{\infty} e^{-\rho t} \ln C \, dt, \tag{3.71}$$

subject to

$$(1-\tau)\left(wL^d + rK + r_b B\right) + \varrho w(L - L^d) = \dot{W} + C + \delta K. \tag{3.72}$$

with ρ the rate of time preference, r the return to capital and r_b gives the interest rate on government bonds. The variable $W \equiv B + K$ denotes wealth of the household which consists of public debt, B, and of private capital, K, that depreciates at the rate δ. The constant income tax rate is denoted by $\tau \in (0, 1)$ and unemployment benefits are not taxed and, as usual, the dot over a variable is the time derivative d/dt.

[22]Again, we omit the time argument t as long as no ambiguity arises.

The household will invest in physical capital and hold governments bond only if the net return to capital equals the net return to government bonds. This requirement yields the following no-arbitrage condition

$$r_b = \frac{r(1-\tau)-\delta}{1-\tau}. \tag{3.73}$$

Using the no-arbitrage condition (3.73), we can rewrite the budget constraint as

$$\dot{W} = (1-\tau)\left(wL^d + rW\right) + \varrho w(L - L^d) - \delta W - C. \tag{3.74}$$

The current-value Hamiltonian for the maximization problem (3.71) subject to (3.74) is given by

$$\mathcal{H} = \ln C + \lambda\left((1-\tau)\left(wL^d + rW\right) + \varrho w(L - L^d) - C - \delta W\right) \tag{3.75}$$

From the Hamiltonian we can derive the necessary optimality conditions:

$$C^{-1} = \lambda \tag{3.76}$$

$$\dot{\gamma}_c = (\rho+\delta)\lambda - \lambda(1-\tau)\,r \tag{3.77}$$

When assets grow at the same rate as consumption, the necessary conditions are also sufficient. This holds because, then, the transversality condition $\lim_{t\to\infty} e^{-\rho t} W/C = 0$ is fulfilled.

Producers and the Labor Market

In analogy to the household sector, the productive sector consists of many identical firms that are price takers and that can be represented by one firm. The firm uses labor and capital as input to produce the final output and it maximizes static profits which, then, determines labor demand and the interest rate. The production function of the firm is given by

$$Y = A\,K^{1-\alpha}\bar{K}^{\alpha}\left(L^d\right)^{\alpha}. \tag{3.78}$$

Output is denoted by Y, A is a constant and $\alpha \in (0,1)$ denotes the elasticity of output with respect to labor and $(1-\alpha)$ gives the private capital share. Finally, $\bar{K}$ gives the average economy-wide level of capital. Maximizing profits gives the labor demand L^d and the interest rate r as

$$L^d = A^{1/(1-\alpha)}\alpha^{1/(1-\alpha)}(w/K)^{1/(\alpha-1)}, \tag{3.79}$$

$$r = (1-\alpha)(Y/K), \tag{3.80}$$

where we used $\bar{K} = K$ in equilibrium in (3.79) and in (3.80).

As mentioned in the introduction, our economy is characterized by wage rigidities. Wage rigidities in our framework result from labor market imperfections that are the outcome of unions setting the wage rate. With respect to the wage setting process we adopt the framework presented in Raurich et al. (2006). There, it is assumed that a large number of unions set the wage rate in order to maximize the expression:

$$\max_{w} \left((1-\tau)w - w^s\right)^{\gamma_w} L^d(\cdot), \tag{3.81}$$

with $L^d(\cdot)$ labor demand determined by (3.79). The variable w^s gives the reference wage and the coefficient $\gamma_w \in (0,1)$ is a measure for the wage gap weight in the trade unions' objective function. Solving the maximization problem (3.81) leads to

$$w = \frac{w^s}{(1-\tau)\left(1-\gamma_w(1-\alpha)\right)}. \tag{3.82}$$

Equation (3.82) shows that the reference wage w^s plays an important role in determining the wage rate w in the economy. In the economics literature, there exist several approaches regarding the determination of the reference wage (see for example Layard et al. (1991), Blanchard and Katz (1999), Blanchard and Wolfers (2000), Collard and de la Croix (2000), or Raurich et al. (2006), Greiner and Flaschel (2009)). In our model we follow Raurich et al. (2006) who posits that the reference wage equals workers' accumulated past average labor income with income further back in time contributing less than more recent labor income. We suppose exponentially declining weights put on average labor income further back in time so that the reference wage is obtained as

$$w^s = \theta \int_{-\infty}^{t} e^{-\theta(t-s)} z_a(s) ds, \tag{3.83}$$

where z_a gives the workers' average income, with $z_a = (1-\tau)wL^d/L + \varrho w(L - L^d)/L$. The parameter $\theta > 0$ determines the weight attributed to more recent income. The higher θ, the larger the weight given to more recent levels of average income relative to income further back in time.

The growth rate of the wage rate is obtained by differentiating (3.82) with respect to time. Doing so and using (3.83), we get

$$\frac{\dot{w}}{w} = \theta \, \frac{(1-\tau)L^d/L + \varrho(L - L^d)/L}{(1-\tau)\left(1-\gamma_w(1-\alpha)\right)} - \theta \tag{3.84}$$

which can be written as

$$\frac{\dot{w}}{w} = \psi_L \left(\frac{L^d - \bar{L}}{L}\right). \tag{3.85}$$

The parameter $\psi_L > 0$ reflects the speed of adjustment that determines how strong actual labor demand relative to the normal level of employment, $\bar{L}$, influences the change in the wage rate. The normal level of employment is defined as that level which implies a constant wage rate. It should be noted that we have set

$$\frac{\bar{L}}{L} = \left(\frac{(1-\tau)(1-\gamma_w(1-\alpha)) - \varrho}{(1-\tau) - \varrho}\right) \text{ and } \psi_L = \frac{\theta(1-\tau) - \theta\varrho}{(1-\tau)(1-\gamma_w(1-\alpha))}$$

in deriving Eq. (3.85) from (3.84). It must also be pointed out that $(1-\tau) > \varrho$ must hold for $\psi_L > 0$ and, thus, $(1-\tau)(1-\gamma_w(1-\alpha)) > \varrho$ for $\bar{L}/L > 0$ that, however, is not a severe limitation of our model.

These considerations demonstrate that the growth rate of the wage rate can be described by a functional relationship with the growth rate being the smaller the higher the unemployment rate is.

The Government

The revenues of the government in our economy are composed of the income tax revenue and of revenues resulting from issuing government bonds. Government spending is used for unemployment benefits, $\varrho w(L - L^d)$, and for public consumption, C_p, that is neither productive nor welfare enhancing.

The accounting identity describing the accumulation of public debt is given by

$$\dot{B} = r_b B(1-\tau) - \left(\tau Y - C_p - \varrho w(L - L^d)\right) = r_b B(1-\tau) - S, \tag{3.86}$$

where S is the government surplus exclusive of net interest payments. Further, the government has to pursue a debt policy such that its intertemporal budget constraint is fulfilled. Formally,

$$B(0) = \int_0^\infty e^{-\int_0^\mu (1-\tau) r_b(\nu) d\nu} S(\mu) d\mu \leftrightarrow \lim_{t\to\infty} e^{-\int_0^t (1-\tau) r_b(\mu) d\mu} B(t) = 0. \tag{3.87}$$

Equation (3.87) is the present-value borrowing constraint which states that public debt at time zero must equal the future present-value surpluses.

Again, we assume that the government sets the primary surplus according to the following rule,

$$S = \phi Y + \psi B. \tag{3.88}$$

The parameter $\psi \in \mathbb{R}_{++}$ determines how strong the primary surplus reacts to changes in public debt and is called the reaction coefficient. The parameter $\phi \in \mathbb{R}$

determines whether the level of the primary surplus rises or falls with an increase in GDP. Thus, the primary surplus relative to GDP can be written as

$$\frac{S}{Y} = \phi + \psi \, \frac{B}{Y} = \frac{\tau Y - C_p - \varrho w(L - L^d)}{Y} \, . \tag{3.89}$$

It should be mentioned that public consumption C_p is set such that Eq. (3.89) holds. Using (3.89), the evolution of public debt is obtained as

$$\dot{B} = r_b B(1 - \tau) - \phi \, Y - \psi \, B. \tag{3.90}$$

3.4.2 The Balanced Growth Path

In this section we analyze the existence and possible uniqueness of balanced growth paths for our model economy. To do so we complete the description of our economy by deriving the growth rate of consumption and by deriving the economy-wide resource constraint. The growth rate of consumption is obtained from (3.76) and (3.77) as

$$\frac{\dot{C}}{C} = -(\rho + \delta) + (1 - \tau)(1 - \alpha)(Y/K). \tag{3.91}$$

with $Y/K = A^{1/(1-\alpha)}\alpha^{\alpha/(1-\alpha)}(w/K)^{-\alpha/(1-\alpha)}$ which is obtained by using the optimality condition (3.79).

The economy-wide resource constraint is derived by combining the budget constraint of the household with that of the government as

$$\frac{\dot{K}}{K} = \frac{Y}{K} - \frac{C}{K} + \psi \, \frac{B}{K} + (\phi - \tau) \, \frac{Y}{K} + \varrho(L - L^d) \, \frac{w}{K} - \delta \, , \tag{3.92}$$

with $L \geq L^d$.

Hence, the economy is completely described by Eqs. (3.85) and (3.90)–(3.92), with the return to capital, r, given by (3.80) and the return to government bonds, r_b, given by (3.73) and with L^d given by (3.79). A balanced growth path (BGP) is obtained when the conditions in Definition 3 are fulfilled.

Definition 3 A balanced growth path (BGP) is a path such that consumption, private capital and the wage rate grow at the same strictly positive constant growth rate, i.e. $\dot{C}/C = \dot{K}/K = \dot{w}/w = g$, $g > 0$, $g = constant$, and either

(i) $\dot{B} = 0$ or
(ii) $\dot{B}/B = g$.

This definition shows that, as usual, consumption, private capital and, thus, output, as well as the wage rate, grow at a constant and strictly positive rate over time. Public debt may be constant over time, which is obtained when the government budget is balanced, or it may grow at the same rate as all other endogenous variables.

Here, it should be recalled and underlined again that the rule modeled in (3.89) with $\psi > 0$ guarantees that the intertemporal budget constraint of the government holds as long as the economy converges to a BGP, where all endogenous variables grow at the same rate. The reason for that is that the primary surplus also grows at the same rate as all other variables along the BGP, thus, assuring solvency of the government. Note that the present value of public debt converges to zero on the balanced growth path because the growth rate of GDP, which is equal to that of the public debt on the BGP, is smaller than the net interest rate on government bonds that is used to discount public debt,[23] $r_b(1-\tau)$.

To get further insight regarding the possible existence and uniqueness of a balanced growth path (BGP), we define the new variables $c := C/K$, $x := w/K$ and $z := B/K$. Differentiating these variables with respect to time gives,

$$\dot{c} = c\left((Y/K)((1-\alpha)(1-\tau) - 1 - (\phi - \tau)) - \rho + c - \psi z - \varrho(L - L^d)x\right) \tag{3.93}$$

$$\dot{x} = x\left(\psi_L(L^d - \bar{L})/L + c - \psi z - (\phi - \tau + 1)(Y/K) - \varrho(L - L^d)\,x + \delta\right) \tag{3.94}$$

$$\dot{z} = z\left(\frac{Y}{K}\left((1-\alpha)(1-\tau) - \frac{\phi}{z} - 1 - (\phi - \tau)\right) - \psi + c - \psi z - \varrho(L - L^d)x\right) \tag{3.95}$$

with $Y/K = A(L^d)^\alpha$ and $L^d = A^{1/(1-\alpha)}\alpha^{1/(1-\alpha)}x^{1/(\alpha-1)}$.

A rest point of (3.93)–(3.95) yields a situation where all endogenous economic variables grow at the same rate, except public debt if the government runs a balanced budget.

Proposition 12 *Assume that the depreciation rate and the time preference are sufficiently small. Then, there exists a unique balanced growth path for $\psi_L\bar{L}/L > \rho + \delta$. For $\psi_L\bar{L}/L < \rho + \delta$ there exists no balanced growth path or there are two balanced growth paths.*

Proof See appendix to this chapter. □

First, we should like to point out that we must make the assumption that the rate of time preference and the depreciation rate are not too large because we can only prove that a rest point for the system (3.93)–(3.95) exists but not that the associated balanced growth, rate given by (3.91), is positive, which, however, is not a rigorous

[23]This is seen from (3.91) together with (3.73) and (3.80).

assumption. Proposition 12 shows that the flexibility of the labor market is decisive as regards existence and uniqueness of the BGP, besides structural parameters. Thus, a rapid adjustment of the wage rate, ψ_L, which implies a flexible labor market and a high threshold of employment above which wages tend to rise, $\bar{L}$, generate a unique BGP, for a given discount rate and depreciation rate of capital. Taking the parameters determining the labor market as given, one can state that patient households with a low value of the discount rate ρ and a low depreciation rate δ generate a unique BGP.

Multiple BGPs, two in our model, imply that there exists a balanced growth path with a relatively high growth rate and low unemployment and a path with a low growth rate and high unemployment which can be termed an underdevelopment trap. Clearly, such an underdevelopment trap is not desirable and we will next discuss how governments can avoid such a situation.

Recalling that $\psi_L > 0$ determines the speed of adjustment on the labor market, such that it can be seen as an indicator for the degree of flexibility of the labor market, we see from Proposition 12 that a more flexible labor market (reflected by a higher ψ_L) tends to give rise to a unique BGP. In our model, the speed of adjustment is a function of the preferences of trade unions and, indirectly, of fiscal policy; we will discuss the effects of these below. First, we should like to mention that interpreting our model in a broader sense implies that the government can avoid multiple BGPs and, thus underdevelopment traps, by a legislation that makes the labor market more flexible, e.g., by allowing free hiring and firing.

As mentioned in the last paragraph, the speed of adjustment in our model is the result of trade unions' preferences. In our economy, trade unions maximize a concave function of the difference between the net wage rate and the reference wage, i.e., of the wage gap, multiplied by labor demand. It can easily be seen that the condition for a unique BGP in Proposition 12 is the sooner fulfilled, the smaller the weight trade unions put on the wage gap in their objective function, i.e. the smaller the parameter γ_w since γ_w negatively affects $\psi_L \bar{L}/L$. This holds because a lower weight on the wage gap in the objective function implies that labor demand receives a higher relative weight in the unions' objective function such that trade unions put more weight on raising labor demand leading to a more flexible labor market. As regards the role of fiscal policy we see that the government affects the optimization problem of trade unions indirectly, by its choice of income tax rate and by fixing unemployment benefits, since the latter affect the wage gap. It is also immediately seen that both the income tax rate, τ, and unemployment benefits, ϱ, have a negative effect on the flexibility of the labor market, i.e. they reduce $\psi_L \bar{L}/L$, because these parameters raise the wage gap. This implies that it will be more important for unions to get higher wages rather than higher employment which leads to a less flexible labor market.

To summarize we can state that governments can avoid underdevelopment traps by raising the flexibility of the labor market. In our model, the relationship between wage changes and (un)employment was derived from trade unions' wage setting behavior and the government can indirectly affect the flexibility of the labor market through (income) tax policy and unemployment benefits since these factors affect trade unions' objective functional. Interpreting our model in a broader sense, we can also state that legislation which makes the labor market more flexible also tends to help avoid underdevelopment traps. The economic mechanism behind that outcome is this: more flexible labor markets imply an economy that comes closer to the production possibility frontier that is obtained with full employment. This holds because wages become more flexible, thus raising labor demand and the incentive to invest.

We should also like to point out that the balanced growth path and, consequently, the long-run growth rate as well as the unemployment rate are independent of the debt policy of the government for a given income tax rate. Proposition 13 states this result.

Proposition 13 *For a given income tax rate the debt policy of the government does not affect the balanced growth path.*

Proof See the appendix to this chapter. □

Proposition 13 demonstrates that public debt in our model is neutral in the sense that it neither affects the question of existence and multiplicity of a BGP nor the balanced growth rate and the unemployment rate, in case of ongoing growth. The reason for this result is that the marginal product of capital and, therefore, the incentive to invest depends on labor demand in our model which, for its part, is a (negative) function of the wage rate relative to the capital stock, $w/K = x$. Since public debt policy does not affect that variable, it has no effect on growth and unemployment. Consequently, if one assumes that the government invests in a productive public capital stock, a higher deficit may lead to less unemployment and higher growth because public debt, per se, does not affect the allocation of resources and because of the positive growth effects of productive public investment which will be shown in detail in Sect. 4.4.3.

The economic intuition behind Proposition 13 is that the wage rate plays the decisive role as concerns the incentive to invest and, thus, as concerns economic growth. Hence, it is the wage policy of trade unions that determines economic growth rather than the debt policy of the government, which has no effect on the wage rate.

Further, we should like to point out that this result changes when we assume that income tax rates rise as public debt increases. This is obvious since the income tax rate is distortionary, such that it affects saving and investment. In our setting, with a fixed income tax rate, however, a higher public debt implies either a decline of public spending or that higher growth raises tax revenues to service the higher debt. Of course, the latter possibility is given only if there occurs a positive exogenous shock that leads to higher growth.

Before we study stability properties of the model we characterize the debt to GDP ratio on the BGP which is the contents of Proposition 14.

Proposition 14 *Assume that the government runs a balanced budget. Then, the debt to GDP ratio equals zero on the balanced growth path. With permanent budget deficits of the government, the debt to GDP ratio on the balanced growth path is* *given by*

$$\frac{B}{Y} = \frac{\phi}{\rho - \psi}$$

Proof See the appendix to this chapter. □

The first part of that theorem is more or less obvious because a balanced budget implies that public debt remains constant. With permanent GDP growth this leads to a steadily declining ratio of public debt relative to GDP so that it converges to zero asymptotically.

The second part of that proposition shows that the debt to GDP ratio is a function of the rate of time preference and of the two parameters that determine public debt policy. When the reaction of the government to higher debt, modeled by the parameter ψ, is small so that $\psi < \rho$ holds, the parameter ϕ must be positive so that sustained growth with a positive public debt to GDP ratio is feasible. A positive ϕ means that the level of the primary surplus rises as GDP grows. If that does not hold, i.e., for a negative ϕ, sustained growth is only possible with a negative government debt, thus implying that the government must have built up a stock of wealth out of which it lends to the private sector and which it uses to finance part of its spending. When the reaction of the government to higher debt is strong, i.e. for $\psi > \rho$, the government puts a high value on stabilizing debt. Then, ϕ must be negative for sustained growth with positive government debt because otherwise primary surpluses become too large and the government builds up a stock of wealth, i.e., government debt becomes negative.

Of course, Proposition 14 only holds ceteris paribus, which implies that changes in parameters go hand-in-hand with changes in the debt-to-GDP ratio. The same holds if the parameters are not constant, but time varying.

In the next section we analyze effects of debt policy on the stability of the economy.

3.4.3 Stability of the Economy

In this section we assume that there exists at least one BGP for our model economy and we analyze its stability properties. We do this first for the model with a balanced government budget and, then, for the model with permanent public deficits.

Balanced Government Budget

To model a balanced government budget we set $\phi = 0$ and $\psi = r_b(1 - \tau)$. Equation (3.90) immediately shows that the government budget is balanced for these parameter values. Proposition 15 gives the result as regards stability of our model economy for this case.

Proposition 15 *Assume that there exists a unique balanced growth path. Then, this path is saddle point stable (one positive, two negative eigenvalues).*

With two balanced growth paths the one associated with high growth is a saddle point and the path with low growth is asymptotically stable (three negative eigenvalues) or there is a one-dimensional manifold leading to that BGP (one negative, two positive eigenvalues).

Proof See the appendix to this chapter. □

This proposition shows that in the case of a unique BGP, this path is saddle point stable with two negative eigenvalues of the corresponding Jacobian matrix, where negative (positive) eigenvalue means negative (positive) real or complex conjugate with a negative (positive) real part. Thus, taking initial public debt as given, there exists a continuum of initial values of private consumption and of the initial wage rate such that the economy converges to this BGP in the long-run. This implies that the transition dynamics depend on the initial values of consumption and of the wage rate. However, in the long-run, as the BGP is approached asymptotically, the growth rate is independent of those initial values.

In the case of two BGPs, the one yielding higher growth has the same stability properties as the BGP when it is unique. The BGP consistent with the smaller growth rate is either stable with three negative eigenvalues or there exists a one-dimensional stable manifold that leads to this BGP (one negative eigenvalue). In the latter case there exists a unique combination of initial private consumption and of the initial wage rate such that the economy converges to this BGP. This implies that the economy does not converge to the low growth BGP unless it just selects that combination which steers it to that BGP. In all other cases there is local divergence.

Permanent Public Deficits

In this subsection we analyze the dynamics of our model economy when the government runs permanent public deficits. In particular, we are interested in the question of how the debt policy of the government affects the stability of the economy.

Proposition 16 *Assume that the government runs permanent deficits. Then, raising the reaction coefficient ψ increases stability of the economy in the sense that it raises the number of negative eigenvalues (or eigenvalues with negative real parts).*

Proof See the appendix to this chapter. □

This proposition shows that with permanent public deficits, stability is more likely when the reaction of the government to public debt, ψ, is large. This holds because a large value of ψ increases the number of negative eigenvalues, implying that convergence to the BGP is assured. It should be noted that this holds both for the case of a unique BGP as well as for the case of two BGPs. From an economic point of view this outcome is very plausible. If the government does not put a sufficiently high value on stabilizing public debt, the public debt-to-GDP ratio will become explosive, thus, destabilizing the whole economy. If, on the other hand, the government controls public debt such that the debt to GDP ratio does not explode convergence to a BGP can be assured.

Conclusion

In this chapter we have first analyzed the basic endogenous growth model with externalities of capital and elastic labor supply and studied how governments can affect stability of the economy and its growth rate through their debt policies. Assuming constant tax rates, we could demonstrate that the model is the more likely to be stable the more weight the government puts on stabilizing public debt. Thus, the balanced budget rule turned out to generate a unique BGP that is always saddle point stable. If the government runs permanent deficits, what is more realistic, and sticks to the intertemporal budget constraint, the BGP is also unique, independent of the governmental reaction to higher public debt. However, in this case convergence to the BGP and, thus stability, is only given if the reaction of the primary surplus to higher public debt is sufficiently large. If the government does not react enough to higher public debt, that is if the increase in the primary surplus is relatively small as debt rises, the economy is unstable. That holds both for the model with a flexible labor market as well as for wage rigidities giving rise to permanent unemployment. We should like to point out that this implies that any discretionary policy, which does not react to increases in the debt to GDP ratio by raising the primary surplus to GDP ratio, violates the intertemporal budget constraint of the government.

Then, we assumed that the primary surplus reacts to cumulated past debt that has given rise to a more complex dynamic outcome. Thus, it turned out that the balanced budget rule yields a stable balanced growth path only if the reaction of the government to higher public debt is sufficiently high and if the weight given to more recent levels of public debt in the function determining the reaction to higher debt is large. In case of permanent public deficits such that public debt grows at the same rate as all other economic variables, the outcome is more complex. In that case, existence of a rest point of the dynamic system and, thus, of a BGP cannot be guaranteed and, in case it exists, its stability properties may crucially depend on how the government reacts to higher debt ratios. In particular, we have seen that higher values of the coefficient determining the reaction of the primary surplus to higher debt again tend to stabilize the economy. When that coefficient is reduced the economy may loose stability and for certain critical values of that coefficient endogenous growth cycles can arise, implying that the economy is characterized by cyclical growth rates and not by a constant balanced growth rate.

(continued)

Further, we could demonstrate that the balanced budget rule and the rule where debt grows but less than all other economic variables, yield the same balanced growth rate in the long-run that exceeds the growth rate of the economy with permanent deficits, in the case of a flexible labor market. The reason for this outcome is that the return to physical capital is smaller when the public debt to GDP ratio is strictly positive compared to the case of a zero debt to GDP ratio. However, that does not hold when the government reduces lump-sum transfers as a consequence of a higher debt ratio. In this case, the reduction of lump-sum transfers can be seen as a lump-sum tax for households that does not affect the allocation of resources. Consequently, public debt does not affect the long-run balanced growth rate.

As regards welfare we could show that the rule with a public debt that grows at the same rate as all other economic variables performs worst. Comparing the other two rules we found that the balanced budget rule yields lower welfare than the rule where public debt grows but less than all other economic variables, provided public spending is sufficiently welfare enhancing. The reason for that outcome is that public spending on the transition path is smaller under the balanced budget rule because the government puts too high a weight on consolidating its budget so that there is too little scope for welfare enhancing public spending.

Integrating money into the model, it turned out that a balanced budget still implies a higher growth rate in the long-run compared to a scenario with permanent deficits. A balanced budget also yields higher welfare than a scenario with permanent deficits if the government puts little weight on stabilizing public debt since the latter implies a high debt to GDP ratio leading to low growth and high inflation. If the government puts a high weight on stabilizing debt in the deficit scenario this may change. Then, the debt to GDP ratio is relatively small such that the negative effects of public debt (low growth, high inflation) are not too drastic. In such a situation, a scenario with permanent deficits can lead to higher welfare than the balanced budget scenario if the initial debt to GDP ratio is large so that it is far away from its value on the balanced growth path. However, if the initial debt ratio is small, a balanced government budget still goes along with higher welfare.

For a given monetary policy in the scenario with permanent public deficits, lower deficits implying smaller debt ratios lead to higher balanced growth and less inflation. Further, if the reaction coefficient is below a certain threshold, sustained growth is not feasible any longer unless the government is a creditor and lends money to the private sector. A stricter debt policy leading to lower debt ratios also generates higher welfare.

For a given public debt policy, raising the nominal money growth rate leads to higher balanced growth and to higher inflation. Thus, the monetary policy can compensate a loose public debt policy. However, it must be underlined

(continued)

that this only holds up to a certain degree. Thus, if the nominal monetary growth rate exceeds a certain threshold sustained growth is not feasible or only if the government is a again a creditor. But a higher nominal money growth rate reduces welfare because the positive welfare effect of higher consumption growth is compensated by the negative welfare effect of higher inflation and of higher labor supply.

Hence, the overall conclusion we can draw from integrating money into that framework is that a stricter debt policy implies both higher growth in the long-run and also higher welfare, in general. The monetary policy can compensate a loose fiscal policy, but only up to a certain point, and it must also be underlined that a higher nominal money growth leads to lower welfare.

Finally, when one allows for wage rigidities in the model without a monetary sector, the most striking different result is that public debt is neutral in the sense that it does not affect economic growth and unemployment in the long-run. The reason why debt is neutral with respect to long-run growth in this case, is that the marginal product of capital and, therefore, the incentive to invest depends on labor demand that is independent of fiscal policy in the model presented.

Further, in the model with wage rigidities an underdevelopment trap may arise. In that case, there are two long-run balanced growth paths where the one yielding the higher growth rate is saddle point stable and the path yielding low growth is asymptotically stable or unstable.[24] However, in this model public debt policy does not affect the possible emergence of an underdevelopment trap. The occurrence of the latter only depends on conditions in the labor market and on structural parameters. In particular, we showed that this phenomenon is more likely to occur when the labor market is less flexible.

In the next chapter, we study an endogenous growth model where the government invests in a productive public capital stock.

[24]In Greiner (2012b) it is proven that this model without public debt can give rise to two BGPs, one being a saddle point and the other being asymptotically stable for a certain parameter constellation.

Appendix

The Elasticity of Labor Supply and the Intertemporal Elasticity of Substitution of Consumption

The Elasticity of Labor Supply

The elasticity of labor supply in this chapter is the so-called Frisch elasticity of labor supply, where labor supply is derived for a constant marginal utility of wealth, i.e. the shadow price of wealth λ is kept constant. Besides the Frisch labor supply, there is the Hicksian labor supply that gives labor supply for a constant level of utility and the Marshallian labor supply that gives labor supply for a constant level of income. The latter two concepts are usually derived from static optimization problems.

To see that $1/\gamma$ gives the Frisch elasticity of labor supply for our model economy, recall that the current-value Hamiltonian for our optimization problem of the household is written as

$$\mathcal{H} = \ln(CC_p^{\kappa}) - L^{1+\gamma}/(1+\gamma) + \lambda((1-\tau)\left(wL + rW + \pi_p\right) - \delta W - C).$$

The necessary optimality conditions with respect to consumption and labor supply are

$$\begin{aligned} C^{-1} &= \lambda \\ L^{\gamma} &= \lambda\,(1-\tau)\,w \end{aligned}$$

Combining those two equations yields the labor supply as

$$L = \left(\frac{(1-\tau)\,w}{C}\right)^{1/\gamma}$$

From the latter equation, one immediately obtains the elasticity of labor supply with respect to changes in w as

$$\frac{\partial L/\partial w}{L/w} = \frac{1}{\gamma}\left(\frac{(1-\tau)w}{C}\right)^{-1+1/\gamma}\left(\frac{1-\tau}{C}\right)\left(\frac{w}{((1-\tau)w/C)^{1/\gamma}}\right) = \frac{1}{\gamma}$$

The Intertemporal Elasticity of Substitution of Consumption

The elasticity of substitution between consumption at two points in time is defined as the relative change of consumption at two points in time as a response to the change in the marginal rate of substitution between consumption at those two points in time (see Havranek et al. 2013, for a survey of empirical estimates of the intertemporal elasticity of substitution).

Assuming that the utility function is time separable, $U = \sum_{j=0}^{\infty}(1+\rho)^{-j} f(C_j)$, with $f'(\cdot) > 0$, $f''(\cdot) < 0$, the marginal rate of substitution between consumption at two points in time t and $t + \Delta t$, $IRS_{(t+\Delta t)/t}$, is obtained from $dU = 0$ as

$$IRS_{(t+\Delta t)/t} := \frac{dC_{(t+\Delta t)}}{dC_t} = -\frac{f'(C_t)}{(1+\rho)^{-\Delta t}\, f'(C_{(t+\Delta t)})}$$

The elasticity of substitution between consumption at two points in time t and $(t + \Delta t)$, $IES_{(t+\Delta t)/t}$, is defined as

$$\begin{aligned} IES_{(t+\Delta t)/t} &:= \frac{d\left(C_{(t+\Delta t)}/C_t\right)/(C_{(t+\Delta t)}/C_t)}{d\, IRS_{(t+\Delta t)/t}/IRS_{(t+\Delta t)/t}} \\ &= -\frac{d\left(C_{(t+\Delta t)}/C_t\right)}{d\left(f'(C_{(t+\Delta t)})/f'(C_t)\right)} \cdot \frac{f'(C_{(t+\Delta t)})/f'(C_t)}{C_{(t+\Delta t)}/C_t} \end{aligned}$$

For continuous time, we get the instantaneous elasticity of substitution of consumption. as follows. First, we note that $IES_{(t+\Delta t)/t}$ can be written as

$$IES_{(t+\Delta t)/t} = -\left(\frac{d\left(f'(\Theta C_t)/f'(C_t)\right)}{d\Theta}\right)^{-1} \cdot \frac{f'(C_{(t+\Delta t)})/f'(C_t)}{C_{(t+\Delta t)}/C_t},$$

$$\text{with} \quad \Theta := \frac{C_{(t+\Delta t)}}{C_t}$$

Letting $\Delta t \to 0$, the instantaneous elasticity of substitution is obtained as

$$IES_{(t+\Delta t)/t} = -\frac{f'(C_t)}{f''(C_t)\, C_t}$$

On the Intertemporal Budget Constraint of the Government with $\psi = 0$

Here, we show that a purely discretionary policy ($\psi = 0$) violates the intertemporal budget constraint along a BGP. To see this, we set $\psi = 0$ which implies that the economy-wide resource constraint does not depend on the public debt ratio. It should be pointed out that this is a general result that does not only hold for the endogenous growth model considered in this chapter. Therefore, we here consider the following utility function that is more general with respect to the intertemporal elasticity of substitution of consumption,

$$U(C) = \frac{C^{1-\sigma} - 1}{1-\sigma}.$$

The debt to private capital ratio, then, evolves according to

$$\dot{b} = b\,r(1-\tau) - \frac{S}{K} - b\left(\frac{\dot{K}}{K}\right) = b\left(\frac{\rho + r(1-\tau)(\sigma-1)}{\sigma}\right) - \frac{S}{K},$$

with S the primary surplus and where we used $\dot{K}/K = (-\rho + r(1-\tau))/\sigma$ on a BGP. Since the primary surplus is not a function of public debt, neither the growth rate of capital nor that of consumption depend on public debt. Further, taking into account that r and S/K are constant on a BGP, the solution to the differential equation is given by,

$$b(t) = \frac{S/K}{(\rho + r(1-\tau)(\sigma-1))/\sigma} + e^{t(\rho + r(1-\tau)(\sigma-1))/\sigma} \times \left(b(0) - \frac{S/K}{(\rho + r(1-\tau)(\sigma-1))/\sigma}\right).$$

Noting that $\dot{K}/K = g = (-\rho + r(1-\tau))/\sigma$ holds on a BGP, we get for the level of public debt

$$B(t) = K_0 e^{gt}\left(C_1 + C_2\, e^{r(1-\tau)t - gt}\right),$$

with $C_1 = \sigma(S/K)/(\rho + r(1-\tau)(\sigma-1))$ and $C_2 = b_0 - \sigma(S/K)/(\rho + r(1-\tau)(\sigma-1))$.

Thus, for $r(1-\tau) > g \leftrightarrow \rho + r(1-\tau)(\sigma-1) > 0$ the limit of the present value of public debt is given by,

$$\lim_{t\to\infty} e^{-r(1-\tau)t} B(t) = K_0\, C_2\,.$$

This shows that the limit of the present value is positive (negative) if the initial primary surplus falls short (exceeds) the initial level of public debt multiplied by the difference between the net interest rate and the balanced growth rate, i.e. if $S_0 < (>) B_0\,(r(1-\tau) - g)$ holds. If the limit of the present value is negative, the private sector is a borrower and fails to pay back its (gross) debt. Only in case $S_0 = B_0\,(r(1-\tau) - g)$ the present value of public debt converges to zero.

For $r(1-\tau) < g \leftrightarrow \rho + r(1-\tau)(\sigma-1) < 0$ the limit of the present value of public debt is obtained as,

$$\lim_{t\to\infty} e^{-r(1-\tau)t} B(t) = +\infty\ (-\infty), \quad \text{for} \quad S < 0\ (S > 0).$$

□

Proof of Proposition 4

To prove this proposition we set $\dot{C}/C = \dot{B}/B$, which must hold on a BGP, giving

$$\phi\,\omega\,c^{-\beta/(1-\beta+\gamma)} b^{-1} = \rho - \psi \tag{3.96}$$

Substituting this relation in $\dot{b}/b$ gives,

$$\dot{b}/b = c - \omega c^{-\beta/(1-\beta+\gamma)}((1-\tau)\alpha + \rho\phi/(\rho-\psi)) - \rho$$

From (3.96) we know that $b > 0$ implies that ϕ and $\rho - \psi$ have the same sign so that $\phi/(\rho-\psi) > 0$ holds. With this, it is easily seen that the following relations hold,

$$\lim_{c\to 0}(\dot{b}/b) = -\infty, \quad \lim_{c\to\infty}(\dot{b}/b) = +\infty, \quad \partial(\dot{b}/b)/\partial c > 0.$$

This proves the existence of a unique $c^\star$ which solves $\dot{b}/b = 0$ and, thus, of a unique BGP for a sufficiently small value of $(\rho+\delta)$.

To study stability, we compute the Jacobian matrix evaluated at the rest point of (3.17)–(3.18). The Jacobian is given by

$$\mathrm{J} = \begin{bmatrix} a_{11} & -\psi\,c \\ a_{21} & \phi\,\omega\,c^{-\beta/(1-\beta+\gamma)} b^{-1} - \psi\,b \end{bmatrix},$$

with c and b evaluated at the rest point $\{c^\star, b^\star\}$ and a_{11} and a_{21} given by

$$\begin{aligned} a_{11} &= c\left(1 + (\beta/(1-\beta+\gamma))\omega\, c^{-1-\beta/(1-\beta+\gamma)}(\phi + (1-\tau)\alpha)\right) \\ a_{21} &= b\left(1 + (\beta/(1-\beta+\gamma))\omega\, c^{-1-\beta/(1-\beta+\gamma)}(\phi(1+b^{-1}) + (1-\tau)\alpha)\right) \end{aligned}$$

The determinant of the Jacobian matrix can be computed as

$$\begin{aligned} \det J = {} & (\rho-\psi)\left(c + (\beta/(1-\beta+\gamma))\omega\, c^{-\beta/(1-\beta+\gamma)}(1-\tau)\alpha\right) + \\ & \rho\,(\beta/(1-\beta+\gamma))\phi\,\omega\, c^{-\beta/(1-\beta+\gamma)} \end{aligned}$$

Using (3.96) we can rewrite the determinant as follows,

$$\begin{aligned} \det J = {} & (\rho-\psi)\left(c + (\beta/(1-\beta+\gamma))\omega\, c^{-\beta/(1-\beta+\gamma)}(1-\tau)\alpha\right) + \\ & \rho\,(\beta/(1-\beta+\gamma))(\rho-\psi)\,b \end{aligned}$$

For $\psi > \rho$ the determinant is negative since $b > 0$ holds.

For $\psi < \rho$ the determinant is positive. To show that the BGP is unstable we have to compute the trace of the Jacobian, tr J, which is given by,

$$\begin{aligned}\operatorname{tr} J &= c - \psi\, b + (\beta/(1-\beta+\gamma))\omega\, c^{-\beta/(1-\beta+\gamma)}(\phi + (1-\tau)\alpha) \\ &\quad + \phi\, \omega b^{-1} c^{-\beta/(1-\beta+\gamma)}.\end{aligned}$$

To see that tr J is positive we first note that a positive value of b implies $\phi > 0$ for $\psi < \rho$. Further, from $\dot{c}/c = 0$ we get $c - \psi\, b = \rho + c^{-\beta/(1-\beta+\gamma)}(\phi + (1-\tau)\alpha) > 0$, so that the trace of the Jacobian is positive, too. Since the trace and the determinant are both positive, the BGP is unstable for $\psi < \rho$. Thus, Proposition 4 is proven. □

Proof of Proposition 5

To prove Proposition 5, we first note that the balanced budget rule implies $b^\star = 0$ since public debt is constant while the capital stock grows over time. Further, $\phi = 0$ and $\psi = (1-\tau)r - \delta$ hold in this case. Using this, the equation $\dot{c}/c$ can be written as

$$\dot{c}/c = \left(c - c^{-\beta/(1-\beta+\gamma)}(1-\tau)\alpha - \rho\right)$$

It is easily seen that the following relations hold,

$$\lim_{c\to 0}(\dot{c}/c) = -\infty, \quad \lim_{c\to\infty}(\dot{c}/c) = +\infty, \quad \partial(\dot{c}/c)/\partial c > 0.$$

This proves the existence of a unique $c^\star$ which solves $\dot{c}/c = 0$ and, thus, of a unique BGP for a sufficiently small value of $(\rho + \delta)$.

The Jacobian is given by

$$\mathrm{J} = \begin{bmatrix} a_{11} & -c(1-\tau)\,(1-\alpha)\,\omega\, c^{-\beta/(1-\beta+\gamma)} \\ 0 & -g \end{bmatrix},$$

with c and b evaluated at the rest point $\{c^\star, 0\}$ and a_{11} given by

$$a_{11} = c + (1-\tau)\alpha\,\omega\,(\beta/(1-\beta+\gamma))\, c^{-\beta/(1-\beta+\gamma)}.$$

One eigenvalue is $a_{11} > 0$, and the second is $-g < 0$ so that the BGP is saddle point stable.

Under rule (ii) we also have $b^\star = 0$ such that uniqueness is shown as above. The Jacobian J is now given by

$$\mathrm{J} = \begin{bmatrix} a_{11} & -\psi\, c \\ 0 & \rho - \psi \end{bmatrix},$$

with c and b evaluated at the rest point $\{c^\star, 0\}$, a_{11} as above and where we used

$$c - (1-\tau)(1-\alpha)\,\omega\, c^{-\beta/(1-\beta+\gamma)} = \rho$$

which follows from $\dot{c} = 0$. Since $\rho < \psi$ holds for rule (ii) one eigenvalue is negative and one is positive implying saddle point stability. Thus, the proposition is proven. □

Proof of Proposition 6

To prove this proposition we note that $\dot{C}/C = \dot{K}/K$ holds on the BGP. With a balanced government budget this is equivalent to,

$$(1-\tau)\,(1-\alpha)\,\omega\, c^{-\beta/(1-\beta+\gamma)} - (\rho+\delta) = (1-\tau)\,\omega\, c^{-\beta/(1-\beta+\gamma)} - c - \delta \tag{3.97}$$

With permanent public deficits $\dot{C}/C = \dot{K}/K$ is equivalent to,

$$\begin{aligned}(1-\tau)\,(1-\alpha)\,\omega\, c^{-\beta/(1-\beta+\gamma)} - (\rho+\delta)\\ = (1-\tau)\,\omega\, c^{-\beta/(1-\beta+\gamma)} - c - \delta + \psi\, b + \phi\,\omega\, c^{-\beta/(1-\beta+\gamma)}\end{aligned} \tag{3.98}$$

Further, with permanent public deficits we get from $\dot{C}/C = \dot{B}/B$,

$$\psi\, b = -\phi\,\omega\, c^{-\beta/(1-\beta+\gamma)} + \rho\, b$$

Inserting this in (3.98) leads to

$$(1-\tau)\,(1-\alpha)\,\omega\, c^{-\beta/(1-\beta+\gamma)} - (\rho+\delta) = (1-\tau)\,\omega\, c^{-\beta/(1-\beta+\gamma)} - c - \delta + \rho\, b \tag{3.99}$$

which holds on a BGP in the economy with permanent budget deficits.

The graph of the left hand side of Eq. (3.97) is the same as the graph of the left hand side of Eq. (3.99). The graph of the right hand side of Eq. (3.97) is below the graph of the right hand side of Eq. (3.99) for $b > 0$. Consequently, the intersection point of the left hand side with the right hand side of Eq. (3.97) is to the left of that of Eq. (3.99) implying that $c^\star$ in the economy with the balanced budget rule is smaller than $c^\star$ in the economy with permanent budget deficits. Therefore, the balanced budget rule yields a higher long-run growth rate. □

Proof of Proposition 7

To prove that proposition we note that $\dot{C}/C = \dot{B}/B$ implies

$$-\phi\,\omega c^{-\beta/(1-\beta+\gamma)} - \psi\, b = -\rho\, b$$

Using that relation we obtain for $\dot{c}/c = (\dot{C}/C) - (\dot{K}/K)$ on the BGP

$$\dot{c} = c\left(c - c^{-\beta/(1-\beta+\gamma)}\,\omega\,(t_p + (1-\tau)\alpha) - \rho b\right) = 0$$

Implicit differentiation of the last equation yields

$$\frac{dc}{db} = \frac{\rho}{c\left(1 + (\beta/(1-\beta+\gamma))c^{-1-\beta/(1-\beta+\gamma)}\omega\,(t_p + (1-\tau)\alpha)\right)} > 0$$

Since $dg/dc < 0$ the first part is proven.

When public transfers are adjusted we immediately see from Eq. (3.25) that this equation does not depend on b. Thus, $c^\star$ that solves $\dot{c} = 0$ is independent of b and, consequently, the balanced growth rate does not depend on the public debt ratio. □

Welfare Effects with a Different Initial Condition and with $\kappa = 1$.

Table 3.9 Welfare F for the different budgetary rules with $\kappa = 0.25$ and $b(0) = 0.5$.

	$\gamma = 0.15$		
	Balanced budget	Asympt. zero debt ratio	Positive debt ratio
F	−10.006	−9.902	−10.624
	$\gamma = 0.3$		
	Balanced budget	Asympt. zero debt ratio	Positive debt ratio
F	−7.028	−6.905	−7.632

Table 3.10 Welfare F for the different budgetary rules with $\kappa = 1$ and $b(0) = 0.32$.

	$\gamma = 0.15$		
	Balanced budget	Asympt. zero debt ratio	Positive debt ratio
F	−17.668	−17.512	−18.812
	$\gamma = 0.3$		
	Balanced budget	Asympt. zero debt ratio	Positive debt ratio
F	−14.182	−13.968	−15.181

Table 3.11 Welfare F for the different budgetary rules with $\kappa = 1$ and $b(0) = 0.5$

	$\gamma = 0.15$		
	Balanced budget	Asympt. zero debt ratio	Positive debt ratio
F	−19.849	−19.35	−20.789
	$\gamma = 0.3$		
	Balanced budget	Asympt. zero debt ratio	Positive debt ratio
F	−16.13	−15.57	−16.881

Proof of Lemma 1

The Jacobian is given by:

$$J = \begin{bmatrix} \partial \dot{c}/\partial c & 0 & -c \\ 0 & \rho & -1 \\ 0 & \psi & -g-\theta \end{bmatrix}$$

with c evaluated at the BGP and where we used $\rho = c - c^{-\beta/(1-\beta+\gamma)}\omega((1-\tau)\alpha + \phi)$ and $-\dot{K}/K - \theta = -g - \theta = c + \delta - \theta - c^{-\beta/(1-\beta+\gamma)}\omega(1-\tau)$. Note that $\partial \dot{c}/\partial c > 0$ and $\psi = \theta(r(1-\tau) - \delta) = \theta(g + \rho)$.

The eigenvalues of the Jacobian can be computed as

$$ev_1 = \partial \dot{c}/\partial c, \; ev_{2,3} = 0.5((\rho - g - \theta) \pm \sqrt{(\rho + g + \theta)^2 - 4\theta(g + \rho)})$$

ev_1 is strictly positive and $ev_{2,3}$ can be written as:

$$ev_{2,3} = 0.5((\rho - g - \theta) \pm \sqrt{(\rho + g - \theta)^2})$$

It is immediately seen that we get $ev_2 = -g < 0$ and $ev_3 = \rho - \theta$. □

Proof of Proposition 10

From $\dot{c}/c = 0$ we get

$$z = c - c^{-\beta/(1-\beta+\gamma)}\omega((1-\tau)\alpha + \phi) - \rho$$

Inserting that in $\dot{b}/b$ and setting $\dot{b}/b = 0$ gives

$$\rho b = c - c^{-\beta/(1-\beta+\gamma)}\omega((1-\tau)\alpha + \phi) - \rho + \phi\omega c^{-\beta/(1-\beta+\gamma)}$$

Using those two expressions to substitute for z and b in $\dot{z}/z$ leads to

$$q = \frac{\psi}{\rho}\left(1 + \frac{\phi\omega}{h(c,\cdot) - \omega((1-\tau)\alpha + \phi)}\right) - c^{-\beta/(1-\beta+\gamma)}\omega(1-\tau)(1-\alpha) + \rho + \delta - \theta,$$

with $h(c,\cdot) = c^{(1+\gamma)/(1-\beta+\gamma)} - \rho c^{\beta/(1-\beta+\gamma)}$. A solution c such that $q(\cdot) = 0$ gives a BGP.

The expression $h(c,\cdot) - \omega((1-\tau)\alpha + \phi)$ is equivalent to $zc^{\beta/(1-\beta+\gamma)} > 0$. Note that we limit the analysis to the case $\omega((1-\tau)\alpha + \phi) > 0$ which implies $h > 0$. The function $q(\cdot)$ has a discontinuity (a pole) at c^{pol} with c^{pol} such that $h(c,\cdot) - \omega((1-\tau)\alpha + \phi) = 0$ for $c = c^{pol}$. Since we only analyze the economy with $z \geq 0$ the BGP value of c, $c^{\star}$, must lie to the right of $\omega((1-\tau)\alpha + \phi)$.

The function $h(c,\cdot)$ has the following properties:

$$h(c,\cdot) = c^{(1+\gamma)/(1-\beta+\gamma)} - \rho c^{\beta/(1-\beta+\gamma)} > 0, \ \lim_{c\to\infty} h(c,\cdot) = \infty,$$

$$\frac{dh}{dc} = \left(\frac{1+\gamma}{1-\beta+\gamma}\right) c^{-1+(1+\gamma)/(1-\beta+\gamma)}$$
$$-\rho\left(\frac{\beta}{1-\beta+\gamma}\right) c^{-1+(\beta/(1-\beta+\gamma))} > 0, \text{ for } h > 0$$

The function $q(\cdot)$ has the following properties:

$$\lim_{c\to\infty} q = (\psi/\rho) + \rho + \delta - \theta, \ \lim_{c\searrow c^{pol}} q = \infty\,(-\infty), \text{ for } \phi > (<)\,0,$$

where $c \searrow c^{pol}$ means that c approaches c^{pol} from above. The derivative of $q(c,\cdot)$ with respect to c is obtained as:

$$\frac{dq}{dc} = \left(\frac{\beta}{1-\beta+\gamma}\right) c^{-1-(\beta/(1-\beta+\gamma))} - \frac{\psi}{\rho}\left(\frac{1}{h(c,\cdot) - \omega((1-\tau)\alpha + \phi)}\right)^2 \phi\,\omega\left(\frac{dh}{dc}\right)$$

Thus, the function $q(c,\cdot)$ does not intersect the horizontal axis for $(\psi/\rho) + \rho + \delta - \theta < 0$ with $\phi < 0$ and, therefore, no BGP exists. For $\phi > 0$ and $(\psi/\rho)+\rho+\delta-\theta < 0$ there exists a unique intersection of $q(c,\cdot)$ with the horizontal axis and, therefore, a unique BGP.

For $(\psi/\rho) + \rho + \delta - \theta > 0$ and $\phi < 0$ there exists a unique intersection of $q(c,\cdot)$ with the horizontal axis and, therefore, a unique BGP.

For $(\psi/\rho) + \rho + \delta - \theta > 0$ and $\phi > 0$ the function $q(c,\cdot)$ starts from $+\infty$ for $c = c^{pol}$ and converges to $(\psi/\rho) + \rho + \delta - \theta > 0$ for $c \to \infty$. Either, $q(c,\cdot)$ does not intersect the horizontal axis (no BGP) or the function is such that there are two points of intersection (2 BGPs) for this case. To show that are maximally 2 BGPs we note that $q(c,\cdot) = 0$ implies $q_1(c,\cdot) = (h(c,\cdot) - \omega((1-\tau)\alpha + \phi)) \cdot q(c,\cdot) = 0$.

Recall that a positive level of outstanding public debt, to which we limit our analysis, implies $h(c,\cdot) - \omega((1-\tau)\alpha + \phi) > 0$. The function $q_1(c,\cdot)$ is given by:

$$q_1 = (h(c,\cdot) - \omega((1-\tau)\alpha + \phi))((\psi/\rho) + \rho + \delta - \theta) + \phi\omega\psi/\rho + \rho\omega(1-\alpha)(1-\tau) + c^{-\beta/(1-\beta+\gamma)}\omega^2((1-\tau)\alpha + \phi)(1-\alpha)(1-\tau)$$

with the properties $\lim_{c\to 0} q_1 = +\infty$, $\lim_{c\to\infty} q_1 = +\infty$. The second derivative of $q_1(c,\cdot)$ is given by

$$\frac{d^2 q_1}{dc^2} = \left(\frac{\beta}{1-\beta+\gamma} + 1\right) c^{-\beta/(1-\beta+\gamma)-2} \cdot C_5 + ((\psi/\rho) + \rho + \delta - \theta)\left(\frac{d^2 h}{dc^2}\right),$$

with $C_5 = \omega^2((1-\tau)\alpha + \phi)(1-\alpha)(1-\tau)\beta/(1-\beta+\gamma) > 0$. The second derivative of $h(c,\cdot)$ is given by

$$\frac{d^2 h}{dc^2} = \frac{\beta}{1-\beta+\gamma}\left(\left(\frac{1+\gamma}{1-\beta+\gamma}\right) c^{((1+\gamma)/(1-\beta+\gamma))-2} + \rho\left(\frac{1+\gamma-2\beta}{1-\beta+\gamma}\right) c^{(\beta/(1-\beta+\gamma))-2}\right)$$

It is positive if and only if

$$\left(\frac{1+\gamma}{1-\beta+\gamma}\right) c^{(1+\gamma)/(1-\beta+\gamma)} - \rho\left(\frac{\beta}{1-\beta+\gamma}\right) c^{\beta/(1-\beta+\gamma)} + \rho\left(\frac{1-\beta+\gamma}{1-\beta+\gamma}\right) c^{\beta/(1-\beta+\gamma)} \geq 0$$

which always holds true since $h(c,\cdot) = c^{(1+\gamma)/(1-\beta+\gamma)} - \rho c^{\beta/(1-\beta+\gamma)} > 0$. Thus, the second derivative of $h(c,\cdot)$ is positive and, therefore, the second derivative of $q_1(c,\cdot)$, too. Consequently, there can be only two points of intersection of $q_1(c,\cdot)$ and, thus, of $q(c,\cdot)$ with the horizontal axis. □

Proof of Lemma 2

From the proof of Proposition 3 we know that along the BGP the following relation holds:

$$0 = c - c^{-\beta/(1-\beta+\gamma)}\omega(1-\tau)\alpha - \rho - \rho b$$

Implicitly differentiating gives:

$$\frac{dc}{db} = \frac{\rho}{1 + (\beta/(1-\beta+\gamma))\, c^{-(\beta/(1-\beta+\gamma))-1}\, \omega\, (1-\tau)\alpha} > 0$$

Since a higher value of c implies a lower long-run growth rate, the lemma is proven. □

Stability of the Balanced Budget Scenario in the Monetary Growth Model

With a balanced government budget that implies $\phi = -\theta z(k/y)$, the Jacobian of the dynamic system (3.62)–(3.64) is given by,

$$J = \begin{bmatrix} \partial \dot{x}/\partial x & \theta x & -\psi x \\ \partial \dot{z}/\partial x & (\theta + \rho + \theta z) & -\psi z \\ 0 & 0 & -g \end{bmatrix},$$

where we also used $\dot{v} = -v(\partial \dot{k}/\partial k)$, $x^\star/z^\star = \theta + \rho$ and $v^\star = 0$ on the BGP and the variables x and z are evaluated at the BGP. Since $\partial \dot{x}/\partial x = xC_2$ and $\partial \dot{z}/\partial x = zC_2 - 1$, with $C_2 = \partial(\dot{x}/x)/\partial x > 0$, we get $(\partial \dot{x}/\partial x)(\theta + \rho + \theta z) - \theta x(\partial \dot{z}/\partial x) = xC_2(\theta + \rho) + \theta x > 0$ as well as $(\partial \dot{x}/\partial x) + (\theta + \rho + \theta z) > 0$, so that there exists one negative eigenvalue of J given by $-g$. □

Proof of Proposition 12

To prove that proposition we set $\dot{x} = 0$ and solve that equation with respect to c and insert that c in $\dot{c}$ which leads to the following equation we denote by f:

$$\begin{aligned} f &= (1-\alpha)(1-\tau)A^{1/(1-\alpha)}\alpha^{\alpha/(1-\alpha)}x^{\alpha/(\alpha-1)} \\ &\quad -\psi_L A^{1/(1-\alpha)}\alpha^{1/(1-\alpha)}x^{1/(\alpha-1)}/L - (\rho+\delta) + \psi_L \bar{L}/L \end{aligned}$$

A solution $f = 0$ with respect to x gives a rest point of (3.93)–(3.95). As regards f we have

$$\lim_{x\to 0} f = -\infty, \;\; \lim_{x\to\infty} f = -(\rho+\delta) + \psi_L \bar{L}/L$$

The first derivative of f is given by

$$\frac{\partial f}{\partial x} = -\left(\frac{\alpha}{1-\alpha}\right) x^{-1+\alpha/(\alpha-1)} A^{1/(1-\alpha)} \alpha^{\alpha/(1-\alpha)} (1-\alpha)(1-\tau) + \left(\frac{1}{1-\alpha}\right) x^{-1+1/(\alpha-1)} \psi_L A^{1/(1-\alpha)} \alpha^{1/(1-\alpha)} / L$$

The second derivative of f is

$$\frac{\partial^2 f}{\partial x^2} = \frac{\alpha}{(1-\alpha)^2} x^{-2+\alpha/(\alpha-1)} A^{1/(1-\alpha)} \alpha^{\alpha/(1-\alpha)} (1-\alpha)(1-\tau) + (-1)\frac{(2-\alpha)}{(1-\alpha)^2} x^{-2+1/(\alpha-1)} \psi_L A^{1/(1-\alpha)} \alpha^{1/(1-\alpha)} / L$$

Setting $\partial f / \partial x = 0$ gives

$$x = x_m = \frac{\psi_L \, \alpha^{1/(1-\alpha)}}{\alpha \, L \, A^{1/(1-\alpha)} \alpha^{\alpha/(1-\alpha)} (1-\alpha)(1-\tau)}$$

Inserting x_m in $\partial^2 f / \partial x^2$ shows that the sign of the resulting expression is equivalent to

$$-\alpha A^{1/(1-\alpha)} \alpha^{\alpha/(1-\alpha)} (1-\alpha)(1-\tau) < 0$$

This demonstrates that the function f reaches a maximum for $x = x_m$ and it has a unique turning point given by

$$x = x_w = x_m \cdot (1 + (1-\alpha))$$

Thus, the function f is concave-convex, starts at $-\infty$, reaches a maximum at $x = x_m$, has a turning point at $x = x_w$ and converges to $-(\rho+\delta) + \psi_L \bar{L}/L$ for $x \rightarrow \infty$. This implies that for $-(\rho + \delta) + \psi_L \bar{L}/L > 0$ there exists a unique rest point of (3.93)–(3.95) and for $-(\rho+\delta) + \psi_L \bar{L}/L < 0$ there exist two rest points for (3.93)–(3.95) or no rest point if f does not intersect the horizontal axis. □

Proof of Proposition 13

We know that a BGP is given for a value of x such that the function f in the proof of Proposition 12 equals zero. Looking at f it is easily seen that this function does neither depend on the ratio of public debt to capital, z, nor on the parameters ψ and ϕ. □

Proof of Proposition 14

The first part is obvious. Since capital and GDP grow at a positive constant rate on the BGP and public debt is constant for a balanced government budget the debt to GDP ratio converges to zero asymptotically.

To see the second part, we solve $\dot{c}/c = 0$ with respect to c and insert the resulting expression in $\dot{z}$. This gives a function that depends on z and on x. Solving that function with respect to $z = B/K$ yields

$$z = \frac{\phi A \left(A^{1/(1-\alpha)}\alpha^{1/(1-\alpha)}x^{1/(\alpha-1)}\right)^{\alpha}}{\rho - \psi}$$

Knowing that $L^d = A^{1/(1-\alpha)}\alpha^{1/(1-\alpha)}x^{1/(\alpha-1)}$ and $Y/K = A(L^d)^{\alpha}$ the second part is immediately seen. □

Proof of Proposition 15

To show saddle point stability, we compute the Jacobian matrix evaluated at the rest point of (3.93)–(3.95). The Jacobian is given by

$$\mathrm{J} = \begin{bmatrix} c & c\left(\partial(\dot{C}/C)/\partial x - \partial(\dot{K}/K)/\partial x\right) & -\psi c \\ x & x\left(\partial(\dot{w}/w)/\partial x - \partial(\dot{K}/K)/\partial x\right) & -\psi x \\ 0 & 0 & -\dot{K}/K \end{bmatrix},$$

where c and x take on their BGP values and where we have used that $z = 0$ holds on the BGP with a balanced government budget. The eigenvalues of that matrix are given by $-\dot{K}/K = -g < 0$ and by the eigenvalues of the matrix J_1 which is

$$\mathrm{J}_1 = \begin{bmatrix} c & c\left(\partial(\dot{C}/C)/\partial x - \partial(\dot{K}/K)/\partial x\right) \\ x & x\left(\partial(\dot{w}/w)/\partial x - \partial(\dot{K}/K)/\partial x\right) \end{bmatrix}$$

The determinant of that matrix is obtained as

$$\det \mathrm{J}_1 = cx\left(\partial(\dot{w}/w)/\partial x - \partial(\dot{C}/C)/\partial x\right) = (-1)\, c\, x\, (\partial f/\partial x),$$

with f from the proof of Proposition 12. If there is a unique rest point of (3.93)–(3.95), f has a positive derivative at $f = 0$ implying that the determinant is negative so that J_1 has one negative and one positive eigenvalue.

If there are two rest points for (3.93)–(3.95), f has a positive derivative at the first intersection (giving the smaller x and, thus, higher growth) implying one negative and one positive eigenvalue of J_1 and f has a negative derivative at the second intersection (giving the higher x and, thus, smaller growth) so that J_1 has either two negative eigenvalues or two positive. The rest point is asymptotically stable if the trace of J_1 is negative.

The trace of J_1 can be computed as

$$\text{tr } J_1 = \left(\frac{1}{1-\alpha}\right) A^{1/(1-\alpha)}\alpha^{1/(1-\alpha)}x^{\alpha/(\alpha-1)}\left((1-\tau)-\varrho - x(1+\psi_L/L)\right) - g$$

where $c = -\delta+\varrho xL-\varrho x^{\alpha/(\alpha-1)}A^{1/(1-\alpha)}\alpha^{1/(1-\alpha)}+x^{\alpha/(\alpha-1)}(1-\tau)A^{1/(1-\alpha)}\alpha^{1/(1-\alpha)}-g$ has been used which holds on the BGP. The trace may have a positive or negative sign depending on the parameters. □

Proof of Proposition 16

In case of permanent deficits the Jacobian matrix is

$$J_2 = \begin{bmatrix} c & c\left(\partial(\dot{C}/C)/\partial x - \partial(\dot{K}/K)/\partial x\right) & -\psi c \\ x & x\left(\partial(\dot{w}/w)/\partial x - \partial(\dot{K}/K)/\partial x\right) & -\psi x \\ z & z\left(\partial(\dot{B}/B)/\partial x - \partial(\dot{K}/K)/\partial x\right) & -\psi z + (\rho-\psi) \end{bmatrix},$$

The determinant is given by

$$\det J_2 = (-1)\, c\, x\, (\rho-\psi)\, (\partial f/\partial x)$$

and the trace, tr J_2, is

$$\text{tr } J_2 = c + x\left(\partial(\dot{w}/w)/\partial x - \partial(\dot{K}/K)/\partial x\right) + (-1)(\psi z - (\rho-\psi)) = C_1 - (\psi-\rho), \tag{3.100}$$

with C_1 containing terms that are independent of ψ and independent of c and z.

Setting $\psi = 0$ we can explicitly compute the eigenvalues ev_i, $i = 1, 2, 3$, as

$$ev_1 = \rho,\ ev_{2,3} = (1/2)\left(\text{tr } J_1 \pm \sqrt{(\text{tr } J_1)^2 - 4\det J_1}\right),$$

with J_1 as for the balanced budget. With a unique BGP we have $(\partial f/\partial x) > 0$ so that J_1 has one positive and one negative eigenvalue. This shows that two eigenvalues of J_2 are positive and one is negative. For reasons of continuity this also holds in an ϵ environment around $\psi = 0$.

If ψ is sufficiently large, i.e. at least larger than ρ, the determinant of the Jacobian J_2 is positive, since $(\partial f/\partial x) > 0$. Because of $\det J_2 = ev_1 \cdot ev_2 \cdot ev_3$ we know that in this case there is no negative eigenvalue or two negative eigenvalues (or eigenvalues with negative real parts in case of complex conjugate eigenvalues). Further, we know that we have for the trace, tr $J_2 = ev_1 + ev_2 + ev_3$. From (3.100) we see that tr J_2

monotonically declines with ψ so that it becomes negative for a sufficiently large ψ implying that there is at least one negative eigenvalue. But, because of det $J_2 > 0$ there must be two negative eigenvalues in that case. We must also point out that, for the analytical model, we cannot exclude det $J_2 < 0$, tr $J_2 <$ which would imply 3 negative eigenvalues (or one negative and two complex conjugate eigenvalues with negative real parts). But numerical examples suggest that this does not occur.

When there exist two BGPs the analysis for the first BGP with the smaller x and, thus, higher growth is equivalent to the analysis for a unique BGP because $(\partial f/\partial x) > 0$ holds at the first BGP. At the second BGP we have $(\partial f/\partial x) < 0$. This implies det $J_2 = ev_1 \cdot ev_2 \cdot ev_3 > 0$ for $\psi = 0$ so that there are either three positive eigenvalues or two negative and one positive. In case of three positive eigenvalues raising ψ sufficiently leads to det $J_2 < 0$ so that there is at least one negative eigenvalue. In the less likely case of one positive and two negative eigenvalues raising ψ sufficiently leads to three negative eigenvalues or to one negative and two positive ones. The latter, however, is extremely unlikely because raising ψ also reduces the trace tr J_2 monotonically so that the sum of the eigenvalues declines. □

Chapter 4
Productive Government Spending, Public Debt and Growth

In the last chapter it was demonstrated that an economy with a balanced government budget or a debt policy such that debt grows less than GDP always generates a higher long-run growth rate compared to an economy where the government runs permanent deficits so that public debt grows at the same rate as all other variables. In addition, it could be shown that, in the case of permanent public deficits, stability of the economy is only given if the reaction of the primary surplus to public debt is sufficiently high. The underlying model was an endogenous growth model with public spending not having productive effects in the sense that it would raise production possibilities in the economy. Now, it could be argued that the results may change when government spending is productive, like investment in public infrastructure for example. In particular, the outcome as regards growth effects might be different. Therefore, in this chapter we study endogenous growth models with productive public spending.

One strand in the endogenous growth literature assumes that the government invests in a productive public capital stock which raises the incentive to invest (see for example Futagami et al. 1993). This approach goes back to Arrow and Kurz (1970) who, however, do not analyze models leading to sustained growth endogenously.

Empirical studies investigating the effect of public spending and public capital on the productivity of economies do not reach definite conclusions. Instead, the outcomes differ in part significantly. However, this is not too surprising because it is to be expected that the time period under consideration as well as the countries which are considered are important as to the results obtained. A survey of the empirical studies dealing with public spending, public capital and the economic performance of countries is given in the paper by Pfähler et al. (1996) and by the more recent contribution by Romp and de Haan (2005), for example.

© Springer International Publishing Switzerland 2015

A. Greiner, B. Fincke, *Public Debt, Sustainability and Economic Growth*,
DOI 10.1007/978-3-319-09348-2_4

Most of the endogenous growth models with productive public spending are characterized by the assumption of a balanced government budget. Exemptions of this are the approaches by Greiner and Semmler (2000) and by Ghosh and Mourmouras (2004). In these contributions it is assumed that the government may finance public expenditures by deficits but the government has to stick to some well-defined budgetary regimes.[1] Greiner and Semmler (2000) study growth effects of fiscal policy and find that stricter regimes generate a higher balanced growth rate because the debt ratio in these regimes is smaller compared to that in less strict budgetary regimes, where the government may run deficits not only to finance public investment. Ghosh and Mourmouras (2004) analyze welfare effects of these regimes and demonstrate that the choice of the budgetary regime does not only affect the long-run growth rate but is also crucial as concerns welfare. An interesting contribution along this line of research is provided by Futagami et al. (2008) who study an endogenous growth model with productive public spending and public debt but assume that government debt must converge to a certain exogenously given debt ratio asymptotically. They demonstrate that there exist two balanced growth paths to which the economy can converge in the long-run, with one being saddle point stable and the other being saddle point stable or asymptotically stable. Further, these authors show that a deficit financed increase in productive public spending raises the low balanced growth rate while it reduces the high balanced growth rate.

While the assumption of budgetary regimes or of a debt ratio to which an economy must converge in the long-run is plausible and can be found in the real world, it may nevertheless be considered as ad hoc. However, this does not hold for the intertemporal budget constraint of the government. This constraint is in a way a natural constraint any government must obey. It should also be pointed out that, given a fixed tax rate and fixed unproductive public spending, a rise in the primary surplus ratio, as a result of a higher debt ratio, can lead to a decline in productive public spending. And there is indeed empirical evidence that public investment is reduced as the debt service rises, instead of other unproductive public spending. Examples of such studies are the ones by Oxley and Martin (1991), Gong et al. (2001) or Heinemann (2002).[2]

It should also be recalled that the fact that an increase in the primary surplus, as debt grows, guarantees sustainability of public debt, is more general than the Ricardo equivalence theorem and contains the latter as a special case. This holds because there are three ways for the government to raise the primary surplus: First, it can raise taxes, second it can reduce spending and, third, the surplus can increase due to a higher GDP leading to more tax revenues.

[1] For a survey of budgetary regimes resorted to in the economics literature, see van Ewijk (1991).

[2] See also the conclusion of Chap. 2.2.

4.1 The Endogenous Growth Model with Full Employment

In this section we take up the approach by Futagami et al. (1993) and allow for public debt and public deficits as in Greiner (2008b). In addition, we posit as in the preceding chapter that the primary surplus relative to GDP is a positive function of the debt to GDP ratio as this guarantees sustainability of public debt. To start with, we present the structure of our growth model.

Our economy consists of three sectors: A household sector which receives labor income and income from its saving, a productive sector and the government. First, we describe the household sector.

4.1.1 Households

The household sector is represented by one household which maximizes the discounted stream of utility arising from per-capita consumption, $C(t)$, over an infinite time horizon subject to its budget constraint, taking factor prices as given. The utility function is assumed to be logarithmic, $U(C) = \ln C$, and the household has one unit of labor, L, which it supplies inelastically, in contrast to the model of the last chapter.[3] The maximization problem can be written as

$$\max_C \int_0^\infty e^{-\rho t} \ln C \, dt, \tag{4.1}$$

subject to

$$(1-\tau)\left(w + rW + \pi_p\right) = \dot{W} + C. \tag{4.2}$$

The parameter ρ is the subjective discount rate, w is the wage rate and r is the interest rate. The variable $W \equiv B + K$ gives wealth which is equal to public debt, B, and private capital, K, and π_p gives possible profits of the productive sector, the household takes as given in solving its optimization problem. Finally, $\tau \in (0,1)$ is the constant income tax rate. The dot gives the derivative with respect to time and we neglect depreciation of private capital in this section.

To solve this problem we formulate the current-value Hamiltonian which is written as

$$\mathcal{H} = \ln C + \lambda((1-\tau)\left(w + rW + \pi_p\right) - C) \tag{4.3}$$

[3] From now on we again omit the time argument t if no ambiguity arises.

Necessary optimality conditions are given by

$$C^{-1} = \lambda \tag{4.4}$$

$$\dot{\lambda} = \rho\lambda - \lambda(1-\tau)\, r \tag{4.5}$$

If the transversality condition $\lim_{t\to\infty} e^{-\rho t} W/C = 0$ holds, which is fulfilled for a time path on which assets grow at the same rate as consumption, the necessary conditions are also sufficient.

4.1.2 Firms

The productive sector is represented by one firm which behaves competitively and which maximizes static profits. The production function of the firm is given by

$$Y = K^{1-\alpha} G^{\alpha} L^{\beta}, \tag{4.6}$$

with $(1-\alpha) + \beta \leq 1$. $(1-\alpha)$ again denotes the private capital share and β gives the labor share. The variable Y denotes output, G is public capital and α gives the elasticity of output with respect to public capital. Using that labor is set to one, $L = 1$, profit maximization gives

$$w = \beta K^{1-\alpha} G^{\alpha} \tag{4.7}$$

$$r = (1-\alpha) K^{-\alpha} G^{\alpha} \tag{4.8}$$

4.1.3 The Government

The government in our economy receives tax revenues from income taxation and has revenues from issuing government bonds it then uses for public investment, I_p, and for public consumption, C_p. As concerns public consumption we here assume that this type of spending does neither yield utility nor raise productivity but is only a waste of resources. Further, the government sets the primary surplus such that it is a positive linear function of public debt which guarantees that public debt is sustainable. We note that the accounting identity describing the accumulation of public debt in continuous time is given by:

$$\dot{B} = rB(1-\tau) - S, \tag{4.9}$$

where S is government surplus exclusive of net interest payments.

The intertemporal budget constraint of the government is fulfilled if

$$B(0) = \int_0^\infty e^{-\int_0^\mu (1-\tau)r(\nu)d\nu} S(\mu)d\mu \leftrightarrow \lim_{t\to\infty} e^{-\int_0^t (1-\tau)r(\mu)d\mu} B(t) = 0 \tag{4.10}$$

holds. Equation (4.10) is the present-value borrowing constraint which states that public debt at time zero must equal the future present-value surpluses.

Again, we assume that the ratio of the primary surplus to GDP ratio is a positive linear function of the debt to GDP ratio and of a constant. The primary surplus ratio, then, can be written as

$$\frac{S}{Y} = \phi + \psi \frac{B}{Y} = \frac{\tau Y - I_p - C_p}{Y}, \tag{4.11}$$

where $\phi \in \mathbb{R}$, $\psi \in \mathbb{R}_{++}$ are constants. The parameter ψ determines how strong the primary surplus reacts to changes in public debt and ϕ determines whether the level of the primary surplus rises or falls with an increase in GDP.

Using (4.11) the differential equation describing the evolution of public debt can be written as

$$\dot{B} = (r(1-\tau) - \psi)\, B - \phi\, Y. \tag{4.12}$$

From Chap. 2.1 we know that a positive linear dependence of the primary surplus to GDP ratio on the debt to GDP ratio, that is $\psi > 0$, guarantees that the intertemporal budget constraint of the government is fulfilled. Therefore, we posit that the government sets the primary surplus according to (4.11) so that the evolution of public debt is given by (4.12).

Defining $C_p/I_p = \zeta$ as public consumption relative to public investment, that is constant, and using that the evolution of public debt is given by $\dot{B} = rB(1-\tau) + I_p(1+\zeta) - \tau Y = rB(1-\tau) - \psi B - \phi Y$ public investment can be written as

$$I_p = \omega(\tau - \phi)Y - \omega\psi B\,, \tag{4.13}$$

where $\omega = 1/(1+\zeta)$. Neglecting depreciation, the differential equation describing the evolution of public capital, then, is written as

$$\dot{G} = I_p = \omega(\tau - \phi)Y - \omega\psi B\,. \tag{4.14}$$

4.1.4 Equilibrium Conditions and the Balanced Growth Path

Before we analyze our model we give the definition of an equilibrium and of a balanced growth path. An equilibrium allocation for our economy now is defined as follows.

Definition 4 An equilibrium is a sequence of variables $\{C(t), K(t), G(t), B(t)\}_{t=0}^{\infty}$ and a sequence of prices $\{w(t), r(t)\}_{t=0}^{\infty}$ such that, given prices and fiscal parameters, the firm maximizes profits, the household solves (4.1) subject to (4.2) and the budget constraint of the government (4.9) is fulfilled with the primary surplus set according to Eq. (4.11).

Resorting to (4.4), (4.5) and (4.8), the growth rate of consumption is derived as

$$\frac{\dot{C}}{C} = -\rho + (1-\tau)(1-\alpha)K^{-\alpha}G^{\alpha} \tag{4.15}$$

The economy-wide resource constraint is obtained by combining (4.12) and (4.2) as

$$\frac{\dot{K}}{K} = -\frac{C}{K} + \frac{K^{1-\alpha}G^{\alpha}}{K} + \psi\frac{B}{K} + (\phi-\tau)\frac{K^{1-\alpha}G^{\alpha}}{K}. \tag{4.16}$$

Thus, in equilibrium the economy is completely described by Eqs (4.15), (4.16), (4.12) and (4.14) plus the limiting transversality condition of the household.

In Definition 5 we give the definition of a balanced growth path for this section.

Definition 5 A balanced growth path (BGP) is a path such that the economy is in equilibrium and such that consumption, private capital and public capital grow at the same strictly positive constant growth rate, that is $\dot{C}/C = \dot{K}/K = \dot{G}/G = g$, $g > 0$, $g = constant$, and either

(i) $\dot{B} = 0$ or
(ii) $\dot{B}/B = g_B$, with $0 < g_B < g$, $g_B = constant$, or
(iii) $\dot{B}/B = \dot{C}/C = \dot{K}/K = \dot{G}/G = g$.

Definition 5 shows that we again consider three different scenarios. Scenario (i) is the balanced budget scenario where the government has at each point in time a balanced budget. But this does not necessarily imply that public debt equals zero. If the level of initial debt is positive, the debt to capital ratio and also the debt to GDP ratio are positive but decline over time and converge to zero in the long-run. Scenario (ii) describes a situation where the government always runs a deficit so that the growth rate of public debt is positive in the long-run. But public debt grows at a smaller rate than capital, consumption and output.[4] This implies that the debt ratio also converges to zero in the long-run since public debt grows at a smaller rate than capital and output. The last scenario, scenario (iii) finally, describes the case which is characterized by public deficits where government debt grows at the same rate as all other endogenous variables in the long-run.

[4]Needless to say that GDP grows at the same rate as capital and consumption on a BGP.

To analyze our economy around a BGP we define the new variables $x := G/K$, $b := B/K$ and $c := C/K$. Differentiating these variables with respect to time leads to a three dimensional system of differential equations given by

$$\dot{x} = x\left((\tau - \phi)x^{\alpha-1}\omega - \omega\psi b/x + c - x^{\alpha} - \psi b + (\tau - \phi)x^{\alpha}\right), \tag{4.17}$$

$$\dot{b} = b\left((1-\alpha)x^{\alpha}(1-\tau) - \psi - \phi x^{\alpha}/b + c - x^{\alpha} - \psi b + (\tau - \phi)x^{\alpha}\right), \tag{4.18}$$

$$\dot{c} = c\left((1-\alpha)x^{\alpha}(1-\tau) - \rho + c - x^{\alpha} - \psi b + (\tau - \phi)x^{\alpha}\right). \tag{4.19}$$

A solution of $\dot{x} = \dot{b} = \dot{c} = 0$ with respect to x, b, c gives a BGP for our model and the corresponding ratios $x^{\star}, b^{\star}, c^{\star}$ on the BGP.[5] In the next section we analyze growth and welfare effects of our scenarios as given in Definition 5.

4.1.5 *Analyzing the Model*

In this section we study the structure of our model as well as growth and welfare effects of the different scenarios. Further, we analyze how a transition from scenario (iii), where the debt ratio is strictly positive in the long-run, to scenario (i) and to scenario (ii), and vice versa, affects growth and welfare.

The Asymptotic Behavior of the Model

First, we analyze scenario (i) and scenario (ii). Scenario (i) is obtained by setting the reaction coefficient ψ equal to the net return on capital, $(1 - \tau)r$, making ψ an endogenous variable. Further, ϕ is set equal to zero for all times, that is $\phi = 0$, for $t \in [0, \infty)$. Scenario (ii) is obtained by setting $\phi = 0$ and by letting ψ be an exogenous parameter which can take arbitrary but strictly positive values. Proposition 17 gives results as concerns existence, uniqueness and stability of a balanced growth path for these two scenarios.

Proposition 17 *There exists a unique saddle point stable balanced growth path for scenario (i). For $\rho < \psi < r(1 - \tau)$, scenario (ii) is also characterized by a unique saddle point stable balanced growth path.*

Proof See the appendix to this chapter.

This proposition demonstrates that both the balanced budget scenario and the scenario with public deficits but an asymptotically zero debt ratio are characterized by unique BGPs which are saddle point stable, where a certain parameter restriction

[5]The $\star$ denotes BGP values and we exclude the economically meaningless BGP $x^{\star} = c^{\star} = 0$.

must be fulfilled for scenario (ii). The restriction $\rho < \psi < r(1-\tau)$ states that, on the one hand, ψ must not be too small, $\psi > \rho$, so that sustained growth is possible. This holds because otherwise public debt would become too large requiring too many resources for the debt service so that ongoing growth would not be possible. The positive effect of ψ on the growth rate can be seen from Eq. (4.16). On the other hand, ψ must not be too large, $\psi < r(1-\tau)$, because otherwise the government would not invest enough in public capital so that sustained growth would not be possible either, which can be seen from (4.14).

Saddle point stability means that there exists a unique value $c(0)$ such that the economy converges to the balanced growth path in the long-run. If one takes both $x(0)$ and $b(0)$ as given, since both x and b are state variables, this implies that the economy is determinate. However, from an economic point of view, it seems plausible to make a difference between capital stocks and public debt. This holds because capital stocks need a longer time period to be built up whereas public debt can be changed faster since it is a financial variable. Therefore, from an economic point of view the assumption that $b(0)$ can be controlled could also be justified.

As concerns scenario (iii), where public debt grows at the same rate as consumption and capital in the long-run, the analytical model turns out to be quite complicated and no unambiguous results can be derived. But it is possible to derive a result as concerns the public debt to private capital ratio for the analytical model. This is the contents of Proposition 18.

Proposition 18 *Assume that there exists a balanced growth path in scenario (iii). Then, the ratio of public debt to private capital is given by*

$$b^\star = \frac{\omega\,(\tau-\phi)(x^\star)^\alpha - g\,x^\star}{\psi\,\omega}.$$

$\phi < \tau$ is necessary for $b^\star$ to be positive and $\phi \geq \tau$ is sufficient for $b^\star$ to be negative.

Proof See the appendix to this chapter.

Proposition 18 shows that the reaction of the primary surplus to variations of GDP is crucial as concerns the question of whether sustained growth is feasible in the long-run together with a positive value of public debt. It should be recalled that the parameter ϕ determines whether, and if so how strongly, the level of the primary surplus rises as GDP increases. Proposition 18 states that for relatively large values of ϕ, that is for $\phi \geq \tau$, sustained growth is only feasible if public debt is negative, that is if the government is a creditor. At first sight, this result may seem counter intuitive. However, if the government puts too high a weight on controlling public debt, by setting ϕ to a high value, it spends too little for public investment so that in this case sustained growth is only feasible if the government has built up a stock of wealth out of which it finances productive public spending. From a technical point of view, this is seen from the differential equation for $\dot{G}$, Eq. (4.14), which shows that public investment would be negative for $\phi \geq \tau$, unless B was negative, too.

In the next subsection we analyze growth effects of the different scenarios.

Growth Effects of the Different Scenarios

Our first concern is to answer the question of which scenario brings about a higher growth rate of consumption and of capital in the long-run. Proposition 19 gives the answer to this question.

Proposition 19 *Assume that the government does not dispose of a stock of wealth and that there exists a balanced growth path with a strictly positive public debt ratio in scenario (iii). Then, the balanced growth rate in scenario (iii) is lower than the balanced growth rate in scenario (i). Further, the balanced growth rate in scenario (i) is equal to the balanced growth rate in scenario (ii).*

Proof See the appendix to this chapter.

The outcome that the balanced growth rate in scenario (i), the balanced budget scenario, is equal to that obtained in scenario (ii), where public debt grows less than capital and output in the long-run, is not too surprising. This holds because asymptotically the debt ratio equals zero in both scenarios, so that both scenarios are described by the same equations.

A more interesting result is the outcome that a balanced budget always leads to a higher growth rate in the long-run compared to a scenario where public debt grows at the same rate as consumption and capital. This is indeed a strong result because it states that, starting from a balanced budget, a deficit financed public investment can never raise the long-run growth rate if it leads to a positive debt ratio in the long-run. The economic intuition behind this result is that a positive debt ratio in the long-run requires resources for the debt service which cannot be used for productive public spending, leading to a lower balanced growth rate. Hence, starting from a balanced government budget, a deficit financed increase in public investment raises the transitional growth rates of private and public capital but brings about a lower growth rate in the long-run, unless the government balances its budget again or lets public debt grow at a smaller rate than GDP in the long-run, so that the debt to GDP ratio converges to zero.

The only possibility to achieve a balanced growth rate exceeding the one of the balanced budget scenario is given if the government has built up a stock of wealth it uses to finance its expenditures and to lend to the household sector. In this case, the government is a creditor implying that b is negative. In a corollary to Proposition 19 we treat this case.

Corollary 1 *Assume that the government has built up a stock of wealth. Then, the balanced growth rate in scenario (iii) exceeds the balanced growth rate of scenario (i).*

Proof See the appendix to this chapter.

It should be noted that there would be no need for the government to stick to the rule defined in (4.11) nor for the balanced budget rule if the government was a creditor. Nevertheless, even for the latter case the primary surplus rule could be justified because it would guarantee that the wealth of the public sector does not explode so that the private sector, to which the government lends, remains solvent. In any case, the result stated in Corollary 1 also holds without rule (4.11), which is shown in the appendix to this chapter.

It must be pointed out that the result in Proposition 19 only states that a balanced government budget, or a scenario where public debt grows at a smaller rate than capital and output in the long-run, gives a higher balanced growth path compared to a scenario where public debt grows at the same rate as capital and output. It does not say anything about long-run growth effects of deficit financed public investment given the scenario where public debt grows at the balanced growth rate in the long-run. Thus, a deficit financed increase in public investment may yield a higher balanced growth rate in the latter scenario and reduce the long-run debt ratio.

In order to see this we resort to a numerical example. As to the parameter values we set the elasticity of output with respect to public capital to 20 %, that is $\alpha = 0.2$. The income tax rate is set to 10 %, $\tau = 0.1$, and the rate of time preference is 15 %, $\rho = 0.15$. Assuming that one time period comprises several years such a high rate can be justified. The reaction coefficient ψ is set to $\psi = 0.05$ and $\omega = 0.1$.

Table 4.1 gives the balanced growth rate, g, and the debt to private capital ratio on the BGP, $b^{\star}$, for different values of ϕ.

To interpret the outcome shown in Table 4.1, it should be noted that a deficit financed increase in public investment is modeled by a decline in ϕ which can be seen from (4.13). Thus, Table 4.1 demonstrates that a deficit financed increase in public investment raises the balanced growth rate. One can also realize that for negative values of ϕ, implying that the primary surplus declines as GDP rises, sustained growth is only feasible with a negative public debt with this parameter constellation. In this case, the government has built up a stock of wealth out of which it finances productive public spending.

It should also be mentioned that the Jacobian matrix of (4.17)–(4.19), with the parameter values underlying Table 4.1, is characterized by one negative eigenvalue and two positive eigenvalues. Thus, the government must be able to control initial public debt, for example by levying a lump-sum tax at $t = 0$, and set $b(0)$ such that the economy starts on the one-dimensional stable manifold leading the economy to the BGP in the long-run.

The economy becomes stable if the reaction coefficient ψ is set to a higher value. Then, the Jacobian matrix is characterized by two negative eigenvalues and one positive eigenvalue. In that case, taking $x(0)$ and $b(0)$ as given, there exists a unique value for initial consumption relative to capital, $c(0)$, such that the economy converges to the BGP in the long-run.

However, with a higher value for ψ that stabilizes the economy, a deficit financed increase in public investment reduces the balanced growth rate. In this case, more

Table 4.1 Balanced growth rate and the debt to private capital ratio for different ϕ with $\psi = 0.05$

	$\phi = 0.005$	$\phi = 0.0025$	$\phi = -0.0025$	$\phi = -0.005$
g	0.189	0.191	0.196	0.198
$b^{\star}$	0.024	0.012	−0.012	−0.024

Table 4.2 Balanced growth rate and the debt to private capital ratio for different ϕ with $\psi = 0.25$

	$\phi = 0.005$	$\phi = 0.0025$	$\phi = -0.0025$	$\phi = -0.005$
g	0.198	0.196	0.191	0.189
$b^\star$	−0.024	−0.012	0.012	0.024

public investments financed through deficits lead to a temporary increase in the growth rate of public capital but to a smaller growth rate in the long-run. The reason is that with a high reaction coefficient, the negative feedback effect of higher debt is larger, because more resources are used for the debt service that cannot be invested in productive public capital. Table 4.2 shows the results of deficit financed increases in public investment that are again modeled by a decrease in ϕ.

Summarizing our results obtained from the simulations up to now, we can state that the higher ψ, that is the stronger the primary surplus and, thus public spending, react to increases in public debt, the sooner the model is stable. But in this case, a deficit financed increase in public investment reduces the balanced growth rate because of the strong feedback effects associated with public debt. Hence, there exists a trade-off between stabilizing the economy and getting positive growth effects of deficit financed public investment.

We should also like to point out the possibility of conjugate complex eigenvalues. For example, with $\psi = -0.025$ there is one positive real eigenvalue and two complex conjugate eigenvalues with negative real parts for $\psi \in (0.1912, 0.25)$. For $\psi = 0.191275$ there are two purely imaginary eigenvalues and for smaller values of ψ the two complex conjugate eigenvalues have positive real parts. Finally, for ψ smaller than about 0.187 the BGP does not exist any longer. This suggests that the system undergoes a Hopf bifurcation that can lead to stable limit cycles.[6]

Before we study welfare effects, we next illustrate the effect resulting from a transition from scenario (iii), where public debt grows at the balanced growth rate in the long-run, to the balanced budget scenario, scenario (i). To do so, we assume that the economy is originally on the BGP when the government decides to balance its budget from $t = 0$ onwards. To do so, we choose the parameter values underlying Table 4.2 with $\phi = -0.005$, so that $b^\star$ is positive and the Jacobian matrix of (4.17)–(4.19) has two negative eigenvalues.

To analyze the effects of a change from scenario (iii) to scenario (i) we study the solution of the linearized system of (4.17)–(4.19) which is given by

$$x(t) = x^\star + C_1 \, v_{11} \, e^{(ev_1)t} + C_2 \, v_{21} \, e^{(ev_2)t}, \tag{4.20}$$

$$b(t) = b^\star + C_1 \, v_{12} \, e^{(ev_1)t} + C_2 \, v_{22} \, e^{(ev_2)t}, \tag{4.21}$$

$$c(t) = c^\star + C_1 \, v_{13} \, e^{(ev_1)t} + C_2 \, v_{23} \, e^{(ev_2)t}, \tag{4.22}$$

[6]More examples, illustrating the results in Tables 4.1 and 4.2 as well as the proof that limit cycles may emerge, are given in Greiner (2007).

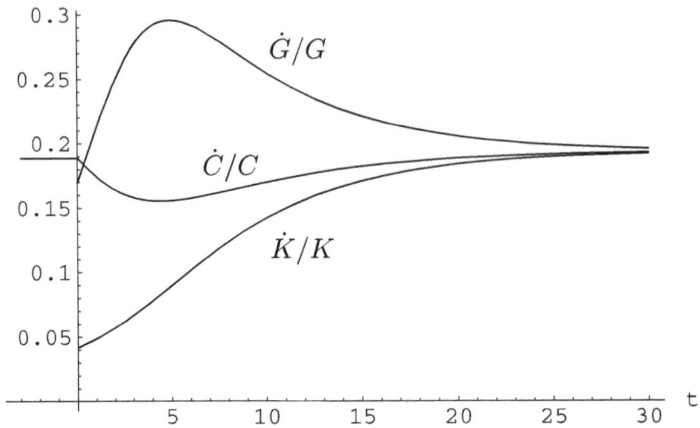

Fig. 4.1 Transitional growth rates of consumption, private capital and public capital after a transition from scenario (iii) to scenario (i) at $t = 0$

with v_{jl} the l-th element of the eigenvector belonging to the negative real eigenvalue ev_j, $j = 1, 2$. C_j, $j = 1, 2$, are constants determined by the initial conditions $x(0)$ and $b(0)$. Setting $t = 0$ gives C_j, $j = 1, 2$, as a function of $x(0)$ and $b(0)$. Inserting these C_j, $j = 1, 2$, in (4.22) gives the unique $c(0)$ on the stable manifold leading to the BGP in the long-run. Given $x(t)$, $b(t)$ and $c(t)$ from (4.20)–(4.22) one can compute the growth rates of C, B, G and K according to (4.15), (4.12), (4.14) and (4.16).

Figure 4.1 shows the transitional growth rates of C, G and K after the government balances its budget at time $t = 0$.

The constant line left of the $t = 0$ axis gives the balanced growth rate of the economy in scenario (iii) which is $g = 0.189$. Switching to a balanced government budget at $t = 0$, by setting $\phi = 0$ and $\psi = (1 - \tau)r$, leads to a downward jump of the growth rate of public capital at $t = 0$ because ϕ is increased from $\phi = -0.005$ to $\phi = 0$ and ψ also rises at $t = 0$ which has a negative effect on public investment, which can be seen from (4.14). Hence, balancing the government budget at $t = 0$ brings about an immediate reduction in public investment, which was to be expected. Since x is fixed at $t = 0$ the growth rate of consumption does not react at $t = 0$. The growth rate of private capital jumps downward at $t = 0$ because the ratio of consumption to private capital rises and compensates the increase in ϕ and ψ. The growth rate of public debt, of course, equals zero from $t = 0$ onward. Over time, the growth rates of consumption, of private capital and of public capital converge to the balanced growth rate of scenario (i) given by $g = 0.193$.

For sake of completeness we want to mention that a change from scenario (iii) to scenario (ii), where public debt grows at a smaller rate than capital in the long-run, gives the same picture as shown in Fig. 4.1 from a qualitative point of view. That is, the growth rate of public capital first jumps down, then rises and overshoots its long-run value before it converges to the balanced growth rate. The growth rate of private consumption declines and then rises again. The private capital stock first jumps down and then rises again and converges to the BGP. But there is a difference in the adjustment path of public debt. Since ϕ rises from $\phi = -0.005$ to $\phi = 0$ the growth rate of public debt jumps down at $t = 0$, but since ψ remains unchanged it is not immediately equal to zero as it is the case when the government switches to the balanced budget scenario. The growth rate of public debt continues to decline for a certain time period and, then, rises again and converges to its new long-run value which is smaller than the growth rates of consumption and capital.

We also want to state that a change from the balanced budget scenario, scenario (i), to scenario (iii), where public debt grows at the same rate as all other variables in the long-run, is just reverse to Fig. 4.1. Thus, both private and public investment jump upwards at $t = 0$ and then converge to the BGP, where the growth rate of public capital overshoots, or better undershoots, its long-run value. The growth rate of consumption rises and then declines again and converges to the balanced growth rate. The growth rate of public debt, which equals zero for $t < 0$, jumps upward at $t = 0$ and then declines again and also approaches the balanced growth rate.

Finally, it should be pointed out that, if one performs a linear analysis around the BGP, the change from one scenario to another scenario is only possible if the BGP values in the old scenario, which are the initial conditions for the new scenario, do not differ too much from the BGP values of the new scenario. For example, setting $\phi = -0.015$ would not allow to study a switch from scenario (iii) to scenario (i) or to scenario (ii). In that case a global analysis would be necessary which, however, is beyond the scope of this book.

In the next subsection we study welfare effects of fiscal policy for our model.

Welfare Analysis

It is well known that growth and welfare maximization are different goals in the endogenous growth model with a productive public capital stock (see Futagami et al. 1993). Therefore, we study welfare effects of fiscal policy in this subsection.

In particular, we are interested in three policy experiments. First, we study the question of whether switching from scenario (iii), where the debt ratio is positive in the long-run, to scenario (i) and scenario (ii) raises welfare. Second, we analyze welfare effects of switching from a balanced budget scenario, scenario (i), to scenario (iii), where the government runs into debt. Third, we calculate welfare for the three scenarios for given initial conditions with respect to the capital stocks and with respect to public debt.

To compute welfare effects we numerically calculate the expression

$$F = \max_{C(t)} \int_0^\infty e^{-\rho t} \ln C(t) dt \,, \tag{4.23}$$

where we set $K(0) = 1$. The value for consumption is obtained by numerically solving Eq. (4.15), with $x(t)$ again given by (4.20)–(4.22).

Table 4.3 Welfare in scenario (iii) and welfare resulting from a transition to scenario (ii) and scenario (i), respectively

	Scenario (iii)	From scenario (iii) to (ii)	From scenario (iii) to (i)
F	−1.174	1.350	1.209

Table 4.4 Welfare in scenario (i) and welfare resulting from a transition to scenario (iii) with $b^{\star} > 0$

	Scenario (i)	From scenario (i) to (iii)
F	−1.037	−8.293

In Table 4.3 we report the outcome of our first policy experiment. As to the parameter values we use those of the last section with $\psi = 0.25$, in scenario (ii) and (iii), and $\phi = -0.005$ in scenario (iii).

Table 4.3 shows that scenario (iii), where debt grows at the balanced growth rate, leads to smaller welfare than a transition from scenario (iii) to scenario (ii), where debt grows in the long-run but at a lower rate than capital and output, and to smaller welfare than a transition to scenario (i), the balanced budget scenario. Comparing scenarios (ii) and (i), one can realize that scenario (i), the balanced budget scenario, yields lower welfare than scenario (ii), where public debt grows in the long-run but less than output.

The reason for this outcome is that the level of consumption at $t = 0$ in scenario (i) rises less than in scenario (ii). On the other hand, the growth rate of consumption temporarily declines and the decline in scenario (ii) is stronger than that in scenario (i). But this transitionally higher growth rate of consumption in scenario (i), compared to scenario (ii), is not sufficient to compensate for the stronger increase of consumption at $t = 0$ in scenario (ii). Therefore, scenario (ii) yields higher welfare than scenario (i) as reported in the table above.

In Table 4.4 we present the outcome of our second policy experiment where the government switches from a balanced budget scenario, scenario (i), to scenario (iii) with a positive government debt. Technically, this is achieved by setting $\phi = -0.005$ giving $b^{\star} = 0.0235$.

Table 4.4 shows that switching from a balanced budget scenario to a scenario where the government runs deficits and accumulates a stock of debt reduces welfare. The reason for this outcome is that the government deficit at $t = 0$ leads to an upward jump of public and private investment and to a decline in the level of consumption at $t = 0$. The growth rate of consumption rises temporarily but the increase is compensated by the decrease in consumption at $t = 0$ and by the lower balanced growth rate so that welfare declines.

In the last experiment, finally, we set the initial conditions with respect to x and b to arbitrary values and, then, compute welfare for the three scenarios. Table 4.5 gives the result of this exercise with $x(0) = 0.03$ and $b(0) = 0.02$.

Table 4.5 confirms the outcome of Table 4.3. It demonstrates that scenario (iii), where public debt grows at the balanced growth rate in the long-run, performs

Table 4.5 Welfare in scenario (i), scenario (ii) and scenario (iii) for given initial conditions $x(0) = 0.03$ and $b(0) = 0.02$

	Scenario (i)	Scenario (ii)	Scenario (iii)
F	1.202	1.317	−1.921

worse than scenario (i) and worse than scenario (ii). Comparing the balanced budget scenario, scenario (i), with scenario (ii), where public debt grows less than capital and consumption in the long-run, shows that scenario (ii) leads to higher welfare than scenario (i).

Hence, the main conclusion we can draw from this subsection is that scenario (iii), where public debt grows at the balanced growth rate in the long-run, performs worse than scenario (i) and worse than scenario (ii) as concerns welfare. Comparing scenario (i) with scenario (ii) shows that scenario (ii) seems to perform better. The reason for this result is that initial private consumption in the balanced budget scenario, scenario (i), is smaller than in scenario (ii), where debt grows but less than output. However, since the difference in welfare is only small, care must be taken in generalizing this result. This holds because it cannot be excluded that the initial conditions of the capital stocks and of government debt may be decisive as to whether scenario (i) or scenario (ii) performs better.

4.2 Effects of a Progressive Income Tax

Up to now we have assumed that the income tax rate is linear. However, in the real world income taxes are typically progressive. Therefore, we now want to analyze effects resulting from a progressive income tax scheme. In the economics literature, Li and Sarte (2004), for example, study an endogenous growth model with heterogeneous households and a balanced government budget but a progressive income tax scheme. They find that a more progressive tax scheme reduces the share of government expenditures, which equals the tax revenue, relative to output because the relative income of the rich household declines. If public spending is productive, a more progressive income tax scheme reduces economic growth through two channels: It reduces both the incentive to invest and the share of productive public spending to output at the same time, implying a smaller growth rate.

In this section, we study the effects of progressive taxation in an endogenous growth model including public debt, where we assume that the primary surplus is an increasing function of public debt, as in the previous section. In contrast to Li and Sarte (2004), however, we analyze a symmetric equilibrium where households have the same capital stock and supply the same amount of labor. Our goal is to study growth effects of progressive tax schemes and to analyze the effects of tax progression on the dynamics of the model.

4.2.1 The Model

Our economy consists of three sectors Greiner (2006): A household sector which receives labor income and income from its saving, a productive sector and the government. First, we describe the household and the productive sector.

4.2.2 The Household and the Productive Sector

The household sector consists of a unit measure of identical households maximizing the welfare functional

$$\max_{c(t)} \int_0^\infty e^{-\rho t} \ln c(t) dt, \tag{4.24}$$

where c is consumption[7] and the utility function is assumed to be logarithmic, $U(c) = \ln c$. The parameter ρ is the subjective discount rate and the household supplies labor l inelastically. The budget constraint is given by

$$(1-\tau)(wl + ra) = \dot{a} + c. \tag{4.25}$$

The variable w is the wage rate and r is the interest rate and $a \equiv b+k$ denotes assets which are equal to public debt held by the household, b, and private capital, k. All variables give per-capita quantities. The parameter $\tau \in (0, 1)$ is the income tax rate. The dot gives the derivative with respect to time and here we neglect depreciation of private capital.

As to the income tax rate we assume a progressive tax scheme where the tax rate τ is given by (cf. Guo and Lansing 1998 and Slobodyan 2005)

$$\tau = 1 - \varsigma \left(\frac{\bar{y}}{y}\right)^{\varepsilon}, \varsigma \in (0, 1],\ \varepsilon \in [0, 1), \tag{4.26}$$

with $\bar{y}$ a base level of income, which is taken as given by households, and y the income of the household. The parameters ς and ε give the level and the slope of the tax schedule. The marginal tax rate τ_m is given by $\tau_m = 1 - \varsigma(1-\varepsilon)(\bar{y}/y)^{\varepsilon}$ and exceeds the average tax rate given by $\tau y/y = 1 - \varsigma(\bar{y}/y)^{\varepsilon}$. For $\varepsilon = 0$ the marginal tax rate is constant and equals the average tax rate.

---

[7] As in the previous section, we omit the time argument t if no ambiguity arises.

The necessary conditions for optimality are obtained as

$$\dot{c} = c\left(\varsigma(1-\varepsilon)\left(\frac{\bar{y}}{y}\right)^{\varepsilon} r - \rho\right) \tag{4.27}$$

$$\lim_{t\to\infty} e^{-\rho t} a/c = 0. \tag{4.28}$$

The productive sector is represented by one firm which behaves competitively and which maximizes static profits. The production function of the firm is given

$$Q = K^{1-\alpha}(LG)^{\alpha}, \tag{4.29}$$

with $\alpha < 1$. The coefficient $(1-\alpha)$ is the private capital share and α gives the labor share and we normalize aggregate labor, L, to be equal to one. The variable G again denotes public capital which is assumed to be a purely public good which is labor augmenting. Normalizing labor by setting $L = 1$, profit maximization yields

$$w = \alpha K^{1-\alpha} G^{\alpha} \tag{4.30}$$

$$r = (1-\alpha)K^{-\alpha} G^{\alpha} \tag{4.31}$$

The Government

The government in our economy receives tax revenues from income taxation and has revenues from issuing government bonds it then uses for governmental investment in a productive public capital stock. Further, the government sets the primary surplus such that it is a positive linear function of public debt which guarantees that public debt is sustainable as shown next above.

The accounting identity describing the accumulation of public debt in continuous time is given by:

$$\dot{B} = rB - S = rB - T + I_p, \tag{4.32}$$

where B stands for public debt, r is the interest rate and S is the government surplus exclusive of interest payments. The variable T gives the tax revenue of the government and I_p is public investment.

As concerns the primary surplus to gross national income ratio, we assume that this ratio is a positive linear function of the debt to gross domestic income ratio and of a constant. The primary surplus ratio, then, can be written as

$$\frac{T - I_p}{Y} = \phi + \psi\left(\frac{B}{Y}\right), \tag{4.33}$$

with $\phi \in \mathbb{R}$, $\psi \in \mathbb{R}_{++}$.

Since the government sticks to rule (4.33) public investment is given by

$$I_p = T - \psi B - \phi Y = Y\left(\left(1 - \varsigma\left(\frac{\bar{Y}}{Y}\right)^{\varepsilon}\right) - \phi\right) - \psi B, \tag{4.34}$$

where we used that $y = Y$ and $\bar{y} = \bar{Y}$ hold in a symmetric equilibrium.

Neglecting depreciation, the differential equation describing the evolution of public capital, then, is written as

$$\dot{G} = I_p = Y\left(\left(1 - \varsigma\left(\frac{\bar{Y}}{Y}\right)^{\varepsilon}\right) - \phi\right) - \psi B. \tag{4.35}$$

It should be mentioned that the budgetary rule (4.33) imposes a constraint on the possibility of the government to control public investment. This holds because a rise in public debt, for whatever reasons, implies that public investment must decrease, for given values of the parameters ϕ and ψ and for a given tax revenue. The reason is that the government must raise the primary surplus such that a fiscal policy remains sustainable when public debt rises. This generates a crowding-out effect of public debt in the model.

Equilibrium Conditions and the Balanced Growth Path

An equilibrium allocation is defined as an allocation such that the firm maximizes profits implying that factor prices equal their marginal products (Eqs. (4.30) and (4.31)), households solve (4.24) subject to (4.25) and the budget constraint of the government is fulfilled. Further, we consider a symmetric equilibrium such that $c = C, b = B, k = K, l = L, y = Y$, and $\bar{y} = \bar{Y}$ hold, where capital letters denote aggregate variables. The variable $\bar{Y}$ is set to the economy-wide average income as in Slobodyan (2005) so that $Y = \bar{Y}$ holds.

The economy-wide resource constraint is obtained from Eqs. (4.25) and (4.32). Thus, the following autonomous system of differential equations completely describes our economy,

$$\frac{\dot{K}}{K} = \left(\frac{G}{K}\right)^{\alpha} - \frac{C}{K} + \psi\left(\frac{B}{K}\right) + \left(\frac{G}{K}\right)^{\alpha}\left(1 + (1-\alpha)\frac{B}{K}\right)(\phi - (1 - \varsigma)) \tag{4.36}$$

$$\frac{\dot{G}}{G} = -\psi\left(\frac{B}{G}\right) - \left(\frac{K}{G}\right)^{1-\alpha}\left(1 + (1-\alpha)\frac{B}{K}\right)(\phi - (1 - \varsigma)) \tag{4.37}$$

$$\frac{\dot{B}}{B} = (1-\alpha)\left(\frac{G}{K}\right)^{\alpha} - \psi - \phi\left(\frac{G}{K}\right)^{\alpha}\left((1-\alpha) + \frac{K}{B}\right) \tag{4.38}$$

$$\frac{\dot{C}}{C} = -\rho + (1-\alpha)\varsigma(1-\varepsilon)\left(\frac{G}{K}\right)^{\alpha} \tag{4.39}$$

A balanced growth path (BGP) is defined as a path on which all endogenous variables grow at the same rate, i.e. $\dot{K}/K = \dot{G}/G = \dot{B}/B = \dot{C}/C$ holds, and the intertemporal budget constraint of the government must hold. Note that the BGP is dynamically efficient[8] and the transversality condition of the household is fulfilled. Since we have posited that the government sets the primary surplus according to (4.33) with $\psi > 0$ any path which satisfies $\dot{K}/K = \dot{G}/G = \dot{B}/B = \dot{C}/C$ is associated with a sustainable public debt.

To analyze our economy around a BGP we define the new variables $x := G/K$, $z := B/K$ and $v := C/K$. Differentiating these variables with respect to time yields a three dimensional system of differential equations given by

$$\dot{x} = x(-\psi z/x - x^{\alpha-1}(1+(1-\alpha)z)(\phi-(1-\varsigma)) - x^{\alpha} - \psi z + v - x^{\alpha}(1+(1-\alpha)z)(\phi-(1-\varsigma))) \tag{4.40}$$

$$\dot{z} = z((1-\alpha)x^{\alpha} - \psi - \phi x^{\alpha}((1+\alpha)+z) - x^{\alpha}(1+(1-\alpha)z)(\phi-(1-\varsigma)) + v - x^{\alpha} - \psi z) \tag{4.41}$$

$$\dot{v} = v((1-\alpha)x^{\alpha}\varsigma(1-\varepsilon) - x^{\alpha} - \rho - x^{\alpha}(1+(1-\alpha)z)(\phi-(1-\varsigma)) + v - \psi z) \tag{4.42}$$

A solution of $\dot{x} = \dot{z} = \dot{v} = 0$ with respect to x, z, v gives a BGP for our model and the corresponding ratios $x^{\star}, z^{\star}, v^{\star}$ on the BGP.[9]

4.2.3 Implications of the Model

In this subsection we first analyze our model for a balanced government budget and no public debt and, then, allowing for public debt.

[8] The difference between the interest rate and the growth on the BGP is strictly positive and constant so that $\lim_{t\to\infty}\int_0^t (r(\mu) - g_y(\mu))d\mu = \infty$ holds.

[9] The $\star$ denotes BGP values and we exclude the economically meaningless BGP $x^{\star} = z^{\star} = v^{\star} = 0$.

The Economy Without Public Debt

To analyze the model for the case of a balanced government budget and where the government has not issued bonds we set $B = \psi = \phi = 0$. The system(4.40)–(4.42) then reduces to a two-dimensional system in x and v given by

$$\dot{x} = x(x^{\alpha-1}(1-\varsigma) - x^{\alpha} + v + x^{\alpha}(1-\varsigma)) \tag{4.43}$$

$$\dot{v} = v(v - \rho + (1-\alpha)x^{\alpha}\varsigma(1-\varepsilon) - \varsigma x^{\alpha}) \tag{4.44}$$

To get insight into our model we first solve (4.44)=0 with respect to v and insert that value in (4.43). Since we exclude the economically meaningless BGP with $x^{\star} = 0$ we can divide the resulting equation by x giving

$$f(x,\cdot) = \rho - (1-\alpha)x^{\alpha}\varsigma(1-\varepsilon) + (1-\varsigma)x^{\alpha-1} \tag{4.45}$$

It is easily seen that $\lim_{x\to 0} f(\cdot) = +\infty$, $\lim_{x\to\infty} f(\cdot) = -\infty$ and $\partial f(\cdot)/\partial x < 0$ holds, implying that there exists a unique positive $x^{\star}$ which solves $f(\cdot) = 0$ and, thus, a unique BGP. It should be noted that this result is independent of the value for ε determining the slope of the tax scheme as long as $\varepsilon < 1$, i.e. as long as a regressive tax scheme is excluded. As concerns the local stability of the BGP it can easily be shown that it is a saddle point.[10]

In order to study growth effects of ε we note that the balanced growth rate is given by Eq. (4.37). Differentiating (4.37) with respect to ε gives

$$\frac{\partial(\dot{G}/G)}{\partial\varepsilon} = (\alpha-1)x^{\alpha-2}(1-\varsigma)\frac{\partial x^{\star}}{\partial\varepsilon}. \tag{4.46}$$

The sign of $\partial x^{\star}/\partial\varepsilon$ is obtained by implicit differentiation from (4.45) as

$$\partial x^{\star}/\partial\varepsilon = -(\partial f(\cdot)/\partial\varepsilon)/(\partial f(\cdot)/\partial x) > 0.$$

This shows that a more progressive tax system leads to a smaller growth rate. It should be mentioned that, in contrast to Li and Sarte (2004), a more progressive tax scheme raises the ratio of public to private capital on the BGP. So, a more progressive tax system implies that the tax revenue rises and, as a consequence, the ratio of public to private capital increases. This effect raises the marginal product of private capital and tends to lead to a higher the growth rate. However, a more progressive tax system has a negative direct effect on the marginal product of private capital and it is this negative direct effect which dominates the positive indirect effect. Thus, a more progressive tax system always reduces the long-run balanced growth rate. That means that we cannot observe an inverted U-shaped relationship

[10]See the appendix to this chapter.

between the growth rate and the degree of progression as in the case of a flat rate income tax (see for example Greiner and Hanusch 1998).

The Model with Permanent Deficits

With public debt, the system (4.40)–(4.42) completely describes the economy. Again, a BGP is a vector $x^\star, z^\star, v^\star$ such that $\dot{x} = \dot{z} = \dot{v}$ holds. To derive a first result for our economy on the BGP we set $\dot{v}/v = 0$ and solve that equation with respect to v. Inserting the resulting value in $\dot{b}/b$ gives

$$h := (\rho - \psi) + x^\alpha((1-\alpha)(1-\varsigma)(1-\varepsilon) - \phi(1-\alpha+1/b)) \tag{4.47}$$

Assuming that b is positive on the BGP, implying that the government is a debtor which is more realistic than the assumption that the government is a creditor, a first result can be derived from (4.47). If the subjective discount rate of the household, ρ, is larger than the coefficient giving the increase in the primary surplus to a marginal increase in public debt, ψ, the parameter ϕ must be positive such that a BGP can exist. This means that the primary surplus must rise with a rising gross domestic income if the government does not raise the primary surplus sufficiently as public debt rises, i.e. if ψ is not sufficiently large. From an economic point of view, this seems plausible. If the government does not react to higher debt, it must raise the primary surplus as the gross domestic income increases in order to stabilize public debt. Otherwise, a BGP cannot exist. Of course, this condition does not hold if the government is a creditor, that is if $b < 0$ holds.

In order to gain further insight into our model we resort to numerical examples. As a benchmark for our simulations we set the elasticity of production with respect to public capital to 25 %, i.e. $\alpha = 0.25$.[11] The rate of time preference is set to 30 %, $\rho = 0.3$. Interpreting one time period as 3 (5, 10) years then gives an annual rate of time preference of 9 (5.4, 2.7) %. ς is set to 0.9 implying an average tax rate of 10 %.

Figure 4.2 shows the average tax rate (10 %) and the marginal tax rate depending on the value of ε. While the average tax rate is constant and only depends on ς, which is set to $\varsigma = 0.9$, the marginal tax rate rises with the value of ε. For example, for $\varepsilon = 0.1$ the marginal tax rate is about 20 % and for $\varepsilon = 0.4$ the marginal tax rate is roughly 45 %.

In Table 4.6 we nest report results of our simulations for $\psi = 0.15$ and $\psi = 0.5$ and for different values of ε with $\phi = 0.015$, where g denotes the balanced growth rate. Recall that $\phi > 0$ means that a higher gross domestic income raises the primary surplus.

Table 4.6 shows that higher values of ε imply a smaller balanced growth rate although the ratio of public capital to private capital, $x^\star$, rises. Thus, the result

[11] For a survey of empirical studies giving estimates for that parameter see e.g. Pfähler et al. (1996).

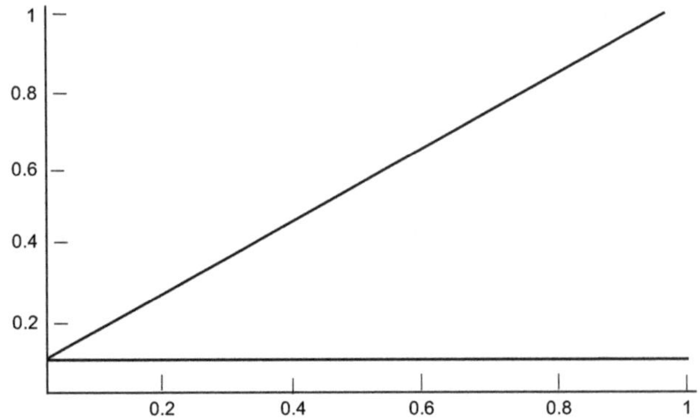

Fig. 4.2 Average tax rate (constant) and marginal tax rate (rising) as a function of ϕ

Table 4.6 Long-run growth rate, endogenous variables on the BGP and eigenvalues for different values of ε and ψ with $\phi = 0.015$

	$\psi = 0.15$				$\psi = 0.5$			
ε	$b^\star$	$x^\star$	g	Eigenvalues	$b^\star$	$x^\star$	g	Eigenvalues
$\varepsilon = 0$	0.06	0.29	0.195	$(+,+,-)$	−0.08	0.43	0.246	$(+,-,-)$
$\varepsilon = 0.1$	0.05	0.36	0.17	$(+,+,-)$	−0.16	0.61	0.232	$(+,-,-)$
$\varepsilon = 0.2$	0.04	0.46	0.144	$(+,+,-)$			no BGP	

obtained for the model without government debt also seems to hold for the model with public debt. On the one hand, a more progressive tax system leads to a higher ratio of public to private capital as Table 4.6 shows. On the other hand, however, a more progressive tax scheme by itself has a distortionary effect and makes the household reduce investment.

As in the model without public debt, it is the negative effect which dominates and, thus, reduces the long-run balanced growth rate. Further, one also realizes that with $\psi = 0.5$ no BGP with sustained growth exists for $\varepsilon \geq 0.2$.

The column 'eigenvalues' in Table 4.6 gives the sign of the eigenvalues of the Jacobian matrix evaluated at the BGP. If there is one negative real eigenvalue, $(+,+,-)$, there exists a one dimensional stable manifold. If one takes $x(0)$ and $z(0)$ as given, this implies that the set of initial conditions$\{x(0), z(0), v(0)\}$ lying on the stable manifold has Lebesgue measure zero. In this case the economy can converge to the BGP in the long-run only if the government levies a lump-sum tax at $t = 0$ which is used to control $B(0)$ implying that $B(0)$, and thus $z(0)$, are not fixed at $t = 0$. The variables $B(0)$ and $C(0)$, then, must be chosen such that $z(0)$ and $v(0)$ lie on the stable manifold and these values are uniquely determined. If there are two negative eigenvalues and $B(0)$ is fixed, the equilibrium is again determinate in the sense that there exists a unique $C(0)$, which can be chosen freely, so that the economy converges to the BGP. If both $B(0)$ and $C(0)$ can be chosen at $t = 0$ there exists a continuum of initial values implying that the equilibrium is indeterminate.

For sake of completeness, we should mention that for $\psi = 0.4$ no BGP exists for $\varepsilon \geq 0.05$. In the next table we make simulations where we set $\phi = -0.015$,

Table 4.7 Long-run growth rate, endogenous variables on the BGP and eigenvalues for different values of ε and ψ with $\phi = -0.015$

	$\psi = 0.15$				$\psi = 0.5$			
ε	$b^\star$	$x^\star$	g	Eigenvalues	$b^\star$	$x^\star$	g	Eigenvalues
$\varepsilon = 0$	-0.056	0.4	0.238	$(+, +, -)$	0.08	0.26	0.184	$(+, Re-, Re-)$
$\varepsilon = 0.1$	-0.04	0.48	0.206	$(+, +, -)$	0.11	0.24	0.126	$(+, Re-, Re-)$
$\varepsilon = 0.2$	-0.04	0.6	0.174	$(+, +, -)$	0.15	0.15	0.035	$(+, Re-, Re-)$
$\varepsilon = 0.3$	-0.03	0.77	0.143	$(+, +, -)$	0.13	0.06	-0.064	$(+, Re+, Re+)$

implying that the primary surplus negatively depends on gross domestic income (Table 4.7).

From a qualitative point of view, the results are the same as those in Table 4.6. Thus, a more progressive tax scheme reduces the balanced growth rate and destabilizes the economy.[12] Further, a higher value of ψ stabilizes the economy. Hence, the differential equation system is stable for $\psi = 0.5$ (except for $\varepsilon = 0.3$) while it is unstable for $\psi = 0.15$ if one takes $B(0)$ as fixed.

In the next section we analyze our model with productive public spending as a flow variable, instead of a stock as we have done up to now.

4.3 Productive Public Spending as a Flow

We begin our presentation with a description of the structure of our model that extends the basic endogenous growth model with productive public spending presented by Barro (1990) by integrating public deficits and public debt. Our model can also be seen as an extension of the model by Kamiguchi and Tamai (2012) by assuming a more general utility function as in Greiner (2013c). In our model, the intertemporal elasticity of substitution of consumption can take more values than 1, in contrast to in Kamiguchi and Tamai (2012) who confine their investigation to the case of a logarithmic utility function.

4.3.1 *The Private Sector*

The private sector in our economy is characterized by a continuum of rational and identical households that have perfect foresight. Rationality in this framework implies that households maximize their utility over an infinite time horizon arising from per-capita consumption, $C(t)$, subject to the budget constraint. Population

[12]The symbol $Re-$ $(Re+)$ means that the eigenvalue is complex with negative (positive) real part. Note that the system does not undergo a Hopf Bifurcation as ψ is varied.

is constant and set equal to one. The maximization problem of the representative household can be written as,

$$\max_{C} \int_{0}^{\infty} e^{-\rho t} \, (C^{1-\sigma} - 1)/(1-\sigma) \, dt, \tag{4.48}$$

subject to

$$\dot{K} + \dot{B} = rB + (1-\tau)Y - C. \tag{4.49}$$

The coefficient ρ is the household's rate of time preference, r is the interest rate and $1/\sigma$ gives the intertemporal elasticity of substitution of consumption and the dot over a variable gives the derivative with respect to time. The variable Y gives GDP which is equal to output in the economy, K denotes private capital where we neglect depreciation, B stands for government bonds and $\tau \in (0,1)$ is the constant tax rate on output.

Output Y is given by

$$Y = K^{(1-\alpha)} G^{\alpha}, \tag{4.50}$$

with $(1-\alpha) \in (0,1)$ the elasticity of output with respect to private capital and α the elasticity of output with respect to productive public spending G that is now a flow variable. In equilibrium the interest rate equals the net marginal product of capital and is given by

$$r = (1-\tau)(1-\alpha)K^{-\alpha} G^{\alpha}. \tag{4.51}$$

4.3.2 *The Government*

Starting point of our considerations is the period budget constraint of the government that is given by the following differential equation,

$$\dot{B} = rB - \tau Y + G: \tag{4.52}$$

In addition, the government sticks to the intertemporal budget constraint that is given by the following expression, $\lim_{t\to\infty} e^{-\int_0^t r(\mu)d\mu} B(t) = 0$, stating that the present-value of public debt converges to zero asymptotically.

In order to fulfill its intertemporal budget constraint, the government sticks to the primary surplus rule which states that the primary surplus, S, relative to GDP, Y, is a function that positively depends on the debt to GDP ratio B/Y and on the term ϕ that reflects the discretionary scope of the government. Thus, this rule can be written as,

$$\frac{S}{Y} = \psi \left(\frac{B}{Y} \right) - \phi, \; \psi \in \mathbb{R}_{++}, \phi \in \mathbb{R}, \tag{4.53}$$

with ψ the average reaction coefficient determining the reaction of the primary surplus to variations in debt, relative to GDP respectively, that is strictly positive and ϕ showing how the level of the primary surplus varies as GDP rises. The coefficient ϕ may be positive or negative. With the primary surplus rule (4.53) the growth rate of public debt is obtained as,

$$\frac{\dot{B}}{B} = r - \psi + \phi\left(\frac{Y}{B}\right). \tag{4.54}$$

The government sticks to the primary surplus rule (4.53) such that the evolution of public debt is given by (4.54). This gives public spending as

$$G = (\tau + \phi)Y - \psi B \tag{4.55}$$

Defining $c_p := G/Y$ as public spending relative to GDP yields $c_p = (\tau + \phi) - \psi(B/Y)$ such that the production function can be rewritten as

$$Y = Kc_p(x, \cdot)^{\alpha/(1-\alpha)}, \tag{4.56}$$

with $x := B/Y \geq 0$ the debt to GDP ratio, where we limit our analysis to the case where public debt is positive.

4.3.3 Analysis of the Model

In this section we analyze our model where we are particularly interested in multiple balanced growth paths. First, we derive the differential equations that describe our economy.

Solving the optimization problem of the household, using $r = (1-\tau)(1-\alpha)K^{(1-\alpha)-1}G^{\alpha} = (1-\tau)(1-\alpha)c_p^{\alpha/(1-\alpha)}$ and (4.54) leads to the following growth rates of consumption and of public debt,

$$\dot{C} = C\left((1-\tau)(1-\alpha)c_p(x,\cdot)^{\alpha/(1-\alpha)} - \rho\right)/\sigma, \tag{4.57}$$

$$\dot{B} = B\left((1-\tau)(1-\alpha)c_p(x,\cdot)^{\alpha/(1-\alpha)} - \psi + \phi/x\right). \tag{4.58}$$

Finally, combining the budget constraint of the household, (4.49), with that of the government, (4.54), gives the economy-wide resource constraint as,

$$\dot{K} = K\left(c_p(x,\cdot)^{\alpha/(1-\alpha)}(1 - c_p(x,\cdot)) - z\right), \tag{4.59}$$

with $z := C/K$. Thus, the economy is completely described by Eqs. (4.57)–(4.59) plus the usual transversality conditions.

To analyze our economy further, we define a balanced growth path.

Definition 6 A balanced growth path (BGP) is a path such that consumption, capital, public spending and output grow at the same strictly positive constant growth rate, i.e. $\dot{C}/C = \dot{K}/K = \dot{G}/G = \dot{Y}/Y = g$, $g > 0$, $g = constant$, and either

(i) $\dot{B} = 0$ (balanced budget) or
(ii) $\dot{B}/B = \dot{C}/C = \dot{K}/K = \dot{Y}/Y = g$ (permanent deficit).

In this section we do not consider the scenario with public debt growing but less than GDP because we are only interested in allocative effects of public debt and deficits and not in welfare effects. Since in the long-run the balanced budget scenario is equivalent to the scenario with debt growing but less than GDP, considering the balanced budget scenario alone is sufficient.

Differentiating the variables z and x with respect to time leads to the following two-dimensional differential equation system

$$\dot{z} = z\big((1-\tau)(1-\alpha)c_p(x,\cdot)^{\alpha/(1-\alpha)}/\sigma - c_p(x,\cdot)^{\alpha/(1-\alpha)}(1-c_p(x,\cdot)) + z - \rho/\sigma\big) \tag{4.60}$$

$$\dot{x} = x\,\varpi(x,\cdot)\left(c_p(x,\cdot)^{\alpha/(1-\alpha)}((1-\tau)(1-\alpha) - 1 + c_p(x,\cdot)) - \psi + \phi/x + z\right), \tag{4.61}$$

with $\varpi(x,\cdot)$ defined as $\varpi := (1-\alpha)(\tau+\phi-\psi x)/((1-\alpha)(\tau+\phi)-\psi x)$ where we used $\dot{Y}/Y = \dot{K}/K + (\alpha/(1-\alpha))\dot{c}_p/c_p$ with $\dot{c}_p = -\psi\dot{x}$.

In the case of a balanced budget we have[13] $x^\star = 0$ and $\dot{z} = 0$ on a BGP so that $\dot{C}/C = \dot{K}/K = \dot{Y}/Y$, $\dot{c}_p = 0$. With permanent deficits a BGP is obtained for $\dot{z} = \dot{x} = 0$ which implies $\dot{C}/C = \dot{K}/K = \dot{Y}/Y = \dot{B}/B$, $\dot{c}_p = 0$ and for the long-run debt to GDP ratio $x^\star > 0$. First, we analyze the balanced government budget, case (i) in Definition 1.

Balanced Government Budget

Proposition 20 demonstrates that in the case of a balanced budget there is a unique saddle point stable BGP.

Proposition 20 *Assume that the government runs a balanced budget. Then, there exists a unique BGP that is a saddle point.*

Proof See the appendix to this chapter. □

Proposition 20 shows that in case of a balanced budget, the BGP is unique and saddle point stable. It can also be shown that the balanced budget scenarios always goes along with a higher balanced growth rate than the scenario with

[13]Again, the star * denotes BGP values.

permanent deficits. The economic mechanism behind that outcome is that a zero debt to GDP ratio implies that the primary surplus relative to GDP also equals zero so that the government does not have to use public resources for unproductive interest payments and for the debt service.[14] The result is stated in the following Proposition 21.

Proposition 21 *A balanced government budget yields a higher balanced growth rate than a scenario with permanent deficits.*

Proof See the appendix to this chapter. □

As concerns the dynamics, the case of permanent public deficits is more interesting because it may give rise to multiple BGPs as will be shown in the next subsection.

Permanent Public Deficits

The following proposition characterizes the long-run behavior of our economy with permanent deficits.

Proposition 22 *For* $1/\sigma < 1$, $\phi > 0$ *and for* $1/\sigma > 1$, $\phi < 0$ *existence of a BGP implies that it is unique. For* $1/\sigma < 1$, $\phi < 0$ *and for* $1/\sigma > 1$, $\phi > 0$ *multiple BGPs can arise.*

Proof See the appendix to this chapter. □

Proposition 22 shows that the intertemporal elasticity of substitution of consumption, $1/\sigma$, and the way how governments set the primary surplus as GDP rises, ϕ, are decisive concerning multiplicity of BGPs. We should like to point out that in this section $\phi > (<) 0$ implies that the primary surplus declines (rises) with a rising GDP meaning that the government puts a small (large) weight on stabilizing public debt. It should also be noted that ϕ reflects the discretionary scope the government has in determining its fiscal policy.

Proposition 22 states that multiple BGPs may occur depending on the intertemporal elasticity of substitution of consumption and on how governments set the primary surplus as GDP rise. In the following corollary to that proposition we give a condition for the emergence of exactly two BGPs.

Corollary 2 *Assume that* $(\tau + \phi)(\rho/\sigma) - \psi\tau < (>) \, 0$ *holds for* $1/\sigma < 1$, $\phi < 0$ $(1/\sigma > 1, \phi > 0)$*. Then, existence of a BGP implies that there are two BGPs.*

Proof See the appendix to this chapter. □

[14] Here, we exclude the situation with a negative government debt.

Before we interpret the outcome we state some results with respect to stability in Proposition 23 where we assume that the condition of Corollary 2 is fulfilled so that there exist two BGPs in case of multiple BGPs.

Proposition 23 *For* $1/\sigma < 1$, $\phi > 0$ *the BGP is saddle point stable if and only if* $x^\star < (1-\alpha)\bar{x}$, *with* $\bar{x} := (\tau + \phi)/\psi$. *For* $1/\sigma > 1$, $\phi < 0$ *the BGP is saddle point stable if and only if* $x^\star > (1-\alpha)\bar{x}$.

For $1/\sigma > 1$, $\phi > 0$ *both BGPs are saddle point stable for* $x_1^\star < (1-\alpha)\bar{x} < x_2^\star$, *with* $x_1^\star$, $x_2^\star$ *the debt to GDP ratio on the first and second BGP, respectively. For* $1/\sigma < 1$, $\phi < 0$ *at most one BGP is saddle point stable.*

Proof See the appendix to this chapter. □

The variable $\bar{x}$ is that value of the debt to GDP ratio for which public spending relative to GDP, c_p, becomes zero. Hence, the debt to GDP ratio cannot exceed the upper bar $\bar{x}$.

Propositions 22 and 23 demonstrate that the BGP is unique and saddle point stable for a relatively small intertemporal elasticity of substitution of consumption, $1/\sigma < 1$, and when the government puts a small weight on stabilizing public debt but instead prefers to raise public spending as GDP grows, $\phi > 0$, provided the debt to GDP ratio on the BGP is relatively small, i.e. lower than $(1-\alpha)\bar{x}$. That makes sense from an economic point of view because with a small debt to GDP ratio, the goal of stabilizing public debt is less important than financing growth enhancing public spending. If, on the other hand, the debt to GDP ratio on the BGP is relatively large, i.e. $x^\star > (1-\alpha)\bar{x}$, the government must put a high weight on stabilizing public debt such that convergence to this BGP can be achieved. In that case, stabilizing public debt is more important than financing productive public spending.

With a high intertemporal elasticity of substitution, $1/\sigma > 1$, there exist two BGPs if the government puts a small weight on stabilizing debt but prefers to invest in productive public spending as GDP rises, $\phi > 0$. In such a situation, the economy converges to the high growth path when the initial debt to GDP ratio is smaller than the threshold $(1-\alpha)\bar{x}$. With an initial debt ratio larger than $(1-\alpha)\bar{x}$ the economy converges to the low growth path in the long-run. In the latter situation, the initial debt ratio is high requiring a lot of public resources that cannot be used for productive public spending so that only convergence to the low growth BGP is feasible. A high intertemporal elasticity of substitution of consumption implies that consumption of the household strongly reacts to variations in the interest rate. Consequently, in contrast to the case $1/\sigma < 1$, $\phi > 0$, there now exists a second saddle point stable BGP since the household is willing to raise initial consumption relative to private capital when the return to capital is small which holds for a high initial debt ratio. Figure 4.3 gives the phase diagram for $1/\sigma > 1$, $\phi > 0$ and illustrates the situation of two saddle point stable BGPs. The arrows on the linearized stable manifold of the two saddle points indicate the direction of movement of the two variables.

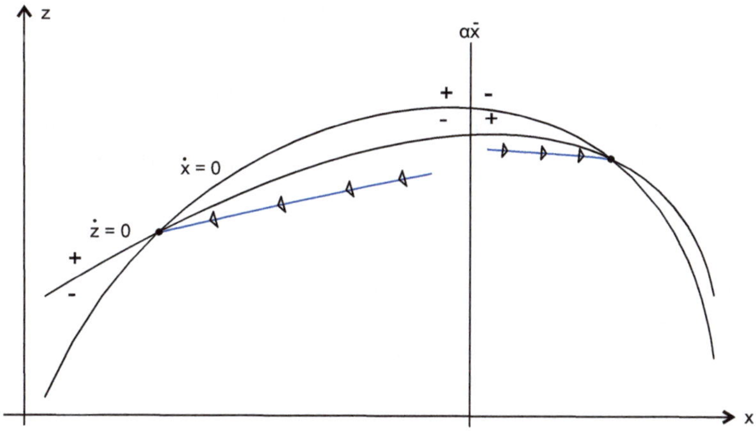

Fig. 4.3 Two saddle point stable BGPs for $1/\sigma > 1, \phi > 0$

If, on the other hand, the government puts a high weight on stabilizing public debt, $\phi < 0$, and the intertemporal elasticity of substitution is large, $1/\sigma > 1$, a saddle point stable BGP is given for a relatively large value of public debt relative to GDP, $x^\star > (1-\alpha)\bar{x}$. In this case the government has to finance productive public spending by deficits such that saddle point stable growth is feasible in the long-run. Note also that there are not two BGPs in this situation, although the intertemporal elasticity of substitution is high, since the household does not expect to get higher income in the future when he renounces to consumption today. The latter holds because the government puts a high weight on stabilizing public debt instead of raising growth enhancing productive public spending as GDP rises, $\phi < 0$.

Finally, when the intertemporal elasticity of substitution is small, $1/\sigma < 1$, multiple BGPs may also arise when the government puts a high weight on stabilizing public debt, $\phi < 0$. In that case, however, at most one of the two BGPs is saddle point stable because the household is not very willing to vary its initial consumption to private capital ratio (due to the small intertemporal elasticity of substitution) for different values of the initial debt to GDP ratio which imply different interest rates. Before we present some numerical examples to illustrate the emergence of multiple BGPs we derive a condition that must be fulfilled such that a deficit financed increase in public investment raises long-run growth.

Proposition 21 in Sect. 4.3.3 has shown that a balanced government budget, where the debt to GDP ratio becomes zero on the balanced growth path, yields maximum growth. However, that does not mean that a deficit financed increase of productive public spending always reduces long-run growth. Instead, a situation is feasible where deficit financed public spending is productive in a way such that the initial increase in public debt is compensated so that the economy ends up with higher long-run growth. In order to get insight into that problem, we next perform comparative statics with respect to a deficit financed increase of productive public spending modeled by an increase in the fiscal parameter ϕ. The result is given in Proposition 24.

Proposition 24 *Assume that a saddle point stable BGP exists. Then, a deficit financed increase in productive public spending raises (reduces) the balanced growth rate if and only if the balanced growth rate falls short of (exceeds) $\bar{g}$ with $\bar{g}$ given by* $\bar{g} = \left((1-\tau)(1-\alpha)c_p((1-\alpha)\bar{x},\cdot)^{\alpha/(1-\alpha)} - \rho\right)/\sigma$.

Proof See the appendix to this chapter. □

Proposition 24 shows that economies with a low balanced growth rate and a high debt to GDP ratio will experience positive growth effects of higher deficit financed productive public spending while the reverse holds for economies with high growth and a low debt to GDP ratio. In the case of two saddle point stable BGPs the balanced growth rate of the BGP with high growth declines while the growth rate of the BGP with low growth rises which is equivalent to the outcome obtained in Futagami et al. (2008). Next, we present some examples to illustrate our analytical results for the case of multiple BGPs.

First we set $1/\sigma = 1.35$ and $\phi = 0.065$ which gives rise to two BGPs. The other parameter values are $(1-\alpha) = 0.7$, $\tau = 0.35$, $\psi = 0.15$ and $\rho = 0.125$. Interpreting one time period to comprise 5 years implies that the annual rate of time preference is about 2.4 %. The first BGP goes along with a growth rate of 18.9 % that corresponds to an average annual growth rate of about 3.5 %. The associated debt to GDP ratio is $x^\star = 0.878$ which is smaller than $(1-\alpha)\bar{x} = 1.94$. The eigenvalues of the Jacobian are given by $ev_1 = 0.171$, $ev_2 = -0.093$. Note that we have $\rho - (1-\sigma)g = 0.076$ for this BGP such that the utility functional (3.1) remains bounded. The second BGP is associated with a growth rate of 0.8 % that corresponds to an average annual growth rate of 0.16 % meaning that this economy is stagnating. The associated debt ratio is $x^\star = 2.4$. The eigenvalues of the Jacobian are $ev_1 = 0.194$, $ev_2 = -0.076$ showing that this BGP is a saddle point, too.

To illustrate the outcome with $1/\sigma < 1$, $\phi < 0$ we set $1/\sigma = 0.3$, $\phi = -0.015$ and $1/\sigma = 0.75$, $\phi = -0.0035$. Table 4.8 shows the results for this numerical example demonstrating that there exists only one saddle point stable BGP for this parameter constellation.[15]

Table 4.8 BGPs for $1/\sigma < 1$ and $\phi < 0$

$1/\sigma, \phi$		Eigenvalues	$x^\star$	g	$(1-\alpha)\bar{x}$
$1/\sigma = 0.3$,	1st BGP:	$ev_1 = 0.368$, $ev_2 = 0.076$	0.189	0.045	1.563
$\phi = -0.015$	2nd BGP:	$ev_1 = 1.413$, $ev_2 = -0.258$	1.518	0.015	1.563
$1/\sigma = 0.75$,	1st BGP:	$ev_1 = 0.293$, $ev_2 = 0.009$	0.295	0.111	1.617
$\phi = -0.0035$	2nd BGP:	$ev_1 = 0.306$, $ev_2 = -0.011$	0.762	0.089	1.617

[15]The given growth rate refers to one time period interpreted as 5 years above.

In the next section we analyze how our results derived up to now change when we assume that the labor market is characterized by wage rigidities giving rise to persistent unemployment.

4.4 The Role of Wage Rigidity and Unemployment

In the previous sections we analyzed the role of public debt and public deficits assuming that the government uses its deficit to finance productive public spending or to finance public investment in a productive public capital stock. In this section we take up the latter approach, but we suppose that labor markets may be characterized by wage rigidities and by unemployment. We then consider two cases. First, we analyze the case with flexible wages as a benchmark implying that the unemployment rate is equal to the natural rate of unemployment. The goal, then, is to analyze the model assuming a balanced government budget and to compare the growth performance to a scenario with persistent deficits. In addition, growth effects of deficit financed public investment are studied as well. In a next step, wages are assumed to be rigid and the growth rate of the wage rate can be described by a Phillips curve that is derived from trade unions' wage setting behavior as in Chap. 3.4. The section again compares a balanced budget scenario to a scenario with permanent deficits and analyzes growth effects of deficit financed public investment.

The motivation to allow for wage rigidities and unemployment in an endogenous growth model is the observation that many European countries experience persistent unemployment in spite of permanently growing GDPs. Therefore, constructing a growth model featuring that characteristic and analyzing effects of fiscal policy within such a model seems to be justified.

The rest of that section is organized as follows. In the next section, we present the basic structure of our model. Then we analyze our model where we assume flexible wages and in the following section we study the model assuming wage rigidities. The following section discusses the economic mechanisms behind the results in detail and compares the outcome to that in the model where unemployment is absent.

4.4.1 The Endogenous Growth Model

Our economy consists of three sectors: A household sector which receives labor income and income from its saving, a productive sector and the government. First, we describe the household sector.

The Household Sector

The household sector is represented by one household which maximizes the discounted stream of utility arising from per-capita consumption, $C(t)$, over an infinite time horizon subject to its budget constraint, taking factor prices as given. The utility function is assumed to be logarithmic, $U(C) = \ln C$, and the household inelastically supplies L units of labor of which L^d is demanded by the productive sector. The rest $L - L^d$ is unemployed and the household receives unemployment benefits of ϱw per unemployed labor, where w is the wage rate and $\varrho \in (0, 1)$.[16] We assume that unemployment payments in our economy are strictly positive and sufficiently high so that unemployed can lead dignified lives. In addition, unemployed must pursue simple activities, organized by the government, that are skill preserving. Hence, unemployment does not lead to a loss of human capital and unemployed labor can again be employed in the production process in the economy. Total labor supply L is constant over time. The maximization problem of the household can be written as,

$$\max_{C} \int_0^{\infty} e^{-\rho t} \ln C \, dt, \tag{4.62}$$

subject to

$$(1-\tau)\left(wL^d + rK + r_B B\right) + \varrho w(L - L^d) = \dot{W} + C + \delta K. \tag{4.63}$$

The coefficient ρ is the household's rate of time preference, r is the return to capital and r_B is the interest rate on government bonds. $W \equiv B + K$ gives wealth which is equal to public debt, B, and private capital, K, which depreciates at the rate δ. Finally, $\tau \in (0, 1)$ is the constant income tax rate and we assume that unemployment benefits are not subject to the income tax. The dot over a variable again gives the derivative with respect to time.

A no-arbitrage condition requires that the return to capital equals the return to government bonds yielding $r_B = r - \delta/(1 - \tau)$. Thus, the budget constraint of the household can be written as

$$\dot{W} = (1-\tau)\left(wL^d + rW\right) + \varrho w(L - L^d) - \delta W - C. \tag{4.64}$$

To solve this problem we formulate the current-value Hamiltonian which is written as

$$\mathcal{H} = \ln C + \lambda\left((1-\tau)\left(wL^d + rW\right) + \varrho w(L - L^d) - C - \delta W\right) \tag{4.65}$$

[16] From now on we again omit the time argument t if no ambiguity arises.

Necessary optimality conditions are given by

$$C^{-1} = \lambda \tag{4.66}$$

$$\dot{\lambda} = (\rho + \delta)\lambda - \lambda(1 - \tau)\,r \tag{4.67}$$

If the transversality condition $\lim_{t\to\infty} e^{-\rho t} W/C = 0$ holds, which is fulfilled for a time path on which assets grow at the same rate as consumption, the necessary conditions are also sufficient.

The Productive Sector and the Labor Market

The productive sector is represented by one firm which behaves competitively and which maximizes static profits. The production function of the firm is

$$Y = K^{1-\alpha}\left(GL^{d}\right)^{\alpha}. \tag{4.68}$$

Y is output, G denotes public capital and $\alpha \in (0,1)$ gives the elasticity of output with respect to public capital and $(1-\alpha)$ is the private capital share. With this formulation public capital is labor augmenting implying that it raises the productivity of labor input. Profit maximization gives the interest rate as

$$r = (1-\alpha)(Y/K) \tag{4.69}$$

In case of flexible wages, implying a vertical Phillips curve, labor demand equals its natural level, L^n, and the wage rate is determined by the marginal productivity rule. Thus, we get

$$w = \alpha(L^n)^{\alpha-1}K^{1-\alpha}G^{\alpha}. \tag{4.70}$$

The unemployment rate, then, is equal to its natural rate and is given by $1 - L^n/L$. At this point we should like to point out that we assume that labor supply exceeds labor demand, that is $L \geq L^d$ holds. Thus, there is no rationing of the productive sector in the economy.

In case of rigid wages, labor demand is again obtained from the firm maximizing profits. This leads to

$$L^d = \alpha^{1/(1-\alpha)}(w/K)^{1/(\alpha-1)}(G/K)^{\alpha/(1-\alpha)}. \tag{4.71}$$

The reason for rigid wages are labor market imperfections due to trade unions setting the wage rate. As concerns the wage setting process we follow Raurich et al. (2006) and assume that there is a large number of unions that set the wage rate in order to maximize the following expression:

$$\max_{w}\left((1-\tau)w - w^s\right)^{\gamma_w} L^d(\cdot) \tag{4.72}$$

with $L^d(\cdot)$ given by (4.71), w^s denoting the reference wage and the coefficient $\gamma_w \in (0,1)$ gives a measure of the weight gap in the unions' objective function. Hence, trade unions maximize the difference between the net wage rate and the reference wage times labor demand. The solution to the optimization problem yields the wage rate as

$$w = \frac{w^s}{(1-\tau)\,(1-\gamma_w(1-\alpha))} \tag{4.73}$$

As concerns the reference wage w^s there exist several approaches in the literature and we again follow Raurich et al. (2006) as in Sect. 3.4. Thus, we the reference wage equals workers' cumulated past average labor income where income further back in time contributes less than more recent labor income. In particular, we assume exponentially declining weights put on average labor income further back in time. Hence, the reference wage can be written as

$$w^s = \theta \int_{-\infty}^{t} e^{-\theta(t-s)} z_a(s)ds, \tag{4.74}$$

with z_a the workers' average income given by $z_a = (1-\tau)wL^d/L + \varrho w(L-L^d)/L$. The parameter $\theta > 0$ determines the weight attributed to more recent income. The higher θ, the larger the weight given to more recent levels of average income compared to income further back in time.

Differentiating (4.73) with respect to time and using (4.74) yields the growth rate of the wage rate as

$$\frac{\dot{w}}{w} = \theta\,\frac{(1-\tau)L^d/L + \varrho(L-L^d)/L}{(1-\tau)\,(1-\gamma_w(1-\alpha))} - \theta \tag{4.75}$$

Defining

$$\frac{\bar{L}}{L} = \left(\frac{(1-\tau)(1-\gamma_w(1-\alpha)) - \varrho}{(1-\tau)-\varrho}\right) \text{ and } \psi_L = \frac{\theta(1-\tau) - \theta\varrho}{(1-\tau)(1-\gamma_w(1-\alpha))}$$

the evolution of the wage rate can be written as[17]

$$\frac{\dot{w}}{w} = \beta_L\left(\frac{L^d - \bar{L}}{L}\right), \tag{4.76}$$

with $\bar{L}$ the normal level of employment in the labor market in the sense that there is no tendency for a change in the wage rate if labor demand is equal to that value. The

[17]Note that $(1-\tau) > \varrho$ must hold for $\psi_L > 0$ and, thus, $(1-\tau)(1-\gamma_w(1-\alpha)) > \varrho$ for $\bar{L}/L > 0$.

parameter $\beta_L > 0$ gives the speed of adjustment determining how strongly actual labor demand relative to the normal level of employment affects the growth rate of the wage rate.

Hence, given the unions' wage setting behavior, the evolution of the wage rate can be described by a simple Phillips curve relationship where the change in the wage rate negatively depends on the rate of unemployment.[18]

We should also point out that there is one good in our economy that can be either consumed or invested. Consequently all variables are real including the return to capital and the wage rate so that Eq. (4.76) describes the evolution of the wage rate. Next, we describe the public sector.

The Government

The government in our economy receives tax revenues from income taxation and has revenues from issuing government bonds. Public spending is composed of public investment, I_p, spending for unemployment benefits, $\varrho w(L - L^d)$, and of public consumption, C_p, that is neither productive nor welfare enhancing. Further, the government sets the primary surplus such that it is a positive linear function of public debt which guarantees that public debt is sustainable. The accounting identity describing the accumulation of public debt in continuous time is given by,

$$\dot{B} = r_B B(1 - \tau) - S, \tag{4.77}$$

where S is government surplus exclusive of net interest payments.

The intertemporal budget constraint of the government is fulfilled if

$$B(0) = \int_0^{\infty} e^{-\int_0^{\mu}(1-\tau)r_B(\nu)d\nu} S(\mu)d\mu \leftrightarrow \lim_{t\to\infty} e^{-\int_0^{t}(1-\tau)r_B(\mu)d\mu} B(t) = 0 \tag{4.78}$$

holds. Equation (4.78) is the present-value borrowing constraint which states that public debt at time zero must equal the future present-value surpluses.

Again, we assume that the ratio of the primary surplus to GDP ratio is a positive linear function of the debt to GDP ratio and of a constant. The primary surplus ratio, then, can be written as

$$\frac{S}{Y} = \phi + \psi\,\frac{B}{Y} = \frac{\tau Y - I_p - C_p - \varrho w(L - L^d)}{Y}, \tag{4.79}$$

[18] An extensive discussion of the role of the Phillips curve in dynamic macroeconomics can be found for example in Flaschel et al. (1997).

where $\phi \in \mathbb{R}$, $\psi \in \mathbb{R}_{++}$ are constants. The parameter ψ determines how strongly the primary surplus reacts to changes in public debt and ϕ determines whether the level of the primary surplus rises or falls with an increase in GDP.

Using (4.79) the differential equation describing the evolution of public debt can be written as

$$\dot{B} = (r_B(1-\tau) - \psi)\, B - \phi\, Y. \tag{4.80}$$

Using that the evolution of public debt is given by $\dot{B} = r_B B(1-\tau) + I_p + C_p + \varrho w(L - L^d) - \tau Y = r_B B(1-\tau) - \psi B - \phi Y$ public investment can be written as

$$I_p = \omega(\tau - \phi)Y - \omega\psi B - \omega\varrho w(L - L^d)\,, \tag{4.81}$$

where we assumed that public consumption relative to public investment is constant, $C_p/I_p = \zeta = constant$, $\omega = 1/(1+\zeta)$.

Denoting by δ_G the depreciation rate of public capital, the differential equation describing the evolution of public capital, then, is written as

$$\dot{G} = \omega(\tau - \phi)Y - \omega\psi B - \omega\varrho w(L - L^d) - \delta_G G\,. \tag{4.82}$$

The Balanced Growth Path

The description of our economy is completed by deriving the growth rate of consumption and by deriving the economy-wide resource constraint. The growth rate of consumption is obtained from (4.66) and (4.67) as

$$\frac{\dot{C}}{C} = -(\rho + \delta) + (1-\tau)(1-\alpha)(Y/K). \tag{4.83}$$

with Y/K given by $Y/K = (L^n)^\alpha (G/K)^\alpha$ in case of a vertical Phillips curve and by $Y/K = \alpha^{\alpha/(\alpha-1)}(w/K)^{-\alpha/(1-\alpha)}(G/K)^{\alpha/(1-\alpha)}$ if the Phillips curve has a negative slope, where the latter is obtained by using the optimality condition (4.71).

The economy-wide resource constraint is derived by combining the budget constraint of the household with that of the government as

$$\frac{\dot{K}}{K} = \frac{Y}{K} - \frac{C}{K} + \psi\,\frac{B}{K} + (\phi - \tau)\,\frac{Y}{K} + \varrho(L - L^d)\,\frac{w}{K} - \delta\,, \tag{4.84}$$

with $L \geq L^d$.

Hence, the economy is completely described by Eqs. (4.80) and (4.82)–(4.84), with r given by (4.69). The wage rate is either determined by (4.70) or by (4.76) with L^d given by (4.71), depending on whether the Phillips curve is vertical or negatively sloped.

A balanced growth path (BGP) is given when the conditions shown in Definition 7 are fulfilled.

Definition 7 A balanced growth path (BGP) is a path such that consumption, private capital, public capital and the wage rate grow at the same strictly positive constant growth rate, that is $\dot{C}/C = \dot{K}/K = \dot{G}/G = \dot{w}/w = g$, $g > 0$, $g = constant$, and either

(i) $\dot{B} = 0$ or
(ii) $\dot{B}/B = g$.

This definition shows that, as usual, consumption, private capital, public capital, and thus output, as well as the wage rate grow at a constant and strictly positive rate over time on the BGP. Public debt may also grow the same rate as output or it may be constant. The latter holds when the government pursues a balanced budget. However, in contrast to the last chapter, we do not consider the case where public debt grows but less than all other economic variables.

In the next two sections we analyze our model, first for the case of a vertical Phillips curve and, second, assuming that the Phillips curve is negatively sloped.

4.4.2 Analysis of the Model with Wage Flexibility

In this section we study the structure of our model assuming that labor demand equals its natural level, $L^d = L^n$, such that the unemployment rate equals its natural rate, $1 - L^n/L$. The wage rate is determined by the marginal productivity rule (4.70).

In this case, the economy is completely described by Eqs. (4.80) and (4.82)–(4.84), with r and w given by (4.69) and (4.70), with $L^d = L^n$. To analyze our economy around a BGP we define the new variables $c := C/K$, $b := B/K$ and $x := G/K$. Differentiating these variables with respect to time leads to a three dimensional system of differential equations given by

$$\dot{c} = c\left((1-\alpha)x^{\alpha}(L^n)^{\alpha}(1-\tau) - \rho + c - x^{\alpha}(L^n)^{\alpha} - (\phi-\tau)x^{\alpha}(L^n)^{\alpha} - \psi b\right) + (-c)\left(\varrho\alpha x^{\alpha}(L^n)^{\alpha-1}(L - L^n)\right), \tag{4.85}$$

$$\dot{b} = b\left((1-\alpha)x^{\alpha}(L^n)^{\alpha}(1-\tau) - \psi - \phi x^{\alpha}(L^n)^{\alpha}/b - x^{\alpha}(L^n)^{\alpha} - (\phi-\tau)x^{\alpha}(L^n)^{\alpha}\right) - b\left(\psi b + \varrho\alpha x^{\alpha}(L^n)^{\alpha-1}(L - L^n) + c\right), \tag{4.86}$$

$$\dot{x} = x\left(\omega(\tau-\phi)(L^n)^{\alpha}x^{\alpha-1} - \omega\psi b/x - \omega\varrho\alpha x^{\alpha-1}(L^n)^{\alpha-1}(L - L^n) - x^{\alpha}(L^n)^{\alpha}\right) + x\left(c + \delta - \psi b - (\phi-\tau)x^{\alpha}(L^n)^{\alpha} - \varrho\alpha x^{\alpha}(L^n)^{\alpha-1}(L - L^n) - \delta_G\right). \tag{4.87}$$

A solution of $\dot{c} = \dot{b} = \dot{x} = 0$ with respect to c, b, x gives a BGP for our model and the corresponding ratios $x^\star, b^\star, c^\star$ on the BGP.[19]

In the following we consider two situations. First, we analyze the economy with a balanced budget, then for the case of permanent deficits.

Balanced Government Budget

The balanced budget scenario, scenario (i), is obtained by setting the reaction coefficient ψ equal to the net return on capital, $(1-\tau)r-\delta$, making ψ an endogenous variable. Further, ϕ is set equal zero for all times, that is $\phi = 0$, for $t \in [0, \infty)$. For this scenario, Proposition 25 gives results as concerns uniqueness and stability of a balanced growth path.

Proposition 25 *Assume that there exists a balanced growth path for scenario (i). Then, the balanced growth path is unique and saddle point stable.*

Proof See the appendix to this chapter.

This proposition demonstrates that the balanced budget scenario is characterized by a unique BGP which is saddle point stable, in case of ongoing growth. The fact that the existence of a BGP cannot be shown for the analytical model is due to unemployment benefits paid by the government and due to depreciation of public capital. Thus, if unemployment benefits exceed a certain threshold sustained growth may not be feasible because public resources devoted to growth enhancing public investment are not sufficiently large.

It should also be pointed out that saddle point stability implies, in case of a vertical Phillips curve, that there exists a unique value $c(0)$ such that the economy converges to the balanced growth path. If one takes both $x(0)$ and $b(0)$ as given, since both x and b are state variables, this means that the economy is determinate, implying that two economies with identical initial capital stocks and the same initial level of public debt have the same transitional growth rates.

Permanent Public Deficits

As concerns scenario (ii), the deficit scenario, where public debt grows at the same rate as consumption and capital in the long-run, the analytical model turns out to be quite complicated and no unambiguous results can be derived. But it is possible to derive a result as concerns the public debt to private capital ratio for the analytical model. This is done in Proposition 26.

[19]The * denotes BGP values and we exclude the economically meaningless BGP $x^\star = c^\star = 0$.

Proposition 26 *Assume that there exists a balanced growth path in scenario (ii). Then, the ratio of public debt to private capital is given by*

$$b^{\star} = \frac{\phi \, (x^{\star})^{\alpha} (L^{n})^{\alpha}}{\rho - \psi} .$$

Proof See the appendix to this chapter.

From Proposition 26 one can realize that in case of a relatively low reaction coefficient ψ, so that $\psi < \rho$, the coefficient ϕ must be positive for sustained growth with a positive government debt to be feasible.[20] This implies that the primary surplus must rise as GDP increases if the reaction of the government to higher public debt is relatively small. If the reverse holds, that is for $\psi > \rho$, the coefficient ϕ must be negative. In this case, the reaction of the government to higher debt is relatively large implying that the government pays too much attention to stabilizing debt and does not attach sufficient weight to fostering economic growth through public investment. Therefore, the primary surplus must decline with a higher GDP, implying that public investment rises, so that sustained growth is feasible.

An interesting result can be obtained when the deficit scenario is compared to the balanced budget scenario. Analogously to the last chapter, it turns out that the balanced budget scenario always is associated with a higher growth rate. Proposition 27 gives the result.

Proposition 27 *The balanced growth rate in scenario (ii), the deficit scenario, is lower than the balanced growth rate in the balanced budget scenario, scenario (i).*

Proof See the appendix to this chapter.

From an economic point of view, the result in Proposition 27 is due to the fact that in the deficit scenario the government must devote resources to the debt service that cannot be used for productive public investment. The latter does not hold for the balanced budget scenario so that this scenario goes along with a higher balanced growth rate.

In order to get additional insight in our model we perform simulations. We should like to point out that our model is a highly stylized one so that we do not intend to make calibration exercises or replicate real economies. The simulations are intended to derive results that cannot be obtained for the analytical model. In particular, we are interested in growth effects of deficit financed public investment and in the question of how the reaction coefficient, ψ, affects stability of the model in order to compare this model to the one of the last chapter, where we performed the same exercise.

In the simulations, the subjective discount rate is set to 3.5 % and the depreciation rates of private and of public capital are 3.5 and 7.5 %, respectively, that is $\rho = 0.035$, $\delta = 0.035$, $\delta_G = 0.075$. Labor supply is normalized to one, $L = 1$, and the

[20]In this section we limit our consideration to $b \geq 0$.

natural rate of employment is 0.98 giving a natural rate of unemployment of 2 %. The parameter ω is set to $\omega = 0.65$ implying that the ratio of public consumption to public investment is about 55 %. The income tax rate is set to 10 % and the unemployment benefit is 80 % of the wage rate, that is $\tau = 0.1$, $\varrho = 0.8$. The elasticity of output with respect to public capital is set to 30 %. It must be pointed out that this implies that the elasticity of output with respect to labor is also 30 % while the elasticity of output with respect to capital is 70 %. This can be justified by supposing that labor is raw labor and that capital is interpreted in a broad sense so that capital comprises both private physical and human capital.[21]

In Table 4.9 we report the balanced growth rate, g, and the signs of the eigenvalues of the Jacobian for different values of ϕ, with ψ set $\psi = 0.01$.

In order to interpret Table 4.9 we note that a deficit financed increase in public investment is modeled by a decline in ϕ which can be seen from Eq. (4.81). Hence, Table 4.9 shows that a deficit financed increase in public investment leads to a higher balanced growth rate with the parameters underlying the simulation. However, it can also be seen that only one eigenvalue is negative implying that the economy is unstable in this case. Consequently, the government must levy an additional non-distortionary tax in order to control public debt so that the economy can converge to the BGP.

If ϕ is further increased in Table 4.9, the balanced growth rate declines and for $\phi \geq 0.068$ no BGP exists any longer. If ϕ is decreased, the balanced growth rate rises and for $\phi \to 0$ the balanced growth rate approaches its maximum value of about 24 % which is equal to the growth rate obtained in the balanced budget scenario.

Next, we choose a higher value for ψ and set $\psi = 0.05$ so that $\rho < \psi$ holds. Table 4.10 gives results for this example.

Table 4.10 shows that with a larger reaction coefficient ψ the economy is stable. For $\psi = 0.05$ there are either two negative real eigenvalues or two complex conjugate eigenvalues with negative real parts. But in this case, a deficit financed increase in public investment reduces the balanced growth rate. The reason is that

Table 4.9 Balanced growth rate, g, and eigenvalues for different ϕ with $\psi = 0.01$

	$\phi = 0.065$	$\phi = 0.055$	$\phi = 0.045$
g (%)	5	11.8	15.2
Eigenvalues	$+;-;+$	$-;+;+$	$-;+;+$

Table 4.10 Balanced growth rate, g, and eigenvalues for different ϕ with $\psi = 0.05$

	$\phi = -0.01$	$\phi = -0.02$	$\phi = -0.03$
g (%)	21.5	18.3	13.8
Eigenvalues	$+;-;-$	$+;-a \pm bi, a, b > 0$	$+;-a \pm bi, a, b > 0$

[21]We made the simulations also with $\alpha = 0.6$. Qualitatively, the results are identical to those presented here.

the initial deficit financed increase in public investment is compensated by the strong reaction of the government to the higher public debt so that the economy ends up with a smaller growth rate. Hence, there is again a trade-off between stability and positive growth effects of deficit financed public investment.

If ϕ is increased the growth rate rises and again approaches its maximum value for $\phi \to 0$. If ϕ is decreased, the balanced growth rate declines and it turns out that for $\phi \leq -0.036$ the balanced growth path becomes unstable, that is the Jacobian matrix has only positive eigenvalues or eigenvalues with positive real parts. For $\phi \leq -0.041$, finally, no BGP exists any longer.

In order to see that a lower reaction coefficient ψ destabilizes the economy, we set $\phi = -0.03$ and continuously decrease ψ starting from $\psi = 0.05$. Doing so shows that for $\psi = \psi_{crit} \approx 0.048$ two eigenvalues are purely imaginary and for values of ψ smaller than ψ_{crit} one eigenvalues is positive and two are complex conjugate with positive real parts, implying that the BGP looses stability. In addition, a Hopf bifurcation can be observed at $\psi = \psi_{crit}$ leading to limit cycles. At the bifurcation point the first Lyapunov coefficient l_1 is negative, $l_1 \approx -1.089$, indicating that the emerging limit cycles are stable.[22]

Figure 4.4 shows a limit cycle in the $(x-b-c)$ phase space. The orientation of the cycle is as indicated by the arrow.

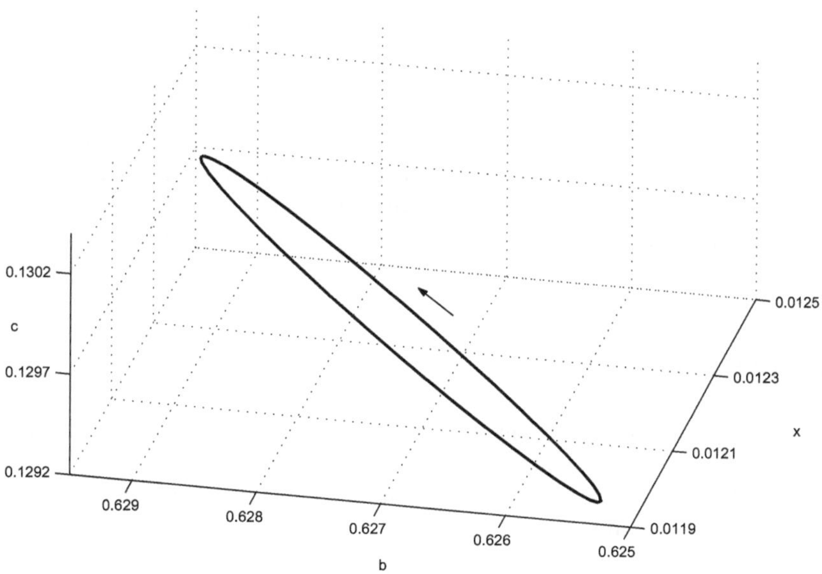

Fig. 4.4 Limit cycle in the $(x - b - c)$ phase space

[22]For those computations as well as for the depiction of the limit cycle we used the software CL_MATCONT, see Dhooge et al. (2003).

4.4.3 *The Model with Wage Rigidities*

In case of wage rigidities, labor demand is given by (4.71) and the wage adjustment is described by the Phillips curve (4.76). This implies that the growth rate of the wage rate is a negative function of the unemployment rate. In this case, the economy is completely described by the Eqs. (4.76), (4.80) and (4.82)–(4.84), with r given by (4.69) and L^d given by (4.71).

In order to analyze the economy around a BGP we proceed as in the last section and define the variables $c := C/K, b := B/K, x := G/K$ and, in addition, $y = w/K$. Differentiating these variables with respect to time gives a four dimensional system of differential equations which is written as,

$$\dot{c} = c\left((1-\alpha)(1-\tau)(Y/K) - \rho - \psi b - \varrho y(L - \alpha^{1/(1-\alpha)} y^{-1/(1-\alpha)} x^{\alpha/(1-\alpha)})\right) + c\left(c - (Y/K)(1-\phi+\tau)\right), \tag{4.88}$$

$$\dot{b} = b\left((1-\alpha)(1-\tau)(Y/K) - \phi(Y/K)/b - \varrho y(L - \alpha^{1/(1-\alpha)} y^{-1/(1-\alpha)} x^{\alpha/(1-\alpha)})\right) + b\left(c - \psi(b+1) - (Y/K)(1-\phi+\tau)\right), \tag{4.89}$$

$$\dot{x} = x\left(\omega(Y/K)(\tau-\phi)/x - w\omega b/x - \delta_G - \omega\varrho y(L - \alpha^{1/(1-\alpha)} y^{-1/(1-\alpha)} x^{\alpha/(1-\alpha)})/x\right) + x\left(c + \delta - \psi b - (Y/K)(1-\phi+\tau) - \varrho y(L - \alpha^{1/(1-\alpha)} y^{-1/(1-\alpha)} x^{\alpha/(1-\alpha)})\right), \tag{4.90}$$

$$\dot{y} = y\left(\beta_L \alpha^{1/(1-\alpha)} y^{-1/(1-\alpha)} x^{\alpha/(1-\alpha)}/L - \beta_L \bar{L}/L - (Y/K)(1-\phi+\tau) + \delta - \psi b\right) + y\left(c - \varrho y(L - \alpha^{1/(1-\alpha)} y^{-1/(1-\alpha)} x^{\alpha/(1-\alpha)})\right), \tag{4.91}$$

with $Y/K = \alpha^{\alpha/(1-\alpha)} y^{-\alpha/(1-\alpha)} x^{\alpha/(1-\alpha)}$. This system is rather complex and it turns out that concrete results cannot be obtained without numerical exercises. In particular, we are again interested in the question of how fiscal policy affects economic growth and stability of the economy. First, we analyze the balanced budget scenario.

Balanced Government Budget

As in the last section, the balanced budget scenario, scenario (i), is obtained by setting the reaction coefficient ψ equal to the net return on capital, $(1-\tau)r - \delta$, and by setting $\phi = 0$. For this scenario, Proposition 28 gives information about stability properties of the dynamic system.

Proposition 28 *Assume that there exists a balanced growth path for scenario (i). Then, there is at least one negative real eigenvalue.*

Proof See the appendix to this chapter.

If there is exactly one negative real eigenvalue the economy is unstable. In this case, the government again has to levy a non-distortionary tax and use the revenue to control public debt such that the economy can converge to the BGP in the long-run. If there are two negative eigenvalues or two eigenvalues with negative real parts, there exist unique initial values of consumption and of the wage rate, the economy can choose, such that it converges to the BGP. In case of more than two negative real eigenvalues, the economy is indeterminate in the sense that the initial consumption and the initial wage rate are not uniquely determined. Next, we study the deficit scenario and try to find how fiscal policy can affect the economy.

Permanent Public Deficits

To analyze the economy with this scenario we again use numerical examples and take the same parameter values as in the last chapter and we set the parameter β_L, determining the adjustment speed of wages, to $\beta_L = 0.07$ and $\bar{L}$ is set to $\bar{L} = 0.75$. This corresponds to $\gamma_w = 0.04$ in (4.72) and to $\theta = 0.6$ in (4.74). In Table 4.11 we study effects of raising deficit financed public investment with a relatively small reaction coefficient ψ.

Table 4.11 shows that for a relatively small value of the reaction coefficient ψ, the model is unstable. In addition, it can be seen that a deficit financed increase in public investment, modeled by a decrease in ϕ, reduces the balanced growth rate and raises the unemployment rate.

If the parameter ϕ is further decreased in Table 4.11, the growth rate becomes negative for $\phi \leq 0.0094$. If ϕ is still further reduced, the balanced growth rate continues to decline and it converges to the value of the balanced budget scenario which is −0.3 % for $\phi \to 0$. Thus, a balanced budget would go along with a negative balanced growth rate and an unemployment rate of 28.9 %. The Jacobian has exactly one negative eigenvalue implying that the BGP is unstable. If ϕ is increased the economy reaches the full employment state for $\phi = 0.0524$ with a growth rate of 2.1 %.

If we set the reaction coefficient ψ to a higher value, implying that the government raises the primary surplus to a larger degree as public debt increases, the situation changes. Then, the economy becomes stable and a deficit financed increase in public investment leads to a higher balanced growth rate and a smaller unemployment rate. Table 4.12 shows the results with ψ set to $\psi = 0.05$.

Table 4.11 Balanced growth rate, g, unemployment rate, u, and eigenvalues for different values of ϕ with $\psi = 0.01$

	$\phi = 0.065$	$\phi = 0.055$	$\phi = 0.045$
g (%)	1.5	1.2	0.8
u (%)	3.1	8.3	13
Eigenvalues	+;−;+;+	+;−;+;+	+;−;+;+

Table 4.12 Balanced growth rate, g, unemployment rate, u, and eigenvalues for different values of ϕ with $\psi = 0.05$

	$\phi = -0.01$	$\phi = -0.02$	$\phi = -0.03$
g (%)	0.07	0.5	1
u (%)	24	17.9	10.7
Eigenvalues	$+;-;+;-$	$+;-;+;-$	$+;-;+;-$

Table 4.12 shows that the economy is saddle point stable with a larger value of ψ. The outcome that a higher reaction coefficient stabilizes the economy is equivalent to the result of the last section with flexible wages and a vertical Phillips curve. But, in contrast to the last section, the trade-off between positive growth effects of deficit financed public investment and stability does not seem to exist any longer when wages are rigid. As Table 4.12 demonstrates, a deficit financed rise in public investment, modeled by a decline in the parameter ϕ, raises the balanced growth rate and the economy is stable.

If we increase the parameter ϕ in Table 4.12 it turns out that for $\phi \geq -0.008$ the balanced growth rate becomes negative. If ϕ is reduced the growth rate rises and for $\phi = -0.0422$ it attains 1.7 % that goes along with an unemployment rate equal to zero. It should also be mentioned that the increase of the balanced growth in Table 4.12 goes along with a higher debt to private capital ratio, in contrast to the latter chapter where a higher balanced growth rate was associated with a smaller debt to capital ratio.

The difference to the outcome of the last section is clearly due to the difference in wage flexibility that determines the shape of Phillips curves. In the next section, we discuss in detail the economic mechanisms behind the different results.

4.4.4 Discussion and Comparison to the Model Without Unemployment

In the last two sections we have derived results for our model and we have seen that the outcome partly depends on the flexibility of the wage rate, that is on whether the Phillips curve is vertical or whether it has a negative slope. In this section we want to identify economic mechanisms that generate the different results.

One result we derived was a trade-off between positive growth effects of higher deficit financed public investment and stability of the model when the Phillips curve is vertical. The reason for that outcome is that a high reaction coefficient ψ implies that the increase in the primary surplus is large as public debt rises, which stabilizes the economy. But, with a large ψ, the initial increase in deficit financed public investment is more than compensated by the rise in public debt implying that public investment declines again, so that the economy is characterized by a smaller growth rate in the long-run. Thus, the higher public debt requires more resources for the debt service which reduces public investment in the end.

If wages are rigid and the Phillips curve has a negative slope, the trade-off does not exist. In this case, when the reaction of the primary surplus to public debt ψ is sufficiently large, a deficit financed increase in public investment raises the ratio of public to private capital and labor demand. As a consequence, unemployment declines reducing unemployment payments of the government which raises public investment. Thus, lower unemployment spending prevents a decline in public investment as public debt rises, even if the reaction coefficient ψ is large. Further, a large reaction coefficient ψ has a positive effect on the growth rate of private capital, which can be seen from the economy-wide resource constraint (4.84). Therefore, a deficit financed increase in public investment raises the balanced growth rate for a large ψ, even if it goes along with a higher debt to private capital ratio in the long-run.

With a small ψ, the positive effect of less unemployment payments on public investment, as a result of higher deficit financed public investment, would be amplified. But, in this case, the crowding-out effect of an increase in public investment dominates in the economy-wide resource constraint so that private investment declines. This is again seen from the economy-wide resource constraint (4.84), where we recall that the initial deficit financed increase in public investment is modeled by a lower ϕ. Therefore, a deficit financed increase in public investment reduces the balanced growth, where $\dot{K}/K = \dot{G}/G$ holds, for a small reaction coefficient ψ in case the Phillips curve has a negative slope.

Hence, the different effects of higher deficit financed public investment in our model are due to the fact that employment is equal to its natural level with flexible wages whereas employment varies if wages are not flexible when deficit financed public investment is increased. It should also be mentioned that a higher balanced growth rate goes along with a higher wage to private capital ratio if wages are flexible. In case of rigid wages, the reverse holds. In this case, a higher balanced growth rate goes along with a smaller ratio of the wage rate to private capital implying a higher employment share and, thus, less unemployment.

Finally, comparing our model with the model where unemployment is not considered, analyzed in the last section, it can be realized that, from a qualitative point of view, the model with flexible wages produces the same results as the model without unemployment. This holds although the differential equations in the two models are of course different, due to unemployment in this model leading to unemployment payments from the government to the household sector. Nevertheless, if wages are flexible and the Phillips curve is vertical, employment is fixed at its natural rate and the wage rate equals the marginal product of labor. Only if wages are rigid and the Phillips curve has a negative slope, fiscal policy affects the unemployment rate and unemployment payments. Then, the model gives rise to different outcomes, as mentioned above.

Conclusion

In this chapter we have presented an endogenous growth model with productive public spending and public debt where the government can run deficits in order to finance public investment. In addition, we have posited, as in the last chapter, that the primary surplus relative to GDP is a positive function of the debt to GDP ratio because this guarantees that public debt remains sustainable. The main results of analyzing our model can be summarized as follows.

It turned out that a balanced budget scenario brings about a higher long-run growth rate than a scenario where public debt grows at the balanced growth rate, that is at the same rate as all other economic variables. Further, a scenario where public debt grows in the long-run, but at a lower rate than the balanced growth rate, yields the same long-run growth rate as the balanced budget scenario. A balanced growth rate exceeding the one of the balanced budget scenario can only be obtained when the government is a creditor. This means that the government must have built up a stock of wealth it uses to finance its expenditures and to lend to the private sector.

Starting from a balanced budget, a deficit financed increase of public investment raises transitional growth rates but leads to a smaller long-run growth rate if this fiscal policy leads to a higher debt to GDP ratio in the long-run. Only if the government switches back to the balanced budget scenario or to the scenario where public debt grows slower than capital and output, a temporarily deficit financed public investment raises transitional growth without leading to smaller growth in the long-run.

The fact that a balanced budget gives the highest possible growth rate in the long-run, unless the government is a creditor, does not imply that a deficit financed increase in public investment always reduces long-run growth. Thus, if the economy is on a balanced growth path where public debt grows at the balanced growth rate, a deficit financed increase in public investment may lead to a higher balanced growth rate and to a smaller debt ratio in the long-run. However, in the model with productive public capital this could only be observed when the response of the primary surplus to public debt is small so that the model is unstable. That implies that the government must impose an additional lump-sum tax to control public debt. In general, it can be said that the stronger the response of the primary surplus to public debt the sooner the model is stable. But, then, a deficit financed increase in public debt leads to a smaller balanced growth rate. Hence, in this model there is a trade-off between stabilizing the economy and getting positive growth effects of deficit financed public investment.

As concerns welfare, numerical examples have shown that the scenario where public debt grows at the balanced growth rate yields smaller welfare

(continued)

than the balanced budget scenario and smaller welfare than the scenario where public debt grows at a smaller rate than capital and output in the long-run. Further, evidence was found that the latter scenario leads to higher welfare than the balanced budget scenario. However, it cannot be excluded that this result depends on the initial conditions with respect to the capital stocks and with respect to public debt. Here, additional research is necessary in order to find how robust this outcome is.

Overall, it can be stated that a scenario where public debt grows at the same rate as capital and output yields smaller growth and welfare in the long-run, compared to the balanced budget scenario and compared to the scenario where debt grows, but less than capital and output. Comparing the latter two scenarios, a balanced budget scenario may perform worse so that the scenario where debt grows, but less than output and capital, makes the economy better off compared to the balanced budget scenario. But even that scenario would require in part drastic changes for countries of the euro area where many economies have difficulties in sticking to the 60 % debt criterion. In any case, changing policies such that debt ratios decline over time instead of remaining constant would benefit economies.

The analysis of the model with progressive income taxation has shown that a more progressive tax schedule leads to a higher ratio of public to private capital but to a smaller balanced growth rate because the direct negative growth effect of a more progressive tax system outweighs the indirect positive growth effect of e relatively higher public capital stock. Hence, there does not exist an inverted U-shaped relation between the growth rate and the parameter determining the slope of the tax schedule as in the model with a flat rate income tax. For the model with a balanced government budget, this could be shown analytically while for the model with public debt we derived this result using numerical examples.

As concerns stability of the system, the model without public debt is characterized by a unique balanced growth path which is saddle point stable, independent of tax parameters. In the version where we allowed for public debt, numerical examples showed that sustained per-capita growth may not be feasible when the degree of progression exceeds a certain threshold. Further, it also turned out that the system may become unstable with more progressive tax schedules, unstable in the sense that the number of negative eigenvalues or eigenvalues with negative real parts decreases.

In the model with productive public spending as a flow, growth effects of public debt and deficit policy are equivalent to the one obtained to the model with a productive stock of public capital. That is the balanced growth rate is the higher, the lower public debt is. But, as in the model with a productive public capital stock, that does not mean that a deficit financed rise of productive public spending must reduce long-run growth. Rather,

(continued)

comparative statics with respect to a deficit financed increase in public spending have demonstrated that the balanced growth rate of the BGP with high growth declines while the growth rate of the BGP with low growth rises which is equivalent to the outcome obtained in Futagami et al. (2008) who conclude that economies with low growth should rely on deficit financed productive public spending while economies with high growth rates should finance productive spending through taxes.

With respect to the long-run dynamics, we could show that the endogenous growth model with productive public spending and public debt can produce a richer dynamic outcome than the model with a productive public capital stock. Then, two saddle point stable balanced growth paths may arise depending on the intertemporal elasticity of substitution of consumption and on the way governments set the primary surplus when GDP grows. A necessary condition for two saddle point stable balanced growth paths is that the household disposes of a high intertemporal elasticity of substitution of consumption and that the government has a preference for productive public spending as GDP rises rather than for reducing public debt. From an economic point of view, this result implies that an underdevelopment trap can emerge. This means that two long-run balanced growth paths exist and the question of whether an economy converges to the high-growth or to the low-growth path in the long-run depends on whether the initial debt to GDP ratio is below or above the threshold value of the debt ratio. If the initial debt to GDP ratio exceeds the critical value, an economy can never converge to the high balanced growth path but, instead, is characterized by low-growth in the long-run, i.e. stuck in the underdevelopment trap.

Further, we have seen that allowing for real wage rigidities leads to a different result regarding growth effects of public deficits and public debt. Therefore, the answer to the question whether the government should run deficits and finance productive public spending in order to promote growth and employment in an economy crucially depends on whether real wages are flexible and the Phillips curve is vertical or whether wages are rigid and the Phillips curve has a negative slope.

With flexible wages, there may be a trade-off between stability and positive growth effects of deficit financed increases in public investment. If a deficit financed increase in public investment raises the balanced growth rate, the government has to levy a lump-sum tax in order to control public debt. Otherwise, convergence to the balanced growth path cannot be assured. If real wages are rigid and the Phillips curve has a negative slope, this trade-off does not exist. The reason for this is that fiscal policy affects the level of employment in this case and, therefore, the feedback effect of higher public debt is different from the situation where employment is fixed at its natural level.

(continued)

A result that holds independent of the flexibility of wages, is that a stronger reaction of the government to higher public debt stabilizes the economy. Hence, if the reaction of the government to higher debt is large, the economy is stable and converges to the balanced growth path asymptotically, independent of whether wages are flexible or rigid.

As concerns stability, our analysis has shown that a strong rise in the primary surplus as a reaction to higher public debt stabilizes the economy. In addition, we have seen that for certain values of the reaction coefficient, cyclical growth can occur in the model with wage rigidities. If the reaction coefficient is set to a larger value, the economy stabilizes and converges to the constant balanced growth rate, if the reaction coefficient is set to a lower value, the economy becomes unstable.

Appendix

Proof of Proposition 17

To prove this proposition with scenario (i), we set $\phi = 0$, $\psi = (1-\tau)(1-\alpha)x^{\alpha}$ and $b = 0$. Setting $\dot{x} = 0$ and solving this equation with respect to c gives c as a function of x and of parameters. Substituting this function for c in $\dot{c}$ gives $q(x,\cdot) = (1-\alpha)x^{\alpha}(1-\tau)-\rho-\omega\tau x^{\alpha-1}$. It is easily seen that $\lim_{x\to 0} q(x,\cdot) = -\infty$, $\lim_{x\to\infty} q(x,\cdot) = +\infty$ and $\partial q(\cdot)/\partial x > 0$. Thus, existence of a unique BGP is shown.

To show saddle point stability, we compute the Jacobian matrix evaluated at the rest point of (4.17)–(4.19). The Jacobian is given by

$$\mathrm{J} = \begin{bmatrix} \partial\dot{x}/\partial x & \partial\dot{x}/\partial b & \partial\dot{x}/\partial c \\ 0 & \partial\dot{b}/\partial b & 0 \\ \partial\dot{c}/\partial x & \partial\dot{c}/\partial b & \partial\dot{c}/\partial c \end{bmatrix}.$$

One eigenvalue of this matrix is given by $ev_1 = \partial\dot{b}/\partial b = -\dot{K}/K = -g$. Thus, we know that one eigenvalue, ev_1, is negative. Further, it is easily shown that $(\partial\dot{x}/\partial x)(\partial\dot{c}/\partial c) - (\partial\dot{x}/\partial c)(\partial\dot{c}/\partial x) < 0$ holds, so that complex conjugate eigenvalues are excluded. The determinant of J is given by $\det \mathrm{J} = \partial\dot{b}/\partial b(\tau(\alpha - 1)x^{\alpha-2}\omega - (1-\tau)(1-\alpha)\alpha x^{\alpha-1})c^{\star}x^{\star} > 0$. Since the product of the eigenvalues equals the determinant, $ev_1 \cdot ev_2 \cdot ev_3 = \det \mathrm{J} > 0$, and because of $ev_1 < 0$, we know that two eigenvalues are negative and one is positive.

For scenario (ii) we set $\phi = 0$ and $b = 0$. Then, we proceed analogously so that existence and uniqueness is readily shown. For $\dot{B}/B < \dot{C}/C$ to hold we must have $\rho < \psi$ and $\psi < (1-\tau)r$ must hold for $\dot{B}/B > 0$. Because of $b^{\star} = 0$

the Jacobian matrix is the same as for scenario (i) except for $\partial \dot{b}/\partial b$. $\partial \dot{b}/\partial b$ now is given by $\partial \dot{b}/\partial b = ev_1 = \dot{B}/B - \dot{K}/K < 0$, because of $\dot{B}/B < \dot{K}/K$ at the BGP. In particular, the determinant is again positive implying that two eigenvalues are negative and one is positive. □

Proof of Proposition 18

To prove Proposition 18, $\dot{c} = 0$ is solved with respect to c giving $c = c(x, b, \cdot)$. Inserting $c = c(x, b, \cdot)$ in $\dot{x}$ and solving $\dot{x} = 0$ with respect to b gives $b^\star$ as shown in Proposition 18. It is immediately seen that $\phi < \tau$ is a necessary condition for $b^\star$ to be positive while $\phi \geq \tau$ is a sufficient condition for $b^\star$ to be negative. □

Proof of Proposition 19

To prove this proposition we note that we set $\phi = 0$, $\psi = (1-\tau)(1-\alpha)x^\alpha$ and $b = 0$ to get scenario (i). Further, the balanced growth rate is given by $\dot{C}/C = -\rho + (1-\tau)(1-\alpha)x^\alpha$. Along a BGP we have $\dot{C}/C = \dot{G}/G$ which implies

$$-\rho + (1-\tau)(1-\alpha)x^\alpha = \tau\,\omega\,x^{\alpha-1} \tag{4.92}$$

The left hand side in (4.92) is monotonically increasing in x and the right hand side is monotonically declining in x. A value $x_i^\star$ such that the left hand side in (4.92) equals the right hand side gives a BGP for scenario (i).

For scenario (ii), $\dot{C}/C = \dot{G}/G$ implies

$$-\rho + (1-\tau)(1-\alpha)x^\alpha = \tau\,\omega\,x^{\alpha-1} - \phi\,\omega\,x^{\alpha-1} - \omega\,\psi\,b/x \tag{4.93}$$

Again, a value $x_{ii}^\star$ such that the left hand side in (4.93) equals the right hand side gives a BGP for scenario (ii).

The function on the left hand side of Eqs. (4.92) and (4.93) are identical. The graph of the function on the right hand side of (4.92), however, is above the graph of the function on the right hand side of (4.93) for all $x \in [0, \infty)$ for $b \geq 0$ and for $\phi > 0$. Therefore, the left hand side and the right hand side in (4.92) intersect at a larger value of x than the left hand side and the right hand side in (4.93), giving a higher balanced growth rate for scenario (i). To show this for $\phi < 0$, we note that on the BGP $b^\star$ is given by $b^\star = \phi(x^\star)^{\alpha-1}/(\rho - \psi)$ which follows from $\dot{C}/C = \dot{B}/B$. Inserting this in the right hand side of (4.93) and deleting the * gives

$$-\rho + (1-\tau)(1-\alpha)x^\alpha = \tau\,\omega\,x^{\alpha-1} - \phi\,\omega\,x^{\alpha-1}\rho/(\rho - \psi) \tag{4.94}$$

If $-\phi\,\omega\,x^{\alpha-1}\rho/(\rho-\psi)<0$, the point of intersection of the left hand side and the right hand side in (4.92) occurs at a larger value of x than in (4.94). For $\psi>\rho$ it is immediately seen that $-\phi\,\omega\,x^{\alpha-1}\rho/(\rho-\psi)<0$ holds (recall that $\phi<0$). For $\psi<\rho$ the reverse holds, but public debt becomes negative because of $b^\star/x^\star=\phi(x^\star)^{\alpha-1}/(\rho-\psi)$. In this case, $x^\star$ in (4.94) is larger than $x^\star$ in (4.92) yielding a higher growth rate for scenario (iii) but this occurs only if public debt is negative.

In scenario (ii) the asymptotic public debt ratio equals zero such that (4.92) holds for both scenario (i) and for scenario (ii) implying that the two scenarios yield the same balanced growth rate. □

Proof of Corollary 1

To prove this corollary we have to show that $\psi>0$ implies $b^\star<0$, with ψ given by $\psi=-\phi\,\omega\,x^{\alpha-1}\rho/(\rho-\psi)$ from the right hand side in (4.94) from the proof of Proposition 19. This holds because $\psi>0$ implies that x which solves (4.92) is smaller than that x which solves (4.94), so that the balanced growth rate of scenario (i) is smaller than the balanced growth rate of scenario (iii). From the proof of Proposition 19 we know that $b^\star$ on the BGP is given by $b^\star=\phi(x^\star)^\alpha/(\rho-\psi)$. It is immediately seen that $b^\star$ and ψ have the opposite sign since ω and x are positive.
□

The Model with Public Infrastructure and with the Government as a Creditor

If the government is a creditor, public debt B is negative. If the government does not stick to the rule modeled in Eq. (4.11) in that case, it is easy to see that the economy, then, is described by the following equations,

$$\dot{C}/C=-\rho+(1-\tau)(1-\alpha)x^\alpha,\qquad \dot{K}/K=x^\alpha-c-i_p\,\omega^{-1}$$

$$\dot{B}/B=(1-\tau)(1-\alpha)x^\alpha-\tau x^\alpha/b+i_p\,\omega^{-1}/b,\qquad \dot{G}/G=i_p/x,$$

with $i_p=I_p/K$, public investment relative to private capital and $c=C/K$, $x=G/K$ and $b=B/K$, as above. The dynamics around a BGP are described by,

$$\dot{c}=c\left(-\rho+(1-\tau)(1-\alpha)x^\alpha-x^\alpha+c+i_p\,\omega^{-1}\right),$$

$$\dot{x}=x\left(i_p/x-x^\alpha+c+i_p\,\omega^{-1}\right),$$

$$\dot{b}=b\left((1-\tau)(1-\alpha)x^\alpha-\tau x^\alpha/b+i_p\,\omega^{-1}/b-x^\alpha+c+i_p\,\omega^{-1}\right),$$

where a BGP is given for $\dot{c} = \dot{x} = \dot{b} = 0$, with $c^\star = x^\star = 0$ again neglected.

Now, assume that a BGP with $b^\star \leq 0$ exists. Then setting $i_p = \omega\,\tau\,x^\alpha - \epsilon\,\omega\,\rho\,b$, $\epsilon \geq 1$, shows that $\dot{B}/B < (=)\,\dot{C}/C$, for $\epsilon > (=)\,1$ and $b^\star = (<)\,0$.

On the BGP, $\dot{C}/C = \dot{K}/K = \dot{G}/G$ holds, so that $b = B/K$ asymptotically converges to zero for $\epsilon > 1$. Hence, $\dot{G}/G$ is given by $\dot{G}/G = \omega\,\tau\,x^{\alpha-1}$, for $\epsilon > 1$, $b = 0$ and by $\dot{G}/G = \omega\,\tau\,x^{\alpha-1} - \omega\,\rho\,b\,x^{-1}$, for $\epsilon = 1, b < 0$.

This shows that the graph of $\dot{G}/G$ with negative public debt ($b < 0$) is above the graph of $\dot{G}/G$ with zero public debt ($b = 0$). Consequently, $\dot{C}/C$ intersects $\dot{G}/G$, which must hold on the BGP, at a larger value of x with $b < 0$ than with $b = 0$. Therefore, $b^\star < 0$ goes along with a higher value of $x^\star$, and thus, with a higher balanced growth rate than $b^\star = 0$.

Stability of the Model with a Progressive Income Tax for the Case of a Balanced Government Budget and No Government Debt

The Jacobian matrix to (4.43)–(4.44) is given by

$$J = \begin{bmatrix} x \cdot \partial\,(\dot{x}/x)/\partial\,x & x \cdot \partial\,(\dot{x}/x)/\partial\,v \\ v \cdot \partial\,(\dot{v}/v)/\partial\,x & v \cdot \partial\,(\dot{v}/v)/\partial\,v \end{bmatrix}$$

where we have used that $\dot{v}/v = \dot{x}/x = 0$ holds on the BGP. The elements of the Jacobian matrix can be computed as

$$x \cdot \frac{\partial\,(\dot{x}/x)}{\partial\,x} = v \cdot \frac{\partial\,(\dot{G}/G)}{\partial\,x} - v \cdot \frac{\partial\,(\dot{K}/K)}{\partial\,x} = -g - \alpha v$$

$$x \cdot \frac{\partial\,(\dot{x}/x)}{\partial\,v} = v \cdot \frac{\partial\,(\dot{G}/G)}{\partial\,v} - v \cdot \frac{\partial\,(\dot{K}/K)}{\partial\,v} = -x$$

$$v \cdot \frac{\partial\,(\dot{v}/v)}{\partial\,x} = v \cdot \frac{\partial\,(\dot{C}/C)}{\partial\,x} - v \cdot \frac{\partial\,(\dot{K}/K)}{\partial\,x} = \alpha v(\rho - v)/x$$

$$v \cdot \frac{\partial\,(\dot{v}/v)}{\partial\,v} = v \cdot \frac{\partial\,(\dot{C}/C)}{\partial\,v} - v \cdot \frac{\partial\,(\dot{K}/K)}{\partial\,v} = v$$

where we have used that $g = \dot{C}/C = \dot{G}/G = \dot{K}/K$ holds at the BGP. For $g > 0$ it can be easily seen that the determinant of the Jacobian is given by $\det J = -v(g + \alpha\rho) < 0$.

Proof of Proposition 20

A balanced government budget implies $x^\star = 0$. Using this it is easily seen that there exists a unique $z^\star > 0$ by solving $\dot{z} = 0$. The Jacobian matrix of (4.60)–(4.61) is

$$\mathrm{J} = \begin{bmatrix} z^\star & \partial\dot{z}/\partial x \\ 0 & -g \end{bmatrix}$$

Since $g > 0$ the determinant is negative. □

Proof of Proposition 21

To prove that proposition we write the balanced growth rate as

$$g = (1/\sigma)(1-\alpha)(1-\tau)(\tau - (S/Y))^{\alpha/(1-\alpha)} - \rho$$

where we used $S/Y = \psi x - \phi$. This shows that g is maximized for $\phi = x = 0$. □

Proof of Proposition 22

To prove that proposition, we solve $\dot{z}/z = 0$ with respect to z and insert the resulting expression into $\dot{x}/(x\varpi(\cdot))$ giving,

$$q_1 := (1-\tau)(1-\alpha)c_p(x,\cdot)^{\alpha/(1-\alpha)}(1-1/\sigma) - \psi + \phi/x + \rho/\sigma.$$

A solution of $q_1(\cdot) = 0$ with respect to x gives a BGP. The function $q_1(\cdot)$ has the following property,

$$\lim_{x\to 0} q_1(\cdot) = +(-)\,\infty, \text{ for } \phi > (<)\, 0,$$

with $\bar{x} := (\tau + \phi)/\psi$. The derivative of $q_1(\cdot)$ is,

$$\frac{\partial q_1(\cdot)}{\partial x} = (-\psi)(1-\tau)\alpha c_p(x,\cdot)^{(1/(1-\alpha))-2}(1-1/\sigma) - \phi/x^2 < (>)\, 0,$$

for $1/\sigma < 1$, $\phi > 0$ ($1/\sigma > 1$, $\phi < 0$). Consequently, if there exists a BGP it is unique. For $1/\sigma > 1$, $\phi > 0$ and for $1/\sigma < 1$, $\phi < 0$ the derivative $\partial q_1(\cdot)/\partial x$ changes signs so that multiple BGPs can arise. □

Proof of Corollary 2

To prove the corollary we define

$$q_2(\cdot) := xq_1(\cdot) = x(1-\tau)(1-\alpha)c_p(x,\cdot)^{\alpha/(1-\alpha)}(1-1/\sigma) - x\psi + \phi + x\rho/\sigma,$$

with

$$\lim_{x\to 0} q_2(\cdot) = \phi, \ \lim_{x\to \bar{x}} q_2(\cdot) = \phi + \bar{x}((\rho/\sigma) - \psi).$$

The condition in the corollary implies $\phi + \bar{x}((\rho/\sigma) - \psi) < 0\ (> 0)$ for $1/\sigma < 1, \phi < 0\ (1/\sigma > 1, \phi > 0)$. Thus, $q_2(\cdot)$ starts at $\phi < (>) 0$ and converges to $\phi + \bar{x}((\rho/\sigma) - \psi) < 0\ (> 0)$ for $1/\sigma < 1, \phi < 0\ (1/\sigma > 1, \phi > 0)$. Consequently, existence of a BGP implies that there are multiple BGPs. To see that there are exactly two BGPs we study the second derivative of $q_2(\cdot)$ that is given by,

$$\begin{aligned}\frac{\partial^2 q_2(\cdot)}{\partial x^2} &= -2(1-\tau)\alpha c_p(x,\cdot)^{-1+\alpha/(1-\alpha)}\psi(1-1/\sigma) + \\ &\quad \psi^2 x\alpha c_p(x,\cdot)^{-2+\alpha/(1-\alpha)}(1-\tau)(1-1/\sigma)(-1+\alpha/(1-\alpha))\end{aligned}$$

With $1/\sigma < 1$ the function $q_2(\cdot)$ is strictly concave for $(1-\alpha) \geq 1/2$. For $(1-\alpha) < 1/2$ there exists a unique point of inflection given by $\tilde{x} = 2(1-\alpha)\bar{x}$ so that there exist at most two values of x that solve $q_2(\cdot) = 0$. For $1/\sigma > 1$ the function $q_2(\cdot)$ is strictly convex for $(1-\alpha) \geq 1/2$. For $(1-\alpha) < 1/2$ there again exists a unique point of inflection given by $\tilde{x} = 2(1-\alpha)\bar{x}$. This proves the corollary. □

Proof of Proposition 23

The Jacobian matrix of (4.60)–(4.61) with permanent deficits is

$$J = \begin{bmatrix} z^\star & \partial\dot{z}/\partial x \\ x^\star\varpi(x^\star,\cdot) & \partial\dot{x}/\partial x \end{bmatrix}$$

with

$$\begin{aligned}\frac{\partial\dot{z}}{\partial x} &= z^\star\left(\psi\alpha c_p(\cdot)^{(\alpha/(1-\alpha))-1}(1-\alpha)^{-1}(1-(1-\tau)(1-\alpha)/\sigma)\right. \\ &\quad \left. -\psi c_p(\cdot)^{(1/(1-\alpha))-1}/(1-\alpha)\right) \\ \frac{\partial\dot{x}}{\partial x} &= x^\star\varpi(\cdot)\left(\psi\alpha c_p(\cdot)^{-1+\alpha/(1-\alpha)}(1-\alpha)^{-1}(1-(1-\tau)(1-\alpha)) - \right. \\ &\quad \left. \psi c_p(\cdot)^{-1+1/(1-\alpha)}/(1-\alpha) - \phi/x^2\right)\end{aligned}$$

The determinant is computed as

$$\det \mathrm{J} = z^{\star} x^{\star} \varpi(\cdot) \left(-\psi \alpha (1-\tau) c_p^{-1+\alpha/(1-\alpha)} (1 - 1/\sigma) - \phi / x^2 \right) = z^{\star} x^{\star} \varpi(\cdot) (\partial q_1 / \partial x),$$

with $\varpi = (1-\alpha)(\tau + \phi - \psi x)/((1-\alpha)(\tau + \phi) - \psi x)$ and q_1 defined in the proof of Proposition 22. Thus we have,

$$\det \mathrm{J} < 0 \leftrightarrow \partial q_1/\partial x < 0 \text{ for } x^{\star} < (1-\alpha)(\tau + \phi)/\psi,$$
$$\det \mathrm{J} < 0 \leftrightarrow \partial q_1/\partial x > 0 \text{ for } x^{\star} > (1-\alpha)(\tau + \phi)/\psi.$$

For $1/\sigma < 1$ and $\phi > 0$ the function q_1 crosses the horizontal axis from above such that $\det \mathrm{J} < 0$ for $x^{\star} < (1-\alpha)(\tau + \phi)/\psi$ and for $1/\sigma > 1$, $\phi < 0$ the function q_1 crosses the horizontal axis from below so that $\det \mathrm{J} < 0$ for $x^{\star} > (1-\alpha)(\tau + \phi)/\psi$.

For $1/\sigma > 1$, $\phi > 0$ the function q_1 first crosses the horizontal axis from above and then from below. Consequently, the first BGP is saddle point stable if and only if $x_1^{\star} < (1-\alpha)(\tau + \phi)/\psi$ and the second BGP is saddle point stable if and only if $x_2^{\star} > (1-\alpha)(\tau + \phi)/\psi$.

For $1/\sigma < 1$, $\phi < 0$ the function q_1 first crosses the horizontal axis from below and then from above. Consequently, the first BGP is saddle point stable if and only if $x_1^{\star} > (1-\alpha)(\tau + \phi)/\psi$ and the second BGP is saddle point stable if and only if $x_2^{\star} < (1-\alpha)(\tau + \phi)/\psi$. Thus, there is only one or no saddle point stable BGP in this case. □

Proof of Proposition 24

To prove that proposition we note that the balanced growth rate rises (declines) for $\partial(S/Y)/\partial\phi < (>) 0$. Since $S/Y = \psi x - \phi$ we get

$$\frac{\partial(S/Y)}{\partial \phi} = -1 + \psi \frac{\partial x}{\partial \phi}$$

The expression $\partial x/\partial \phi$ is obtained by implicit differentiation as

$$\frac{\partial x}{\partial \phi} = -\frac{\partial q_1/\partial \phi}{\partial q_1/\partial x}$$

with q_1 from the proof of Proposition 22 which gives

$$\frac{\partial(S/Y)}{\partial \phi} = \frac{C_1 + \phi/x^2 - \psi/x - C_1}{\partial q_1/\partial x} = \frac{\psi x - \phi}{(-x^2)\,(\partial q_1/\partial x)}$$

with $C_1 = \psi(1-\tau)\alpha(\tau+\phi-\psi x)^{(1/(1-\alpha))-2}(1-1/\sigma)$. Since $\psi x - \phi = S/Y > 0$ the balanced growth rate rises (declines) for $\partial q_1/\partial x > (<)0$ which holds for $x^\star > (<)(1-\alpha)\bar{x}$ for a saddle point stable BGP (see the proof of Proposition 23). Inserting $(1-\alpha)\bar{x}$ in Eq. (4.57) gives the result. □

Proof of Proposition 25

The strategy of the proof is analogous to that of the proof of Proposition 17. Hence, we set $\phi = 0$, $\psi = (1-\tau)(1-\alpha)x^\alpha(L^n)^\alpha - \delta$ and $b = 0$. Setting $\dot{x}/x = \dot{c}/c$ gives $q(x,\cdot) = (1-\alpha)x^\alpha(L^n)^\alpha(1-\tau) - (\rho+\delta) + \delta_G - \tau x^{\alpha-1}(L^n)^\alpha + \varrho\alpha x^{\alpha-1}(L^n)^{\alpha-1}(L-L^n)$. In case of sustained growth we have $g = \tau x^{\alpha-1}(L^n)^\alpha - \delta_G - \varrho\alpha x^{\alpha-1}(L^n)^{\alpha-1}(L-L^n) > 0$ which is only possible for $\tau > \varrho\alpha(L-L^n)/L^n$. With this, it is easily seen that $\lim_{x\to 0} q(x,\cdot) = -\infty$ and $\lim_{x\to\infty} q(x,\cdot) = +\infty$. Further, we have $\partial q(\cdot)/\partial x > 0$. Thus, uniqueness of a BGP is shown.

To show saddle point stability, we compute the Jacobian matrix evaluated at the rest point of (4.85)–(4.87). The Jacobian is given by

$$\mathrm{J} = \begin{bmatrix} c\ \partial\dot{c}/\partial b & \partial\dot{c}/\partial x \\ 0\ \partial\dot{b}/\partial b & 0 \\ x\ \partial\dot{x}/\partial b & \partial\dot{x}/\partial x \end{bmatrix},$$

with $c = c^\star$ and $x = x^\star$. One eigenvalue of this matrix is given by $\varrho_1 = \partial\dot{b}/\partial b = -\dot{K}/K = -g < 0$. Thus, we know that one eigenvalue, ϱ_1, is negative. Further, $c(\partial\dot{x}/\partial x) - x(\partial\dot{c}/\partial x)$ can be computed as follows, $c(\partial\dot{x}/\partial x) - x(\partial\dot{c}/\partial x) = -\alpha(1-\alpha)x^{\alpha-1}(L^n)^\alpha(1-\tau) + (\alpha-1)x^{-1}\left(\tau x^{\alpha-1}(L^n)^\alpha - \varrho\alpha x^{\alpha-1}(L^n)^{\alpha-1}(L-L^n)\right)$. $g > 0$ implies $\tau x^{\alpha-1}(L^n)^\alpha - \varrho\alpha x^{\alpha-1}(L^n)^{\alpha-1}\ (L-L^n) > \delta_G > 0$. Consequently, the determinant of J is negative. Since the product of the eigenvalues equals the determinant, $ev_1 \cdot ev_2 \cdot ev_3 = \det \mathrm{J} > 0$, and because of $ev_1 < 0$, we know that two eigenvalues are negative and one is positive. □

Proof of Proposition 26

To prove Proposition 26, equation $\dot{b}/b = 0$ is solved with respect to c giving $c = c(x,b,\cdot)$. Inserting $c = c(x,b,\cdot)$ in $\dot{c}/c$ and solving $\dot{c}/c = 0$ with respect to b gives $b^\star$ as in Proposition 26. □

Proof of Proposition 27

To prove this proposition we note that we set $\phi = 0$, $\psi = (1-\tau)(1-\alpha)x^\alpha(L^n)^\alpha - \delta$ and $b = 0$ to get scenario (i). Further, the balanced growth rate is given by $\dot{C}/C = -(\rho+\delta) + (1-\tau)(1-\alpha)x^\alpha(L^n)^\alpha$. Along a BGP we have $\dot{C}/C = \dot{G}/G$ which implies

$$(1-\tau)(1-\alpha)x^\alpha(L^n)^\alpha - (\rho+\delta) = \omega\,\tau x^{\alpha-1}(L^n)^\alpha - \omega\,\varrho\alpha x^{\alpha-1}(L^n)^{\alpha-1}(L-L^n) - \delta_G \tag{4.95}$$

A value $x_i^\star$ such that the left hand side in (4.95) equals the right hand side gives a BGP for scenario (i).

Using that b on the BGP is given by $b = \phi\cdot(x^\star)^\alpha(L^n)^\alpha/(\rho-\psi)$, the condition $\dot{C}/C = \dot{G}/G$ can be written for scenario (ii) as

$$(1-\tau)(1-\alpha)x^\alpha(L^n)^\alpha - (\rho+\delta) = \omega\tau x^{\alpha-1}(L^n)^\alpha - \omega\varrho\alpha x^{\alpha-1}(L^n)^{\alpha-1}(L-L^n) - \delta_G - \rho\omega b/x \tag{4.96}$$

A value $x_{ii}^\star$ such that the left hand side in (4.96) equals the right hand side gives a BGP for scenario (ii).

The function on the left hand side of Eqs. (4.95) and (4.96) are identical. The graph of the function on the right hand side of (4.95), however, is above the graph of the function on the right hand side of (4.96) for all $b > 0$. Therefore, the left hand side and the right hand side in (4.95) intersect at a larger value of x than the left hand side and the right hand side in (4.96), giving a higher balanced growth rate for scenario (i). □

Proof of Proposition 28

To prove this proposition, we compute the Jacobian matrix evaluated at the rest point of system (4.88)–(4.91). The Jacobian has the following form,

$$\mathrm{J} = \begin{bmatrix} c\ \partial\dot{c}/\partial b & \partial\dot{c}/\partial c & \partial\dot{c}/\partial y \\ 0\ \partial\dot{b}/\partial b & 0 & 0 \\ x\ \partial\dot{x}/\partial b & \partial\dot{x}/\partial c & \partial\dot{x}/\partial y \\ y\ \partial\dot{y}/\partial b & \partial\dot{y}/\partial c & \partial\dot{y}/\partial y \end{bmatrix},$$

with $c = c^\star$, $x = x^\star$ and $y = y^\star$. One eigenvalue of this matrix is given by $ev_1 = \partial\dot{b}/\partial b = -\dot{K}/K = -g < 0$. □

Chapter 5
Government Debt and Human Capital Formation

In this chapter, we focus on another important source of sustained growth, namely human capital formation. Therefore, we study two endogenous growth models with human capital accumulation that is the result of public spending. The government hires teachers and finances additional expenditures for human capital formation. As in the last section, it may run deficits but sets the primary surplus again such that it is a positive function of public debt.

The seminal papers in the field of endogenous growth with human capital are the contributions by Uzawa (1965) and by Lucas (1988) that are basically the same. There, the representative individual decides how much of his available time is spent for producing physical output and how much is used for the formation of human capital. Human capital is modeled as a production factor that raises aggregate production possibilities as well as the marginal product of physical capital and, thus, the long-run growth rate. Rebelo (1991) extended this class of models by assuming that both physical capital and human capital enter the production process of human capital, in contrast to the model by Uzawa and Lucas who posit that human capital formation is the result of human capital input alone.

However, neither of these models allows for public spending in the process of human capital formation. Contributions, which take into account that the public sector can stimulate the formation of human capital by devoting public resources to schooling, are for example Glomm and Ravikumar (1992), Ni and Wang (1994), Beauchemin (2001), Blankenau and Simpson (2004) and Greiner (2008c). In those contributions, human capital accumulation results either from both private and public services, as in Glomm and Ravikumar and in Blankenau, or from public spending alone, as in Ni and Wang, in Beauchemin and in Greiner.

As concerns the empirical relevance of human capital, there is evidence that education is positively correlated with income growth. At the microeconomic level the positive correlation seems to be quite robust. On the macroeconomic level the findings are more fragile (see for example Krueger and Lindahl 2001) which, however, may be due to measurement errors. Thus, Krueger and Lindahl

© Springer International Publishing Switzerland 2015

A. Greiner, B. Fincke, *Public Debt, Sustainability and Economic Growth*,
DOI 10.1007/978-3-319-09348-2_5

demonstrate that cross-country regressions indicate that the change in education is positively correlated with economic growth if measurement errors are accounted for. Further, in the study by Levine and Renelt (1992) the secondary school enrollment rate is also positively correlated with economic growth and is even robust. Robust means that the variable human capital is always significantly correlated with economic growth independent of which other variables are present in the estimated equation. Barro and Sala-i-Martin (2003) find that the average years of both the male and female secondary and higher schooling, observed at the start of each decade, are significantly correlated with the average growth rates of per-capita GDP over the considered time periods. Greiner et al. (2005) also find evidence that human capital is an important factor that helps explain economic growth and that a basic model featuring human capital can replicate the time series of economic variables for the US and for the German economy after World War II. Therefore, building endogenous growth models with human capital as the engine of growth seems to be justified.

5.1 The Structure of the Growth Model with Human Capital

Our economy consists of three sectors: A household sector which receives labor income and income from its saving, a productive sector and the government. First, we describe the household and the productive sector.

5.1.1 The Household and the Productive Sector

Overall population in the economy is assumed to be constant and the household sector is represented by one household which maximizes the discounted stream of utility resulting from consumption, C, over an infinite time horizon subject to its budget constraint.[1] The utility function is assumed to be given by $U(C) = (C^{1-\sigma} - 1)/(1-\sigma)$ and labor, L, is supplied inelastically. The maximization problem, then, can be written as

$$\max_C \int_0^{\infty} e^{-\rho t} \, (C^{1-\sigma} - 1)/(1-\sigma) dt, \tag{5.1}$$

subject to

$$(1-\tau)\,(wuL + rW) = \dot{W} + C. \tag{5.2}$$

[1]Note that we again omit the time argument t if no ambiguity arises.

We denote by ρ the subjective discount rate, $1/\sigma$ is the intertemporal elasticity of substitution of consumption between two points in time, w is the wage rate and r is the interest rate. Assets are denoted by $W \equiv B + K$ which are equal to public debt, B, and physical capital, K, and $\tau \in (0, 1)$ is the income tax rate. The dot gives the derivative with respect to time and we neglect depreciation of private capital.

Further, u gives that part of available time used of production and $1-u$ is that part of time used for education, which builds up a human capital stock. We assume that the part of time used for human capital formation is determined by the government through mandatory attendance laws so that the household takes u as exogenously given.

To solve this problem we formulate the current-value Hamiltonian which is now written as

$$\mathcal{H} = (C^{1-\sigma} - 1)/(1-\sigma) + \lambda((1-\tau)(wuL + rW) - C). \tag{5.3}$$

Necessary optimality conditions are given by

$$\lambda = C^{-\sigma} \tag{5.4}$$

$$\dot{\lambda} = \rho\lambda - \lambda(1-\tau)\, r. \tag{5.5}$$

If the transversality condition $\lim_{t\to\infty} e^{-\rho t}\lambda W = 0$ holds the necessary conditions are also sufficient.

The productive sector is represented by one firm which behaves competitively and which maximizes static profits. The production function of the firm is given by

$$Y = K^{1-\alpha}(uh_c L)^{\alpha}, \tag{5.6}$$

with $0 < \alpha < 1$. The parameter $(1-\alpha)$ denotes the private capital share and α gives the labor share. Human per-capita capital is denoted by h_c, which is labor augmenting, and u is that part of the labor force employed in the final goods sector. Profit maximization yields

$$w = \alpha(uL)^{-1} Y \tag{5.7}$$

$$r = (1-\alpha)K^{-1} Y. \tag{5.8}$$

Using (5.4)–(5.6) and (5.8), which must hold in equilibrium, the growth rate of consumption is derived as

$$\frac{\dot{C}}{C} = -\frac{\rho}{\sigma} + \frac{(1-\tau)(1-\alpha)K^{-\alpha}(uh_c L)^{\alpha}}{\sigma}. \tag{5.9}$$

5.1.2 Human Capital Formation

Human capital in our economy is produced in the schooling sector where we assume that the government decides about the time the household has to spend for education. Additionally, the government uses public resources for education in the schooling sector, like expenditures for books and other teaching material, which is an input in the process of human capital formation, too. Thus, the input in the schooling sector is composed of time spent for education by the household and of school expenditures by the government. We assume decreasing returns to scale in each input alone and constant returns to scale in both inputs together.

As concerns the production function for human capital formation we assume a Cobb-Douglas specification. Normalizing labor to one, $L = 1$, which holds from now on, the differential equation describing the change in human per-capita capital can be written as

$$\dot{h}_c = \xi((1-u)h_c)^{\beta_h} I_e^{1-\beta_h}, \tag{5.10}$$

with I_e public resources used in the schooling sector, $\xi > 0$ a technology parameter and $\beta_h \in (0,1)$ is the elasticity of human capital formation with respect to the time spent for education.

5.1.3 The Government

The government in our economy receives tax revenues from income taxation and has revenues from issuing government bonds it then uses for public spending in the schooling sector and for interest payments on public debt. Thus, the period budget constraint of the government is given by

$$\dot{B} = rB + I_e - T, \tag{5.11}$$

with T denoting tax revenue.

Further, as in the preceding sections the government fixes the primary surplus to GDP ratio such that it is a positive linear function of the debt to GDP ratio. The primary surplus ratio, then, can be written as

$$\frac{S}{Y} = \phi + \psi \frac{B}{Y}, \tag{5.12}$$

where $\phi, \psi \in \mathbb{R}$ are constants and $\psi > 0$ holds.

Using (5.12), the differential equation describing the evolution of public debt, Eq. (5.11), can be rewritten as

$$\dot{B} = (r - \psi)B - \phi Y. \tag{5.13}$$

It should be recalled that, as in the model of the last chapter, this assumption brings a feedback effect of higher government debt into the model. If the government increases public debt, for whatever reasons, it must raise the primary surplus so that fiscal policy remains sustainable. This, however, means that more resources must be used for the debt service implying that the government has less scope for other types of spending, for example for the formation of human capital as in this model. In the next subsection we define equilibrium conditions and the balanced growth path.

5.1.4 Equilibrium Conditions and the Balanced Growth Path

An equilibrium allocation is defined as an allocation such that the firm maximizes profits implying that factor prices equal their marginal products (Eqs. (5.7) and (5.8)), the household solves (5.1) subject to (5.2) and the budget constraint of the government (5.11) is fulfilled and the government sticks to the rule defined in (5.12).

Using (5.11) and (5.13) we get the amount of public resources used in the schooling sector, I_e, in equilibrium. Inserting the resulting value in (5.10), the growth rate of human capital is described by the following differential equation,

$$\frac{\dot{h}_c}{h_c} = \xi \frac{((1-u)h_c)^{\beta_h}}{h_c} \left(\left(\frac{uh_c}{K} \right)^{\alpha} K(\tau - \phi) - B(\psi - \tau r) \right)^{1-\beta_h}, \tag{5.14}$$

with r given by (5.8).

The economy-wide resource constraint is obtained by combining Eqs. (5.2) and (5.13) as

$$\frac{\dot{K}}{K} = \frac{Y}{K}(1 + \phi - \tau) - \frac{C}{K} - \frac{B}{K}(r\,\tau - \psi). \tag{5.15}$$

Thus, the economy is completely described by Eqs. (5.9) and (5.13)–(5.15) plus the limiting transversality condition of the household.

A balanced growth path (BGP) is here defined as a path on which all endogenous variables grow at the same rate, that is $\dot{K}/K = \dot{B}/B = \dot{C}/C = \dot{h}_c/h_c$ holds, and the intertemporal budget constraint of the government is fulfilled. Assuming that $\sigma > (1-\tau) - \rho/r$ holds, so that the difference between the interest rate and the growth rate on the BGP is strictly positive, and positing that the government sets the primary surplus according to (5.12) with $\psi > 0$, any path which satisfies $\dot{K}/K = \dot{B}/B = \dot{C}/C = \dot{h}_c/h_c$ is associated with a sustainable public debt.

It should be noted that, in this section, we do not consider a balanced government budget nor a growth rate of public debt that is positive but smaller than the balanced growth rate. Instead, we are interested in how fiscal policy affects growth and stability on a path where public debt grows at the same rate as all other variables. Hence, in contrast to our earlier analyses, we only consider the situation where the long-run growth rate of public debt is positive and equal to that of the GDP so that the debt to GDP ratio remains constant.

To analyze our economy around a BGP we define the new variables $h := h_c/K$, $b := B/K$ and $c := C/K$. Differentiating these variables with respect to time yields a three dimensional system of differential equations given by

$$\dot{h} = h\xi(1-u)^{\beta_h}\left(u^\alpha h^{\alpha-1}(\tau-\phi) + (b/h)(\tau(1-\alpha)h^\alpha u^\alpha - \psi)\right)^{1-\beta_h} + h(c + b(\tau(1-\alpha)h^\alpha u^\alpha - \psi) - u^\alpha h^\alpha(1+\phi-\tau)), \tag{5.16}$$

$$\dot{b} = b(c + b(\tau(1-\alpha)h^\alpha u^\alpha - \psi) - u^\alpha h^\alpha(1+\phi-\tau)) - \phi u^\alpha h^\alpha + (1-\alpha)u^\alpha h^\alpha b - b\psi, \tag{5.17}$$

$$\dot{c} = c\left((1-\tau)(1-\alpha)u^\alpha h^\alpha/\sigma - \rho/\sigma - u^\alpha h^\alpha(1+\phi-\tau) + c\right) + c\,b(\tau(1-\alpha)h^\alpha u^\alpha - \psi). \tag{5.18}$$

A solution of $\dot{h} = \dot{b} = \dot{c} = 0$ with respect to h, b, c gives a BGP for our model and the corresponding ratios $h^\star, b^\star, c^\star$ on the BGP.[2] In the next section we derive some economic implications of our model and numerically study its dynamics.

5.1.5 *Analysis of the Model*

To get insight into our model we first solve (5.18) with respect to c, insert that value in (5.17) and set Eq. (5.17) equal to zero giving

$$b^\star = \frac{\phi\, u^\alpha (h^\star)^\alpha}{(r-g)-\psi}, \tag{5.19}$$

with $r = (1-\alpha)(uh^\star)^\alpha$ and g given by (5.9). From Eq. (5.19) we can derive a first result.

Since $b^\star$ is an endogenous variable, it can be positive or negative, with the latter implying that the government is a creditor. However, a positive value of government debt is more realistic since most real world economies are characterized by public debt and we limit our analysis to this case.

Assume that $\phi < 0$ holds. This implies that the primary surplus declines as GDP rises and the government raises its spending for education with higher GDP. In this case, ψ must be sufficiently large, more concretely $\psi > r - g$ must hold, so that the debt-capital ratio is positive on the BGP, which can be seen from (5.19). This means that the reaction of the government to increases in public debt must be sufficiently

[2]The $\star$ denotes BGP values and we exclude the economically meaningless BGP $h^\star = c^\star = 0 = b^\star$.

strong such that a BGP with public debt is feasible. If this does not hold, that is if the reaction of the government to higher public debt is relatively small, the government must be a creditor for the economy to achieve sustained growth.

If $\phi > 0$, that is if the primary surplus rises as GDP increases, the contrary holds. In this case, ψ must not be too large, that is $\psi < r - g$ must hold, so that sustained growth with positive public debt is feasible. This holds because a positive ϕ and a high ψ imply that the government does not invest sufficiently in the formation of human capital, which is the source of economic growth in our model. Consequently, if $\phi > 0$ and if ψ is relatively large, the government must be a creditor in order finance its investment in the schooling sector in order to achieve sustained growth. This can be seen from (5.14) which shows that for a positive ϕ and for a sufficiently large ψ, a negative government debt has a positive effect on the growth rate of human capital.

These considerations have shown that neither a too severe nor a too loose budgetary policy are compatible with sustained growth if the government is a debtor. On the one hand, if the government does not control public debt sufficiently, public debt becomes too high leading to a crowding-out of private investment, making sustained growth impossible. In this case, sustained growth is only possible if the government is a creditor.

On the other hand, the government must not conduct a too strict budgetary policy. This holds because with a too strict budgetary policy the government does not invest enough in the formation of human capital, which is the source of economic growth. In this case, sustained growth is not feasible either and the government again must be a creditor, so that it can finance necessary investment in the schooling sector to build up human capital.

Next, we resort to numerical examples in order to gain additional insight into our growth model.

Results for the Model on the BGP

To analyze our model further, we resort to simulations. We do so because the analytical model turns out to become too complex to derive further results.

As a benchmark for our simulations we set the income tax rate to 20 %, $\tau = 0.2$, and the elasticity of production with respect to physical capital is set to 30 %, $1 - \alpha = 0.3$. The rate of time preference is set to 5 %, $\rho = 0.05$, and we assume a logarithmic utility function, $\sigma = 1$. Further, 90 % of the available time is assumed to be used in the final goods sector, $u = 0.9$, and 10 % for human capital formation. As concerns the elasticity of human capital formation with respect to time we consider two values, $\beta_h = 0.75$ and $\beta_h = 0.5$. This implies that a marginal increase in time used for human capital formation raises human capital by 75 % and by 50 %, respectively. It also implies that time spent for education is more important compared to educational spending of the government. Finally, we set $\xi = 0.15$.

In Tables 5.1 and 5.2 we report results of our simulations for different values of ϕ and for values of ψ which are smaller than the subjective discount rate ρ. For

Table 5.1 Long-run growth rate and endogenous variables on the BGP for different ϕ and small values of ψ with $\beta_h = 0.75$

	$\psi = 0.015$				$\psi = 0.035$			
ϕ	$b^\star$	$h^\star$	g (%)	$I_e^\star/Y^\star$	$b^\star$	$h^\star$	g (%)	$I_e^\star/Y^\star$
$\phi = 0.05$	0.27	0.19	1.86	0.15	0.44	0.18	1.76	0.11
$\phi = 0.01$	0.06	0.19	1.96	0.2	0.09	0.19	1.94	0.2
$\phi = -0.01$	−0.06	0.19	2.01	0.23	−0.09	0.19	2.02	0.24
$\phi = -0.05$	−0.28	0.19	2.09	0.28	−0.45	0.2	2.14	0.32

Table 5.2 Long-run growth rate and endogenous variables on the BGP for different ϕ and small values of ψ with $\beta_h = 0.5$

	$\psi = 0.015$				$\psi = 0.035$			
ϕ	$b^\star$	$h^\star$	g (%)	$I_e^\star/Y^\star$	$b^\star$	$h^\star$	g (%)	$I_e^\star/Y^\star$
$\phi = 0.05$	0.28	0.2	2.27	0.15	0.45	0.19	2.06	0.11
$\phi = 0.01$	0.06	0.21	2.52	0.21	0.09	0.21	2.49	0.2
$\phi = -0.01$	−0.06	0.22	2.63	0.23	−0.09	0.22	2.66	0.24
$\phi = -0.05$	−0.3	0.22	2.84	0.28	−0.48	0.23	2.97	0.32

$\sigma = 1$, the latter implies that $(r - g) - \psi > 0$ holds on the BGP. The balanced growth rate g is given in percent and $E^\star/Y^\star$ gives education expenditures relative to GDP.

Tables 5.1 and 5.2 confirm the result derived for the analytical model that for small values of the reaction coefficient ψ, ϕ must be positive so that sustained growth with positive public debt is feasible. In this case, the primary surplus must rise as GDP rises, otherwise endogenous growth with a positive government debt is not possible. If this does not hold, that is if ϕ is negative, the government must be a creditor and the level of public debt is negative.

If ϕ is negative and ψ is small and if the government was a debtor, public debt would become extremely large and the government would require too large a fraction of the resources in the economy for interest payments on public debt. This would lead to a crowding-out of private investment, which can be seen from the economy-wide resource constraint (5.15). From Eq. (5.15), one realizes that private investment relative to capital, $I/K = \dot{K}/K$, will be low if ϕ is negative and if ψ is smaller than the product $r\,\tau$ (in case B is positive). Therefore, sustained growth is not feasible with a negative ϕ and a small ψ unless the government is a creditor.

Further, one realizes that for a given value of ψ the growth rate rises as ϕ is decreased. This means that a decrease in ϕ, which reflects a deficit financed increase in public spending for education since it implies that the government reduces its primary surplus at the expense of government spending for human capital formation, leads to higher growth. Thus, higher spending for human capital enhances long-run growth even if financed through public deficits in this case.

The reason for this outcome is to be seen in the fact that ψ, giving the reaction of the primary surplus to higher public debt, is small. A small ψ implies small negative feedback effects of higher debt and, consequently, a deficit financed increase in public spending for human capital formation raises the balanced growth rate. However, it must be pointed out that, if the government is a debtor, this policy is only feasible as long as the government raises its primary surplus with increases in GDP, that is as long as $\phi > 0$ holds. If ϕ is negative the government must be a creditor so that sustained growth is possible at all and so that this fiscal policy leads to higher long-run growth.

These qualitative results hold for both $\beta_h = 0.75$ and $\beta_h = 0.5$. Further, the smaller the value of β_h the more important is educational spending of the government relative to time as input. Therefore, the balanced growth rate g is the higher the smaller β_h for a given value of educational spending to GDP, $E^\star/Y^\star$, which can be clearly seen from Tables 5.1 and 5.2.

As to stability, the BGP is unstable in all cases, because the Jacobian has two positive eigenvalues and one negative. This means that the economy can converge to the BGP in the long-run only if the government levies a lump-sum tax at time zero which is used to control initial public debt, $B(0)$. Then, initial debt and initial consumption, $B(0)$ and $C(0)$, must be chosen such that the economy converges to the BGP in the long-run and these values are uniquely determined.

To gain further insight into our model we next set $\psi > \rho$ implying that $(r - g) - \psi < 0$ holds on the BGP. The results of the simulations are shown in Tables 5.3 and 5.4.

Tables 5.3 and 5.4 demonstrate that for relatively large values of ψ the situation changes. In this case, the government must be a creditor if ϕ is positive. A large value of ψ implies that the government raises the primary surplus to a great extent as public debt rises. Thus, a deficit financed increase in public spending for schooling,

Table 5.3 Long-run growth rate and endogenous variables on the BGP for different ϕ and large values of ψ with $\beta_h = 0.75$

	$\psi = 0.075$				$\psi = 0.1$			
ϕ	$b^\star$	$h^\star$	g (%)	$I_e^\star/Y^\star$	$b^\star$	$h^\star$	g (%)	$I_e^\star/Y^\star$
$\phi = 0.05$	−2.65	0.22	2.61	0.8	−0.46	0.2	2.15	0.32
$\phi = 0.01$	−0.41	0.2	2.13	0.31	−0.09	0.19	2.02	0.24
$\phi = -0.01$	0.36	0.18	1.81	0.13	0.09	0.19	1.95	0.2
$\phi = -0.05$	no BGP				0.43	0.18	1.77	0.12

Table 5.4 Long-run growth rate and endogenous variables on the BGP for different ϕ and large values of ψ with $\beta_h = 0.5$

	$\psi = 0.075$				$\psi = 0.1$			
ϕ	$b^\star$	$h^\star$	g	$I_e^\star/Y^\star$	$b^\star$	$h^\star$	g (%)	$I_e^\star/Y^\star$
$\phi = 0.05$	no BGP				−0.56	0.23	3.03	0.34
$\phi = 0.01$	−0.73	0.24	3.15 %	0.37	−0.1	0.22	2.67	0.24
$\phi = -0.01$	0.41	0.2	2.11 %	0.12	0.1	0.21	2.48	0.2
$\phi = -0.05$	no BGP				0.45	0.19	2.05	0.11

modeled by a decrease in ϕ, goes along with strong feedback effects of the higher public debt, so that in the end the economy ends up with less education spending per GDP and, consequently, with a lower long-run growth rate. In this case, one can state that the government policy is too strict, in the sense that it pays too much attention to the control of public debt, instead of fostering economic growth by investing into education. Therefore, sustained growth with a positive government debt for large values of ψ is only possible if ϕ is negative, that is if the government does not raise the primary surplus as GDP rises but invests in education. If this does not hold, the government must be a creditor with a certain stock of wealth out of which it finances necessary investment in the schooling sector.

As for Tables 5.1 and 5.2 we get a higher balanced growth rate in Tables 5.3 and 5.4 for a smaller value of β_h. Again, the reason is that with a higher elasticity of human capital production with respect to educational spending, reflected by a lower β_h, a given level of educational spending leads to a higher balanced growth rate.

As concerns stability, the economy is stable for all situations considered in Tables 5.3 and 5.4, with two eigenvalues of the Jacobian being negative or having negative real parts, in case they are complex conjugate, and one eigenvalue being positive. This means that, for any given value of public debt at time zero, $B(0)$, there exists a unique value of consumption at time zero, $C(0)$, which can be chosen freely, such that the economy converges to the BGP in the long-run. Thus, the long-run equilibrium is determinate. In this case, the government does not have to control public debt at time zero so that convergence to the BGP is assured.

Hence, from Tables 5.1 to 5.4 we can conclude that a strong reaction of the primary surplus to higher public debt, expressed by a large ψ, tends to stabilize the economy. On the other hand, high values of ψ imply that the feedback effect of public debt is large so that deficit financed expenditures for human capital formation, modeled by decreases in ϕ, lead to lower growth, whereas for small values of ψ the reverse holds. Thus, there is a monotonic relationship between growth and deficit financed spending for human capital formation which is negative for large values of ψ and positive for small values of ψ.

These considerations show that there is again a trade-off between stabilizing the economy, by choosing a high value for ψ, and getting positive growth effects of deficit financed spending for human capital, which is achieved by setting ψ to a low value.

Sensitivity Analysis of the Dynamics

The dynamic system in the last subsection was characterized by a unique economic reasonable BGP which is either stable or unstable. In the latter case, the government must intervene at time zero and control public debt such that the economy converges to the BGP in the long-run. Now, we look at the dynamics of our growth model in more detail. It turns out that for $\psi < \rho$, existence of a BGP implies that it is unique. For $\psi > \rho$ and for a sufficiently large difference $\psi - \rho$, the BGP is also unique.

If the difference $\psi - \rho$ is small, we can observe a situation which is characterized by two BGPs, where one is unstable, while the other is stable. In this case, the economy converges to the second BGP unless the government intervenes at $t = 0$ by levying a lump-sum tax, which is used to control $B(0)$ such that the economy converges to the first BGP.

In addition, if we continuously vary the parameter ψ, the second BGP may undergo a Hopf bifurcation leading to persistent cycles. In this case, the BGP is stable for certain values of ψ. If we decrease ψ the system becomes unstable and for a certain range of the parameter ψ in between stability and instability, sustained cycles occur. This implies that the economy is characterized by endogenously oscillating growth rates and does not converge to a constant long-run BGP.

We should like to point out that, as in the last subsection, higher values of ψ tend to stabilize the economy, which seems to be intuitively clear. Thus, the stronger the reaction of the government to higher public debt, more concretely, the stronger the increase in the primary surplus as public debt rises, the more likely it is that the dynamic system describing the economy is stable. Thus, we can state that the economy is locally stable for relatively large values of ψ. As ψ is continuously decreased, the BGP looses stability and, before becoming unstable, persistent cycles can emerge.

5.2 A More Elaborate Model with Human Capital

Another source of sustained growth in endogenous growth models is learning by doing. This type of growth theory goes back to the development literature of the 1950s and was revived by Romer (1986), who presented an endogenous growth model in which capital shows decreasing returns to scale on the microeconomic level of an individual firm but increasing returns on the macroeconomic level, due to spillovers.[3] Because of increasing returns to capital on the economy-wide level, the model predicts positive sustained per-capita growth. However, Romer did not focus on pure physical capital but on knowledge, as a more general concept of capital. But applying the concept of positive externalities of investment to physical capital alone makes sense, too. That holds true because DeLong and Summers (1991), for example, have demonstrated that investment, particularly in machinery, is associated with strong positive externalities. Further, Levine and Renelt (1992) have shown that the investment share is a robust variable in explaining economic growth. This positive and statistically significant effect of investment on the growth rate of countries suggests that investment not only affects the stock of physical capital but also increases intangible capital, such as knowledge, so that the social return to investment is larger than the private return. Cooley et al. (1997) and Greenwood et al. (1997) argue that investment in physical capital has a larger

[3]It was also that mechanism that generated ongoing growth in the models presented in Chap. 3.

influence on economic growth than is suggested by its factor share. This relationship holds because technological improvements are incorporated in physical capital that are not reflected in the share paid to physical capital. For those reasons, building a theoretical model that relates positive externalities of investment to physical capital seems to be a reasonable approach.

In this section we intend to combine the human capital model of endogenous growth with the learning by doing approach. To do so we present an endogenous growth model with learning by doing and human capital formation where human capital does not enter the aggregate production function directly but affects the ability of individuals to generate knowledge as a by-product of investment as in Greiner (2012c). With respect to human capital formation we again posit that the government plays a decisive role by financing school expenditures. Thus, it is public education that is at the center of our consideration, as in the last section. In addition, we allow for deficit finance of the government but, again, we assume the primary surplus to GDP ratio is a positive linear function of the debt to GDP ratio so that the debt ration becomes a mean-reverting process. This assumption as regards governmental behavior implies that public debt is sustainable.

The contribution of the model presented in this section relative to the existing literature on endogenous economic growth is to highlight the importance of learning by doing as a source for the formation of knowledge capital (see the seminal articles by Arrow 1962 and by Romer 1986), on the one hand, and of human capital formation (see Uzawa 1965 and Lucas 1988), on the other hand. Since human capital is formed in the schooling sector with the input financed by the government, public spending plays an important role in generating ongoing growth. In this respect, our approach resembles endogenous growth models with productive public spending (see Barro 1990, Futagami et al. 1993, or Glomm and Ravikumar 1997, and Chap. 4 of this book). However, the way how human capital is generated differs significantly from that of building up a stock of productive public capital so that these two approaches are to be seen as fundamentally different in nature, which is reflected by the different equations describing the formation of human capital and of public capital. Further, we allow for deficit financing and analyze repercussions of public debt so that our study also contributes to the analysis of the role of public finance in economic growth.

5.2.1 The Structure of the Growth Model

Our economy consists of three sectors: A household sector which receives labor income and income from its saving, a productive sector, and the government. In this section, lowercase letters give per-capita quantities and uppercase letters denote aggregate variables. First, we describe the household.

The Household

The household sector is represented by one household which maximizes the discounted stream of utility resulting from per-capita consumption, c, times the total number of household members over an infinite time horizon subject to its budget constraint. The utility function is assumed to be logarithmic, $U(c) = \ln c$ and labor, L, is supplied inelastically and constant over time. The maximization problem, then, can be written as follows

$$\max_{c} \int_{0}^{\infty} e^{-\rho t} L \ln c \, dt \tag{5.20}$$

subject to

$$(1-\tau)(wL + rK + rB) = \dot{K} + \dot{B} + C. \tag{5.21}$$

We denote by ρ the subjective discount rate, w is the wage rate, and r is the interest rate. Assets are given by public debt, B, and by physical capital, K, and $\tau \in (0, 1)$ is the income tax rate. We neglect depreciation of physical capital and the dot over a variable gives the derivative with respect to time.

Denoting by $a \equiv k + b$ per-capita assets, the budget constraint of the household in per-capita terms can be rewritten as

$$\dot{a} = (1-\tau)(w + ra) - c \tag{5.22}$$

The solution to this optimization problem gives the growth rate of per-capita consumption as

$$\frac{\dot{c}}{c} = -\rho + (1-\tau)r \tag{5.23}$$

In addition, the usual transversality condition $\lim_{t\to\infty} e^{-\rho t} a/c = 0$ must hold.

The Productive Sector and the Learning by Doing Mechanism

The productive sector is represented by one firm which behaves competitively and which maximizes static profits. The production function of the firm is given by

$$Y = K^{1-\alpha}(vuL)^{\alpha} \tag{5.24}$$

with $0 < \alpha < 1$. The coefficient $(1-\alpha)$ is the private capital share and α gives the labor share. The variable v gives the stock of knowledge that is formed as a by-product of cumulated investment and that is a purely public good. Further, we denote by u that part of the labor force that is employed in the final goods sector.

Dividing both sides of Eq. (5.24) by L gives the per-capita production function as

$$y = k^{1-\alpha}(uv)^{\alpha} \tag{5.25}$$

Profit maximization yields

$$w = \alpha k^{1-\alpha} v^{\alpha} u^{\alpha-1} \tag{5.26}$$

$$r = (1-\alpha)k^{-\alpha} v^{\alpha} u^{\alpha}. \tag{5.27}$$

As mentioned in the last paragraph the stock of knowledge is a by-product of cumulated investment. Thus, we adopt the idea of learning by doing as first brought into the economics literature by Arrow (1962) and Levhari (1966). According to Arrow (1962) the acquisition of knowledge, that is learning, is strongly related to experience and a good index of experience is cumulated past investment. The reason is that any new investment contains the latest level of technology so that any new investment raises the productivity of workers, provided they are capable of handling newly installed machines one should add. An important aspect about this learning by doing process is also that the knowledge raises the efficiency of each worker but, once formed, is a public good in the sense that the efficiency of any number of workers ca be raised equally.

In addition, workers must dispose of a certain stock of human capital in order to build up knowledge capital. The reason for that is that employees must dispose of certain capabilities in order to be able to operate the latest technologies so that the latter can raise labor productivity. Thus, workers must dispose of human capital in order to be able to produce with modern physical capital goods and it is the combination of these two factors that determines their productivity. Hence, human capital that is acquired in school does not immediately raise production possibilities of the economy but only when combined with practice.

We would like to point out that we focus on the average level of human capital in the economy rather than on that of high-skilled employees. That is also one reason why we assume that it is public schooling, financed by the government, where human capital is formed.[4]

Formally, the change in knowledge is a function of per-capita capital, h, and of cumulated past investment, that is of the physical capital stock, k, with the production function being Cobb-Douglas. Neglecting depreciation of knowledge, the differential equation can be written as

$$\dot{v} = \varphi k^{\beta} h^{1-\beta} \tag{5.28}$$

[4]A more formal reason is that knowledge is a purely public good that requires human capital for its formation, see the next subsection for details.

with $\varphi > 0$ an efficiency index and $\beta \in (0, 1)$ and $(1 - \beta)$ giving the contribution of cumulated past investment and of human capital to the formation of knowledge capital, respectively.

Human Capital Formation and the Public Sector

Human capital in our economy is produced in the schooling sector that is publicly financed. The structure is identical to that of the last section. The government hires $(1-u)$ of the active labor force as teachers. Additionally, the government uses public resources for education in the schooling sector, like expenditures for books and other teaching material, which is an input in the process of human capital formation, too. Thus, the input in the schooling sector is composed of teachers and of school expenditures and we assume decreasing returns to scale to each input but constant returns to both inputs.

With respect to human capital accumulation we assume that employees spend a fixed fraction of one time period for learning. Hence, our framework can be considered to model life-long learning of workers raising their individual human capital. Another possible interpretation of the model is that total population consists at each point in time of students, workers and teachers. When students graduate they become themselves either workers or are hired by the government as teachers, thus replacing the old generation, with a new generation of students going to school.

As concerns the production function for human capital formation we assume a Cobb-Douglas specification. The differential equation describing the change in aggregate human capital can be written as

$$\dot{H} = \xi((1 - u)hL)^{\beta_h} I_e^{1-\beta_h}, \tag{5.29}$$

with I_e public resources used in the schooling sector, $\xi > 0$ a technology parameter and $0 < \beta_h < 1$ is the elasticity of human capital formation with respect to teachers. Since population is constant, per-capita human capital $h = H/L$ evolves according to

$$\dot{h} = \xi((1 - u)h)^{\beta_h} i_e^{1-\beta_h}. \tag{5.30}$$

It should be noted that human capital is embodied in the workforce and is a private good, in contrast to knowledge. The government finances schooling because it is aware that education, that is, the formation of human capital, is necessary for the accumulation of knowledge capital. Hence, although human capital is a private good, education is publicly financed because it is a prerequisite for the accumulation of knowledge that is a public good and that determines aggregate productivity.

The government in our economy receives tax revenues from income taxation and has revenues from issuing government bonds it then uses for public spending in the schooling sector and for interest payments on public debt. Thus, the period budget constraint of the government is given by

$$\dot{B} = r(1-\tau)B + I_e + (1-u)wL - \tau(rK + wL) \tag{5.31}$$

with $(1-u)wL$ expenditures for teachers and I_e school expenditures. Further, S denotes that primary surplus given by $S \equiv T - I_e - (1-u)wL$, with T the tax revenue resulting from taxing labor and capital income of the household. It means that the primary surplus is defined as tax revenue minus government spending exclusive of net interest payments, as usual.

The budget constraint can be rewritten in per-capita terms as

$$\dot{b} = r(1-\tau)b + i_e + (1-u)w - \tau(rk + w) = rb(1-\tau) - s, \tag{5.32}$$

Further, the government sets the primary surplus to GDP ratio such that it is a positive linear function of the debt-GDP ratio, that is

$$s/y = \phi + \psi(b/y), \quad \phi \in \mathbb{R}, \quad \psi \in \mathbb{R}_{++}. \tag{5.33}$$

If the government was a creditor that lends to the private sector[5] the rule specified in Eq. (5.33) would guarantee that the private sector does not accumulate too much debt. Although the case with the government a lender to the private sector is of less relevance for real world economies, that rule can nevertheless be justified on economic grounds. Taking into account that the severe financial crisis that had begun in 2008 in the USA, was in part also due to the accumulation of huge debt by private households, that rule does make sense even if the government is not a debtor.

Using Eq. (5.33), the evolution of public debt per-capita is described by

$$\dot{b} = r(1-\tau)b - \psi b - \phi y. \tag{5.34}$$

Taking other fiscal policy instruments as given, school expenditures per-capita, i_e, are obtained from Eq. (5.32) as

$$i_e = \tau(rk + w) - (1-u)w - \psi b - \phi y. \tag{5.35}$$

Before we analyze our model we give the definition of an equilibrium and of a balanced growth path for this extended model. An equilibrium allocation is defined as an allocation such that the firm maximizes profits implying that factor prices equal their marginal products, the household solves (5.20) subject to (5.21) and the budget constraint of the government (5.32) is fulfilled and the government sticks to the rule defined in (5.33). Formally, an equilibrium allocation for our economy is defined as follows.

[5] Recall that in this case public debt B would be negative.

Definition 8 An equilibrium is a sequence of variables $\{c(t), v(t), h(t), b(t), k(t)\}_{t=0}^{\infty}$ and a sequence of prices $\{w(t), r(t)\}_{t=0}^{\infty}$ such that

(a) Equations (5.22) and (5.23) hold,
(b) Equations (5.26)–(5.28) hold and
(c) Equations (5.29), (5.34) and (5.35) hold.

The economy, then, is completely described by the differential equations $\dot{c}$, given by Eq. (5.23), $\dot{v}$, Eq. (5.28), $\dot{h}$, given by Eq. (5.30), $\dot{b}$, Eq. (5.34), and by the economy-wide resource constraint that is obtained by combining the budget constraint of the household, (5.22), with that of the government, (5.34). The system of differential equations describing the economy is obtained as

$$\dot{c} = c(-\rho + (1-\tau)(1-\alpha)k^{-\alpha}v^{\alpha}u^{\alpha}) \tag{5.36}$$

$$\dot{v} = \varphi k^{\beta}h^{1-\beta} \tag{5.37}$$

$$\dot{h} = \xi((1-u)h)^{\beta_h}(\tau(rk+w) - (1-u)w - \psi b - \phi k^{1-\alpha}v^{\alpha}u^{\alpha})^{1-\beta_h} \tag{5.38}$$

$$\dot{b} = (1-\tau)rb - \psi b - \phi k^{1-\alpha}v^{\alpha}u^{\alpha} \tag{5.39}$$

$$\dot{k} = (1-\tau)\left((1-\alpha)k^{1-\alpha}v^{\alpha}u^{\alpha} + \alpha k^{1-\alpha}v^{\alpha}u^{\alpha-1}\right) - c + \psi b + \phi k^{1-\alpha}v^{\alpha}u^{\alpha}, \tag{5.40}$$

with w and r given by Eqs. (5.26) and (5.27), respectively.

We are interested in a situation where the economy is characterized by ongoing growth. A balanced growth path (BGP) is defined as a path on which all economic variables grow at the same rate, with the exception of public debt possibly that may be constant or grow at a smaller rate. The next definition gives the exact definition of a BGP.

Definition 9 A BGP is a path such that the economy is in equilibrium and such that consumption, physical capital, knowledge and human capital grow at the same strictly positive constant rate, that is $\dot{c}/c = \dot{k}/k = \dot{v}/v = \dot{h}/h = g$, $g > 0$, $g =$ *constant*, and either

(i) $\dot{b} = 0$ or
(ii) $\dot{b}/b = g_b$, with $0 < g_b < g, g_b =$ constant or
(iii) $\dot{b}/b = \dot{c}/c = \dot{v}/v = \dot{h}/h = \dot{k}/k = g$

5.2.2 *Analyzing the Model*

To analyze our model for the case of ongoing growth we first note that the right hand side of the differential equation system (5.36)–(5.40) does not have a rest point. To be able to study our model we therefore introduce the new variables $x := c/k$, $q := h/k$, $z := v/k$ and $p := b/k$. Differentiating these variables with respect to time leads to a new four-dimensional system of differential equations given by

$$\dot{x} = x(\dot{c}/c - \dot{k}/k) \tag{5.41}$$

$$\dot{q} = q(\dot{h}/h - \dot{k}/k) \tag{5.42}$$

$$\dot{z} = z(\dot{v}/v - \dot{k}/k) \tag{5.43}$$

$$\dot{p} = p(\dot{b}/b - \dot{k}/k) \tag{5.44}$$

In the next subsection we will first analytically analyze the characteristics of the balanced growth path in our model.

The Balanced Growth Path

To start with we note that a rest point of (5.41)–(5.44), that is, values $x^\star, q^\star, z^\star$ and $p^\star$ such that $\dot{x} = \dot{q} = \dot{z} = \dot{p} = 0$, gives a BGP[6] where $\dot{c}/c = \dot{k}/k = \dot{h}/h = \dot{v}/v =: g$ holds. Further, in case (iii) of Definition 9 public debt grows at the same rate as all other economic variables yielding $\dot{b}/b = g$. In case (i) and (ii) of the Definition 9, public debt is constant or grows at a smaller rate.[7]

The first result stated in Proposition 29 excludes the possibility of multiple balanced growth paths for our model.

Proposition 29 *Existence of a balanced growth path implies that it is unique.*

Proof See the appendix to this chapter. □

This proposition demonstrates that the BGP is unique if it exists. Hence, the model does not give rise to development traps modeled as global indeterminacy where one economy converges to a BGP with high growth while another one may converge to a BGP with low growth. As regards the existence of a BGP, we cannot answer this question for the analytical model. Therefore, we resort to a numerical example in the next subsection in order to get additional insight into our model. As concerns the balanced growth rate, g, we note that this variable is given by Eq. (5.36). It is immediately realized that the balanced growth rate negatively depends on the level of physical capital and positively on the level of knowledge. Hence, those economies will experience high growth rates in the long-run that have a high ratio of knowledge relative to physical capital. The stock of knowledge for its part positively depends on human capital in this economy that is formed through public education.

---

[6]The * denotes the values on the BGP. We exclude $x^\star = z^\star = 0$ and $q^\star = 0$ is not feasible since it would imply division by zero in $\dot{h}/h$.

[7]Equation (5.34) shows that case (i) is obtained with $\phi = 0$ and $\psi = (1-\tau)r$, case (ii) is obtained for $\phi = 0$ and $\psi < (1-\tau)r$. Further, in case (ii) $\rho < \psi$ must hold so that $\dot{C}/C < \dot{B}/B$ on the BGP.

We would also like to point out that public expenditures for schooling are productive so that there exists a growth maximizing value for the income tax rate, as in the seminal contributions by Barro (1990) or Futagami et al. (1993) who analyzed an endogenous growth model with productive public spending as a flow and as a stock, respectively. The same holds for the amount of human capital that is employed by the government as teachers in the schooling sector. On the one hand, more teachers imply better education. On the other hand, more teachers mean that fewer labor force is producing final goods, thus reducing the marginal product of physical capital, and that less resources are available for educational spending. These results are rather obvious so that we do not state them as propositions. Nevertheless, we want to mention them for the sake of completeness.

More interesting is the relation between public debt and the balanced growth rate that we will address next. In Lemma 3 we first present an important result as concerns the relation between the balanced growth rate and the ratio of public debt to physical capital on the BGP, $p^\star$.

Lemma 3 *On the BGP the following property holds:* $\mathrm{d}g/\mathrm{d}p^\star < 0$.

Proof See the appendix to this chapter. □

This lemma shows that there is a negative correlation between public debt and the long-run growth rate, that is, the higher public debt the lower is the long-run growth rate. Given this lemma, we can state the following proposition.

Proposition 30 *The balanced growth rate becomes maximal when the government builds up a stock of wealth. If the government does not build up a stock of wealth the balanced growth rate becomes maximal for a zero debt to physical capital ratio.*

Proof Follows immediately from Lemma 3. □

The economic mechanism behind this outcome is that a higher stock of public debt requires more resources for the debt service that cannot be used for human capital formation. When the government can use more resources for education the level of human capital in the economy will be higher. As a consequence, any new investment is more productive in the sense that it raises knowledge to a stronger degree. This, for its part, raises the marginal product of physical capital and, thus, the incentive to invest. The long-run growth rate is highest when the government has built up a stock of wealth it can use to finance human capital formation in addition to the tax revenue it receives.

Proposition 30 gives the relation between the long-run growth rate and the ratio of public debt to physical capital. In order to build up a stock of wealth, the government must run surpluses over a certain time period. Leaving aside this case that seems to be rather unrealistic if one looks at real world economies, the balanced growth rate is maximized with a zero ratio of public debt to physical capital. The latter can be achieved either with a public deficit such that public debt rises less than physical capital, case (ii) in Definition 9, or with a balanced government budget, case (i) in Definition 9. Both budgetary policies are equivalent as regards their implication for the long-run growth rate because in both cases public debt relative to physical capital, and also relative to GDP, converges to zero asymptotically.[8] We state this result as corollary to Proposition 30.

Corollary 3 *Assume that the government is a debtor. Then, the balanced growth rate becomes maximal when public deficits are such that public debt rises less than the balanced growth rate or when the government budget is balanced.*

Proof $\dot{b}/b = g_b$, with $0 < g_b < g$, implies $p(t) = e^{(g_b - g)t} p(0) \rightarrow 0$ for $t \rightarrow \infty$, with $p(0)$ the initial value of public debt relative to physical capital on the BGP. Further, we also have that $\dot{b}/b = 0$ implies $p(t) = e^{-gt} p(t_0) \rightarrow 0$ for $t \rightarrow \infty$. □

Up to now we have analyzed different budgetary strategies as regards their effect on the balanced growth rate. In a next step, we consider the situation where public debt grows at the same rate as all other variables on the BGP, case (i), and we study whether a deficit financed increase in public educational spending can raise the balanced growth rate. We state the result in Proposition 31.

Proposition 31 *Assume that public debt grows at the balanced growth rate. Then, a deficit financed increase of educational spending raises the balanced growth rate if and only if $\psi < \rho$ holds.*

Proof See the appendix to this chapter. □

In order to understand the economic mechanism that generates this result we note that, in a first step, more (deficit financed) educational spending implies better education and, thus, raises the accumulation of human capital. A higher stock of human capital leads to a better acquisition of knowledge that spurs economic growth. In a second step, the additional public debt exerts a negative feedback effect by absorbing more public resources for the debt service that cannot be used for educational purpose. If the reaction of the primary surplus to higher public debt, ψ, is large (small), that is, if it exceeds (falls short of) the subjective discount rate of the household, ρ, the feedback effect is so strong that it dominates the initial increase in public educational spending leading to a lower (higher) balanced growth rate. It should also be pointed out that in the case of a positive growth effect of a deficit financed increase in educational spending, the ratio of public debt to private physical capital declines, which is an immediate consequence of Lemma 3. Thus, in this case the higher balanced growth rate leads to higher tax revenues that reduce the long-run debt to capital ratio.

In the next subsection we analyze transition dynamics and welfare in order to gain additional insight into the structure of our growth model.

---

[8]The public debt to GDP is given by $p^{\star}/(z^{\star}u)^{\alpha}$.

Transition Dynamics and Welfare Effects

First, we analyze the transitional behavior of our model economy to the long-run balanced growth path.

The dynamics of our growth model around a BGP are described by Eqs. (5.41)–(5.44). To study that system we perform a local stability analysis where we proceed as usual and linearize that system and then compute the eigenvalues of the corresponding Jacobian matrix. Unfortunately, that matrix is rather complex so that no results can be obtained for die analytical model.

Nevertheless, it is possible to get some insight by focusing on the differential equation describing the ratio of public debt to physical capital and assuming that the growth rates of consumption, knowledge and physical capital are the same. Proposition 32 gives the result.

Proposition 32 *Assume that a BGP exists and that consumption and knowledge grow at the same rate as physical capital. Then, the debt to physical capital ratio converges to its BGP value if and only if* $\psi > \rho$ *holds.*

Proof See the appendix to this chapter. □

This proposition demonstrates that the debt to physical capital ratio converges to its BGP value only if the reaction of the primary surplus to a higher public debt is sufficiently large, that is, for $\psi > \rho$. That makes sense because the parameter ψ determines the degree of mean-reversion in the differential equation giving the evolution of public debt. Thus, Proposition 32 states that the debt to physical capital ratio converges only if the government puts a sufficiently high value on controlling public debt so that the degree of mean-reversion of the public debt to private capital ratio is sufficiently large.

To be more concrete, we note that the balanced growth rate is given by Eq. (5.36) implying that $\rho = (1 - \tau)r - g$ holds on the BGP. Hence, the condition in Proposition 32 states that the reaction coefficient ψ must exceed the difference between the net interest rate on public debt and the balanced growth rate for convergence to be given, which makes sense from an economic point of view.

Recalling Proposition 31 from the last subsection, we know that the government can achieve a higher balanced growth rate by running into debt in order to finance school expenditures in case of $\psi < \rho$. However, Proposition 32 suggests that in this case the debt ratio does not converge to its new BGP value by itself. Hence, the government has to levy an additional non-distortionary tax, possibly at a later point in time, in order to control the level of outstanding debt so that convergence may be achieved. Consequently, Proposition 32 suggests that there is a trade-off between stability and positive growth effects of deficit financed investment in human capital formation.

We would also like to point out that in the case of a balanced government budget and in the case where public debt grows but less than all other variables, convergence of the public debt ratio to its BGP value is given with the assumptions of Proposition 32. In these cases we have $\phi = 0$ and $\psi = (1 - \tau)r > \rho$ and $\psi > \rho$, respectively (see Footnote 7). Further, in both cases the debt to GDP ratio on the balanced growth path equals zero since public debt is constant or grows less than the stock of physical capital.

Proposition 32 gives a clue how the reaction coefficient ψ affects convergence of the debt to physical capital ratio and, thus, the stability of the complete model. However, it does not give a complete characterization of the dynamics of our growth model which is not possible for the analytical model. Nevertheless, resorting to a numerical example in order to gain additional insight into the dynamics confirms the conjecture of Proposition 32.[9]

Next, we address the question of which fiscal policy set forth in Definition 9 leads to highest welfare. In order to answer that question we have to compute the utility functional (5.20). If there were no transition dynamics that could be done analytically. However, in our model transition dynamics arise due to its nonlinear structure so that we have to resort to numerical examples in order to gain insight into welfare properties of different fiscal policies.

In our numerical examples we take as a benchmark the following parameter values. The subjective discount rate ρ is set to 3.5 %, that is, $\rho = 0.035$. The labor share in the production function is 60 % giving $\alpha = 0.6$ and total labor is set to one, $L = 1$. The parameters determining the external effect of investment and the efficiency of human capital formation are set to $\varphi = 0.05$ and to $\xi = 0.05$, respectively. The elasticity of human capital formation with respect to teachers is 50 %, $\beta_h = 0.5$, and we also set $\beta = 0.5$. The income tax rate is set to 15 %, $\tau = 0.15$. Finally, the share of human capital employed in the education sector is set to 10 %, that is, $1 - u = 0.1$. These parameters are left unchanged throughout the simulations.

We consider two different cases. First, we take arbitrary initial conditions of the variables human capital relative to physical capital, q, knowledge relative to physical capital, v, and public debt relative to physical capital, p, and analyze which of the three fiscal policies specified in Definition 9 leads to highest welfare. After that, we assume that the economy is on the balanced growth path and the government runs permanent deficits such that public debt grows at the same rate as physical capital and GDP, scenario (iii). Then, we compare welfare obtained for that situation with welfare which results when the government switches to a balanced budget, scenario (i), and which results when the government runs only slight deficits such that the debt to GDP ratio converges to zero asymptotically, scenario (ii). Of course, in the latter two cases we must again take into account transition dynamics.

To compute the value of the functional (5.20) we proceed as follows. First, we numerically solve the linearized system of the differential equation system (5.41)–(5.44) which gives the time path of the variable $z(t)$ for $t \in [0, \infty)$. Given that variable we can solve the differential equation (5.23) and insert the resulting time path for the level of consumption, $C(t)$, in Eq. (5.20). In order to get an initial value

[9]The results are given in the appendix to this chapter.

Table 5.5 Welfare in scenario (i), scenario (ii), and scenario (iii) for given initial conditions $q(0) = 0.0032,\ p(0) = 0.1,\ z(0) = 0.035$

	Scenario (i)	Scenario (ii)	Scenario (iii)
Welfare	−54.8605	−55.1642	−59.5031

Table 5.6 Welfare in scenario (iii) on the BGP and welfare resulting from a transition to scenario (ii), and scenario (i), respectively

	Scenario (iii)	From scenario (iii) to (ii)	From scenario (iii) to (i)
Welfare	−24.86991	−24.7471	−24.52635

for the time path of $C(t)$ we set $K(0) = 1$ such that $C(0) = x(0)$ holds. Tables 5.5 and 5.6 give the results.[10]

The tables show that in both cases scenario (iii) where debt grows at the same rate as physical capital and GDP yields the lowest welfare. This holds because that scenario goes along with a smaller balanced growth rate compared to the other two scenarios where the debt to GDP ratio equals zero in the long-run. Comparing the scenario (ii), where debt grows but less than capital and GDP, with the balances budget scenario, scenario (i), one realizes that in both cases the balanced budget scenario performs better. That holds, because the balanced budget scenario (i) implies a higher initial value of consumption than scenario (ii) and the balanced growth rate is the same in both scenarios so that the utility functional (5.20) takes on a higher value in the balanced budget scenario.

Conclusion

The analysis of the first endogenous growth model with human capital in this chapter has demonstrated that a loose fiscal policy, where the government does not pay great attention to stabilizing debt, does not permit sustained growth in the long-run, unless the government is a creditor. In this case, there is a crowding-out of private investment and sustained growth is not feasible, unless the government is a creditor and lends to the private sector, so that the latter can finance the necessary investments in physical capital. On the other hand, if the government puts a large weight on debt stabilization and does not invest sufficiently in the formation of human capital, sustained growth is not possible either, unless the government is again a creditor. In this case, the government must use its wealth in order to finance necessary investment in the formation of human capital. It should be noted that those results were

(continued)

[10] The parameters ϕ and φ are $\phi = -0.01,\ \varphi = 0.05$ in scenario (iii), $\phi = 0,\ \varphi = 0.05$ in scenario (ii), and $\phi = 0,\ \varphi = (1 - \tau)r$ in scenario (i).

derived under the assumption that public debt grows at the same rate as all other economic variables on the balanced growth path.

The second endogenous growth model we presented was more elaborate. There, it was the combination of learning by doing and human capital formation that generates ongoing growth. In contrast to the usual human capital approach in the endogenous growth theory, we did not assume that human capital directly affects production possibilities in the economy. Instead, human capital is necessary for the formation of knowledge that results as a by-product of cumulated past investment. Hence, it is the combination of learning and practical experience that determines labor productivity and that is decisive for economic growth.

For that model, we could show that the balanced growth path is unique in case it exists. As regards the long-run growth rate we found that the latter is the smaller the higher the debt to GDP ratio. If one excludes the unrealistic case that the government is a net lender to the private sector, the long-run growth rate is maximized for a zero debt to GDP ratio. That can be achieved either through a balanced budget or through public deficits such that the government debt grows at a smaller rate than GDP.

Further, evidence was found that convergence to the balanced growth path is given only if the reaction of the primary surplus to higher public debt is sufficiently large. Otherwise, the time path of the debt to GDP ratio does not display mean-reversion such that divergence of the debt to GDP ratio cannot be avoided. This leads to an unstable situation for the whole economy so that convergence to a balanced growth path cannot be achieved.

Finally, we have seen that a balanced budget does not only lead to the highest balanced growth rate in the long-run but also to highest welfare in our model. Comparing the three scenarios (balanced budget, debt growing but less than GDP and debt growing at the same rate as GDP), it turned out that the balanced budget gives the highest value for welfare, followed by the scenario where debt grows but less than GDP, followed by the scenario where debt grows at the same rate as GDP in the long-run.

Hence, as regards policy recommendations we can state that a scenario where debt grows at the same rate as GDP yields the lowest long-run growth rate as well as lowest welfare. Thus, governments should reduce their debt to GDP ratios that can be either achieved by balanced government budgets or by public deficits such that government debt grows less than GDP. Such scenarios generate both higher growth in the long-run as well as higher welfare.

Appendix

Proof of Proposition 29

The balanced growth rate is given by Eq. (5.23) as $g = \dot{c}/c = -\rho + (1-\tau)(1-\alpha)z^{\alpha}u^{\alpha}$ with $z = z^{\star}$. Solving Eqs. (5.41), (5.44) and (5.42) with respect to x, p and q leads to $x = x(z,\cdot)$, $p = p(z,\cdot)$ and $q = q(p(z,\cdot), z, \cdot)$, respectively. Inserting that x, p, and q in Eq. (5.43) gives $\dot{z}$ as function of z. Dividing $\dot{z}$ by z leads to the function f_1 given by

$$f_1(\cdot) = \rho - (1-\tau)(1-\alpha)u^{\alpha}z^{\alpha} + z^{\alpha(1-\beta)-1}\varphi \cdot C_1^{1-\beta} \cdot \left(\frac{(1-\alpha)(1-\tau)u^{\alpha}z^{\alpha} - \rho}{\xi}\right)^{-\frac{1-\beta}{1-\beta_h}},$$

with

$$C_1 = \left(\frac{\alpha(1-\tau)(u-1) + u\tau}{u^{1-\alpha}(1-u)^{\beta_h/(\beta_h-1)}} + \frac{\phi\rho u}{u^{1-\alpha}(1-u)^{\beta_h/(\beta_h-1)}(\psi-\rho)}\right)$$

On a BGP we must have $f_1(\cdot) = 0$.

Differentiating $f_1(\cdot)$ with respect to z leads to

$$\frac{df_1(\cdot)}{dz} = (1-\tau)(\alpha-1)\alpha z^{\alpha-1}u^{\alpha} - \varphi z^{-2}C_1^{1-\beta}\left(\frac{(1-\alpha)(1-\tau)u^{\alpha}z^{\alpha} - \rho}{\xi}\right)^{\frac{1-\beta}{1-\beta_h}}$$
$$+ \frac{\alpha(\beta-1)\varphi C_1^{1-\beta}\left(\frac{(1-\alpha)(1-\tau)u^{\alpha}z^{\alpha}-\rho}{\xi}\right)^{-\frac{1-\beta}{1-\beta_h}}(\rho(1-\beta_h) + \beta_h(1-\tau)(1-\alpha)u^{\alpha}z^{\alpha})}{(1-\beta_h)z^2((1-\alpha)(1-\tau)u^{\alpha}z^{\alpha} - \rho)}$$

Existence of BGP implies $C_1^{1-\beta}((1-\alpha)(1-\tau)u^{\alpha}z^{\alpha}/\xi - \rho/\xi)^{-\frac{1-\beta}{1-\beta_h}} > 0$, $(1-\alpha)(1-\tau)u^{\alpha}z^{\alpha} - \rho > 0$ so that $\lim_{z\to\infty} f_1(\cdot) = -\infty$ and $\lim_{z\searrow u^{-1}\rho^{1/\alpha}((1-\alpha)(1-\tau))^{-1/\alpha}} f_1(\cdot) = +\infty$, where $z \searrow u^{-1}\rho^{1/\alpha}((1-\alpha)(1-\tau))^{-1/\alpha}$ means that z approaches that value from above. We can restrict the range of z to $z > u^{-1}\rho^{1/\alpha}((1-\alpha)(1-\tau))^{-1/\alpha}$ because otherwise there would be no positive balanced growth rate. Further, for $z \in \left(u^{-1}\rho^{1/\alpha}((1-\alpha)(1-\tau))^{-1/\alpha}, \infty\right)$ we have $df_1(\cdot)/dz < 0$ so that there is a unique z that solves $f_1(\cdot) = 0$ and, thus, a unique BGP. □

Proof of Lemma 3

From the proof of Proposition 29 we know that $f_1(\cdot) = 0$ must hold on the BGP. Solving (5.41) with respect to x leads to $x = x(z, \cdot)$. Inserting that x in Eq. (5.44) and solving the resulting equation with respect to p yields

$$p = -u^\alpha z^\alpha \left(\frac{\phi}{\psi - \rho}\right) \leftrightarrow \frac{\phi}{\psi - \rho} = \frac{-p}{u^\alpha z^\alpha}$$

Substituting $\phi/(\psi - \rho)$ in $f_1(\cdot) = 0$ (from the proof of Proposition 29) leads to

$$f_2(\cdot) = \rho - (1-\tau)(1-\alpha)u^\alpha z^\alpha + \varphi \cdot \left(\frac{(1-\alpha)(1-\tau)u^\alpha z^\alpha - \rho}{\xi}\right)^{-\frac{1-\beta}{1-\beta_h}} \cdot$$

$$\left(z^{\alpha-1/(1-\beta)}\frac{\alpha(1-\tau)(u-1)+u\tau}{u^{1-\alpha}(1-u)^{\beta_h/(\beta_h-1)}} + \frac{\rho u}{u(1-u)^{\beta_h/(\beta_h-1)}} z^{-1/(1-\beta)}(-p)\right)^{1-\beta}$$

The function $f_2(\cdot)$ is continuous in x and p and this function has the following properties, $\lim_{z \searrow u^{-1}\rho^{1/\alpha}((1-\alpha)(1-\tau))^{-1/\alpha}} f_2(\cdot) = +\infty$, $\lim_{z \to \infty} f_2(\cdot) = -\infty$. From Proposition 29 we know that existence of a BGP implies that it is unique so that $\partial f_2(\cdot)/\partial z < 0$ holds for $f_2(\cdot) = 0$. Further, $\partial f_2(\cdot)/\partial p < 0$ is immediately seen. Implicitly differentiating $f_2(\cdot)$ then gives

$$\frac{dz}{dp} = -\frac{\partial f_2(\cdot)/\partial p}{\partial f_2(\cdot)/\partial z} < 0.$$

Since the balanced growth rate rises with z the balanced growth rate and the debt ratio are negatively correlated. □

Proof of Proposition 31

The balanced growth rate is given by $g = \dot{c}/c = -\rho + (1-\tau)(1-\alpha)z^\alpha u^\alpha$. A deficit financed increase in educational spending can be modeled by a decline in ϕ which is immediately seen from Eqs. (5.35) and (5.34). Differentiating g with respect to $-\phi$ gives

$$\frac{\partial g}{\partial(-\phi)} = (1-\tau)(1-\alpha)u^\alpha \alpha z^{\alpha-1} \frac{\partial z}{\partial(-\phi)},$$

with z evaluated on the BGP, that is, at $z = z^\star$.

The derivative $\partial z/\partial(-\varphi)$ is obtained by implicit differentiation of $f_1(\cdot)$ (from the proof of Proposition 29) as

$$\frac{\partial z}{\partial(-\phi)} = -\frac{\partial f_1(\cdot)/\partial(-\phi)}{\partial f_1(\cdot)/\partial z} = \frac{z^{\alpha(1-\beta)-1}\varphi(1-\beta)C_1^{-\beta}\left(\frac{(1-\alpha)(1-\tau)u^\alpha z^\alpha-\rho}{\xi}\right)^{-\frac{1-\beta}{1-\beta_h}}\rho u^\alpha}{(1-u)^{\beta_h/(\beta_h-1)}(\psi-\rho)(\partial f_1(\cdot)/\partial z)}.$$

Because of $\partial f_1(\cdot)/\partial z < 0$ for all relevant z (see the proof of Proposition 29) we get

$$\frac{\partial z}{\partial(-\phi)} > (<)0 \quad \text{for } \psi < (>)\rho$$

□

Proof of Proposition 32

To prove that proposition we note that $\dot{c}/c = \dot{k}/k$ implies $\dot{k}/k = -\rho + (1-\tau)r$. Using this, the debt to physical capital ratio evolves according to $\dot{p}/p = (\rho - \psi) - \phi(y/k)p^{-1}$. Thus, the differential equation describing the evolution of public debt relative to physical capital is obtained as

$$\dot{p} = p(\rho - \psi) - \phi\left(\frac{y}{k}\right),$$

where $y/k = u^\alpha(v/k)^\alpha$ is constant if knowledge v and physical k grow at the same rate. Setting $\dot{p} = 0$, the debt to physical capital ratio on the BGP is computed as $p^\star = (y/k)\phi/(\rho - \psi)$.

For $p^\star > 0$ we have $\phi < (>)0$ for $\rho < (>)\psi$. In addition, $\phi < (>)0$ gives $\dot{p} > (<)0$ for $p = 0$. Further, $\partial\dot{p}/\partial p = \rho - \psi < (>)0$ for $\rho < (>)\psi$. This demonstrates that p converges to the unique $p^\star(> 0)$ if and only if $\rho < \psi$.

For $p^\star < 0$ we have $\varphi > (<)0$ for $\rho < (>)\psi$. Further, $\phi > (<)0$ yields $\dot{p} < (>)0$ for $p = 0$. Again we have $\partial\dot{p}/\partial p = \rho - \psi < (>)0$ for $\rho < (>)\psi$ so that p converges to the unique $p^\star(< 0)$ if and only if $\rho < \psi$. □

Transition Dynamics

Since the initial conditions with respect to q, z, and p are given, that is, $q(0) = q_0$, $z(0) = z_0$ and $p(0) = p_0$, the economy is saddle point stable if the Jacobian matrix of the differential equation system (5.41)–(5.44) has three negative eigenvalues or

Table 5.7 Balanced growth rate, g, debt to capital ratio on the BGP, $b^{\star}$, and the signs of the eigenvalues of the Jacobian for different values of ψ and ϕ

(ψ, ϕ)	(0.025, −0.01)	(0.025, 0.01)	(0.05, −0.01)	(0.05. 0.01)
g (%)	3.9	3.3	3.5	3.8
$b^{\star}$	−0.22	0.2	0.14	−0.14
Eigenvalues	$+,-,-,+$	$+,-,-,+$	$+,-,-,-$	$+,-,-,-$

Table 5.8 Balanced growth rate, g, growth rate of public debt, g_b, and the signs of the eigenvalues of the Jacobian for $\phi = 0$ and for different values of ψ

	$\psi = 0.05$	$0.035 < \psi < 0.072$
g (%)	3.7	3.7
g_b	0	$0.072 - \psi$
Eigenvalues	$+,-,-,-$	$+,-,-,-$

three eigenvalues with negative real parts. In that case, there exists a unique value for $x(0)$ such that the economy converges to the BGP.

Table 5.7 gives the balanced growth rate, the debt to capital ratio on the BGP and the signs of the eigenvalues of the Jacobian for different values of ψ and ϕ with the benchmark parameter values used in Sect. 5.2.2.

Table 5.7 suggests that the threshold of the reaction coefficient ψ, which determines whether the economy is stable or unstable, is determined by the subjective discount rate ρ such that for values of ψ larger (smaller) ρ the economy is stable (unstable). It should also be noted that ϕ must not become too small (large) so that a BGP exists in the case of $\psi > (<)\rho$. In our example underlying Table 5.7, existence of a BGP is given for $\phi > -0.04(\phi < 0.027)$ in case of $\psi = 0.05 > \rho(\psi = 0.025 < \rho)$.

Table 5.8 gives the result for the situation where public debt grows but less than GDP, case (ii) in Definition 9, and the situation of a balanced government budget, case (i) in Definition 9.

Chapter 6
Debt and Growth: Empirical Evidence

In the last chapters, we have analyzed endogenous growth models assuming that the government sticks to the intertemporal budget constraint and seen how different debt policies affect economic growth and welfare. In this chapter, we intend to contribute to the empirical research studying the relation between debt and economic growth where we proceed as in Fincke and Greiner (2013).

The correlation between public debt and public deficits, on the one hand, and economic growth, on the other hand, has been the subject of a great many studies in the recent past. A frequently cited contribution is the one by Reinhart and Rogoff (2010) who, using histograms, find a threshold of public debt relative to GDP of about 90 % beyond which the relationship between debt and growth becomes negative. Although that paper seems to contain a spreadsheet coding error[1] that led to a miscalculation of the growth rates of some economies, there are other studies that support this outcome by detecting an inverted U-shaped relation between debt and growth. For example, Caner et al. (2010) analyze 101 countries over the time period 1980–2008 and detect a critical value for the debt ratio beyond which the relation between debt and growth becomes negative.[2] The threshold of the debt to GDP ratio is about 77 % and it depends on which countries are included in their sample. Checherita and Rother (2010) perform regression analyses for 12 euro area countries over the period 1970–2011, where they distinguish between annual growth rates and growth rates over a time span of 5 years. For both cases, these authors also find an inverted U-shaped relation between debt and growth, with the threshold of public debt being at 70–80 % of GDP. In addition, Checherita-Westphal et al. (2012) estimate regressions for various subsamples of OECD countries and find values for

[1]See also the critique in Herndon et al. (2014).

[2]Earlier studies using time series data for the USA find a growth maximizing debt to GDP ratio of about 40–50 %, cf. Smyth and Hsing (1995) and the literature cited in that paper.

© Springer International Publishing Switzerland 2015

A. Greiner, B. Fincke, *Public Debt, Sustainability and Economic Growth*,
DOI 10.1007/978-3-319-09348-2_6

the threshold of the debt to GDP ratio that range between 43 and 63 % of GDP.[3] Egert (2012) extends the time period of the sample in Reinhart and Rogoff back to 1790 and detects a small negative correlation between debt and growth. Using an endogenous threshold model, he finds some evidence of a non-linear relationship between debt and growth. Further, Egert (2012) points out that both the presence and the level of the thresholds are not robust to small changes in country coverage, data frequency and to changes in the assumptions on the minimum number of observations included in each regime. Dreger and Reimers (2013) study the effect of the debt ratio on the real GDP per capita growth rate for two groups of countries, euro-zone members and non-euro-zone European economies, and further separate the situations in sustainable and non-sustainable debt states. They utilize a pooled panel regression and also find a negative effect of the debt ratio on economic growth.

On the other hand, there exist empirical studies that only find a negative correlation between the debt to GDP ratio and economic growth. Ferreira (2009), for example, performs Granger causality tests for 20 OECD countries over the time period from 1988–2001, where he studies annual growth rates. It turns out that higher debt to GDP ratios exert a negative effect on the growth rates of economies. This effect is statistically significant and it goes in both directions, that is higher public debt reduces economic growth and less growth implies higher government debt. Kumar and Woo (2010) analyze 19 countries over the time span from 1970 to 2007, where they estimate growth regressions with the growth rate over 5 years as the dependent variable. The result of their estimations is a definitely negative relationship between the debt to GDP ratio at the beginning of a period and the growth rate of that period. In addition, they investigate the relation between public deficits and economic growth and detect a negative correlation, too. Their study also reveals nonlinearities such that higher public deficits and higher debt to GDP ratios go along with disproportionately negative growth rates. Ballasone et al. (2011) analyze the relation between the ratio of public debt relative to GDP and the growth rate of real per capita income in Italy over the period 1861–2009. They detect a negative correlation between government debt and economic growth, where the negative effect seems to work mainly through reduced investment. Eberhardt and Presbitero (2013) find evidence for systematic differences in the debt-growth relationship across countries, but, they could not find evidence for non-linearities within countries. Rather, the relation between debt and growth seems to be characterized by a linear function. Further, the debt coefficients seem to be smaller in countries with high debt burdens and the average debt coefficient across countries was positive. In particular, they assert that the debt-growth relationship differs across countries, so that appropriate policies for one country may be seriously misguided in another one. Finally, Pescatori et al. (2014) analyze the medium-run relationship existing between public debt and economic growth. They find no evidence for a debt threshold beyond which the relation between debt and growth

[3]However, within a theoretical endogenous growth model, one needs extreme assumptions to get an inverse U-shaped relation between debt and growth (cf. Greiner 2013d).

changes. Further, the association between debt and medium-term growth becomes rather weak at high levels of debt. But they assert that high levels of debt are associated with higher volatility implying that high levels of debt tend to destabilize economies.

Panizza and Presbitero (2013) present a survey of papers dealing with debt and growth. They find that the presence of thresholds and, more generally, of a non-monotonic relationship between public debt and economic growth is neither robust to changes in data coverage nor to the empirical techniques resorted to. They maintain that empirical studies dealing with that subject should, in particular, put a strong emphasis on cross-country heterogeneity.

In the next section, we first describe the estimation procedure.

6.1 The Estimation Procedure and the Data

In order to analyze how the public debt to GDP ratio at a certain point in time affects economic growth in subsequent periods, we perform panel data estimation with annual data from seven selected countries (Austria, France, Germany, Italy, the Netherlands, Portugal and the USA) covering the years from 1970 until 2012. All those countries are developed economies and display similar patterns with respect to the time series of public debt and economic growth. Thus, although the countries differ as concerns their legal regulations and institutions they are relatively homogeneous so that the estimation results are not expected to be biased due to systematic differences in the debt-growth relationship across countries. With six European economies the focus is set on this region, where Germany and France represent the two largest Euro zone economies. Further, the Netherlands and Austria are two smaller central European economies, of which Austria suffered from an almost steadily rising debt to GDP ratio over the observation period whereas the Netherlands were able to remarkably reduce their debt ratio in the 1990s. Italy and Portugal have been included because they both have been strongly affected by the 2008 financial and public debt crisis. In order to draw meaningful conclusions we also include the USA in our sample as one of the largest economies world wide. Moreover, taking data until 2012 allows us to take into consideration the influence of the financial and public debt crisis that started in 2008.

Following the approach in Kumar and Woo (2010), we divide the whole observation period into sub-periods with non-overlapping intervals. As concerns growth, we distinguish three types of intervals (5 years $q = 5$, 3 years $q = 3$ and 1 year $q = 1$). This implies that we analyze the question of how the public debt to GDP ratio at time $t - q$ affects the growth rate for the following q years. Consequently, for $q = 5$ the seven intervals are (1970–1975), (1976–1981), ..., (2000–2005) and (2006–2011), while for $q = 3$ the eleven sub-periods start with (1970–1973) and end with (2010–2012), where the last interval comprises only 2 years.

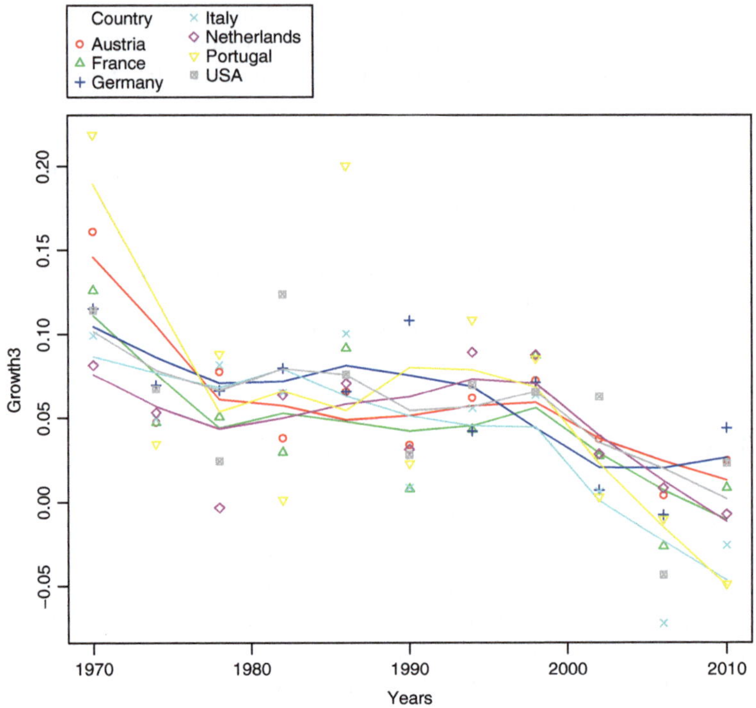

Fig. 6.1 Three-years growth rate

The following Figs. 6.1 and 6.2 show the GDP growth rates over an interval of 3 years ($q = 3$), calculated as the difference of the natural logarithm of real GDP per capita, and the public debt to GDP ratio, measured at the beginning of the period.[4]

The figures have been plotted using *scatterplot* implemented in the package *car*. The lines represent a nonparametric regression smooth (see for instance Fox et al. 2013), whereas the dots and crosses etc. represent the actual observations. Obviously, there is a generally decreasing trend with respect to the GDP growth rate across all seven economies, while the debt to GDP ratio basically increases over time. Thus, our sample seems to represent rather a homogeneous set of economies. Certainly, both figures are significantly shaped by the financial and public debt crisis visible in the more recent time intervals. This graphical illustration suggests a negative relationship between public debt and economic growth.

To get a more profound idea about the relationship between public debt and economic growth, we first estimate the following pooled regression model, where

[4]For the data see OECD (2013) and IMF (2013). The figures and the estimations have been performed using R 2.5.0., except when a newer version was necessary to implement a certain package.

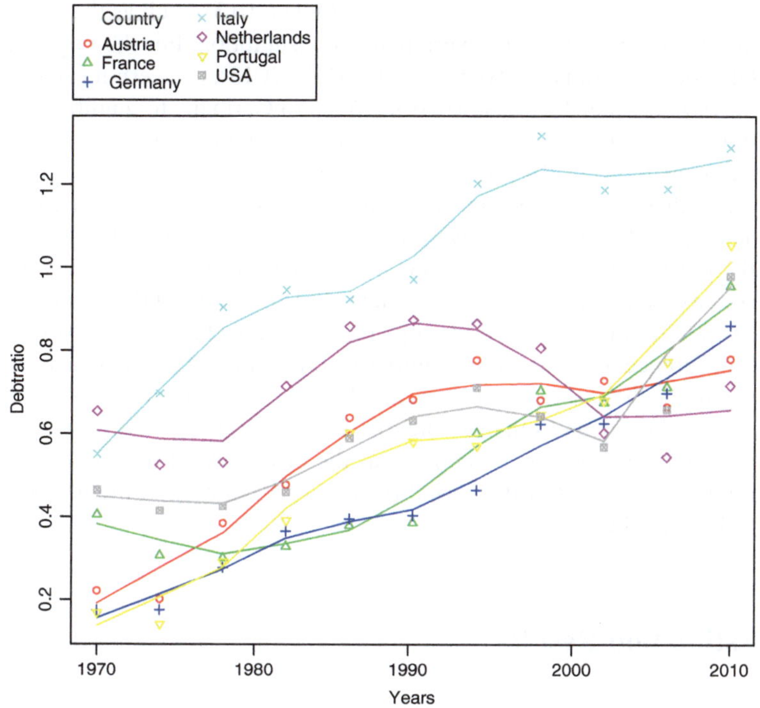

Fig. 6.2 Public debt to GDP ratio

we proceed as in Kumar and Woo (2010) and Dreger and Reimers (2013),

$$y_{i,t} - y_{i,t-q} = \phi_0 + \psi\, b_{i,t-q} + \sum_j \phi_j C_{j,i,t-q} + \epsilon_{i,t}, \tag{6.1}$$

with $y_{i,t}$ the natural logarithm of real GDP per capita for country i at time t. Further, b is the public debt to GDP ratio, C gives the vector of the control variables and ϵ is the error term. All regressors are measured at the beginning of a period, i.e. at $t - q$. This allows us to analyze the effect of the initial explanatory variable on economic growth in subsequent periods. Concerning the control variables we include the initial real GDP per capita ($y_{i,t-q}$) expressed in log units, foreign trade ($Trade_{i,t-q}$) proxied by the difference between exports and imports (i.e. the external trade balance or net exports) relative to GDP, government consumption ($GCons_{i,t-q}$) calculated as government consumption expenditures relative to GDP and the initial annual inflation rate ($Infl_{i,t-q}$). In order to check for robustness, the log of the population ($Pop_{i,t-q}$) had initially been included, too, but it did not yield a significant effect or change the results essentially.

The data set contains variables for the seven selected economies Austria, France, Germany, Italy, the Netherlands, Portugal and the USA for the years from 1970 until 2012. The data are mainly taken from OECD (2013), such as the GDP, public debt, imports and exports and governmental consumption. For the population and for the GDP deflator statistics, we resorted to IMF (2013). Concerning Germany, the change in 1992 reflects the transition from Western Germany to reunified Germany. For Portugal, in order to get a long time series of public debt, the data have been merged into one series in 1996. Further, the Portuguese GDP deflator has been taken from OECD (2013) which has the base year 2006 instead of 2005 (as the IMF data). Since the data for EU economies were in part only available in national currencies, before the introduction of the Euro, they have been transformed to Euro according to the fixed exchange rates, e.g. for Germany 1 € = 1.95583 DM or for Portugal 1 € = 200.482 Escudos. For the trade (openness) variable the net exports or external balance (difference of exports minus imports), on a national account basis, has been used. Originally, these series were measured in US \$. A transformation to Euro has been performed using an exchange rate of 1 US \$ = 0.75 € (as of August 2013).

All growth rates have been computed as the difference of the natural logarithm of a variable x at the end of the period (t) and the beginning of the period ($t - q$), i.e. $g_x = \ln(x_t) - \ln(x_{t-q})$.

6.2 Estimation Results

Figures 6.1 and 6.2 in the last section suggest a negative relationship between economic growth and the public debt to GDP ratio. Neglecting for the moment all control variables, the relation between the public debt to GDP ratio and the subsequent economic growth rate for all seven economies can be estimated according to

$$y_{i,t} - y_{i,t-q} = \phi_0 + \psi\, b_{i,t-q} + \epsilon_{i,t}. \tag{6.2}$$

for which we use the R package *plm* (see for instance Croissant and Millo 2008, or Kleiber and Zeileis 2008). Table 6.1 summarizes the results.

The results in Table 6.1 are distinguished by type, i.e. pooled OLS regression (first block), a fixed effects model (second block) and a random effects model (third block). All estimation results indicate a statistically significant negative relationship between the public debt to GDP ratio and the subsequent economic growth. This also holds true for all three time period periods ($q = 5$ 5-year growth, $q = 3$ 3-year growth and $q = 1$ annual growth, respectively). Further, the estimation results suggest that the negative effect of the debt to GDP ratio is stronger for the 5-year period than for the 3-years interval and the 3-year period effect is larger than the effect on the annual economic growth rate, which may be due to the fact that the first interval, $q = 5$ ($q = 3$), is much longer than the latter, $q = 3$ ($q = 1$). The Durbin Watson statistic, *DW*, suggests non-autocorrelated residuals for the 5-years interval and for the 3-years period, whereas there is a slight positive autocorrelation in the estimations with annual growth rates.

Table 6.1 Plain panel estimation results

	Pooled model		
	$q = 5$ $(N = 49)$	$q = 3$ $(N = 77)$	$q = 1$ $(N = 294)$
Constant	0.139***	0.100***	0.029***
b_{t-q}	−0.089**	−0.076***	−0.018***
R^2(adj)	0.16	0.16	0.04
DW	1.72	2.26	1.62
	Fixed effects model		
	$q = 5$	$q = 3$	$q = 1$
b_{t-q}	−0.132**	−0.104***	−0.025***
R^2(adj)	0.16	0.17	0.04
DW	1.96	2.40	1.65
F test	F=0.68, p-val.=0.67	F=0.66, p-val.=0.69	F=0.75, p-val.=0.61
	Random effects model		
	$q = 5$	$q = 3$	$q = 1$
Constant	0.149***	0.107***	0.031***
b_{t-q}	−0.105**	−0.087***	−0.020***
R^2(adj)	0.16	0.17	0.04
DW	1.80	2.31	1.63
Hausman test	$\chi^2 = 1.03$ p-val.=0.31	$\chi^2 = 1.49$ p-val.=0.22	$\chi^2 = 1.46$ p-val.=0.23
***(0.1 % level)	**(1 % level)	*(5 % level)	•(10 % level)

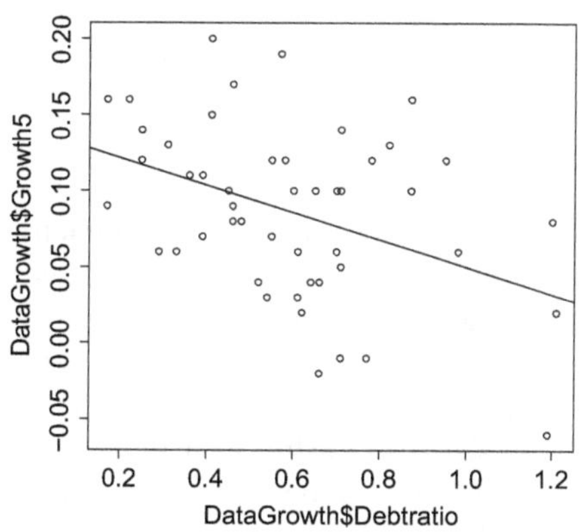

Fig. 6.3 Pool, $q = 5$

Despite the rather modest fit there is, nevertheless, substantial empirical evidence for a negative relationship between the two variables debt and growth. This result is also supported and visualized in the corresponding scatterplots with the linear regression line from the pooled OLS estimation in Figs. 6.3–6.5. Finally, the model selection tests (the F-test tests if the pooled or the fixed effects model is more appropriate and the Hausman test studies whether a random or fixed effects model should be applied) suggest the use of the pooled or the random model for this data set. However, all three estimations yield the same qualitative outcome anyway.

Fig. 6.4 Pool, $q = 3$

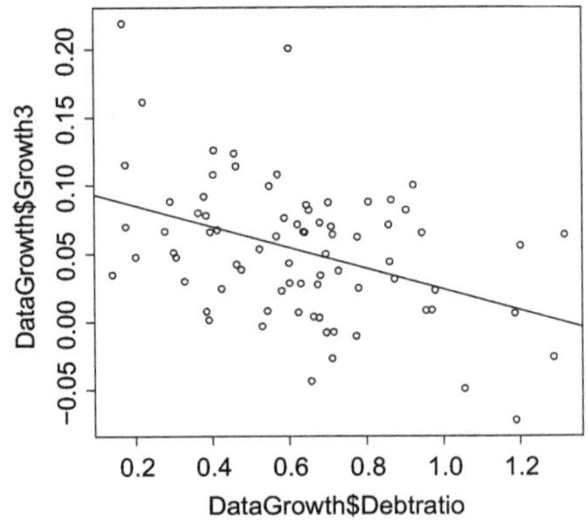

Fig. 6.5 Pool, $q = 1$

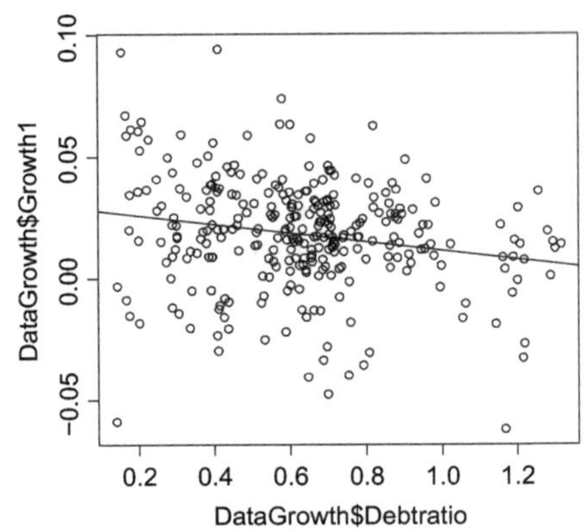

Next, we perform a non-parametric estimation for the plain model from above, i.e. including only the two variables debt and growth. Neglecting for the moment that the data come from different countries and treating the whole sample as one data set, allows us to study the (potentially) non-linear relationship between the two variables. Here, a spline estimation is applied to the data set, dealing with the relationship in a fairly unrestricted (non-parametric) manner. Basically, it approximates the systematic link between the variables with a flexible function, here denoted by s, that is only required to be continuous and differentiable.[5]

$$y_t - y_{t-q} = s(b_{t-q}) + \epsilon_t. \tag{6.3}$$

The estimation is performed with the *mgcv* package in R. Table 6.2 summarizes the estimation results identifying potential non-linearities. Non-linearities are indicated by the estimated degrees of freedom, *edf*, where high values imply a wiggly function while a value near 1 suggests a linear fit. The second interesting part is

[5]For a short introduction to the method, see Kauermann (2006) or Greiner (2009) for instance.

Table 6.2 Spline estimation results, plain model

	$q = 5$ $(N = 49)$	$q = 3$ $(N = 77)$	$q = 1$ $(N = 294)$
edf	4.12*	1***	1***
R^2(adj)	0.21	0.15	0.04
DW	1.88	2.26	1.62
***(0.1 % level)	**(1 % level)	*(5 % level)	•(10 % level)

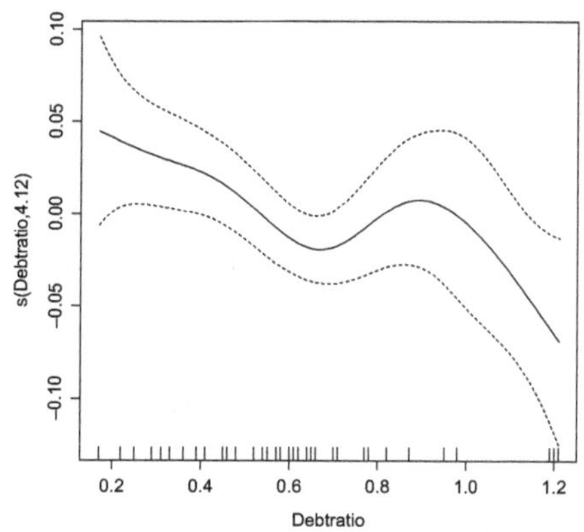

Fig. 6.6 Spline, $q = 5$

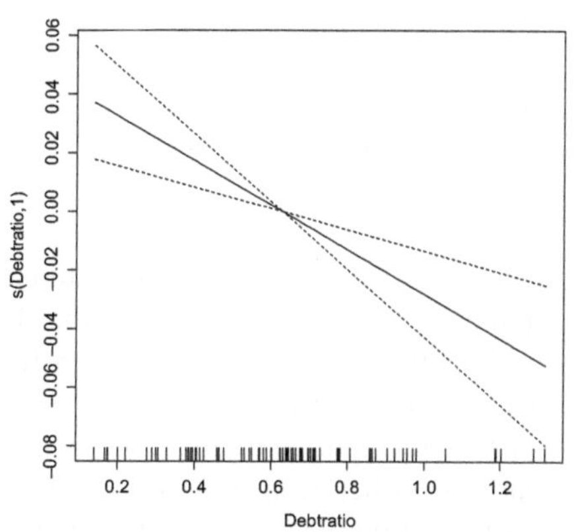

Fig. 6.7 Spline, $q = 3$

the visualization of the estimation outcome. The plots of the estimated functions are shown in Figs. 6.6–6.8.

As Table 6.2 and Figs. 6.6–6.8 show, only for the 5-years interval the relationship might be non-linear. Basically, all three time periods are characterized by a negative relation, with a linear shape for the 3-years growth rate and for the annual growth rate. The 5-years interval also reveals a mainly negative form, however with a bump at a debt to GDP ratio of about 90 %. However, this is statistically significant only at the 5 % level. For the 3-years interval and for annual growth the estimations do not show any evidence for non-linearities. Further, we also estimated an OLS regression including a quadratic term, $b_{i,t-q}^2$, and a cubic term, $b_{i,t-q}^3$, as regressors. None

Fig. 6.8 Spline, $q = 1$

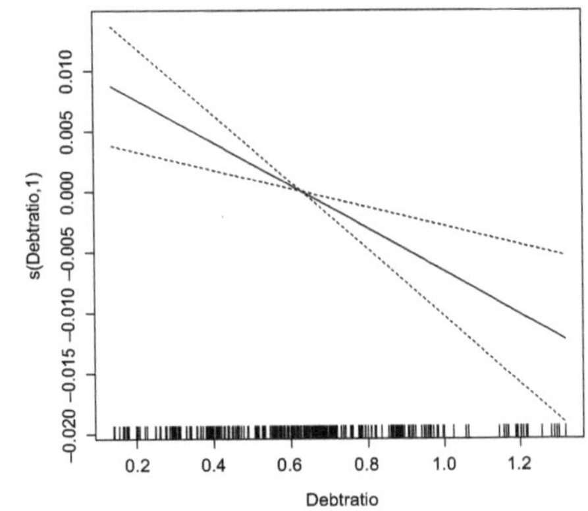

Table 6.3 Panel estimation results, pooled OLS

	$q = 5$ $(N = 49)$	$q = 3$ $(N = 77)$	$q = 1$ $(N = 294)$
Constant	0.853**	0.921***	0.313***
b_{t-q}	−0.051	−0.050*	−0.012*
y_{t-q}	−0.067*	−0.072***	−0.025***
$Trade_{t-q}$	0.193•	0.223***	0.086***
$GCons_{t-q}$	−0.390	−0.560**	−0.188***
$Infl_{t-q}$	0.029	−0.194	−0.093**
R^2(adj)	0.27	0.39	0.15
DW	1.78	2.02	1.73
***(0.1 % level)	**(1 % level)	*(5 % level)	•(10 % level)

of these higher-order terms was statistically significant in the estimations, neither for the 5-years interval, nor for the 3-years or 1-year time period. Therefore, we conclude that the evidence for a non-linear relation between debt and growth is very weak in our sample.

From the outcomes in Table 6.1 and Figs. 6.3–6.5 one can conclude that the relationship between the public debt to GDP ratio and the economic growth rate over the following year(s) is negative. However, for those plain estimations the only regressor was the debt to GDP ratio. In order to see how robust that result is, we next include the control variables in our estimations. Thus, the following regression equation is now estimated for the data of the seven selected economies:

$$y_{i,t} - y_{i,t-q} = \phi_0 + \psi\, b_{i,t-q} + \phi_1 y_{i,t-q} + \phi_2 Trade_{i,t-q} + \phi_3 GCons_{i,t-q} + \phi_4 Infl_{i,t-q} + \epsilon_{i,t}, \tag{6.4}$$

with the variables according to the explanations above. Table 6.3 presents the outcome.

As the results in Table 6.3 demonstrate, the data suggest empirical evidence for a negative relationship between the public debt to GDP ratio and subsequent economic growth. Although the coefficient of interest for b_{t-q} is not statistically

Table 6.4 Panel estimation results, random effects

	$q = 5$ $(N = 49)$	$q = 3$ $(N = 77)$	$q = 1$ $(N = 294)$
Constant	1.388***	0.957***	0.324***
b_{t-q}	0.018	−0.049*	−0.011*
y_{t-q}	−0.125***	−0.075***	−0.026***
$Trade_{t-q}$	0.159	0.225***	0.087***
$GCons_{t-q}$	−0.399	−0.582**	−0.196***
$Infl_{t-q}$	0.022	−0.206	−0.098**
R^2(adj)	0.36	0.41	0.17
DW	1.75	2.03	1.74
***(0.1 % level)	**(1 % level)	*(5 % level)	•(10 % level)

significant for the 5 year growth interval (first column), the 3-years period (second column) and the annual growth rates (last column) indicate a negative relationship between debt and growth. The estimation results also suggest again that the negative effect of the debt to GDP ratio is stronger for the 3-years period than for the annual economic growth rate, which may be due to the fact that the first interval ($q = 3$) is much longer than the latter ($q = 1$). The other control variables show the expected signs. For instance, the negative coefficient of the initial real GDP per capita demonstrates that a higher initial GDP per capita reduces growth in subsequent periods, suggesting convergence. As above, this holds true for all three time specifications, i.e. for $q = 5$, $q = 3$ and $q = 1$. Moreover, trade (openness), shown in the fourth line, has a positive effect on subsequent growth for all three estimations. The estimation also reveals that higher government consumption seems to lower economic growth in the following years, as does higher inflation in the initial year.

Since the fixed effects model did not yield significant results concerning the debt and growth relationship we, next, estimate the random effects model for our panel data. Table 6.4 presents the estimation results.

Basically, the estimation of the random effects model confirms the results from the pooled OLS estimation of our model. The estimations suggest a significant negative relationship between the initial public debt to GDP ratio and the subsequent 3-years or annual growth rate of GDP. Further, the coefficients are quite similar in size. The control variables show the expected signs and also support the results from the pooled model in Table 6.3. Again, for both estimations, pooled and random effects, the hypothesis of non-autocorrelated residuals cannot be rejected, except for the 1-year time interval.

Concerning model suitability, the F test suggests the pooled model for $q = 5$ and the fixed effects model for $q = 3$ and $q = 1$. The Hausman test supports the suitability of the random effects model for the first two specifications. Especially for $q = 3$, it yields a p-value of 0.9994 (see Table 6.5). For $q = 1$, the fixed effects model may be more appropriate. However, the estimated coefficient for the debt

Table 6.5 Model selection tests

	$q = 5$	$q = 3$	$q = 1$
F test	F=1.92, p-val.=0.104	F=3.85, p-val.=0.002	F=3.60, p-val.=0.002
Hausman test	$\chi^2 = 3.86$ p-val.=0.57	$\chi^2 = 0.17$ p-val.=0.999	$\chi^2 = 21.08$ p-val.=0.0008

ratio in the fixed effects model is insignificant, which is contrary to the majority of the outcomes presented in this section.

Conclusion

In this chapter we have empirically analyzed the relationship between public debt and economic growth. Our regression results yield evidence for a negative relationship between the public debt to GDP ratio and the growth rate of the economies in subsequent periods. This means that a high public debt to GDP ratio at the beginning of the period tends to reduce the real GDP per capita growth rate in the following years.

We performed panel data estimations where we estimated several regression models. When the control variables are neglected, all models yield a significant negative relation between the public debt to GDP ratio and economic growth in the subsequent period for the 5-years time interval, for the 3-years time interval and for the annual interval. When control variables are included in the regression, this statistically significant negative correlation between debt and growth becomes smaller but is still present for the pooled and for the random effects model for the 3-years time interval and for the 1-year time interval, whereas the effect of public debt becomes statistically insignificant for the 5-years interval. Further, the link between debt and growth seems to be characterized by a linear relationship since the empirical evidence for non-linearities is very weak. In particular, we could not find any indication of non-linearities for the 3-years time interval and for annual growth rates.

Chapter 7
Conclusion

In this book we have analyzed the effects of public debt with respect to economic growth and welfare. Whereas the allocative consequences of distortionary taxation can be readily derived, that does not hold for public debt since the latter does not directly affect the allocation of resources in the economy. The decisive aspect about public debt is the intertemporal budget constraint the government must fulfill if it does not want to default on its debt. The intertemporal budget constraint states that the amount of the outstanding public debt must equal the present value of the expected future primary surpluses at any moment in time. This implies that the government must run higher primary surpluses in the future if the level of public debt rises as a result of higher deficits today. That principle can be used to test for sustainability of a given time series of public debt by analyzing the reaction of the primary surplus relative to GDP to changes in the debt to GDP ratio. If the estimated reaction coefficient is positive on average and sufficiently large so that the upper bound of the primary surplus relative to GDP does not become binding, a given debt policy is sustainable. The primary surplus relative to GDP is bounded from above because it must be financed out of GDP so that the primary surplus cannot exceed a certain fraction of GDP. If the reaction coefficient is positive but smaller than the difference between the interest rate on public debt and the GDP growth rate, the debt to GDP ratio increases over time and becomes asymptotically unbounded. But, an unbounded debt to GDP ratio is not compatible with a sustainable public debt policy since it would require permanently rising primary surpluses relative to GDP. The latter, however, is excluded because the primary surplus relative to GDP is bounded from above. In case of a permanently rising debt to GDP ratio, the upper bound of the primary surplus to GDP ratio becomes binding and the government fails to service its debt, sooner or later. Therefore, a sustainable debt policy requires that the ratio of public debt to GDP becomes constant and only transitionally rising debt ratios are compatible with sustainability.

Our empirical tests have demonstrated that most of the countries we analyzed positively react to higher debt ratios by raising their primary surplus to GDP ratios.

© Springer International Publishing Switzerland 2015

A. Greiner, B. Fincke, *Public Debt, Sustainability and Economic Growth*,
DOI 10.1007/978-3-319-09348-2_7

Therefore, in a next step we studied theoretically how public debt affects economic growth and welfare with the help of endogenous growth models, where we assumed that the government sticks to the intertemporal budget constraint and raises the primary surplus as a response to higher public debt relative to GDP, respectively. To achieve a higher primary surplus the government can raise taxes, it can reduce public spending or the tax revenue may increase of its own due to a higher GDP growth. If the government raises a distortionary tax rate to generate a higher primary surplus, like the income tax rate for example, it is obvious that a higher debt implies negative growth effects. If, on the other hand, the government levies a non-distortionary tax or reduces non-distortionary transfer payments, public debt is neutral in the sense that is does not affect the allocation of resources and, consequently, economic growth is not affected by public debt, which is basically the same as the Ricardian equivalence principle. Because of that, we have fixed the tax rate throughout our analyses. Besides those possibilities to achieve higher revenues, in a monetary model the central bank can raise the nominal money supply and, thus, seignorage to generate additional public revenues and a higher inflation rate yields an inflation tax revenue.

Analyzing our models, we have found that a higher public debt to GDP ratio goes along with a smaller balanced growth rate in the long-run, as long as wages are flexible such that there is no involuntary unemployment in the economy. The economic mechanism behind that outcome is that higher public debt implies that the government has less spending available for productive public investment in infrastructure or for the formation of human capital since the higher debt service requires more public resources. But it must be underlined that this does not mean that deficit financed public investments lead to a lower balanced growth rate in the long-run. If deficit financed public investments are productive such that the ensuing rise in GDP leads to higher tax revenues that compensate the initial increase of the outstanding public debt, this fiscal policy leads to a lower debt to GDP ratio and, thus, to higher growth. Further, the balanced growth is the smaller the higher is the ratio of public debt relative to GDP, even if public spending is unproductive. In that case, a higher public debt implies that less of the aggregate savings can be used for private investment in capital. This implies that the shadow price of savings and labor supply are smaller, so that the return to capital declines and, therefore, economic growth will be lower compared to a situation with less public debt. In the case of rigid wages giving rise to permanent unemployment, public debt is neutral in the sense that it does not affect the allocation of resources. The reason for that outcome is that the marginal product of capital and, as a consequence, the incentive to invest depend on the labor demand that is determined by the wage policy of the trade unions. Consequently, if the government runs a deficit to finance productive public spending, this policy measure can raise the balanced growth rate in the long-run and reduce unemployment, even if it goes along with a higher debt to GDP ratio. When a monetary sector is integrated, we have seen that the monetary policy can compensate a loose public debt policy because it can reduce the debt to GDP ratio so that the growth rate rises. However, that goes at the expense of higher inflation and it must be underlined that this only holds up to a certain degree. This means that sustained growth is not possible or only if the government is a creditor once the nominal monetary growth rate exceeds a certain threshold.

One policy recommendation we can draw from our analyses is that governments should reduce the public debt to GDP ratio in order to spur economic growth and set the general conditions such that the labor market is sufficiently flexible to avoid involuntary unemployment. A decline in the debt to GDP ratio can be obtained by running a balanced budget or by setting public deficits in a way such that the debt to GDP ratio declines over time. Asymptotically, those two fiscal policies are equivalent from an allocative point of view and imply the same balanced growth rate because they both lead to a zero debt to GDP ratio in the long-run. Only on the transition path, those two scenarios differ and the debt to GDP ratio declines faster in the balanced budget scenario than in the scenario with a slight deficit. However, from the aspect of welfare maximization the scenario with a slight deficit may perform better than the balanced budget scenario, in the case when public spending is not welfare enhancing. The reason is that the initial level of consumption in the balanced budget scenario is lower than in the scenario with a slight deficit. But, when one allows for positive welfare effects of public spending this can change. Then, there exists a threshold for the coefficient that determines the welfare effects of public goods so that the balanced budget performs better than the scenario with a slight deficit if that coefficient falls short of the threshold value. But, in any case, both of those two regimes that lead to a zero debt to GDP ratio in the long-run yield higher welfare than the scenario where public debt grows at the same rate as GDP. The latter also holds for the monetary growth model in general, unless the government puts a high weight on debt stabilization, i.e. unless the reaction coefficient is high, and if the initial debt to GDP ratio is large. Then, a balanced budget may perform worse. In addition, for the case of permanent public deficits we have seen that monetary policy can compensate a loose public debt policy up to a certain degree by reducing the debt ratio, thus, fostering economic growth. But that policy goes at the cost of welfare since the associated rise in the labor supply and the higher growth rate of money, that leads to higher inflation, generate negative welfare effects that exceed the positive one of a higher growth rate.

As concerns stability, we have detected that a higher reaction coefficient tends to stabilize the economy. That is, the stronger the rise in the primary surplus relative to GDP is as the debt to GDP ratio increases, the sooner the model will be stable. This holds independent of whether wages are flexible or rigid and also independent of whether public spending is unproductive or productive, when it is spent for human capital formation or for public infrastructure capital. The reason for that outcome is that a strong increase in the primary surplus as public debt rises makes the debt to GDP ratio a mean-reverting process avoiding that public debt relative to GDP becomes explosive. If, on the other hand, the reaction of the primary surplus is small as debt rises, public debt will explode and the economy becomes unstable implying its collapse. This implies that a purely discretionary policy, where the reaction coefficient is equal to zero, leads to a violation of the intertemporal budget constraint of the government. Hence, any fiscal policy is unsustainable unless it is a rule based policy, in the sense that the primary surplus sufficiently rises as public debt increases, or unless it imposes some other sort of constraint that prevents the debt to GDP ratio from exploding. However, it should be noted that this does not imply that the government has no discretionary scope at all because even in the rule based policy the government has some discretionary scope, although the latter is limited. We have also seen that in some model versions the economy does not converge to a balanced growth path with a constant growth rate, but is rather characterized by persistent growth cycles, for a certain range of the reaction coefficient. Further, we could show that an underdevelopment trap may arise, depending on the preferences of the household and on the fiscal policy of the government, implying that an economy cannot achieve a high growth rate in the long-run if its initial debt to GDP ratio exceeds a certain critical threshold. Only if the debt ratio is below the critical value, the economy can converge to the high balanced growth path. An underdevelopment trap may also arise in the growth model with rigid wages. There, however, it is the labor market that is decisive as to whether this phenomenon occurs or not. The less flexible labor markets are the sooner an underdevelopment trap can arise, while more flexible labor markets tend to give rise to a unique balanced growth path.

Finally, we also empirically estimated the relation between public debt and economic growth. We performed panel data estimations where we estimated several regression models. All models yield a significant negative relation between the public debt to GDP ratio and economic growth in the subsequent period for the 5-years time interval, for the 3-years time interval and for the 1-year time interval, when the control variables are neglected. When control variables are included in the regression, this statistically significant negative correlation between debt and growth is still present for the 3-years time interval and for the 1-year time interval, whereas the effect of public debt becomes statistically insignificant for the 5-years interval. Further, the link between debt and growth seems to be characterized by a linear relationship since the empirical evidence for non-linearities is very small. Overall, our empirical tests support the hypothesis of a negative relationship between public debt and economic growth that has been derived in the theoretical growth models with flexible labor markets.

Appendix A
Non-parametric Estimation

The subsequent algorithm is based on Wood (2000) and implemented in the public domain software package R (see Ihaka and Gentleman 1996). The program and more information about it can be downloaded from http://www.r-project.org/. We exemplify the fit with the simplified model (see also Greiner and Kauermann 2008)

$$s_t = \phi_0 + \psi_t b_{t-1} + \tilde{\varepsilon}_t$$

Let s_t and b_{t-1} be the observed values for $t = 2, 3, \ldots$. For fitting we replace the functional shape ψ_t by the parametric form

$$\psi_t = \psi_{00} + \psi_{01} t + Z(t)\boldsymbol{\gamma} \tag{A.1}$$

where $Z(t)$ is a high dimensional basis in t. A typical setting is to choose $Z(t)$ as cubic spline basis functions allocated at the observed time points $t = 2, 3, \ldots$. However, numerically more efficient is to work with a reduced basis as suggested in O'Sullivan (1986) or Wood (2000). The latter proposal is implemented in R. The idea is to construct only those basis functions corresponding to the largest eigenvalues of $Z(t)Z(t)^T$ (see Wood (2000) for more details).

In principle, with replacement (A.1) one ends up with a parametric model. However, fitting the model in a standard OLS fashion is unsatisfactory due to the large dimensionality of $Z(t)$ which will lead to highly variable estimates. This can be avoided by imposing an additional penalty term on γ, shrinking its values to zero. To be more specific, we obtain an estimate by minimizing the penalized OLS criterion

$$\sum_t \{s_t - d_t \psi_d - Z(d_t)\gamma\}^2 + \lambda \gamma^T P \gamma$$

with λ called the smoothing or penalty parameter and $\gamma^T P \gamma$ as penalty. Matrix P is thereby chosen in accordance to the basis and for cubic splines the penalty

© Springer International Publishing Switzerland 2015

A. Greiner, B. Fincke, *Public Debt, Sustainability and Economic Growth*,
DOI 10.1007/978-3-319-09348-2

corresponds to the integrated square derivative of ψ_t (see also Ruppert et al. 2003, for more details). It is easy to see that choosing $\lambda = 0$ yields an unpenalized OLS fit, while $\lambda \to \infty$ typically implies $\gamma = 0$ depending on the choice of P. Hence, λ steers the amount of smoothness of the function with a simple linear fit as one extreme and a high dimensional parametric fit as the other extreme.

Let $\boldsymbol{\psi} = (\psi_1, \psi_2, \dots)^T$ be the time varying effect stacked up to a column vector and assume for simplicity of presentation that $\phi_0 \equiv 0$. Let $\mathbf{t}$ be the vector of observed points in time and $Z(\mathbf{t})$ the spline basis evaluated at these points. With the spline approximation we set $\boldsymbol{\psi} = B(\mathbf{t})\boldsymbol{\theta}$ where $B(\mathbf{t}) = (\mathbf{1}, \mathbf{t}, Z(\mathbf{t}))$ and $\boldsymbol{\theta} = (\psi_{00}, \psi_{01}, \boldsymbol{\gamma})^T$. The estimate $\hat{\boldsymbol{\psi}}$, say, is then available in analytic form via $\hat{\boldsymbol{\psi}} = H(\lambda)\mathbf{s}$, with $\mathbf{s} = (s_1, s_2, \dots)^T$ and $H(\lambda)$ as hat or smoothing matrix, respectively, defined through

$$H(\lambda) = B(\mathbf{t}) \left(B^T(\mathbf{t})B(\mathbf{t}) + \lambda \begin{pmatrix} 0 & 0 \\ 0 & P \end{pmatrix} \right)^{-1} B^T(\mathbf{t})$$

Note that $H(0)$ and $H(\infty)$ are classical hat matrices while $H(\lambda)$ for $0 < \lambda < \infty$ is a penalized version. The trace of $H(\lambda)$ is usually understood as the degree of the fit where $2 = \text{tr}(H(\infty)) \leq \text{tr}(H(\lambda)) \leq \text{tr}(H(0)) = p + 2$ with p as dimension of $Z(\mathbf{t})$. The linear operator also allows to easily calculate variances of the estimate via

$$\text{Var}\left(\hat{\boldsymbol{\psi}}\right) = H(\lambda)\Sigma(s)H^T(\lambda)$$

with $\Sigma(s)$ as covariance matrix of $\mathbf{s}$. Assuming uncorrelated and homoscedastic residuals we get $\text{Var}\left(\hat{\boldsymbol{\psi}}\right) = \hat{\sigma}^2 H(\lambda)H^T(\lambda)$ with $\hat{\sigma}^2$ as residual variance estimate. Finally, if additional covariates are in the model, like in (2.9) for example, we pursue the same estimation like above but with hat matrix $H(\lambda)$ being supplemented by the additional covariate vectors.

To obtain a reliable fit, λ should be chosen data driven. One possibility is to use a generalized cross validation criterion defined through

$$GCV(\lambda) = \sum_t \left(\frac{s_t - \phi_0 - \hat{\psi}_t b_{t-1}}{1 - tr(H)/n} \right)^2$$

with n as overall sample size. A suitable choice for λ is achieved by minimizing $GCV(\lambda)$. This can be done iteratively using a Newton-Raphson algorithm, as has been pointed out and implemented by Wood (2000, 2001). In principle there are numerous other routines to select λ, like an Akaike Information Criterion or Cross Validation (see e.g. Hastie and Tibshirani 1990). The generalized cross validation however has proven to be numerically quite stable and is therefore the default choice used in the implemented version in R.

Appendix B
Basic Theorems from Optimal Control Theory

In this book we have assumed that economic agents are rational, behave intertemporally and perform dynamic optimization. In this appendix we present some basics of the method of dynamic optimization using Pontryagin's maximum principle and the Hamiltonian.

Let an intertemporal optimization problem be given by

$$\max_{u(t)} W(x(0), 0), W(\cdot) \equiv \int_0^\infty e^{-\rho t} F(x(t), u(t)) dt \tag{B.1}$$

subject to

$$\frac{dx(t)}{dt} \equiv \dot{x}(t) = f(x(t), u(t)), x(0) = x_0 \tag{B.2}$$

with $x(t) \in \mathbb{R}^n$ the vector of state variables at time t and $u(t) \in \Omega \in \mathbb{R}^m$ the vector of control variables at time t and $F : \mathbb{R}^n \times \mathbb{R}^m \to \mathbb{R}$ and $f : \mathbb{R}^n \times \mathbb{R}^m \to \mathbb{R}^n$. ρ is the discount rate and $e^{-\rho t}$ is the discount factor.

$F(x(t), u(t))$, $f_i(x(t), u(t))$ and $\partial f_i(x(t), u(t))/\partial x_j(t)$, $\partial F(x(t), u(t))/\partial x_j(t)$ are continuous with respect to all $n + m$ variables for $i, j = 1, \ldots, n$ Further, $u(t)$ is said to be admissible if it is a piecewise continuous function on $[0, \infty)$ with $u(t) \in \Omega$.

Define the current-value Hamiltonian $\mathcal{H}(x(t), u(t), \lambda(t), \lambda_0)$ as follows:

$$\mathcal{H}(x(t), u(t), \lambda(t), \lambda_0) \equiv \lambda_0 F(x(t), u(t)) + \lambda(t) f(x(t), u(t)) \tag{B.3}$$

with $\lambda_0 \in \mathbb{R}$ a constant scalar and $\lambda(t) \in \mathbb{R}^n$ the vector of co-state variables or shadow prices. $\lambda_j(t)$ gives the change in the optimal objective functional W^o resulting from an increment in the state variable $x_j(t)$. If $x_j(t)$ is a capital stock $\lambda_j(t)$ gives the marginal value of capital at time t. Assume that there exists a solution for (B.1) subject to (B.2). Then, we have the following theorem.

© Springer International Publishing Switzerland 2015

A. Greiner, B. Fincke, *Public Debt, Sustainability and Economic Growth*,
DOI 10.1007/978-3-319-09348-2

Theorem B.1 *Let $u^o(t)$ be an admissible control and $x^o(t)$ is the trajectory belonging to $u^o(t)$. For $u^o(t)$ to be optimal it is necessary that there exists a continuous vector function $\lambda(t) = (\lambda_1(t), \ldots, \lambda_n(t))$ with piecewise continuous derivatives and a constant scalar λ_0 such that:*

(a) $\lambda(t)$ and $x^o(t)$ are solutions of the canonical system

$$\dot{x}^o(t) = \frac{\partial}{\partial \lambda}\mathcal{H}(x^o(t), u^o(t), \lambda(t), \lambda_0)$$

$$\dot{\lambda}(t) = \rho\lambda(t) - \frac{\partial}{\partial x}\mathcal{H}(x^o(t), u^o(t), \lambda(t), \lambda_0),$$

(b) For all $t \in [0, \infty)$ where $u^o(t)$ is continuous, the following inequality must hold: $\mathcal{H}(x^o(t), u^o(t), \lambda(t), \lambda_0) \geq \mathcal{H}(x^o(t), u(t), \lambda(t), \lambda_0)$,

(c) $(\lambda_0, \lambda(t)) \neq (0, 0)$ and $\lambda_0 = 1$ or $\lambda_0 = 0$.

Remarks

1. If the maximum with respect to $u(t)$ is in the interior of Ω, $\partial\mathcal{H}(\cdot)/\partial u(t) = 0$ can be used as a necessary condition for a local maximum of $\mathcal{H}(\cdot)$.
2. It is implicitly assumed that the objective functional (B.1) takes on a finite value, that is $\int_0^\infty e^{-\rho t} F(x^o(t), u^o(t)) < \infty$. If x^o and u^o grow without an upper bound[1] $F(\cdot)$ must not grow faster than ρ.
3. Working with the present-value Hamiltonian that contains the discount factor $e^{-\rho t}$ gives necessary conditions that are equivalent to those of Theorem B.1 after suitable transformation. Working with the current-value Hamiltonian instead of the present-value Hamiltonian implies that the differential equations are autonomous and do not explicitly depend on time.

Theorem B.1 provides us only with necessary conditions. The next theorem gives sufficient conditions.

Theorem B.2 *If the Hamiltonian with $\lambda_0 = 1$ is concave in $(x(t), u(t))$ jointly and if the transversality condition $\lim_{t\to\infty} e^{-\rho t}\lambda(t)(x(t) - x^o(t)) \geq 0$ holds, conditions (a) and (b) from Theorem B.1 are also sufficient for an optimum. If the Hamiltonian is strictly concave in $(x(t), u(t))$ the solution is unique.*

Remarks

1. If the state and co-state variables are positive the transversality condition can be written as stated in the above chapters, that is as $\lim_{t\to\infty} e^{-\rho t}\lambda(t)x^o(t) = 0$.
2. Given some technical conditions it can be shown that the transversality condition is also a necessary condition.

Theorem B.2 requires joint concavity of the current-value Hamiltonian in the control and state variables. A less restrictive theorem is the following.

[1] Note that in the book we did not indicate optimal values by ^{o}.

Theorem B.3 *If the maximized Hamiltonian*

$$\mathcal{H}^o(x(t), \lambda(t), \lambda_0) = \max_{u(t)\in\Omega} \mathcal{H}(x(t), u(t), \lambda(t), \lambda_0)$$

with $\lambda_0 = 1$ *is concave in* $x(t)$ *and if the transversality condition* $\lim_{t\to\infty} e^{-\rho t}\lambda(t)$ $(x(t)-x^o(t)) \geq 0$ *holds, conditions (a) and (b) from Theorem B.1 are also sufficient for an optimum. If the maximized Hamiltonian* $\mathcal{H}^o(x(t), \lambda(t), \lambda_0)$ *is strictly concave in* $x(t)$ *for all* t, $x^o(t)$ *is unique (but not necessarily* $u^o(t)$*).*

Since the joint concavity of $\mathcal{H}(x(t), u(t), \lambda(t), \lambda_0)$ with respect to $(x(t), u(t))$ implies concavity of $\mathcal{H}^o(x(t), \lambda(t), \lambda_0)$ with respect to $x(t)$, but the reverse does not necessarily hold, Theorem B.3 may be applicable where Theorem B.2 cannot be applied.

The above three theorems demonstrate how optimal control theory can be applied to solve dynamic optimization problems. The main role is played by the Hamiltonian function (B.3). It should be noted that in many economic applications, as in this book, interior solutions are optimal so that $\partial\mathcal{H}(\cdot)/\partial u(t) = 0$ can be presumed. For further reading and more details concerning optimal control theory we refer to the books by Feichtinger and Hartl (1986), Seierstad and Sydsæter (1987) or Beavis and Dobbs (1990).

Appendix C
The Hopf Bifurcation Theorem

The Hopf bifurcation theorem is stated in Hassard et al. (1981) for example. Here, we present the Hopf bifurcation theorem as it can be found in Guckenheimer and Holmes (1983), pp. 151–52.

Theorem C.4 *Suppose that the system* $\dot{x} = G(x, \omega), x \in \mathbb{R}^n, \ \omega \in \mathbb{R}$ *has an equilibrium* (x_0, ω_0)*, at which the following properties are satisfied:*

(i) $D_x\, G(x_0, \omega_0)$ *has a simple pair of purely imaginary eigenvalues and no other eigenvalues with zero real parts.*

Then (i) implies that there is a smooth curve of equilibria $(x(\omega), \ \omega)$ *with* $x(\omega_0) = x_0$*. The eigenvalues* $\lambda(\omega), \ \bar{\lambda}(\omega)$ *of* $D_x\, G(x(\omega), \omega_0)$ *which are imaginary at* $\omega = \omega_0$ *vary smoothly with* ω*. If, moreover,*

$$\frac{d}{d\omega} Re(\lambda(\omega)) = d_1 \neq 0, \ \text{für } \omega = \omega_0,$$

then there is a unique three-dimensional center manifold passing through (x_0, ω_0) *in* $\mathbb{R}^n \times \mathbb{R}$ *and a smooth system of coordinates (preserving the planes for* $\omega = const.$*) for which the Taylor expansion of degree 3 on the center manifold is given by*

$$\dot{x}_1 = [d_1\omega + \beta_1(x_1^2 + x_2^2)]x_1 - [d_4 + d_2\omega + d_3(x_1^2 + x_2^2)]x_2,$$
$$\dot{x}_2 = [d_4 + d_2\omega + d_3(x_1^2 + x_2^2)]x_1 + [d_1\omega + \beta_1(x_1^2 + x_2^2)]x_2.$$

If $\beta_1 \neq 0$*, there is a surface of periodic solutions in the center manifold which has quadratic tangency with the eigenspace of* $\lambda(\omega_0), \ \bar{\lambda}(\omega_0)$ *agreeing to second order with the paraboloid* $\omega = -(\beta_1/d_1)(x_1^2 + x_2^2)$*. If* $\beta_1 < 0$*, then these periodic solutions are stable limit cycles, while if* $\beta_1 > 0$*, the solutions are repelling.*

© Springer International Publishing Switzerland 2015

A. Greiner, B. Fincke, *Public Debt, Sustainability and Economic Growth*,
DOI 10.1007/978-3-319-09348-2

Data Sources

Government of Gibraltar. (2013). Information services, statistics, key Indicators http://www.gibraltar.gov.gi/statistics, last access January 8, 2013.

International Statistical Yearbook. (2006). IMF database. *DSI data service & information.*

International Statistical Yearbook. (2009). IMF database, via StatistikNetz.de, January 2009. DSI data service & information.

IMF. (2010). International statistical yearbook, IMF's international financial statistics, via StatistikNetz.de, DSI data service and information.

IMF. (2013). International financial statistics, via StatistikNetz.de, DSI data service and information.

Japan Statistics Bureau. (2009). Ministry of Internal Affairs and Communications, Japan; Historical Statistics of Japan, http://www.stat.go.jp/english/data/chouki/index.htm, last access January 15, 2009, extended by Japan Statistical Yearbook 2009 data.

OECD. (2003). *OECD economic outlook statistics and projections*, Databasis: OECD economic outlook 73, June 2003, especially all "Government Account" Data.

OECD. (2009). Gross domestic product in National Account Data. http://www.oecd.org/statsportal/0,3352,en_2825_293564_1_1_1_1_1,00.html, last access April 20, 2010.

OECD. (2009a). OECD databases, OECD Publications, via StatistikNetz.de, October 2009. DSI Data Service & Information.

OECD Databases. (2010). "Economic outlook statistics and projections" also "fiscal positions and business cylcles (historical ed.)," via StatistikNetz.de, DSI data service and information.

OECD Databases. (2013). "Economic outlook statistics and projections" also "fiscal positions and business cylcles (historical ed.)," via StatistikNetz.de, DSI data service and information.

Statistisches Bundesamt. (2008). *Statistisches Jahrbuch 2008 Volkswirtschaftliche Gesamtrechnungen, Bruttoinlandsprodukt*. Wiesbaden: Statistisches Bundesamt.

SVR (2007) Sachverstaendigenrat zur Begutachtung der gesamtwirtschaftlichen Lage, Staatsverschuldung wirksam begrenzen, Wiesbaden: Statistisches Bundesamt.

SVR. (2008). Sachverstaendigenrat zur Begutachtung der gesamtwirtschaftlichen Lage, Lange Reihen zum Downloaden, Nationale Tabellen, Öffentliche Finanzen, Verschuldung der öffentlichen Haushalte, http://www.sachverstaendigenrat-wirtschaft.de/timerow/tabdeu.php, last access January 16, 2009.

United States Government. (2008). *Office of management and budget. Historical tables, budget of the United States Government, fiscal year 2009*. Washington: U.S. Government Printing Office. Access via www.gpoaccess.gov

World Bank. (2008a). Data & statistics, country at a glance tables, 9/28/07, http://go.worldbank.org/3516WI4UM0, last access on September 9, 2008.

© Springer International Publishing Switzerland 2015

A. Greiner, B. Fincke, *Public Debt, Sustainability and Economic Growth*,
DOI 10.1007/978-3-319-09348-2

World Bank. (2008b). Data & statistics, country classification, http://web.worldbank.org/WBSITE/EXTERNAL/DATASTATISTICS/0,,contentMDK:20420458~menuPK:64133156~pagePK:64133150~piPK:64133175~theSitePK:239419,00.html, last access on March 13, 2008.

World Bank. (2013). Worldbank selection data, via StatistikNetz.de, DSI data service and information.

Bibliography

Acemoglu, D. (1997). Technology, unemployment and efficiency. *European Economic Review, 41*, 525–533.

Afonso, A. (2005). Fiscal sustainability: the unpleasant European case. *Finanzarchiv, 61*, 19–44.

Aghion, P., & Howitt, P. (1992). A model of growth through creative destruction. *Econometrica, 60*, 323–51.

Aghion, P., & Howitt, P. (1994). Growth and unemployment. *Review of Economic Studies, 61*, 477–494.

Aiyagari, S., & Gertler, M. (1985). The backing of government bonds and monetarism. *Journal of Monetary Economics, 16*, 19–44.

Arico, F. (2003). Growth and unemployment: Towards a theoretical integration. *Journal of Economic Surveys, 17*, 419–455.

Arrow, K. J. (1962). The economic implications of learning by doing. *Review of Economic Studies, 29*, 155–173.

Arrow, K. J., & Kurz M. (1970). *Public investment, the rate of return, and optimal fiscal policy*. Baltimore: John Hopkins.

Asako, K., Ito, T., & Sakamoto, K. (1991). The rise and fall of deficit in Japan, 1965–1990. *Journal of the Japanese and International Economies, 5*, 451–472.

Askenazy, P. (2003). Minimum wage, exports and growth. *European Economic Review, 47*, 147–164.

Bajo-Rubio, O., Diaz-Roldan, C., & Esteve, V. (2004). Searching for threshold effects in the evolution of budget deficits: An application to the Spanish case. *Economic Letters, 82*, 239–243.

Ballabriga, F. C., & Martinez-Mongay, C. (2005). Sustainability of EU public finances. *European Economy. Economic Papers, 225*. Brussels: European Commission.

Ballasone, F., Francese, M., & Pace, A. (2011, October). *Public debt and economic growth in Italy* (Quaderni di Storia Economica/Economic History Working Papers No. 11). Rome: Banca d'Italia.

Barro, R. J. (1979). On the determination of public debt. *Journal of Political Economy, 87*, 940–971.

Barro, R. J. (1990). Government spending in a simple model of endogenous growth. *Journal of Political Economy, 98*, S103–S125.

Barro, R. J., & Sala-i-Martin, X. (2003). *Economic growth* (2nd ed.). Cambridge: MIT.

Beauchemin, K. R. (2001). Growth or stagnation? The role of public education. *Journal of Development Economics, 64*, 389–416.

© Springer International Publishing Switzerland 2015

A. Greiner, B. Fincke, *Public Debt, Sustainability and Economic Growth*,
DOI 10.1007/978-3-319-09348-2

Benhabib, J., & Farmer, R. (1994). Indeterminacy and increasing returns. *Journal of Economic Theory, 63*, 19–41.

Benhabib, J., & Perli, R. (1994). Uniqueness and indeterminacy. *Journal of Economic Theory, 63*, 113–142.

Beavis, B., & Dobbs, I. M. (1990). *Optimization and stability theory for economic analysis*. Cambridge: Cambridge University Press.

Blanchard, O. J., & Fischer, S. (1989). *Lectures on macroeconomics*. Cambridge: MIT.

Blanchard, O., & Katz, L. F. (1999). Wage dynamics: Reconciling theory and evidence. *American Economic Review, 89*, 69–74.

Blanchard, O., & Wolfers, J. (2000). The role of shocks and institutions in the rise of European unemployment: The aggregate evidence. *The Economic Journal, 110*, C1–C33.

Blankenau, W. F., & Simpson, N. B. (2004). Public education, expenditures and growth. *Journal of Development Economics, 73*, 583–605.

Bohn, H. (1995). The sustainability of budget deficits in a stochastic economy. *Journal of Money, Credit and Banking, 27*, 257–271.

Bohn, H. (1998). The behavior of U.S. public debt and deficits. *Quarterly Journal of Economics, 113*, 949–963.

Bohn, H. (2008). The sustainability of fiscal policy in the United States. In R. Neck & J.-E. Sturm (Eds.), *Sustainability of public debt* (pp. 15–50). Cambridge: MIT.

Bräuninger, M. (2005). The budget deficit, public debt, and endogenous growth. *Public Economic Theory, 7*, 827–840.

Breuss, F. (2007). *Globalization, EU enlargement and income distribution* (FIW Working Paper Nr. 8), University of Economics and Business Administration. Vienna: FIW.

Buiter, W. H. (1982). *Predetermined and non-predetermined variables in rational expectation models* (Technical Paper No. 21). Cambridge: National Bureau of Economic Research.

Buiter, W. H. (2002). The fiscal theory of the price level: A critique. *The Economic Journal, 112*, 459–480.

Canzoneri, M. B., Cumby, R. E., & Diba, B. T. (2001). Is the price level determined by the needs of fiscal solvency? *American Economic Review, 91*, 1221–1238.

Cahuc, P., & Michel, P. (1996). Minimum wage unemployment and growth. *European Economic Review, 40*, 1463–1482.

Caner, M., Grennes, T., & Koehler-Geib, F. (2010). *Finding the tipping point – When sovereign debt turns bad* (Policy Research Working Paper 5391). The World Bank.

Checherita, C., & Rother, P. (2010). *The impact of high and growing debt on economic growth. An empirical investigation for the euro area* (ECB Working Paper Series No. 1237).

Checherita-Westphal, C., Hallett, A. H., & Rother, P. (2012). *Fiscal sustainability using growth-maximising debt targets* (ECB Working Paper Series No. 1472).

Collard, F., & de la Croix, D. (2000). Gift exchange and the business cycle: The fair wage strikes back. *Review of Economic Dynamics, 3*, 166–193.

Cooley, J. F., Greenwood, J., & Yorukoglu, M. (1997). The replacement problem. *Journal of Monetary Economics, 40*, 457–499.

Croissant, Y., & Millo, G. (2008). Panel data econometrics in R: The plm package. *Journal of Statistical Software, 27*(2), 1–43. http://www.jstatsoft.org/

DeLong, B. J., & Summers, L. H. (1991). Equipment investment and economic growth. *Quarterly Journal of Economics, 106*, 445–501.

Dickey, D. A., & Fuller, W. A. (1981). Likelihood ratio statistics for autoregressive time series with a unit root? *Econometrica, 49*, 1057–1072.

Dhooge, A., Govaerts, W., Kuznetsov, Y.A., Maestrom, W., & Riet, A. M. (2003). CL_MATCONT: A continuation toolbox in Matlab. *Ghent University*. Last access April 27, 2013, http://www.matcont.ugent.be/

Dreger, C., & Reimers, H.-E. (2013). Does euro area membership affect the relation between GDP growth and public debt? *Journal of Macroeconomics*. Available online August 22, 2013 and *DIW Discussion Paper 1249, 2012*.

Eberhardt, M., & Presbitero, A. F. (2013). *This time they're different: Heterogeneity and nonlinearity in the relationship between debt and growth* (Centre for Finance, Credit and Macroeconomics, Working Paper 13/10). Nottingham.

Egert, B. (2012). Public debt, economic growth and nonlinear effects: Myth or reality? (OECD Economics Department Working Papers 993). OECD Publishing.

Embassy of the Republic of Mauritius. (2008). Economy of Mauritius. Last access on September 3, 2008, http://www.mauritius-embassy.de/economy.php

Enders, W. (2004). *Applied econometric time series* (2nd ed.). Hoboken: Wiley.

European Union. (1992). Treaty on European Union. Last access November 27, 2007, http://europa.eu.int/eur-lex/lex/en/treaties/dat/11992M/htm/11992M.html

European Union. (1997). Consolidated version of the treaty on European Union. *Official Journal of the European Communities, C 340, 10. November 1997.* Access via: http://eur-lex.europa.eu/en/treaties/index.htm html version. Last access June 1, 2011.

van Ewijk, C. (1991). *On the dynamics of growth and debt.* Oxford: Oxford University Press.

Feichtinger, G., & Hartl, R. F. (1986). *Optimale Kontrolle Ökonomischer Prozesse: Anwendungen des Maximumprinzips in den Wirtschaftswissenschaften.* Berlin: De Gruyter.

Ferreira, C. (2009). Public debt and economic growth: A granger causality panel data approach (Working Paper 24/2009). School of Economics and Management, Technical University of Lisbon.

Fincke, B. (2013). *Sustainable debt policies despite the crisis? Empirical evidence for Iberian economies* (Bielefeld Working Papers in Economics and Management No. 16–2013). Available at SSRN: http://ssrn.com/abstract=2323323

Fincke, B., & Greiner, A. (2008). How to assess debt sustainability? Some theory and empirical evidence for selected euro area countries. *Applied Economics, 44*, 3717–3724.

Fincke, B., & Greiner, A. (2009). Do governments in developing countries pursue sustainable debt policies? Empirical evidence for selected countries in Africa and Latin America. *Journal of Development Studies, 46*, 745–770.

Fincke, B., & Greiner, A. (2011a). Do large industrialized economies pursue sustainable debt policies? A comparative study for Japan, Germany and the United States. *Japan and the World Economy, 23*, 202–213.

Fincke, B., & Greiner, A. (2011b). Debt sustainability in selected euro area countries. Empirical evidence estimating time-varying parameters. *Studies in Nonlinear Dynamics & Econometrics, 15*(3), article 2.

Fincke, B., & Greiner, A. (2013). *On the relation between public debt and economic growth: An empirical investigation* (Bielefeld Working Papers in Economics and Management No. 24–2013). Available at SSRN: http://ssrn.com/abstract=2362788

Flaschel, P., Franke, R., & Semmler, W. (1997). *Dynamic macroeconomics: Instability, fluctuations and growth in monetary economies*. Cambridge: MIT.

Flaschel, P., & Greiner, A. (2011). Dual labor markets and the impact of minimum wages on atypical employment. *Metroeconomica, 62*, 512–531.

Fox, C., Weisberg, S., Adler, D., Bates, D., Baud-Bovy, G., Ellison, S., Firth, D., Friendly, M., Gorjanc, G., Graves, S., Heiberger, R., Laboissiere, R., Monette, G., Murdoch, D., Nilsson, H., Ogle, D., Ripley, B., Venables, W., Zeileis, A., & R-Core. (2013). Package 'car'. Last access on November 6, 2013, http://cran.r-project.org/web/packages/car/car.pdf

Fuller, W. A. (1976). *Introduction to statistical time series*. New York: Wiley.

Futagami, K., Morita, Y., & Shibata, A. (1993). Dynamic analysis of an endogenous growth model with public capital. *Scandinavian Journal of Economics, 95*, 607–625.

Futagami, K., Iwaisako, T., & Ohdoi, R. (2008). Debt policy rule, productive government spending, and multiple growth paths. *Macroeconomic Dynamics, 12*, 445–462.

Ghosh, S., & Mourmouras, I. (2004). Endogenous growth, welfare and budgetary regimes. *Journal of Macroeconomics, 26*, 363–384.

Gillman, M., & Kejak, M. (2005). Contrasting models of the effect of inflation on growth. *Journal of Economic Surveys, 19*, 113–136.

Glomm, G., & Ravikumar, B. (1992). Public versus private investmentin human capital: Endogenous growth and income distribution. *Journal of Political Economy, 100*, 818–834.
Glomm, G., & Ravikumar, B. (1997). Productive government expenditures and long-run growth. *Journal of Economic Dynamics and Control, 21*, 183–204.
Gomme, P. (1993). Money and growth revisited: Measuring the costs of inflation in an endogenous growth model. *Journal of Monetary Economics, 32*, 51–77.
Gong, G., Greiner, A., & Semmler, W. (2001). Growth effects of fiscal policy and debt sustainability in the EU. *Empirica, 28*, 3–19.
Government of Botswana. (2008) Economic information. Last access on September 3, 2008, http://www.gov.bw/index.php?option=com_content&task=view&id=63&Itemid=74
Granger, C. W. J. (2008). Non-linear models: Where do we go next – Time varying parameter models? *Studies in Nonlinear Dynamics & Econometrics, 12*(3), article 1: 1–9.
Greenwood, J., Hercowitz, Z., & Krusell, P. (1997). Long-run implications of investment specific technological change. *American Economic Review, 87*, 342–362.
Greiner, A. (2006). Progressive taxation, public capital and endogenous growth. *Finanzarchiv, 62*, 353–366.
Greiner, A. (2007). An endogenous growth model with public capital and sustainable government debt. *Japanese Economic Review, 58*, 345–361.
Greiner, A. (2008a). Sustainability of public debt: Some theoretical considerations. *Economics Bulletin, 33*, 2357–2364.
Greiner, A. (2008b). Does it pay to have a balanced government budget? *Journal of Institutional and Theoretical Economics, 164*, 460–476.
Greiner, A. (2008c). Human capital formation, public debt and economic growth. *Journal of Macroeconomics, 30*, 415–427.
Greiner, A. (2009). Estimating penalized spline regressions: Theory and applications to economics. *Applied Economics Letter, 16*, 1831–1835.
Greiner, A. (2011a). Economic growth, public debt and welfare: Comparing three budgetary rules. *German Economic Review, 12*, 205–222.
Greiner, A. (2011b). Environmental pollution, the public sector and economic growth: A comparison of different scenarios. *Optimal Control Applications & Methods, 32*, 527–544.
Greiner, A. (2012a). Public debt in a basic endogenous growth model. *Economic Modelling, 29*, 1344–1348.
Greiner, A. (2012b). Transition dynamics in an AK growth model under wage rigidity. *Mathematical Social Sciences, 63*, 50–56.
Greiner, A. (2012c). Human capital formation, learning by doing and the government in the process of economic growth. *Scottish Journal of Political Economy, 51*, 71–89.
Greiner, A. (2013a). How to test for debt sustainability? Some theoretical reflections on an empirical test. *Economics Bulletin, 33*, 2357–2364.
Greiner, A. (2013b). Sustainable public debt and economic growth under wage rigidity. *Metroeconomica, 64*, 272–292.
Greiner, A. (2013c). *Public debt, productive public spending and endogenous growth.* (Bielefeld Working Papers in Economics and Management No. 23–2013). Available at SSRN: http://ssrn.com/abstract=2357882, forthcoming in: *Japanese Economic Review*.
Greiner, A. (2013d). Debt and growth: Is there a non-monotonic relation? *Economics Bulletin, 33*, 340–347.
Greiner, A. (2014a). Public debt and the dynamics of economic growth. *Annals of Economics and Finance, 15*, 185–204.
Greiner, A. (2014b). Fiscal and monetary policy in a basic endogenous growth model. *Computational Economics*. doi: 10.1007/s10614-014-9421-3.
Greiner, A., & Fincke, B. (2009). *Public debt and economic growth.* Berlin: Springer.
Greiner, A., & Flaschel, P. (2009). Public debt and public investment in an endogenous growth model with real wage rigidities. *Scottish Journal of Political Economy, 51*, 71–89.
Greiner, A., Gong, G., & Semmler, W. (2005). *The forces of economic growth: A time series perspective*. Princeton: Princeton University Press.

Greiner, A., & Hanusch, H. (1998). Growth and welfare effects of fiscal policy in an endogenous growth model with public investment. *International Tax and Public Finance, 5*, 249–261.

Greiner, A., & Kauermann, G. (2008). Debt policy in euro-area countries: Empirical evidence for Germany and Italy using penalized spline smoothing. *Economic Modelling, 25*, 1144–1154.

Greiner, A., Köller, U., & Semmler, W. (2007). Debt sustainability in the european monetary union: Theory and empirical evidence for selected countries. *Oxford Economic Papers, 59*, 194–218.

Greiner, A., & Semmler, W. (2000). Endogenous growth, government debt and budgetary regimes. *Journal of Macroeconomics, 22*, 363–384.

Greiner, A., & Semmler, W. (2008). *The global environment, natural resources and economic growth*. New York: Oxford University Press.

Guckenheimer, J., & Holmes, P. (1983). *Nonlinear oscillations, dynamical systems and bifurcation of vector fields*. New York: Springer.

Guo, J.-T., & Harrison, S. G. (2004). Balanced-budget rules and macroeconomic (in)stability. *Journal of Economic Theory, 119*, 357–363.

Guo, J.-T., & Lansing, K. J. (1998). Indeterminacy and stabilization policy. *Journal of Economics Theory, 82*, 481–490.

Hamilton, J. D., & Flavin, M. (1986). On the limitations of government borrowing: A framework for empirical testing. *The American Economic Review, 76*, 808–819.

Haskamp, U. (2013). Was Spanish fiscal policy sustainable? *Empirica*, 1–14. doi: 10.1007/s10663-013-9211-5.

Hassard, B. D., Kazarinoff, N. D., & Wan, Y.-H. (1981). *Theory and applications of Hopf bifurcation*. Cambridge: Cambridge University Press.

Hastie, T. J., & Tibshirani, R. J. (1990). *Generalized additive models*. London: Chapman and Hall.

Havranek, T., Horvath, R., Irsova, Z., & Rusnak, M. (2013). *Cross-country heterogeneity in intertemporal substitution* (IES Working Paper: 11/2013). Institute of Economic Studies, Faculty of Social Sciences, Charles University in Prague.

Heinemann, F. (2002). Factor mobility, government debt and the decline in public investment (ZEW Discussion Paper No. 02–19). http://zew.de/

Herndon, T., Ash, M., & Pollin, R. (2014). Does high public debt consistently stifle economic growth? A critique of Reinhart and Rogoff. *Cambridge Journal of Economics, 38*, 257–279.

Ihaka, R., & Gentleman, R. (1996). R: A language for data analysis and graphics. *Journal of Computational and Graphical Statistics, 5*, 299–314.

Ihori, T., Doi, T., & Kondo, H. (2001). Japanese fiscal reform: Fiscal reconstruction and fiscal policy. *Japan and the World Economy, 13*, 351–370.

International Monetary Fund. (1995). *IMF approves stand-by credit for Panama* (IMF Press Release No. 95/60). Last access on September 3, 2008, http://www.imf.org/external/np/sec/pr/1995/pr9560.htm

International Monetary Fund. (2008). Heavily indebted poor countries (HIPC) debt initiative all publications. Last access on September 5, 2008, http://www.imf.org/external/np/hipc/index.asp

Jones, L. E., & Manuelli, R. E. (1995). Growth and the effects of inflation. *Journal of Economic Dynamics and Control, 19*, 1405–1428.

Kamiguchi, A., & Tamai, T. (2012) Are fiscal sustainability and stable balanced growth simultaneously attainable? *Metroeconomica, 63*, 443–457.

Kauermann, G. (2006). Nonparametric models and their estimation. *Allgemeines Statistisches Archiv, 90*(1), 137–152.

Khibnik, A., Kuznetsov, Y., Levitin, V., & Nikolaev, E. (1993) Continuation techniques and interactive software for bifurcation analysis of ODE's and iterated maps. *Physica D, 62*, 360–371.

Kleiber, C., & Zeileis, A. (2008). *Applied econometrics with R*. Use R! New York: Springer.

Krueger, A. B., & Lindahl, M. (2001). Education for growth: Why and for whom? *Journal of Economic Literature, 39*, 1101–1136.

Kumar, M. S., & Woo, J. (2010). *Public debt and growth* (IMF Working Paper No. WP/10/174).

Layard, P. R. J., Nickell, S. J., Jackman, R. (1991). *Unemployment: Macroeconomic performance and the labor market*. Oxford: Oxford University Press.

Leeper, E. M. (1991). Equilibria under 'active' and 'passive' monetary and fiscal policies. *Journal of Monetary Economics, 27*, 129–147.
Legrenzi, G., & Milas, C. (2011). *Debt sustainability and financial crises: Evidence from the GIIPS* (CESifo Working Paper No. 3594).
Levhari, D. (1966). Extensions of arrow's learning by doing. *Review of Economic Studies, 33*, 117–131.
Levine, R., & Renelt, D. (1992). A sensitivity analysis of cross-country growth regressions. *American Economic Review, 82*, 942–963.
Li, W., & Sarte, P.-D. (2004). Progressive taxation and long-run growth. *American Economic Review, 94*, 1705–1716.
Lucas, R. E. (1988). On the mechanics of economic development. *Journal of Monetary Economics, 22*, 3–42.
Martin, G. M. (2000). US deficit sustainability: A new approach based on multiple endogenous breaks. *Journal of Applied Econometrics, 15*, 83–105.
McCallum, B. C. (2003). Is the fiscal theory of the price level learnable? *Scottish Journal of Political Economy, 50*, 634–649.
McCallum, B. C., & Nelson, E. (2006). *Monetary and fiscal theories of the price level: The irreconcilable differences*. (Federal Reserve Bank of St. Louis Working Paper 2006-010A).
Minkner-Buenjer, M. (1999). Costa Rica: Internationalisierung der Wirtschaft mit Bananen und Mikroprozessoren. *Brennpunkt Latainamerika. Politik Wirtschaft Gesellschaft, Institut für Iberoamerika-Kunde Hamburg, 19*, 162–172.
Neck, R., & Sturm, J.-E. (2008). Sustainability of public debt. Introduction and overview. In R. Neck & J.-E. Sturm (Eds.). *Sustainability of public debt* (pp. 1–14). Cambridge: MIT.
Ni, S., & Wang, X. (1994). Human capital and income taxation in an endogenous growth model. *Journal of Macroeconomics, 16*, 493–507.
Nsouli, S. M., Eken, S., Duran, P., Bell, G., & Yucelik, Z. M. (1993). *The path to convertibility and growth the tunisian experience*. (IMF Occasional Paper 109).
O'Sullivan, F. (1986). A statistical perspective on Ill-posed inverse problems (C/R:P 519–527). *Statistical Science, 1*, 502–518.
Oxley, H., & Martin, J. P. (1991). Controlling government spending and deficits; trends in the 1980s and prospects for the 1990s. *OECD Economic Studies, 17*, 145–189.
Panizza, U., & Presbitero, A. F. (2013). Public debt and economic growth in advanced economies: A survey. *Swiss Journal of Economics and Statistics, 149*, 175–204.
Paul, E. C. (1987). *Fisheries development and the food needs of Mauritius*. Rotterdam: A.A. Balkema.
Payne, J. E., Mohammadi, H., & Cak, M. (2008). Turkish budget deficit sustainability and the revenue-expenditure nexus. *Applied Economics, 40*, 823–830.
Pescatori, A., Sandri, D., Simon, J. (2014). *Debt and growth: Is there a magic threshold*? (IMF Working Paper No. WP/14/34).
Pfähler, W., Hofmann, U., Bönte, W. (1996). Does extra public capital matter? An appraisal of empirical literature. *Finanzarchiv N.F., 53*, 68–112.
Piergallini, A., & Rodano, G. (2012). *Public debt, distortionary taxation, and monetary policy* (CEIS Tor Vergata, Research Paper Series, 10(2), 220).
Pissarides, C. A. (1990). *Equilibrium unemployment theory*. Oxford: Blackwell.
Raurich, X., Sala, H., & Sorolla, V. (2006). Unemployment, growth, and fiscal policy: New insights on the hysteresis hypothesis. *Macroeconomic Dynamics, 10*, 285–316.
Rebelo, S. (1991). Long-run policy analysis and long-run growth. *Journal of Political Economy, 99*, 500–521.
Reinhart, C. M., & Rogoff, K. S. (2010). *Growth in a time of debt* (NBER Working Paper No. 15639).
Romer, P. M. (1986). Increasing returns and long-run growth. *Journal of Political Economy, 94*, 1002–1037.
Romer, P. M. (1990). Endogenous technological change. *Journal of Political Economy, 98*, S71–S102.

Romp, W., & de Haan, J. (2005). Public capital and economic growth: A critical survey. *EIB Papers, 10*(1), 40–70.

Ruppert, R., Wand, M. P., & Carroll, R. J. (2003). *Semiparametric regression*. Cambridge: Cambridge University Press.

Sawada, Y. (1994). Are the heavily indebted countries solvent?: Tests of intertemporal borrowing constraints. *Journal of Development Economics, 45*, 325–337.

Schmitt-Grohé, S., & Uribe, U. (1997). Balanced-budget rules, distortionary taxes, and aggregate instability. *Journal of Political Economy, 105*, 976–1000.

Seierstad, A., & Sydsæter, K. (1987) *Optimal control with economic applications*. Amsterdam: North-Holland.

Sims, C. A. (1994). A simple model for study of the determination of the price level and the interaction of monetary and fiscal policy. *Economic Theory, 4*, 381–399.

Slobodyan, S. (2005). Indeterminacy, sunspots, and development traps. *Journal of Economic Dynamics and Control, 29*, 159–185.

Smyth, D. J., & Hsing, Y. (1995). In search of an optimal debt ratio for economic growth. *Contemporary Economic Policy, 13*, 51–59.

Stork, J. (1990). Europe's other frontier: North Africa faces the 1990s. *Middle East Report, 163*(44), 4–8.

Tanner, E. (2013). *Fiscal sustainability: A 21st century guide for the perplexed* (IMF Working Paper No. WP/13/89).

Trehan, B., & Walsh, C. E. (1991). Testing intertemporal budget constraints: theory and applications to U.S. Federal budget and current account deficits. *Journal of Money, Credit and Banking, 23*, 206–223.

Uzawa, H. (1965). Optimum technical change in an aggregative model of economic growth. *International Economic Review, 6*, 18–31.

Wang, P., & Yip, C. K. (1992). Alternative approaches to money and growth. *Journal of Money, Credit and Banking, 24*, 553–562.

Westerlund, J., & Prohl, S. (2010). Panel cointegration tests of the sustainability hypothesis in rich OECD countries. *Applied Economics, 42*, 1355–1364.

Wilcox, D. W. (1989). The sustainability of government deficits: Implications of the present-value borrowing constraint. *Journal of Money, Credit and Banking, 21*, 291–306.

Wood, S. N. (2000). Modelling and smoothing parameter estimation with multiple quadratic penalties. *Journal of the Royal Statistical Society, Series B, 62*, 413–428.

Wood, S. N. (2001). mgcv: GAM's and generalized ridge regression for R. *R News, 1*(2), 20–25.

Woodford, M. (1994). Monetary policy and price level determination in a cash-in-advance economy. *Economic Theory, 4*, 345–380.

Wu, Y., & Zhang, J. (1998). Endogenous growth and the welfare costs of inflation: A reconsideration. *Journal of Economic Dynamics and Control, 22*, 465–482.

Yakita, A. (2008). Sustainability of public debt, public capital formation, and endogenous growth in an overlapping generations framework. *Journal of Public Economics, 92*, 897–914.

Index

© Springer International Publishing Switzerland 2015

A. Greiner, B. Fincke, *Public Debt, Sustainability and Economic Growth*,
DOI 10.1007/978-3-319-09348-2

MIX
Papier aus verantwortungsvollen Quellen
Paper from responsible sources
FSC® C105338

If you have any concerns about our products,
you can contact us on
ProductSafety@springernature.com

In case Publisher is established outside the EU,
the EU authorized representative is:
Springer Nature Customer Service Center GmbH
Europaplatz 3, 69115 Heidelberg, Germany

Printed by Libri Plureos GmbH
in Hamburg, Germany